The Lower Animals

LIVING INVERTEBRATES OF THE WORLD

With photographs by

RALPH BUCHSBAUM

DOUGLAS P. WILSON

FRITZ GORO

and others

Line drawings by

KENNETH GOSNER

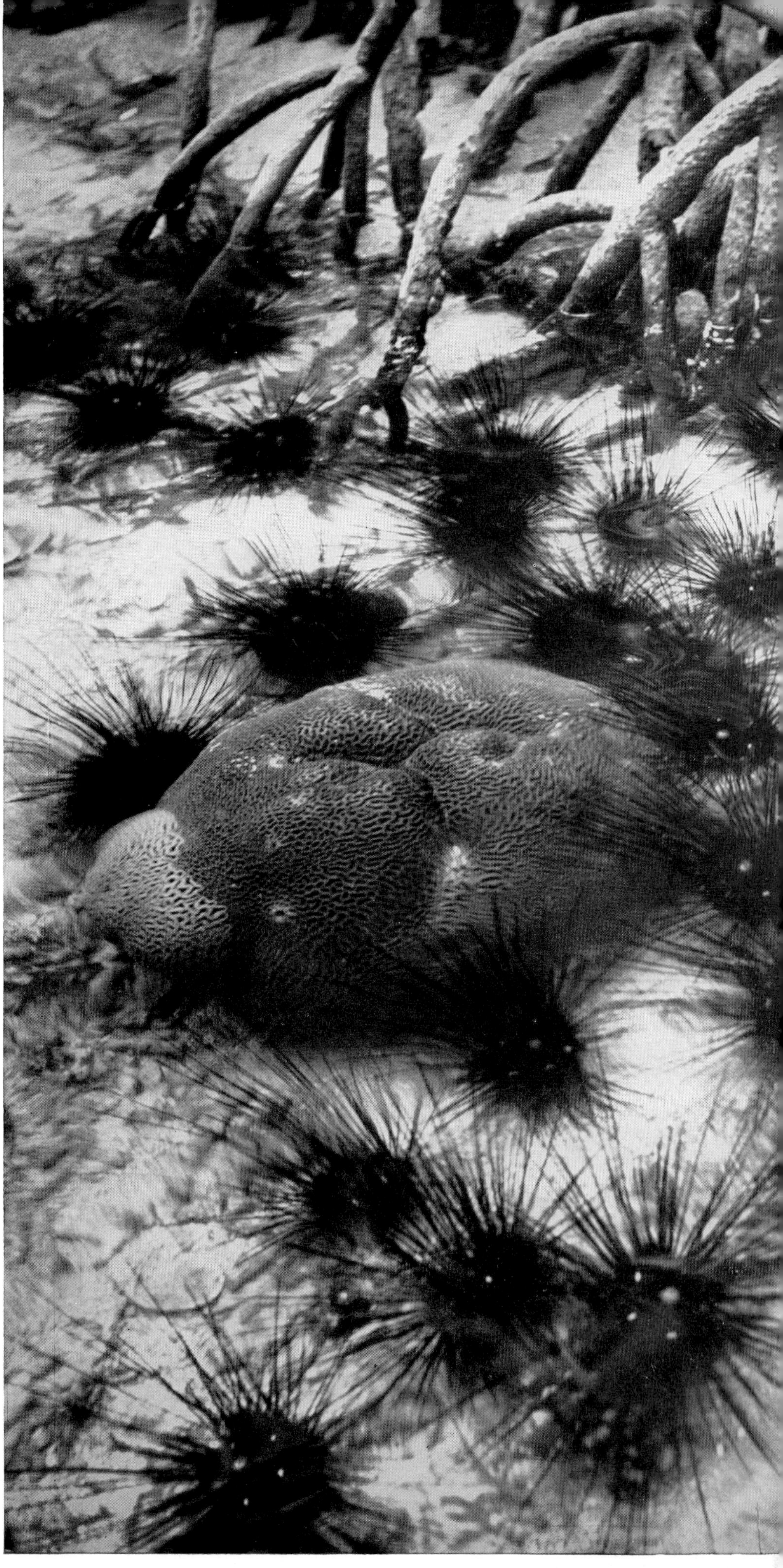

FRITZ GORO

The Lower Animals

LIVING INVERTEBRATES OF THE WORLD

by *Ralph Buchsbaum*

Professor of Zoology, University of Pittsburgh

and *Lorus J. Milne*

Professor of Zoology, University of New Hampshire

*in collaboration with Mildred Buchsbaum
and Margery Milne*

A CHANTICLEER PRESS EDITION

DOUBLEDAY & COMPANY Inc., *Garden City, New York*

PUBLISHED BY DOUBLEDAY & COMPANY, INC. 1960

Garden City, New York

SECOND PRINTING 1961

PLANNED AND PRODUCED BY CHANTICLEER PRESS, INC., NEW YORK

THE WORLD OF NATURE SERIES

Living Mammals of the World by Ivan T. Sanderson

Living Reptiles of the World by Karl P. Schmidt
and Robert F. Inger

Living Birds of the World by E. Thomas Gilliard

Living Insects of the World by Alexander B. Klots
and Elsie B. Klots

*The Lower Animals: Living Invertebrates of the
World* by Ralph Buchsbaum and Lorus J. Milne,
in collaboration with Mildred Buchsbaum
and Margery Milne

Living Fishes of the World by Earl S. Herald

Living Amphibians of the World by Doris M. Cochran

Library of Congress Catalog Card No. 60–10650

PRINTED IN THE UNITED STATES OF AMERICA

THIS BOOK IS DEDICATED TO

all those who have helped to found, to maintain, to direct, and to carry on the work of the field laboratories of the world. To their efforts we owe much of our knowledge of the invertebrates.

A few of the larger marine laboratories have become veritable universities by the seashore, with summer classes, good research facilities, and fine libraries. They maintain displays of living animals that are of interest to any serious amateur naturalist who may stop to visit. The smaller marine laboratories, as well as those beside fresh waters or located in many terrestrial habitats from the tundra to the tropical forest or desert, have more modest facilities but are equally hospitable. Large or small, these field laboratories, or biological stations, make their greatest contribution by enabling scientists to live and work in places where animals can be studied in their natural surroundings.

Contents

Preface

THE oldest pictures of living invertebrates that have come down to us, from about 1500 B.C., are of the octopuses that Cretan artists painted on their beautiful vases, and of the cockles and nautiluses that they worked into the designs of their frescoes and faiences. The first book illustrations of animals were those of Aristotle, who made many diagrams to support the descriptions of animal structure in his texts. The diagrams were lost long ago, but many of them have been reconstructed from his references to them and from his excellent descriptions in the *Historia Animalium*. Since Aristotle's day no better way has been devised for communicating details of anatomical structure or embryological development than the well-designed drawing or diagram.

No diagram, however, could have helped Aristotle to impart to his students the full attraction of the world of invertebrates that had kept him for much of two years on the island of Lesbos. He became so enamored of the shore invertebrates that he passed day after day leaning over the edge of a boat intent on what he could see in the still, clear, shallow, sunlit waters. The graceful stances, the variety of behavioral postures, the delicate textures, the subtle and rich colorings, and whatever it is that so completely fascinates those who see invertebrates at first hand in their natural surroundings—all these are not easily communicated to others.

After Aristotle, interest in marine invertebrates declined; scientific inquiry into animals was first neglected and then actively discouraged. During the Middle Ages people of religious outlook tended to look upward, and the birds were of primary interest. Then came the new age of marine discovery: the sea was once more in fashion, and interest in fishes and in marine invertebrates returned. From Renaissance to modern times, artists mobilized every skill to depict living animals as they saw and enjoyed them. Wood engravings, steel engravings, and color printing inevitably fell far short of the reality. Artistic effort in biological books declined during the first half of this century, as artists found more lucrative outlets for their skills and as book-production costs soared. Photographers seemed the natural successors to artists, but technical limitations made them train their heavy cameras on domestic animals or on the same big-game mammals of Africa that were already known to us through the displays of zoos. Not only were the smaller invertebrates more difficult to photograph because of their size and timidity, but many of the most attractive ones lived below the surface of the sea or were accessible to a camera only a few days in the year, when the lowest tides happened to coincide with the sunniest mornings.

More than two decades ago a few photographers rejected the methods of the wire-and-pin school of nature photography with its long bellows extensions and fixed lighting equipment used to photograph dead, propped-up insects. Armed with faster lenses and the newest flashbulbs, they went whenever possible into the field, turning up logs in the tropical rain forest and following the tides out on dark, foggy mornings. The black-and-white photographs made by this group were a vast improvement over earlier ones, and they revived an interest in invertebrates and in books on invertebrates. Then suddenly, in the last decade, there was a major advance in the photography of animals. Faster color films and newly portable electronic lighting equipment have sent naturalist-photographers into the field in greater numbers than ever. The aqualung has taken the skin-diving photographer to the ocean bed to bring back beautiful images of one of the last unexplored "landscapes" on our planet. The aqualung has itself brought the enchantment of marine invertebrates to many thousands in areas and at depths that once were accessible only to a handful of swimmers. This has helped to add many to the increasing audience for books on invertebrates. Most of the new books that treat at all of invertebrates are limited to those of the seashore or of shallow marine waters and deal with the animals from an ecological viewpoint and according to their habitat. This is a much needed approach, and many such books are listed in the bibliography. But the series of which this is the fifth volume (earlier volumes have covered mammals, reptiles, birds and insects, and forthcoming volumes will cover fishes and amphibians) is designed to supply the need for a new set of illustrated natural histories arranged systematically, group by group, and proceeding from the primitive forms to the most specialized ones. Thus the present volume is a natural history of the invertebrates (excepting the insects). But it necessarily presents the animals on a different scale from that of the other volumes, which dealt with no more than a single class of animals. The authors have had to cope with the many invertebrate phyla without allowing the extreme limitations of space for such a project to turn it into a mere catalogue, lacking the vivid detail and discursiveness that make for readability. The plan adopted here seems a reasonable compromise: the smaller phyla are covered only in generalized accounts followed by a treatment of a few typical or better-known examples. The large phyla are described in general accounts, as are all of their living classes. Below the level of class the treatment is not completely systematic; however, where possible, the specific examples are selected so as to give some representation to all the important orders. Internal structure and embryological evidence are mentioned only when indispensable for understanding of some aspect of behavior or of an animal's position in the evolutionary sequence. For the most part the evidences for classification are only alluded to; they cannot be adequately expounded in a book of such broad scope.

It should be noted that the inserts of color plates involve special technical problems and so do not necessarily adjoin the corresponding text, nor do they in all cases follow exactly the sequence of the text. The black-and-white photographs accompany the text and follow the same sequence.

Natural history is the oldest and the most diffuse of all the branches of biology. A realistic acknowledgement of the written sources of the material in this book would have to begin with Aristotle, who supplemented his own experience by drawing on every possible source, including fishermen, peasants, and mere hearsay. From his time to ours these same informants have been contributing, along with better-trained or professional observers. This has weighted down natural history with much unreliable information, but it also has given it advantages in a day in which most branches of biology have become so specialized and so experimental as to create an unbridgeable gulf between the professional worker and the interested layman. Although much of the material of natural history is first published in scientific journals, and the authors have drawn mostly on these sources as a matter of habit, the field is one in which original material is also published for the first time in natural history books or even in popular magazines.

The first half of the text, that covering the protozoans through the entoprocts, was written by Ralph and Mildred Buchsbaum; the second half, that dealing with the chaetognaths through the invertebrate chordates was written by Lorus and Margery Milne.

The Lower Animals

LIVING INVERTEBRATES OF THE WORLD

Introduction

To develop a really friendly feeling for a jelly-fish or a flatworm takes a lively imagination. And even to tell head from tail in many invertebrates one also needs some information. This poses for the writer on invertebrates special problems of presentation that do not arise in quite the same way in books on the natural history of vertebrates. Show anyone a vertebrate, even so lowly a one as a goldfish, and he can immediately identify himself with it, for it has the same "two-sided" or bilateral symmetry as himself. He not only knows head from tail but back from belly and right side from left. He knows where to approach it with an offering of food, and which end will go first when it swims away. Gazing into its two symmetrically placed eyes, he does not doubt that the fish is looking at him, and he may even imagine that his image evokes a psychological response that is closely akin to his own feeling of relatedness.

Not so with many of the lower invertebrate groups. Their bodies may be spherical, as in many of the floating protozoans, or they may be radial in symmetry, as in jellyfishes and corals. Even in bilateral invertebrates like mollusks and insects, the legs may wrap around the head, the multiple eyes may encircle most of the body, or the ears may be mounted in the legs. There are groups of invertebrates that superficially are difficult to distinguish from seaweeds and are almost as unresponsive. Many of the most fascinating invertebrate groups require the use of a hand lens or a microscope to be seen at all. Yet it is the very strangeness of invertebrates—in contrast to the relative sameness and predictability of the gen-erally four-limbed vertebrates—that attracts us so strongly. Whether we are exploring the sea bottom with an aqualung, eagerly following a receding tide, or merely wading about in a brook, the constant expectation of coming upon some hitherto unimagined living shape or some undreamed-of way of life is an exciting challenge—but a challenge on a purely aesthetic or intellectual level. For there is little emotional warmth to be derived from fondling a beautiful jellyfish or a colorful crab. Though there is great sensual enjoyment in the kaleidoscopic variety of invertebrate shapes and color patterns, this has its limits—even with animals as lovely or as bizarre as are many of the invertebrates.

The inexhaustible possibilities for intellectual enrichment through contact with invertebrate animals must come mostly through knowing something of their habits, their distribution, their role in the natural communities in which they live, their variety of structure, the basic relationships of even the most seemingly diverse forms, their relative structural complexity, and their origins in the grand scheme of evolutionary history. The last four matters, it must be added, can only be touched on in a book of this kind.

The authors hope only to give the reader, through both text and photographs, some vicarious familiarity with the external appearance of invertebrates (excepting the insects) and some understanding of their habits, their environmental adaptations, and a few of the more interesting ways in which they enter into our own lives.

What is an Invertebrate?

The word "invertebrate" is a semantic blanket that covers most of animal kind and reveals nothing of the varied shapes that have been thrust under it. To lift one corner and glimpse a few of the more familiar invertebrates—worms, starfishes, snails, clams, crabs, and butterflies—is a mere beginning toward appreciating a variety of creatures that range in size and in complexity from microscopic protozoans to giant squids 50 feet long, and that comprise 97 per cent of the nearly a million different kinds of animals that scientists have so far described and named. About 685,000 of the invertebrate species are built very much alike and are grouped together as the class Insecta. They are treated in a separate volume in the series of which this book is a part.

To be called an invertebrate, an animal need have no one special shape, nor any specific structure, nor any single positive attribute. It need only, for lack of a vertebral column or backbone, be excluded from the select company of the vertebrates. All vertebrates, including man, have down the middle of the back a row of articulated bones or sometimes cartilages. Each of these pieces, called a vertebra, is rigid; but since the vertebrae are movable upon one another, they provide just that combination of high tensile strength and flexibility needed to support the large body size, the marked muscularity, and the speed that characterize the vertebrate way of life. In contrast, the invertebrate groups generally lack any kind of rigid internal skeleton to which powerful muscles can be attached, and many of the groups consist of small, soft-bodied, flabby animals that drift, crawl, burrow, glide, or inch their way along. Some, like the clams and the arthropods, do have hard skeletons that support and protect the body and provide a rigid surface against which muscles can pull, but these are external encasing skeletons; and a hard covering that must enclose the whole body grows disproportionately heavy with increase in body size. Many invertebrates move swiftly, but mostly in bodies of very small size.

A striking difference between vertebrates and invertebrates has been apparent to man at least since the prehistoric time when he was a primitive nomad, managing a precarious existence as a fisher, a hunter, and a gatherer of seeds and fruits. We can imagine him one day stalking a wolf and getting nothing for all his skill and courage but a few slashing bites from the sharp teeth of his big, fast, and intelligent vertebrate adversary. Then, coming out of the woods to a rocky seashore at low tide, he discovers that the rocks are covered with a very different kind of creature—a shelled animal that neither flees nor turns on its attacker but lies quiet and defenseless within its hard shell until this is split open, with a rock, to expose the soft, flabby, deliciously edible, bite-size invertebrate within. Seashores in many parts of the world bear witness to such scenes of long ago as this. On the shores of Denmark, for example, there are huge mounds that are filled mostly with the shells of mussels, periwinkles, and cockles, but also contain charred bones, stone tools, and other kinds of refuse discarded in these prehistoric kitchen middens. There is no difficulty for us today in distinguishing invertebrate remains from vertebrate, for no substance quite like bone is found in any invertebrate group (though they do sometimes have cartilage-like materials). The texture and detailed structure of bone is unique to vertebrates; and even the deposited salts, of calcium phosphate, are seldom found in invertebrate skeletons, which are typically of calcium carbonate.

In radially symmetrical invertebrates there is no head, and the central nervous system is a ring of tissue encircling the animal. But in the much more numerous bilateral invertebrates the central nervous system is a pair of solid nerve cords that run along the midline of the belly (not the back, as in vertebrates). Each cord has swellings, the nerve ganglia, that are concentrations of nerve cells and that act as nerve centers. In those invertebrates that have heads, the largest ganglion is in the head, where the sense organs are concentrated, and it is called the brain. The small invertebrate brain has room for few cells

that are free to do much except coordinate the muscles and relay information from sense organs to muscles. Even if the tiny brain were capable of handling much learning, there would scarcely be time for such a luxury in the great majority of invertebrates, for most have brief life cycles. They usually feed, grow, reproduce, and die within a few weeks or, at most, months. To do this, they must come into the world equipped with instinctive behavior patterns, and these are promptly elicited by the stimuli of their environment. Only to a very limited extent can they take advantage of the adaptive possibilities and of the flexibility of learned behavior. Though we can demonstrate, even in the one-celled protozoans, some capacity to modify behavior as a result of experience, it is instinct, not learning, that dominates behavior in the invertebrate world. This is true even in the generally highly developed line of evolution that led to the insects.

All invertebrates are cold-blooded; that is, they have no mechanism for controlling their internal body temperature, which in turn controls the rate at which bodily activities can take place. At all seasons they must adjust to the temperature of the external environment—living actively when temperatures are moderately high, becoming dormant or dying when temperatures are very low or very high. None has the capacity to be up and about at either of the temperature extremes to which a warm-blooded vertebrate like man can adjust. This does distinguish them from the warm-blooded birds and mammals— but not from the lower classes of vertebrates, the fishes, amphibians, and reptiles, which also are cold-blooded. In a desert at high noon or on an arctic tundra in the dead of winter, we would see none but birds and mammals on the move. Only in tropical regions, where cold-blooded animals can remain active at all seasons, or in all the great seas of the world, where the water masses themselves act as thermal regulators for the animals that live in them, is it readily evident that ours is indeed an invertebrate world.

One may seriously question whether it is logical to divide the animal kingdom into animals with and animals without backbones, since there are only some 55,000 species of vertebrates and nearly a million known species of invertebrates—perhaps several million when zoologists have finally named and described all of them. The vertebrates are admittedly a highly successful group; and many of them, such as man, are big, cunning, aggressive, and noisy, and attract an undue amount of attention to themselves. From the viewpoint of a zoologist, though, the five kinds of vertebrates—fishes, amphibians, reptiles, birds, and mammals—are all so similar that they must be considered only as five of the classes of one major phylum or group, the phylum Chordata. Sharing the same phylum with the vertebrates (in most classifications) are three small subphyla of invertebrate chordates built on the same basic body plan but lacking the vertebrated backbone and other internal bones.

The union of invertebrate animals, on the other hand, is not a natural grouping but merely a convenient device for talking about at least twenty-eight different phyla—some say more—with as many different basic designs for living. The discrepancy in number of phyla results from differences of opinion as to just what constitutes a body plan distinctive enough to entitle a group to a phylum of its own.

Classifying animals in neat cubicles labeled with long, resounding names tends to obscure the fact that such names designate phyla of very different size and importance, and that the characteristics used to differentiate the groups are not always of equal magnitude. To emphasize these points, the list of phyla given below has apposed to it rough approximations of the number of living species and also a few subheadings that indicate either deep cleavages or broad

Subkingdom Protozoa	Subkingdom Metazoa
Phylum Protozoa: 30,000	(continued)
Subkingdom Parazoa	*Phylum Entoprocta: 60*
Phylum Porifera: 4,500	*Phylum Chaetognatha: 30*
Subkingdom Metazoa	*Phylum Hemichordata: 100*
Phylum Coelenterata:	*Phylum Pogonophora: 22*
9,000	*Phylum Phoronida: 15*
Phylum Ctenophora: 80	*Phylum Bryozoa: 6,000*
Phylum Mesozoa: 7	*Phylum Brachiopoda: 260*
Phylum Platyhelminthes:	*Phylum Sipunculoidea:*
9,000	*250*
Phylum Nemertea: 570	*Phylum Echiuroidea: 60*
Phylum Nematoda: 10,500	*Phylum Mollusca: 40,000*
Phylum Rotifera: 1,200	*Phylum Annelida: 6,000*
Phylum Gastrotricha: 100	*Phylum Arthropoda (ex-*
Phylum Kinorhyncha: 30	*clusive of insects): 65,000*
Phylum Priapulida: 6	*Phylum Echinodermata:*
Phylum Nematomorpha: 80	*5,500*
Phylum Acanthocephala:	*Phylum Chordata (exclu-*
400	*sive of vertebrates): 1,320*

bonds. The numbers given here are only tentative and all of them are subject to change as new forms are found, described, and named. Occasionally a group even loses a species or two because a specialist finds that two or more named species are really variants of the same species. In practice it is not easy to decide how much variation can be allowed within the bounds of a single species or of higher ranks in the classificatory scheme, so that the "lumpers" and the "splitters" among taxonomists often engage in spirited arguments over criteria. If there are difficulties even at the species level, where the specialists are dealing with the more or less natural category that we think of as "a kind of animal"— a man or a dog or a honeybee—it is little wonder

that the disagreement increases as we approach the larger and more arbitrary groupings.

It is apparent that the "great divide" in the animal kingdom is not that between vertebrates and invertebrates, even though this distinction was first made by Aristotle. He did not use those terms, but mistakenly divided the animal kingdom into the "enaima" ("bloody animals") equivalent to our vertebrates, and the "anaima" ("bloodless animals") corresponding to our modern concept of invertebrates. In his limited experience with invertebrates he did not happen to examine one with red blood, and the colorless blood of invertebrates he did not recognize as blood at all. Though he also recorded that "all sanguineous animals have a backbone," his error of classification stood for more than two thousand years. Then in the early part of the nineteenth century Lamarck used the terms "vertebrate" and "invertebrate," and his fellow Frenchman, the great comparative anatomist Cuvier, made the correct distinction based on the fundamental difference in body plan.

The really wide gap in the animal kingdom, however, is that which separates the one-celled animals, the Protozoa, from the other phyla which we call the Metazoa because they are many-celled. More will be said of this in the next chapter. Here it is also important to point out the setting apart of the many-celled sponges, or Porifera, as a phylum so different from other Metazoa that we feel it must have had a separate origin from the Protozoa. Among metazoans an important distinction sunders the two-layered coelenterates and ctenophores from all the groups which have three well-developed primary embryological layers. This third layer appears between the original two, and it produces those firm and bulky tissues which are so conspicuously lacking in the more fragile kinds of coelenterates.

The pattern of animal evolution is not a ladder on which the various groups have ascended rung by rung, but a three-dimensional tree with branches that diverge at various levels. For lack of evidence we cannot make out the exact connections of some of the branches. But looking up along the main trunk of the tree we see clearly that it soon splits into two main branches. One of these is the main line of invertebrate evolution, which gives rise to the segmented worms or annelids; to the two largest invertebrate phyla, the mollusks and arthropods; and also to most of the smaller groups. The other main branch is a minor diversion as far as invertebrates go, for it has only one sizeable invertebrate phylum, the Echinodermata, which includes the starfishes and their allies. These are sluggish creatures, lacking a head, losing their two-sided symmetry, and possessing the most feeble kind of nervous system. Yet from this stock, man and the vertebrates appear to have come.

CHAPTER I

The Protozoans

(*Phylum Protozoa*)

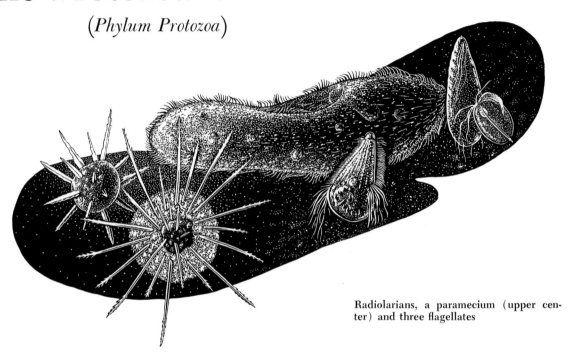

Radiolarians, a paramecium (upper center) and three flagellates

THE protozoans belong to a microscopic world into which we may peer, but only through a glass darkly. We have no hope of coming face to face with the problems of their microcosm because our faces are too big and our sense organs are scaled accordingly. This difference in size, however, does not deter the protozoans from entering very importantly into the natural economy of which we are a part, or from invading our bodies and living there as parasites or as uninvited commensal guests that share the organic matter we ingest. For many thousands of years men have been dying of protozoan-caused amebic dysentery and African sleeping sickness. The Roman Empire is often said to have fallen victim not so much to political events as to the protozoans that cause malaria. Again and again epidemics of protozoan-caused disease have returned to decimate the animals that man has taken into his economic household, causing widespread distress among those who tend silkworms, honeybees, or domestic flocks and herds. Yet the microscopic organisms—at least 100,000 kinds of them, protozoan and otherwise, and many of them occurring on everything men

touched or ate—went unknown and unsuspected during almost all of man's long history on earth.

Then, in 1674, a minor Dutch official named Leeuwenhoek trained a simple lens of his own making on some water from a small inland lake near his home in Delft and became the first to observe and describe living protozoans.

By 1816, when Baron Cuvier was putting together *Le Regne Animal,* the first important modern work on animal classification, he had to write in his preface that "infusorians, offering no field for anatomical investigations, will be briefly disposed of." By infusorians he meant protozoans and rotifers (p. 137), because they were the most numerous of the microscopic forms to be found in infusions, standing water containing decaying organic matter. He disposed of the infusorians in two and one-half pages in a book that ran to about two thousand. Today our knowledge of protozoans is a major branch of biology and fills many hundreds of published volumes. The introduction of achromatic lenses for the microscope has made it possible to see the detailed structure of Leeuwenhoek's "very little animalcules," whose extraordinary variety and complexity first fascinated and then overawed the earlier microscopists. Though some workers delineated the protozoans in superb engravings which we still admire, they also put curious interpretations upon what they saw, because they tried to find stomachs and intestines and kidneys in little animals that they visualized always in terms of vertebrate anatomy. Only when it was realized that protozoans are not miniatures of the larger beasts but animals organized in a very different way from all the other groups did biologists begin to make real headway. Now we understand the protozoan body to consist of a minute bit of a complex mixture of substances known as protoplasm, bounded externally by a membrane and containing at least one formed body, the nucleus. In all other animals the body is built up of a very large number of such nucleated units of protoplasm, called cells. Whether to think of a protozoan as a single cell, or to consider it noncellular (or acellular) because the body is not partitioned up into units as in the many-celled metazoan groups, is a matter still debated by specialists. For our purpose it is enough to keep in mind that a protozoan is not comparable to a single cell of a man but to his whole body.

Size is not the criterion for putting protozoans into a special subkingdom Protozoa apart from all the animals of the other subkingdoms. As we shall see later, there are groups of metazoans that are entirely microscopic, and some as big as lobsters that have free-swimming microscopic stages when they first hatch from the egg. The larger protozoans regularly capture and devour adult metazoans related to the lobster, though sometimes not without a truly heroic struggle. The important distinction, as has already been pointed out, is that of body design. And it is at least as remarkable that protozoans are able to carry on all the complex processes of life within a single microscopic globule as that many-celled animals can do the same thing through the combined activities of vast numbers of walled-off and specialized units.

Having just settled the protozoans comfortably in their place, it seems a little belated to point out that some zoologists have tossed them out of the animal kingdom altogether. The problem of their status began to puzzle microscopists from the moment that Leeuwenhoek first saw green globules swimming under their own power. Today many zoologists still maintain that green unicellular forms that move about actively are properly members of the irritable, restless animal kingdom. Equally firm are the botanists who claim that such forms belong to the plant kingdom, since the green color is that of chlorophyll. Those who feel less sure about what to do with sedentary one-celled plants that have actively swimming sex cells, or where to place swimming green

forms that can lose their pigment and feed like any animal when conditions change, decline to take sides in this tug of war. They prefer to set up a third kingdom of living organisms, the Protista, that admits any form not divided into separate cells. Colonial forms are included because they do not show enough division of labor among the aggregated cells to be considered truly multicellular.

The very existence of modern plant-animals that are green but swim actively and that can shift from plantlike to animal-like feeding habits suggests that there was at one time a primitive stock of green motile organisms, perhaps very much like modern green flagellates (p. 22) from which both plant and animal kingdoms have arisen. Because this book is about animals, it is more convenient here to put flagellated organisms that swim about actively, whether green or colorless, in the phylum Protozoa. This first great grouping in the animal kingdom, as mentioned earlier, is set aside in a special subkingdom of its own.

Numbers

The protozoans or "first animals" deserve their name in more than just the chronological sense. Every larger animal that we carefully examine turns out to harbor one or more species of protozoans, and protozoans themselves may play host to even smaller uninvited protozoans. So it is quite safe to guess that the number of individual protozoans in the world exceeds by far that of all other animal species combined. In the seas, which cover three-quarters of the globe, free-living protozoans occur from top to bottom. The billions upon billions of protozoans in such masses of water are really incomprehensible to our simple mammalian minds.

Despite the inconceivable numbers of protozoans in all bodies of water and in all surface soils, and the intimate association enjoyed by some twenty-five different species of protozoans that live in man, no large grouping of animals is so unfamiliar at first hand to all but professional biologists. In the nineteenth century in England and on the Continent, every gentleman of wealth who had any pretensions to intellectual curiosity displayed a microscope in his living room and perhaps belonged to a microscope club in which he could exchange his latest observations with like-minded friends. This has gone out of fashion, and the only microscopes found in most homes are toylike versions for children. The almost incredible fairyland of beautiful and bizarre creatures that swim, feed, pursue each other, and reproduce—unabashed by the gaze of anyone who chooses to look at them through a microscope—may some day again become a source of entertainment and intellectual satisfaction after we have pushed most of the bigger animals to near extinction. For protozoans are accessible to anyone who can spare

Long and slender *Spirostomum*, a giant among protozoans, dwarfs the smaller, slipper-shaped *Paramecium*. Two rotifers in this same microscope field are many-celled animals, yet are barely larger than the paramecia. (General Biological Supply House, Chicago)

the space for a jar of water from a bird bath, a stagnant pool, or the plant-invaded edge of a pond. There are known to us roughly thirty thousand species of protozoans, and new ones are reported almost every day. But there are also presumably respectable ones that are suddenly dispossessed of their status and have to move in with their relatives because they are shown not to be different enough to be considered separate species.

Size

Protozoan predominance in number loses some of its overwhelming impressiveness when we consider that almost all protozoans are minute and that most of them are microscopic. The smallest forms, parasites that live within other animal cells, are only 2 microns (1 micron = $\frac{1}{25,000}$ of an inch) in their longest diameter. To learn much about the structure of such animals is difficult even for the most experienced microscopists using the best microscopes. Fortunately, most of the free-living forms come in larger packages, but even these are invisible to the naked eye except when a colored species multiplies so fast that through sheer density it colors sea water pink, a rain pool blood-red, forms green scum on ponds, or gives a pink or greenish cast to large snow banks.

Paramecium caudatum is of moderate size (180 to 300 microns or $\frac{1}{250}$ to $\frac{1}{100}$ of an inch) and can barely be seen by the unaided eye as a white speck darting about in a dish of pond water. Ten times larger than this are such fresh-water giants as *Spirostomum* and *Stentor*, which often measure more than $\frac{3}{25}$ of an inch. Even these are dwarfed by the shelled foraminiferans of marine waters. If we admit to the phylum Protozoa the slime molds (the Mycetozoa), which many botanists classify as fungi, then these super-amebas, with hundreds of nuclei but without cellular partitions, are by far the largest protozoans. During the multinuclear stage the ameboid body may extend for several feet as it crawls slowly over a rotten log on the forest floor. The size of any particular protozoan may vary with nutritional state and with changing conditions in the environment. It depends also upon consistent hereditary differences that mark the many races or strains of any one species. So size is not always a dependable criterion for identifying a protozoan. Nevertheless, a fairly definite adult size does characterize each species, as well as each stage of its life cycle.

Gross Structure

Though it will save time to consider the protozoans as a whole before going on to separate accounts of the classes, generalizations come hard about a group that matches all of the rest of the animal kingdom in its range of sizes, shapes, habitats, structural specializations, feeding habits, and life cycles. Only the basic body plan brings all of these extraordinarily varied creatures into a single grouping. The body consists of one undivided mass of living substance, or protoplasm, bounded by an external membrane that regulates exchanges of materials with the outside environment. Near the center of the protoplasm is a formed body, the nucleus, which is in control of essential chemical processes. If an ameba is deprived of its nucleus by accidental or experimental manipulation, the part without the nucleus may move about for a time, but it cannot feed and it soon dies. There is usually only one nucleus, but when there are two or more, no one nucleus is in sole charge of any particular portion of the protoplasm. In some species the division of the original mass results in a group of cells that remain attached to each other as a protozoan colony. Such a colony differs from a multicellular body in that the cells are usually all alike except during reproduction and in that any one can live independently of the others.

Body Symmetry

Protozoans come in every major type of symmetry known in the animal kingdom. In this they differ from all other groups, for in each multicellular phylum the members are consistent in having some one kind of symmetry. The freely floating protozoans, such as the radiolarians, are likely to be spherically symmetrical, with organs of locomotion and feeding, or protective spines, projecting from the whole surface and meeting life in every direction. Bottom-living forms that grow attached by a stalk are usually radially symmetrical, with a mouth at the free end surrounded by a ring of food-trapping organs. The fast swimmers, various ciliates and flagellates, are usually bilaterally symmetrical, with front and rear end, top and bottom surfaces. They may have an asymmetrical spiral twist at the front. Finally, many protozoans can be described only as asymmetrical.

Habitats

Protozoan habitats are all essentially aquatic, though the amount of water required by a microscopic animal may sometimes be no more than the merest film between particles of damp soil or of rain-moistened desert sand. Parasitic protozoans find adequate moisture between or within the living cells of their plant or animal hosts. The free-living protozoans abound in all bodies of water, large or small: in puddles of standing rain water and in rain-filled tree holes or hollow stumps; in bird baths or flower urns; in ditches and canals; in brooks and rivers; in swamps, ponds, and lakes; and in all the seas of the world. Even the melting surfaces of icebergs, glaciers, and snow banks have active populations of flagellates, as one can tell at a distance by the greenish or reddish cast of such snow. At the other temperature extreme are the protozoans that live in hot springs (at up to 133°F. in one place in Japan). This is highly exceptional, of course, and most protozoans die when their external environment reaches temperatures between 97°F. and 104°F. They lack the internal controls that enable a warm-blooded (really temperature-constant) animal like man to keep his body temperature from rising much above 98.6°F. even when his surroundings rise to temperature levels that kill living protoplasm. The optimum temperature range for activity and growth of protozoans seems to be between 61°F. and 77°F.

Distribution

The common protozoan species are ubiquitous. A schoolboy who scoops up pond water in Australia is likely to find the same species of *Paramecium* as will a boy in Germany or California. Soil samples all the way from Greenland to Argentina have yielded *Amoeba proteus*. Apparently, animals that are as small as protozoans and have the habit of encysting (encasing themselves in a dormant condition within a waterproof, resistant wall) are readily transported about the world by wind, animals, and the slightest movement in bodies of water. Thus protozoans, and especially those that live in large bodies of water,

show very little of the limitations in geographic distribution that are due to mechanical barriers and that we expect in dealing with the larger animals. This does not mean that protozoan species do not differ where conditions of life make different demands. In the seas there are characteristic species of warm and of cold waters, of shallow and of deep waters, of surface waters and of sandy or muddy bottoms. Where fresh waters move rapidly, protozoans are sparse; but where such water is slow-moving or stagnant, especially if there is much organic matter present, protozoans come into their own.

The numbers of protozoans, contrary to what many people suppose, are greatest in arctic and antarctic waters, which are richest in the nitrogenous compounds necessary for protoplasmic growth. Tropical seas are home to a great variety of species, including most of the really bizarre protozoans, but these do not occur in the dense populations that make cold waters a kind of protozoan soup.

The salt content (salinity) of waters also determines what species will be found there. Especially versatile species are at home in marine, brackish, and fresh waters; but most are restricted to one of these habitats, or even to a particular level of salt content. Brine pools or large salty bodies such as Great Salt Lake contain some species of flagellates, amebas, and ciliates that are not found elsewhere.

More critical than salt content for many protozoans is the acidity or alkalinity of the water or moist soil in which they must thrive. A few species are regularly found in extreme situations, such as in the highly acid drainage from mines, but most grow best under conditions that hover close about the neutrality point. If grown above or below their most favorable range, some species are not only smaller but have a very different body shape.

In soils protozoans live mostly within six inches of the surface, but they can be found in small numbers even at depths of several feet. Their numbers vary mainly with the supply of bacterial food, and in moist, rich soils the density of amebas and flagellates may reach a million per gram of soil, even though you cannot see anything alive about the soil as you pass it through your fingers. Whether protozoans play a role in enriching the soil, or whether they are harmful to the soil by destroying soil-enriching bacteria, we do not really know, even though this is a matter of great economic importance.

Encystment

Where the sun beats down on desert sands protozoans are scarce. They stay quietly within their cyst walls except immediately after a rain, when they emerge to feed actively—perhaps for no more than a single hour during a whole year. As the sand dries the protozoan rounds up and appears to lose its specialized structures. It extrudes any undigested food, and then shrinks by expelling water. Finally it secretes around itself outer and then inner cyst walls. Many encyst also when they are regenerating injured parts, reproducing, or simply digesting a big meal. Dry cysts have in extreme cases been shown to be capable of returning to active life again at any time during half a century if proper conditions are supplied. For most species the period of viability lasts only for several months to several years. Encystment is characteristic of parasitic protozoans, for these must temporarily leave their comfortable berths inside moist and nutritious hosts in spreading the species from one host to another. In the oceans encysting protozoans are rare, for the tremendous volume of the marine habitat acts as a great stabilizing mechanism against changes of any kind. Bodies of fresh water are smaller and so less stable as aquatic environments. In temporary ponds and marshes protozoans regularly encyst and excyst with the round of dry and wet seasons. Not all forms can do this, and among the exceptions, as far as we know, is the familiar *Paramecium caudatum.*

The capacity to encyst has opened to protozoans a tremendous assortment of land-based but irregularly moist niches which would otherwise be too unreliable for aquatic organisms. Such are the bark on the shady side of trees, the cavities of insectivorous plants and of cup-shaped flowers, the axils of leaves, the crevices in beds of moss, and the surfaces of grasses and other vertical vegetation that are regularly wet by dew. A special fauna inhabits the freshly laid feces of animals, remaining active until the sun bakes the feces dry, then encysting again.

Nutrition

The protozoan approach to nutrition runs the entire gamut of possibilities. There are green flagellated forms able to use the energy of sunshine to synthesize their food, like any green plant, from simple materials in water and soil. And there are colorless protozoans that roam, chase, and capture prey like any carnivorous animal. Between these wholly plantlike or wholly animal-like methods are a series of intermediate solutions to the problem of earning a living. Some forms absorb already synthesized and dissolved foods through their external surface and are known as saprozoic feeders. These include many free-living flagellates as well as most of the parasitic protozoans. Others turn from "independent" or photosynthetic habits to saprozoic feeding when occasion permits, thus availing themselves of an alternative source of food whenever it presents itself. By far the greatest number of free-living protozoans earn their living by ingesting whole organisms or large particles of organic debris. They feed on bacteria, yeasts, algae, wood particles, and small animals, either other protozoans or certain small metazoans.

Reproduction

Reproduction in the protozoans is essentially the same as in the multicellular groups, for in all animals the basic process is cell division. Sexual processes are widespread among protozoans, and in some species must take place at intervals or the strain will die out, but they do not occur in all species. As far as we have been able to determine, *Amoeba proteus,* for example, has only asexual reproduction. When the animal has reached a certain size and maturity, it divides into two cells, each containing half of the nucleus and of the hereditary materials of the nucleus. This division of the parent cell into two halves (binary fission) is the most common method of reproduction in protozoans. Two other main types of asexual division are known. One is budding, in which the parent cell retains its individuality while producing, by division, one or more "daughter" cells, usually much smaller in size and less differentiated than the parent. Either before or after it is freed, the bud grows to resemble the parent in size and structure. Budding is typical of the Suctoria but is rare in other groups. Multiple fission, or sporulation, is an asexual process in which the nucleus divides many times, and then the protoplasm divides into as many offspring as there are newly formed nuclei. This is the protozoan version of mass production, and it results in extremely rapid multiplication. It is seen especially in forms like the sporozoans. Through the various asexual processes a species is assured rapid multiplication and the maintenance of its numbers. Through sexual processes there arises a steady supply of new variants, individuals with new combinations of hereditary characteristics. Each sexually produced individual has the possibility of being better adapted in some way than were either of its parents. Thus sexual processes provide the hereditary variations upon which natural selection may act. Their significance for adaptation and evolution is the same in the protozoans as in higher animals. In animals as small as protozoans growth and reproduction take place on a time scale measured in hours, not years. *Paramecium* may undergo binary fission as often as three times a day, the smaller ciliate, *Glaucoma,* eight times a day.

Behavior

Anyone who observes the speed with which protozoans dart backward after striking an obstruction, or the persistency with which they squeeze through a narrow passageway between two algal filaments, or the ingenuity with which a sluggish ameba captures a fast-moving ciliate, will want to credit protozoans with a full share of the irritability and modifiability that are characteristic of all living protoplasm. Whether this involves "consciousness" is something we can only guess about. A single cell cannot provide the complex sense organs or nervous system that we see in higher animals, but protozoans apparently do use flagella, pseudopods, and cilia as tactile organs, and probably also as chemoreceptors to detect food or chemical changes in the water. Near the front end of many green flagellates there is a specialized photoreceptor in connection with the red-pigmented eyespot or stigma. Many ciliates, including *Paramecium,* have been shown to have a neuromotor system, a counterpart, within the cell, of a nervous system, which conducts information from one point to another and which coordinates the beating of the cilia. Nevertheless, we know that perception, conduction, and responsiveness can all occur in what appears to be undifferentiated protoplasm. Protozoans in general probably are sensitive over the entire surface of the cell to such stimuli as light, contact, excesses of heat and cold, concentration of chemicals, or presence of food. And when they respond, they usually do so by a movement of the whole animal. The responses of protozoans are stereotyped, but no more so than the reflexes of higher animals. And they are not invariable.

Body Structure

In touching briefly on the ways in which protozoans move about, feed, grow, and reproduce, we are reminded again that they perform all of the same life activities as do the other animals among which they must live and compete. The clear implication is that the "simple protozoans" are not as simple as they appear to the human eye, even though some of them have little visible structure. There are, moreover, some protozoans that are among the most complex cells known. One ciliate, *Epidinium ecaudatum,* displays at least forty-eight protoplasmic structures that can be described and named. This exceeds the complexity of some of the lower metazoans. The endless variety of protozoan structural specializations can hardly be discussed adequately in anything less than a good-sized treatise. Those merely alluded to here are the ones that are visible in the accompanying photographs.

The nucleus is the one structural specialization or organelle that is consistently present and indispensable. It is not always easy to see in the living protozoan, especially in a photograph. In a stained preparation it usually stains much darker than the unspecialized protoplasm or cytoplasm. The nucleus may appear quite different during the various stages of the life cycle. A protozoan that has recently fed contains conspicuous food-filled globules, the food vacuoles. These are not specialized structures but merely droplets of water containing ingested food in various stages of digestion. The surrounding protoplasm secretes digestive enzymes into these food vacuoles, and as the food body undergoes digestion it gradually dissolves, the dissolved substances passing into the protoplasm to be used there for supplying energy or growth needs. Flagellates that manufacture their own food by photosynthesis have no food vacuoles (with rare exception), but instead have one or more prominent pigment bodies, the chromatophores ("color-bearers"). These may be bright green, yellow, green, or brown—depending upon how much yellow or red pigment is present to mask the bright green color of the photosynthetic pigment, chlorophyll. A conspicuous organelle is the contractile vacuole, a pulsating clear globule that accumulates and expels to the exterior excess fluid from the protoplasm of many protozoans, especially fresh-water species. Such vacuoles are usually absent in marine or parasitic forms other than ciliates. In ciliates the feeding habits tend to increase the amount of fluid taken into the body. There is no very good evidence for supposing that the contractile vacuole also acts as a special device for ridding the organism of metabolic wastes, in the manner of the vertebrate kidney. And in any case this could not be its major role, since so many protozoans are able to do without a contractile vacuole. Usually there is only one such vacuole, as in *Amoeba proteus,* but *Paramecium* has two, and some protozoans have many. The locomotor organelles, and an extraordinary array of skeletal structures that encase or support the delicate protoplasm, especially of the flagellate and ameboid types, will be described in connection with the groups in which they occur.

The Flagellates

(*Class Flagellata* or *Mastigophora*)

The flagellated protozoans or "whip-bearers" are the most widely distributed of the protozoans, occurring in every place that it is moist, from hot springs to the melting surfaces of glaciers. In all seas the greatest portion of the protozoan component of the floating surface population consists of flagellates. Almost any bit of unlovely green scum from the surface of a pond, when mounted in a drop of water on a microscope slide, will suddenly become transformed into a field of shimmering, green, ovate creatures that swim rapidly but with a jerkiness that distinguishes them from their more smoothly gliding ciliated relatives. The jerkiness is not due to an intermittent supply of power but to the rotation and gyration of the flagellate body as the flagellum is thrust forward with a whiplike motion that draws the animal along. It usually cuts a spiral path in the water but moves in a fairly straight line.

Now that spindles are no longer so common as they used to be, words like "fish-shaped" or "submarine-shaped" are replacing "spindle-shaped" in descriptions of these little animals, which tend to be widest in the middle and tapering toward both ends. The front end may be more rounded than the rear, or just the reverse. In either case the end that goes first in locomotion has some sort of depression into which the flagella (usually one to four in number, but sometimes eight or many) are inserted. The outer layer of most flagellates is firm enough to maintain a constant body shape. The surface covering may be a stiff pellicle handsomely sculptured with spiral or longitudinal ridges, or it may be thin and plastic and allow for squirming "euglenoid movements," named for the familiar fresh-water *Euglena* in which they are most often seen. A completely constant shape is shown by those dinoflagellates that are enclosed in hard skeletons. When a hard surface layer is absent altogether, the animal may be ameboid, at times even losing the flagellum and moving about by extending pseudopods.

The flagellates are the only group in either plant or animal kingdoms that utilizes all three main methods of feeding: photosynthesis, saprozoism, and ingestion of solid food. Even a single flagellate species may use the whole repertoire. The photosynthetic flagellates feed like plants, and all have pigmented bodies containing the green pigment chlorophyll; but the green may be masked by additional pigments that make it appear red, yellow, or brown. Even flagellates that lack chlorophyll may show, in the protoplasm, refractive bodies which contain reserves of starch or a similar substance. These have a pale bluish green tinge and should be easily distinguishable from the bright green color of chlorophyll. Food reserves also include oil and fats. Photosynthetic flagellates usually have a pigmented eyespot or stigma, near the base of the flagellum, that partly shades a highly light-sensitive region of the protoplasm and enables these animals to orient readily to light and to remain as much as possible in the degree of light intensity at which they carry on photosynthesis most advantageously. Parasitic flagellates are entirely saprozoic, absorbing dissolved nutrients through the body surface. Most free-living colorless flagellates are animal-like feeders that take in solid food.

Reproduction is almost entirely asexual in flagellates, though some species do show sexual reproduction. In the usual asexual method the body splits lengthwise down the middle, beginning at the front end and proceeding toward the rear. Often this occurs at a definite hour of the day. Some always divide while in an encysted state; others reproduce within cysts only at certain times. Resistant cysts are formed readily if conditions change. Colony formation is widespread, especially among green forms, and in such colonies there may be division of labor between ordinary feeding individuals and those that can reproduce, and between reproductive cells that form male or female sex cells.

Some of the green (zoochlorellae) and the much more common yellow or brown algalike cells (zooxanthellae) seen in the bodies of a great variety of protozoans and metazoans, most of them marine, have been shown to be modified flagellates. These live imprisoned within the bodies of their hosts and escape as free-living forms only at certain times. Within the transparent host body they enjoy a place in the sun, yet they are well protected and have all about them a steady supply of carbon dioxide and more especially of other waste products of the host. From these they can obtain the nitrogenous compounds that are at such a premium in the tropical or warm waters that are home to most of such flagellates. The host receives oxygen and probably benefits from the removal of its wastes. Whether it also receives food or uses the pigmented cells as a food reserve is not clear in most cases.

As a group the flagellates lie somewhere between the algae and the amebas, overlapping somewhat at the edges with both groups. The nature of the overlap makes it quite plausible that the green flagellates are the ancestral group from which both plant and animal kingdoms have been derived. The ancestral group has remained, on the whole, the most primitive of the five classes of protozoans, but particular members are among the most complex protozoans that we know about. There are many different orders of both plantlike and animal-like flagellates, but only some examples can be given, of species most commonly seen or of some interest for the ways in which they benefit or annoy man.

THE PLANTLIKE FLAGELLATES
(*Subclass Phytomastigina*)

THE CHRYSOMONADS

Typical of the chrysomonads ("golden units") is the oval *Chromulina,* with two large pigment bodies in which the golden-brown color masks the green chlorophyll. When it is abundant enough in fresh waters, the water appears brown. Any single individual, however, is less than $\frac{1}{10,000}$ of an inch long. Its one flagellum whips the water, pulling the body along in the fast vibratory glide characteristic of flagellates; but there are times when it uses pseudopods to move like an ameba. *Dinobryon* has two unequal flagella which protrude from the transparent, vase-shaped cellulose case that encloses the animal. It lives either as a solitary individual or as a branching attached colony, and if abundant in water reservoirs, imparts a fishy odor to the water, like that of cod-liver oil. Also colonial is *Synura,* with the individuals attached at their inner ends and the flagellar ends extending out radially in all directions. *Synura* may be very numerous under the ice of ponds in winter. When it is the dominant form in a pond, the water has an odor like that of ripe cucumbers or muskmelon and tastes both bitter and spicy. The odors and tastes imparted by flagellates are due to aromatic oils stored as food reserves and liberated when the animals die. One part of oil from *Synura* can be detected in twenty-five million parts of water, so that it may be necessary to filter the water or to add to it minute quantities of copper sulphate which inhibits the growth of the small organisms without doing readily detectable harm to man or other animals. Marine chrysomonads often are enclosed in beautiful latticed cases or have the body surface covered or embedded with secreted plates of calcium carbonate called coccoliths. These range from flat oval disks to plates ornamented with long rodlike or trumpetlike extensions. The coccoliths of bottom deposits from tropical and subtropical seas were well known to biologists long before the living flagellates that produced the skeletons had ever been seen. The disintegrated skeletons continue to be deposited at a rate that is estimated for an area in the North Atlantic, at a depth of 7200 feet, to be sixty billions of shells per square meter (about ten square feet) annually. They add their bulk to the more numerous and more durable shells of ameboid protozoans (forams and radiolarians).

THE CRYPTOMONADS

Cryptomonas, of fresh water, is a photosynthetic cryptomonad with two flagella protruding from a distinct opening at the front, and two yellowish or brownish green pigment bodies. The very similar but colorless and saprozoic *Chilomonas* is the commonest and most familiar cryptomonad of stagnant fresh waters. We know a great deal about its remarkable nutrition. It can synthesize protoplasm from inorganic material provided that certain chemicals are present.

THE DINOFLAGELLATES

The numerous dinoflagellates are distinguished by the two flagella seen in all the typical forms. In these a long flagellum trails downward with the long axis of the body from a hole in a longitudinal groove, and another flagellum undulates in steady waves in a groove that encircles the body at right angles to the upright axis. They swim in a bouncy sort of way, and occur in incalculable numbers, providing the nutritional basis for the surface-floating animal populations in all seas and in ponds and

lakes. Some cause the destructive "red tides" referred to below. Most of them are photosynthetic, usually have an eyespot, and have green, yellow, or brown pigment bodies. The single nucleus is very large. Some dinoflagellates live as floating rounded forms that look like algae. Many are believed to be the yellow alga-like bodies seen inside marine protozoans, especially in tropical radiolarians. Others are external or internal parasites. The colorless forms engulf small organisms in ameboid fashion.

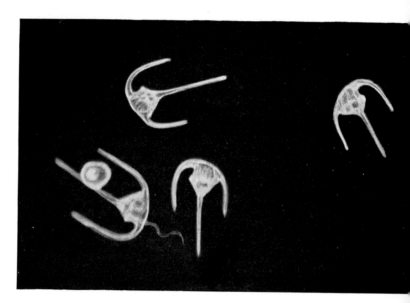

Marine dinoflagellates, *Ceratium tripos,* with three long spines on the encasing armor, are tremendously abundant in surface waters. One extrudes a long flagellum. (England. D. P. Wilson)

The typical dinoflagellates, all with two grooves and two flagella, may be either armored or unarmored, the latter kind either naked or enclosed in a cellulose membrane. Most are marine, but some genera are also numerous in fresh waters. *Gymnodinium brevis,* a marine species, suddenly "bloomed" in 1947 in concentrations higher than five million to a quart, causing a "red tide" off the Florida coast. The toxin provided by such large numbers of dinoflagellates killed coastal marine animals over a wide area, and littered the beaches for many miles with a hundred pounds of rotting fish per running foot. Off the southern and Lower California coast destructive red tides are caused in certain summers by the rise of *Gonyaulax polyhedra,* a heavily armored dinoflagellate whose toxin kills fishes, shrimps, crabs, barnacles, oysters, and clams. Similar dinoflagellate-caused red tides also occur off the Atlantic coast of Spain and Portugal, and either red or yellow tides cause serious local problems in many other parts of

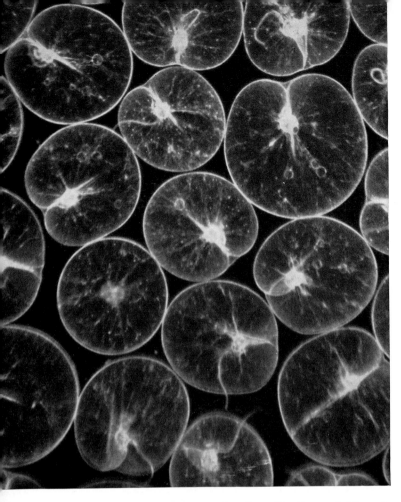

Luminescent dinoflagellate, *Noctiluca scintillans*, is noted for tinting the sea surface pink in the daytime, lighting it at night. (England. D. P. Wilson)

head-sized, nearly spherical, and mostly gelatinous bodies are colorless, pale pink, or yellowish, and when dense can make extensive areas of the sea appear, in the daytime, like pale tomato soup. At night this protozoan is a major cause of the luminescence of seas. As ships plow through the water, disturbing billions of *Noctiluca,* the waves that they set up flame in the darkness, and the trailing wake scintillates with minute flashes. Where *Noctiluca*-laden waters are thrown with great force against steep rocky shores, the nighttime displays are truly spectacular, suggesting fireworks set off under water, though this bioluminescence, or animal light, gives off no measurable heat and dissipates little of the animal's energy. In marine waters that enter plumbing installations, the luminescent effects can be startling. Inshore winds may compact *Noctiluca* to a surface crust on the waters and also bring them ashore, where they are seen, on sand beaches, as a red scum at high tide mark. A noctiluca was once described by T. H. Huxley as looking like a little peach, with a waving, finger-like tentacle as long as the body, emerging from the place where the stalk of a peach might be. Under the microscope we see that the curling tentacle emerges from one end of a pouchlike depression. The animal floats mostly with the feeding pouch down, and the tentacle wafts diatoms and dinoflagellates toward the mouth, or even manages to cram in the larvae of copepods or other crustaceans, which distort the enclosing *Noctiluca* body. Digestion goes on in the protoplasmic mass that lies at the bottom of the pouch, and that branches and rebranches into fine filaments radiating out through the thin gelatinous bulk that adds to the buoyancy of the animal. Organisms too small to be easily strained out of the water by larger animals are thus converted into packages of *Noctiluca* size. These are then available to small crustaceans, which form the next links in the chains of animals of increasing size that make up the network of animal feeders of the seas.

THE EUGLENOID FLAGELLATES

Distance lends no enchantment to *Euglena* in the mass, and to many people a green pond scum of this flagellate is not pleasing. But close up, under the magnifying powers of a microscope, a single euglena, propelled gracefully across a lighted microscope field, rich green in color and often beautifully sculptured with surface ornamentation, is as lovely a sight as any living organism. In the various species of *Euglena* the pellicle may be striated, or ridged with rows of spines or knobs, often spirally arranged; and it is highly elastic, permitting the wormlike creeping "euglenoid" movements named for this common genus. In euglenoids of other genera the pellicle may be rigid. At the front end of a spindle-shaped euglena is a flasklike depression, the gullet, and from

the world. On the California coast several epidemics of shellfish poisoning in men have been attributed to the eating of a common California mussel, *Mytilus californianus,* which may in summer become loaded with *Gonyaulax catenella,* known to produce a very toxic substance.

The most significant of all dinoflagellates are the typical genera *Peridinium* and *Ceratium,* of both fresh and salt water, which have large numbers of species and of individuals. *Ceratium* has three spines on its enclosing armor, and these tend to be short and thick in cold, highly saline waters and very thin and long in warm, less salty waters. The greater surface of the longer, thinner spines retards sinking in the less dense low-salinity warmer water, so that it is actually easier, in certain oceanographic studies, to use the species of *Ceratium* as a "biological indicator" of salinity than it is to make actual measurements of salt content.

Noctiluca is one of the largest, most aberrant, and most conspicuous of the flagellates. What is usually considered a single species, preferably called *Noctiluca scintillans* ("night light that scintillates"), occurs off oceanic shores all over the world. The pin-the narrow neck of the flask there emerges the single long flagellum. Into the rounded base of the flask a large contractile vacuole discharges its fluid content at frequent intervals. No one has ever seen a green euglena take particles of food into its gullet, but if placed in the dark the animal does lose its green pigment, chlorophyll, and lives by absorbing nutrient material through the surface. Next to the gullet is a bright red eyespot, and if a dish of euglenas is placed near a window they gather quickly in the lighted side of the dish if the light intensity is not too great. They are negative, however, to very strong sunlight.

This special sensitivity to light plays a major role in the life of animals that must use the energy of sunlight to synthesize their food supply. *Euglena gracilis* is small as euglenoids go, $\frac{1}{500}$ of an inch, and the flagellum is shorter than the body. It is one of the most common species, apparently because it can adapt to a wider range of acid or alkaline conditions than can others. *Euglena rubra* contains thousands of red granules, which may be concentrated in one central area, allowing the green color of the pigment bodies to predominate, or which may be distributed through the protoplasm, covering the green bodies and giving a red color to the animal and to the scum it forms on barnyard ponds, especially in very hot weather. During sunlight hours a pond may appear red, then turn green when the sun goes down. Colorless euglenoids live by devouring bacteria, algae, diatoms, and the smaller protozoans. Reproduction in *Euglena* is by asexual fission only, with the body splitting down the middle and parallel to the long axis of the body. Division may occur in the free-swimming animal, but the encysted reproductive stage is so common that it may be the sole content of the green scum covering a pond. If examined under a microscope it looks more like an alga.

THE PHYTOMONADS

The most plantlike of the flagellates are the phytomonads ("plantlike units"), which resemble algae in having, typically, a rounded shape, a rigid cellulose wall, and grass-green pigment bodies. *Chlamydomonas* is common in ponds and ditches and often so numerous there as to render the water an almost opaque green. Especially abundant in waters contaminated by manure, it probably supplements its mostly photosynthetic nutrition with saprophytic feeding, absorbing dissolved nutrients through the body surface. It is small ($\frac{1}{1250}$ of an inch), ovate, has two equal flagella protruding through the cellulose cell membrane, a red eyespot, and a large cup-shaped pigment body. *Carteria* resembles *Chlamydomonas* but has four flagella. It is probably a species of this genus that lives in the tissues of the marine acoel flatworm *Convoluta roscoffensis* (Plate

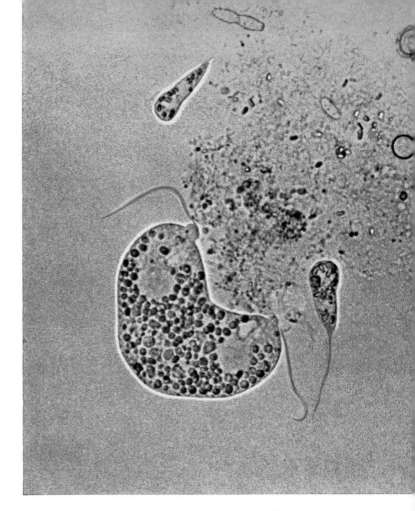

Euglena, in the midst of dividing, shows a split front end, each half with a long flagellum. A smaller flagellate, *Peranema*, is at the right. (Ralph Buchsbaum)

36). *Haematococcus* looks like a reddish *Chlamydomonas* with a loosely fitting outer wall that is attached to the organism by radiating threads of protoplasm. Its red hematochrome granules may be so numerous as to mask the green, giving a red color to standing rain water or to fresh-water ponds in which *Haematococcus* abounds. In the Alps and in the American Rockies *Haematococcus* is well known for imparting a reddish or pinkish color to melting snow drifts.

Colonial phytomonads, all fresh-water forms, are remarkable for the way in which the various species can be arranged in a series showing every stage from a simple flat disk of four cells, as in *Gonium*, that look alike and reproduce in the same way, to complex colonies of many thousands of cells, as in *Volvox*, where cells differ in appearance and in function yet are coordinated into a single behavior unit. Though developed to a lesser degree, these are certainly the beginnings of the multicellularity and the individuality we see in higher plants and animals. *Volvox* is large enough ($\frac{1}{10}$ of an inch in diameter) to be seen in fresh-water ponds as a small green ball that rolls smoothly through the water. Under the microscope this rolling motion (*volvere* is Latin for

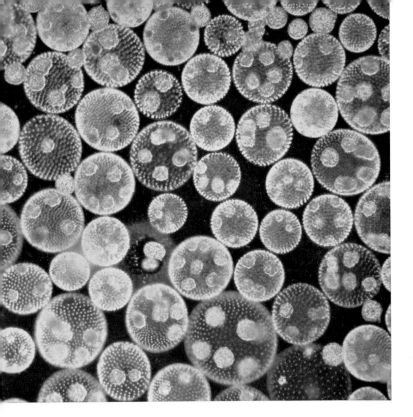

Colonies of *Volvox*, with small daughter colonies showing within the parental spheres. (General Biological Supply House, Chicago)

"roll") comes to be understood as the coordinated beating of thousands of flagella protruding outward from the surface of a fluid-filled gelatinous ball. Each flagellated individual imbedded in the outer layer of the jelly ball is something like *Chlamydomonas*, with an oval body, two equal flagella, a large cup-shaped pigment body, and a red eyespot. If the flagella were not in some way coordinated, such a ball could get nowhere and would simply tumble this way and that. If we watch carefully we see that the same end of the sphere is always the one that goes forward, and careful study has indeed revealed protoplasmic strands that traverse the jelly and connect the individual flagellates with each other. Only particular zooids in the rear half of the sphere can divide asexually, while still others produce small motile sperms or large food-laden eggs. Tumbling about within the fluid-filled interior of a *Volvox* colony are usually to be seen small asexually-produced daughter colonies, which are released to a life of their own when the mother colony breaks down after the spring period of rapid asexual multiplication. In sexual reproduction eggs and sperms are not produced at the same time in any one colony, so that whether the species has both kinds of sex cells in one colony or not, fertilization occurs only between sex cells from different colonies. The resulting fertilized eggs develop a thick, spiny covering, often orange or deep red. They lie dormant during the winter months, but in the spring the covering bursts, releasing the young colony.

THE ANIMAL-LIKE FLAGELLATES
(*Subclass Zoomastigina*)

For admission to the clearly animal-like flagellates (the technical name means "animals with whips") a species must lack photosynthetic pigment bodies and must not be otherwise practically identical with one of the green flagellates. It must never store starch or starch-related carbohydrate reserves, and often it will have more than the two flagella that are characteristic of most plantlike flagellates. In this group of flagellate orders are many of the important parasites of man and his domestic animals.

Most likely to be seen are the free-living *Monas* and *Bodo,* abundant among decaying vegetation and in the infusions examined by students. Extremely small, and active in a microscope field, they do not make for easy examination and are usually dismissed quickly as "common monads." Both have two unequal flagella, but in *Bodo* the longer one trails behind and is used for temporary anchoring. Food is ingested at a spot near the base of the flagella. *Oikomonas,* of fresh waters and of soil, is similar but has only one flagellum. Also with one flagellum are the choanoflagellates ("collar flagellates"), which are generally fixed by a stalk, either singly as in *Monosiga,* or by a branching stalk that unites many zooids as in *Codosiga.* There is a large, delicate protoplasmic collar around the base of the flagellum. Food particles attracted by currents set up by the flagellum adhere to the outside of the collar and are ingested at its base.

Important from the human point of view are the trypanosomes, many of which cause serious or fatal disease in man and in his domestic animals. An African form of trypanosome disease has been known to us at least since the days when the slave traders learned not to accept as captives any Negroes with swollen neck glands, an important symptom of African sleeping sickness. A similar disease in cattle is known as nagana. These are not the same as the epidemics of virus-caused sleeping sickness that strike in the United States during certain summers. The African trypanosomes have no doubt been introduced into the Western Hemisphere many times, and only the lack of their insect carrier, the tsetse fly, prevents our part of the world from suffering the dreadful human and economic losses that so heavily afflict Africa. Large parts of Africa have long been uninhabitable for men and for any of their domestic animals except poultry because of certain trypanosomes and the flies that carry them. It has been a long, seesaw struggle, with men now gaining control after many years of intensive medical and ecological work by many investigators. But it remains a staggering problem. As recently as 1949 about a fourth of Africa was still completely denied to man.

The African disease in man begins with anemia and fever as the flagellates begin to multiply, and then manifests itself as swollen lymph glands, extreme lethargy, and finally coma as they invade the lymph glands and then enter the fluids surrounding the spinal cord and the brain. After this last stage death may ensue. Two closely related forms of the human disease are known: one caused by *Trypanosoma gambiense,* and another more acute form of the disease caused by *Trypanosoma rhodiense.* Whether these are really separate species of *Trypanosoma,* or whether both are only variant strains of *Trypanosoma brucei,* which causes nagana in cattle, is not yet settled. If we examine the blood of a victim we see long, slender flagellates propelled about among the red corpuscles by a delicate ruffled membrane along one side of the body. The single long flagellum is attached along the outer border of this undulating membrane, and it may extend free like a little tail at the front end of the animal, the end that goes first as it swims. Many years of patient investigation have shown that the flagellates in human blood are injected into the blood stream with the saliva from the bite of the tsetse fly (*Glossina*). The same flagellates are also found in the blood of almost all the large wild game of Africa. In the wild hosts, such as antelopes, however, there are no obvious signs of disease. And we can only conclude that an amicable relationship has been worked out between antelope and flagellate, who were introduced to each other a very long time ago. They have had ample time to adjust, apparently by a steady elimination of the most susceptible hosts and also of those trypanosomes that abused their hosts too severely and so were killed when their hosts died. Where unbalance occurs, such that a parasite kills its host, it is likely that host and guest have been very recently introduced and have not yet worked out the biological amenities.

Trypanosomes probably infested only invertebrates at first, and many still do, but in their long history some have come to use their invertebrate hosts as a means of gaining entrance to the bodies of vertebrates. In the Western Hemisphere, where there are no tsetse flies, *Trypanosoma cruzi,* of South America, can be transmitted to man from its natural hosts (armadillos, opossums, rodents) and also from cats, dogs, monkeys, and other mammals, by the bite of triatomid bugs that regularly live in houses, like bedbugs, and suck blood from the human inhabitants. Having gained entrance to human tissues, *Trypanosoma cruzi* causes the anemia and the nervous symptoms of Chagas's disease in scattered areas from northern Argentina to Mexico. In some parts of Brazil, Bolivia, Chile, and Argentina, 10 to 20 per cent of the population is infected. The same flagellate is found in many species of triatomid bugs in the scrub woods and farms of Texas and in the deserts and canyons of Arizona and California; but natural infections, if they occur, must be rare. Some trypanosomes have dispensed with the invertebrate host altogether and can be transmitted directly; for example, *Trypanosoma equiperdum,* which is passed from horse to horse in coitus, and causes dourine disease. It is found in all regions except Australasia.

The family Trypanosomidae also includes such forms as *Herpetomonas,* parasitic in the intestine of invertebrates, and *Leishmania,* which causes kala azar and Oriental sore in people living in warm parts of the world. *Phytomonas,* from the milky latex of many plants, can be found abundantly in our common milkweeds, and infection is carried from one plant to another by sucking bugs that visit the plants. For the amateur wishing to see trypanosomes, an easily obtained form is in the blood of frogs and of crimson-spotted newts. The transmitting agent for flagellates that live in such aquatic hosts is often a pond leech. Fortunately, flagellates parasitic in the lower vertebrates do not infect man. Details about such disease-causing protozoans are best sought in the specialized books on human parasitology or on the parasitology of domestic animals, as listed in the bibliography. Information on the protozoan parasites of animals other than man or his pets and flocks will be found in books on protozoology.

The most highly organized of the flagellates are the polymastiginads, which usually have more than three flagella, often many. The trichomonads are common in the digestive tracts of vertebrates, and also in the urinogenital passages. They are pear-

Trypanosomes among red blood cells in a stained blood smear. Those shown here, *Trypanosoma gambiense,* cause African sleeping sickness. (General Biological Supply House, Chicago)

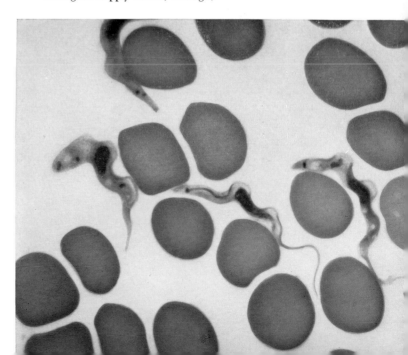

shaped, and have at the front end several flagella, one of which extends backward along the edge of an undulating membrane. The body is supported by an internal stiff rod, projecting at the rear, which also anchors the animal in feeding. *Trichomonas vaginalis* is found in the vagina of from 20 to 40 per cent of all women examined and in 50 to 70 per cent of those who complain of leucorrhea. It sometimes causes irritation and discomfort, but whether it does more serious harm we do not definitely know. Since the flagellate does not thrive in the acid condition of the normal vagina, weak acetic acid is the usual treatment; but it does not always help, and then various drugs or antibiotics are tried. This flagellate also occurs in the male urinary tract, in the urethra and in the prostate. *Trichomonas tenax* lives in the mouth of man and may be involved in some way in pyorrheal conditions. *Trichomonas hominis* is present suspiciously often in cases of human diarrhea.

The diplomonads, which have paired sets of organelles and look as if two simpler flagellates were joined together in the middle, include *Giardia intestinalis* and other species of *Giardia* that live in all kinds of vertebrates. They inhabit the upper part of the small intestine instead of the large intestine, which attracts the other intestinal protozoans. Seen from the side, *Giardia* looks like a half-pear with the broad end directed forward and the flat side indented by a concavity, which helps the animal to adhere tightly to the intestinal lining. The eight flagella, attached at the middle and at the hind end, are in active use when the animal is seen in the liquid feces that attend the diarrhea it apparently causes. The lashing of these flagella was vividly described by the indefatigably curious Leeuwenhoek. Ill with mild diarrhea, he was not content merely to complain, like the rest of us. Instead he set about to examine his watery feces and in them saw *Giardia*. In the absence of diarrhea, only the cysts of *Giardia* are found

in the feces. In one case a single stool was estimated to contain 14 billion cysts, but in a moderate infection the number would be closer to 300,000,000. An effective cure for *Giardia*-caused diarrhea is atebrin or other drugs used also for malaria. A group of related flagellates, the hypermastiginads, which live in the gut of termites, cockroaches, and woodroaches, are certainly among the most remarkable of protozoans both in the complexity of their structure and in their habits. *Trichonympha campanula,* from the gut of termites, is pear-shaped, with the fore end narrower than the rear, and is covered with hundreds of long flagella. The front end of the body is very complex and composed of structurally specialized layers. The large, rounded rear end has thin protoplasm and engulfs the minute wood particles that surround the animal in the termite gut. The flagellate has enzymes that digest the cellulose in wood to soluble carbohydrates. These are then shared with the termite host, which eats wood but cannot digest its chief constituent, cellulose, without the intervention of its protozoan guests. Such mutualistic relationships, in which two organisms are so closely associated for mutual benefit, are fairly unusual in the animal kingdom, but they are common in this group of flagellates that inhabit wood-eating insects.

The Ameboid Protozoans

(*Class Sarcodina or Rhizopoda*)

The word "ameba" is derived from a Greek word meaning "change," and the ameboid protozoans are those that move about and capture their food by means of "false feet" or pseudopods, temporary extensions of the body, that may never appear the same from moment to moment, or may appear stiff and fixed yet show a constant streaming of the protoplasm. Members of this group never move by flagella in the principal phase of the life cycle, though they may have flagellated stages or sex cells. Most are free-living in fresh and salt waters and in soil. Some are parasitic or live as supposedly harmless commensals, mostly in the digestive tracts of larger animals. A few very small amebas live as parasites within the bodies of other protozoans.

THE LOBOSE AMEBAS

The lobose amebas have no fixed shape and move along by extending lobose or finger-like pseudopods, now at one point, now at another. As new pseudopods form, the old ones flow back into the general mass of protoplasm, and the animal appears to flow about in irregular fashion with no permanent front or rear. Lobose amebas may at times have long, pointed pseudopods, especially when they are floating in water. But typically they are bottom-dwellers

An ameba is never the same from moment to moment as it moves along by protoplasmic flow. (Ralph Buchsbaum)

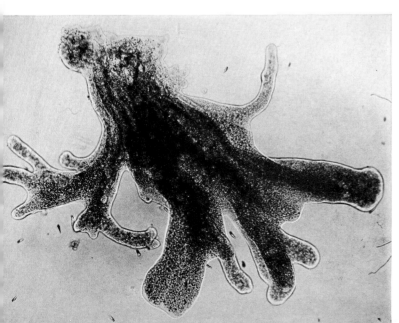

that glide over the substrate or on vegetation or decaying organic debris in fresh and salt waters. Most of the soil amebas are members of this group. *Amoeba proteus* is one of the largest ($\frac{1}{50}$ of an inch) of the common pond amebas. It has a disk-shaped nucleus, longitudinally ridged pseudopods, and the habit of advancing through a flow of all the protoplasm into the leading pseudopod. Pseudopods are used not only in moving about but also in engulfing food and in taking it into the body, surrounded by a minute quantity of water that then forms the food vacuole we see within the protoplasm. Anyone tempted to speak of "the simple ameba" should watch one moving about and capturing prey. If the food is a motionless algal cell, the ameba's body flows closely about the alga as a flowing drop of oil might surround a glass bead. But if the food is a rapidly swimming protozoan, something quite different occurs. The ameba sends out long pseudopods, in a wide embrace, but at no point in contact with the prey until it has been completely surrounded on the sides and over the top so that it is trapped against the substratum. Only then is it closely enveloped and finally incorporated into the body. Amebas can also tell food particles from nonnutritive ones and show a preference for one species of prey over another. The giant ameba, *Pelomyxa carolinensis,* has several hundred small nuclei and may be up to $\frac{1}{5}$ of an inch long when moving actively. Though rarely found in nature, it is readily obtainable from biological supply houses and is very convenient to watch because of its large size. It ingests paramecia, one after another, as many as twenty in one food vacuole. (The naming of the fresh-water amebas is still being debated, quite unknown to the amebas themselves, so that you may find them called by different names in different books.)

About half a dozen species of naked amebas live in man; but only one, the dysentery ameba, *Entamoeba histolytica,* is unquestionably harmful. Small and very active, it is able to dissolve the intestinal lining and to enter the connective tissue and muscle layers of the large intestine; and when present in numbers it causes abscesses, diarrhea (liquid feces) and dysentery (bloody feces). Human amebiasis is a worldwide disease—not confined to the tropics as many people believe—and it is spread by the contamination of food or of drinking water with the resistant cysts of an ameba that is itself too delicate to be passed around. We do not have immunizing techniques for amebiasis, as we do for typhoid, and when traveling in countries where soil is likely to be fertilized with human manure, or water contaminated with human sewage, or food handled by people with unsanitary habits, it is best to avoid foods that cannot be peeled or cooked. Ordinary chlorination of drinking water will not always kill the cysts. Ame-

biasis is better avoided than cured, but we do have several drugs that are effective in most cases. *Entamoeba coli* is a harmless commensal that lives in the human colon, feeding mostly on bacteria but occasionally on intestinal protozoans that come its way. The mouth ameba, *Entamoeba gingivalis,* does not form resistant cysts so can only be spread directly from mouth to mouth in eating or in kissing. Even so, by the time they are forty years old about 75 per cent or more of the human population have managed to obtain some of them. These amebas feed on bacteria and loose cells, and when pyorrhea is present they cluster about the bases of the teeth, probably aggravating the condition.

Closely allied to the naked amebas of fresh waters are the shelled amebas which have single-chambered coverings. The covering may be vase-shaped or bowl-shaped, and has an opening at the bottom through which the lobose, in some cases filose (long and thin), pseudopods are protruded. Some coverings are soft and gelatinous; others harden after they are secreted. They may consist entirely of secreted silicious plates or prisms, or they may be constructed of foreign particles, such as sand grains or diatom shells cemented together by a secretion. These shelled amebas live mostly in somewhat foul fresh-water ponds, in sphagnum bogs or peaty soil, and in animal feces. Most often seen is *Arcella vulgaris,* which lives in the ooze and vegetation of stagnant water and also in damp soil. It secretes about itself a hard, bowl-shaped, yellow or brown transparent covering. Viewed from above, the covering appears circular, and the animal is seen not to fill the interior completely but to be attached to the walls by thin protoplasmic strands. Two nuclei, several contractile vacuoles, and numerous food vacuoles are visible in the protoplasm. Viewed from the side, the hemispherical covering is seen to have a concave funnel-shaped opening at the bottom, through which pseudopods extend. When an *Arcella* divides, one daughter inherits the cover; the other has to secrete a new one. Also likely to turn up in organic ooze in fresh water is *Difflugia,* which at first glance may be mistaken for a little mass of sand grains. This ameba gathers sand grains and cements them about itself into a pear-shaped (in some species vase-shaped) covering into which it can withdraw completely whenever necessary.

THE FORAMS

The "pore-bearers" or foraminiferans (called "forams" for short) are amebas with shells that typically are many-chambered and perforated all over with small pores through which extend long and fine branching pseudopods. These fuse and fork over and over again, forming a spreading network of living, sticky threads that entangle and digest small organ-

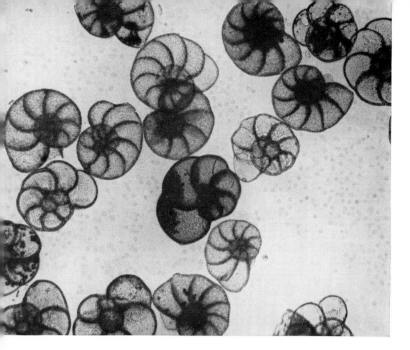

When enlarged under the microscope and viewed by transmitted light, foraminiferan shells of certain species look like snail shells. (West Germany. Kurt Herschel)

isms. The protoplasm extends not only through the pores but out of the mouth of the shell as well, pouring out in all directions and flowing over the surface of the shell. In the pseudopods, granules can be seen streaming constantly toward the tips and then returning along their outer edges.

In contrast to the predominantly fresh-water ameboid protozoans just discussed, forams are almost exclusively marine. Most of the species move about on the ooze of the muddy bottom or attach themselves loosely to debris on the ocean floor, usually in shallow waters but sometimes at depths of even 18,000 feet. Of more than twelve hundred living species, only about twenty-six are pelagic and float in the surface waters of the seas, mostly in the warmer parts of the world, where the high alkalinity of the water facilitates the extraction of calcium carbonate from the sea. But these are the most prolific of the forams, and when they die their innumerable shells fall in a steady rain to the ocean floor, contributing about 65 per cent by weight to the gray mud known as "Globigerina ooze," from the genus of forams that predominates in its formation. The most common foram species in the ooze is *Globigerina bulloides,* but shells of other species of *Globigerina* are well represented, as are other foram genera, other shelled ameboid protozoans, and especially the skeletal parts, called coccoliths (p. 23), which make up nearly 30 per cent by weight of the ooze. Globigerina ooze occupies nearly fifty million square miles of the deep-sea bottom. Below fifteen thousand feet, however, the lime content of the ooze begins to thin out because the calcite shells of the common foram species become dissolved, and below eighteen thousand feet calcareous shells are rare.

The presence of *Globigerina* in fossil beds has been used as an indication that the beds were deposited originally at a depth of between about three thousand and twelve thousand feet. *Operculina* shells indicate a depth of less than 180 feet. The rate of deposition of *Globigerina* ooze has been calculated, for some areas, to be about four-tenths of an inch in a thousand years. Though this is a rate in modern times, it gives those who can comprehend such stupendous figures some idea of the time it must have taken to deposit the marine beds that, when uplifted, form such great chalk formations (as much as 90 per cent calcium carbonate) as the white cliffs of Dover in England, the chalk beds of Europe, and the thousand-foot-deep chalk beds of Mississippi and Georgia in the United States. Modern species of forams are for the most part just visible to the naked eye ($\frac{1}{25}$ of an inch), but many are of the size of a pinhead and the largest one has a long, slender, tube-like shell that may be 2 inches long. In geological times past, when forams were more abundant than at present, some members of the genus *Nummulites* had shells several inches across. Many large forms flourished on the sea bottom in Tertiary times, and their fossil shells, mostly about as big and flat as a United States quarter-dollar, can be seen in limestone now exposed in Asia, in the Alps, and also in northern Africa, where such limestone was used to build the pyramids of Gizeh, near Cairo.

Limestones are produced instead of chalk when foraminiferan ooze is deposited in waters close enough to shores to become admixed with deposits washed in from the land. The gradual change in foram species from Tertiary times to the present makes their shells very valuable as index fossils for paleontologists trying to determine the age of various sedimentary rocks. And because of their minute size foram shells can be recovered undamaged, from rocks far below the surface, in the borings made by oil-well drills. By comparing the species of shells brought up from different levels with species from layers known to be oil-bearing, paleontologists are able to direct oil-well drilling operations.

A detection scheme on a much grander scale is now unfolding in many laboratories around the world, where foram shells are being used in studies of world-wide glaciation, for piecing together the jigsaw puzzle of the evolution and distribution of animals, and for understanding long-term climatic trends.

Globigerina bulloides has a shell (about $\frac{1}{25}$ of an inch) of spherical chambers spirally arranged and perforated by many pores. When the foram is alive and near the surface the shell is covered with long, needle-like spines; these dissolve away when it later falls to the bottom and is found in the ooze. The protoplasm is said to be a rosy pink color when seen through the shell of an animal that has withdrawn on being lifted out of the sea in a tow net. When undisturbed it spreads its pseudopodial network in surface waters and feeds on diatoms and algae, other protozoans, and occasionally even larger animals. *Elphidium crispa* is another pelagic form, and is a giant among modern species. Its flattened, spiral, sculptured, many-chambered shell reaches a diameter of ⅛ of an inch and superficially resembles a small snail shell, so that originally it was classed as a mollusk. Leeuwenhoek first found this genus in the stomach of a shrimp, but *Elphidium* can ingest, along with its unicellular plant diet, the small copepods that are relatives to the shrimp.

Many forams harbor green or yellow bodies believed to be modified flagellates. Reproduction in forams takes place by multiple division and involves an alternation of asexual and sexual forms. In the typical many-chambered species the forms that reproduce asexually have shells of small size, those that reproduce sexually have larger shells. The sex cells are usually flagellated but sometimes are ameboid. The life cycles of forams are marvelously complex, but details must be sought in advanced treatises.

THE HELIOZOANS

The "sun animalcules" or heliozoans, found mostly in fresh waters, are spherical ameboid protozoans with stiff radiating pseudopods that serve only for feeding, not for moving about. The pseudopods are supported by stiff internal protoplasmic rods and covered with thin, clear, streaming surface protoplasm. In many species the body has a gelatinous covering in which foreign particles or secreted plates or needles of silica are imbedded. Or it may be enclosed, as in the common but lovely *Clathrulina,* in a spherical latticed cage. *Clathrulina* is fastened by a stalk to the substrate, and the pseudopods protrude through the lattice openings. The more typical free-floating forms are motionless or move only very slowly. Passing organisms that happen to touch the outstretched stiff pseudopods adhere to them and are quickly paralyzed, as if by a toxin. The pseudopods may shorten and carry the prey to the main body mass, or several may surround the victim first and then slowly withdraw into the main body. The two most familiar heliozoans of pond water are both free-floating. The small *Actinophrys sol* has one nucleus and a body that is not clearly divided into two regions. The much larger *Actinosphaerium eichhorni,* visible to the naked eye, has a distinct outer layer surrounding a granular interior in which one can usually see recently eaten diatoms or other algae, and small protozoans or crustaceans. A number of small heliozoans may unite temporarily when they capture and ingest large prey. Asexual reproduction is by fission or budding.

THE RADIOLARIANS

The radiolarians are all marine and pelagic ameboid protozoans, abundant especially in warm seas. They nearly always have siliceous skeletons, many of these so exquisitely shaped that Haeckel, the great German biologist and student of the radiolarians, once called them the miniature jewelry of the abyss. Mostly spherical, they extend long, fine, usually stiff raylike pseudopods from which they take their name. The pseudopods are sticky and capture diatoms, protozoans, and copepods that adhere to them. Radiolarians are of large size as protozoans go. The giant *Thalassicola nucleata* is about ⅕ of an inch in diameter, and its closely related colonial relatives reach 1 inch or more in length. *Thalassicola* has no skeleton, but in most radiolarians siliceous needles are fused into a beautifully symmetrical latticework. The lattice is most often spherical, and in some species there are a number of concentric latticed spheres, one within the other, like the balls made to show off the skills of Chinese ivory carvers. There is also a bewildering variety of helmet-shaped, disk-shaped, and bell-shaped lattices—all combined in every possible way with beautiful and bizarre ornamentations of spines, hooks, branching thorns, and long, gracefully curved extensions. The almost endless differences in radiolarian skeletons, each produced in a consistent inherited pattern by what appears to be a relatively formless blob of protoplasm, makes one wonder if this protoplasm is as unorganized and as similar in the various species as its appearance in the naked amebas might lead us to believe.

A great variety of shell shapes can be seen in many samples of foraminiferan material. (Otto Croy)

Radiolarians can be distinguished from their fresh-water counterparts, the heliozoans, by the definite membrane that separates the outer highly vacuolated protoplasm from the inner more granular protoplasm—though these are continuous with each other through pores in the membrane. The outer layer is gelatinous, with large fluid-filled vacuoles (none of them contractile) that give it a frothy appearance; and it usually contains yellow bodies, which are thought to be flagellates that exchange favors with their hosts.

When the weather grows rough or the temperature rises too high, the buoyancy of radiolarians is said to be reduced by a withdrawal of the pseudopods and a bursting of some of the fluid-filled vacuoles in the frothy layer. Surface-living animals can thus descend into deeper water, restoring their vacuoles later.

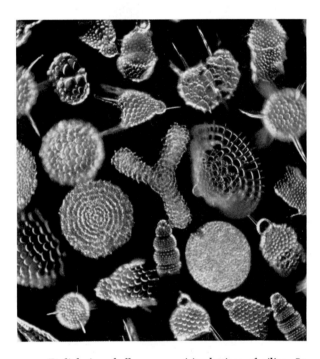

Radiolarian shells are exquisite lattices of silica. In life, the protozoans that secrete the shells extend stiff pseudopods from many openings. (Otto Croy)

Some species regularly float at great depths (sixteen thousand feet or three miles). In the deeper parts of the ocean, where the calcareous shells of foraminiferans soon dissolve, the bottom ooze may contain siliceous skeletons only: radiolarian lattices, sponge spicules, and diatom cases. When the radiolarian content reaches at least 20 per cent, bottom deposits are called "radiolarian ooze." In the Pacific and Indian oceans such ooze covers almost three million square miles of ocean bottom. Upon being up-lifted, radiolarian beds become sedimentary rock layers on land, and the small but well-preserved radiolarian skeletons, like those of the foraminiferans, serve as convenient index fossils for dating rock layers and for guiding oil-well digging operations. Radiolarian deposits occur as siliceous inclusions in other rocks, forming flint or chert. And radiolarian skeletons contribute to the abrasiveness of the "Tripoli stone" used in metal-polishing powders.

The Spore-Formers

(*Class Sporozoa*)

The sporozoans include some of man's worst enemies, the spore-forming parasitic protozoans that cause malaria, various cattle fevers, coccidiosis in chickens, diseases of halibut, salmon, and other fishes, epidemic death in cultivated honeybees and silkworms. Yet one hesitates to hold a grudge against a whole class of animals that is itself so impartial as to parasitize every major group in the animal kingdom, not excepting other protozoans. Each species of parasite is more or less limited to a specific host or to a few closely related hosts, and the parasite lives within or between the host cells, absorbing food through its body wall. Feeding in this way, sporozoans can take only dissolved food, sometimes that digested by the host but more often the dissolved protoplasm or body and tissue fluids of the host itself. An animal that lives protected from the external environment and surrounded on all sides by materials for abundant feasting has little or no need to move about, and the adult or main feeding stage of sporozoans has no external organs of locomotion. Besides this negative criterion, which is used to separate them from other protozoans, all sporozoans share the habit of producing very large numbers of spores as transfer stages to new hosts, and this has suggested the name of the group. The young transfer stage produced by sporulation is usually enclosed in a resistant wall, but in the blood-inhabiting species, like the malarial parasite, the spores are naked and they are never exposed to the rigors of the external world, being transferred from one final host to another by a blood-sucking intermediate host. The life cycles of sporozoans can be extraordinarily complex, involving both asexual and sexual processes, each of these with one or more cycles of multiple fission. The nucleus splits repeatedly by rapidly ensuing divisions, and each new nucleus becomes surrounded by a tiny share of the protoplasm, so that when the cell finally breaks up there are as many offspring as there were nuclei. The simultaneous hatching of billions of slender parasites in each such cycle is

[continued on page 49]

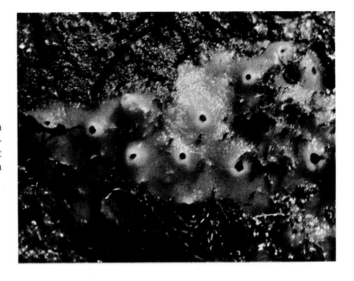

1. The **breadcrumb sponge**, *Halichondria panicea*, can be crumbled like stale bread. The thin patches that encrust shaded rocks on the shore are usually greenish but may be creamy or orange. (Brittany, France. Ralph Buchsbaum)

2. This **globular commensal sponge**, *Suberites*, overgrows the shells inhabited by certain hermit crabs. It repels predators by its distastefulness, and benefits from being carried about to new feeding grounds. (Banyuls, France. Ralph Buchsbaum)

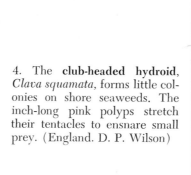

3. A **yellow branching sponge**, *Axinella*, and an **irregular reddish-orange sponge**, *Polymastia*, are both common in the shore waters off South Devon, England, at depths of sixty feet or more. (D. P. Wilson)

4. The **club-headed hydroid**, *Clava squamata*, forms little colonies on shore seaweeds. The inch-long pink polyps stretch their tentacles to ensnare small prey. (England. D. P. Wilson)

5. A **colony of oaten-pipes hydroid**, *Tubularia larynx*. It gets its name from the yellowish tubes that encase the stems holding aloft the many flower-like but carnivorous polyp "heads." (England. D. P. Wilson)

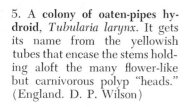

6. A **hydrozoan medusa**, *Polyorchis*, common on the American Pacific coast, is shown here about three times natural size. The trumpet-shaped feeding tube, with the mouth at its tip, is mostly obscured by the stringlike sex organs. At the bases of the tentacles are pigmented sense organs. (Woody Williams)

7. A true or **scyphozoan jellyfish**, *Dactylometra pacifica,* whose lovely appearance belies the danger of its stringing threads. Some members of this genus can cause illness or death. (Sagami Bay, Japan. Y. Fukuhara)

8. The **Portuguese man-of-war**, *Physalia,* was probably named by English sailors who first sighted its floating bladder, up to a foot or more long, in Portuguese waters. The trailing tentacles of this coelenterate usually ensnare fishes and can inflict fatal stings on swimmers. (Florida. Charles Lane)

9. **Sea fingers**, a kind of soft coral, deserves its name when seen, as here, with the body limp and the polyps withdrawn. Compare this contracted colony of *Alcyonium palmatum* with the fully expanded sea pen overleaf. (Banyuls, France. Ralph Buchsbaum)

10. A simple kind of **sea pen**, *Veretillum cynomorium*, with fully expanded polyps arising from its fleshy body. To its right is a white **sea squirt**, *Phallusia mamillata*. (Banyuls, France. Ralph Buchsbaum)

11 and 12. **A common sea fan** of European waters, *Eunicella verrucosa*, still attached to a small boulder, is shown just after being dredged from the sea bottom off Plymouth, England. (Ralph Buchsbaum.) Below, the enlarged portion shows the many polyps, each with eight feathery tentacles. (D. P. Wilson)

13. The **aggregated anemone**, *Anthopleura elegantissima*, is the commonest anemone of the American Pacific coast. About 3 inches across when fully expanded, it lives in dense beds, often attached to rock in sand. (Woody Williams)

14. The **snakelocks anemone**, *Anemonia sulcata*, is usually pinkish brown but may be a soft apple green, from the algal cells in its tissues. Unlike most anemones, it displays its snaky tentacles in the sun. (Brittany, France. Ralph Buchsbaum)

15. A **commensal anemone** of European waters, *Calliactis parasitica*, attaches to whelk shells inhabited by the **large hermit crab**, *Eupagurus bernhardus*. Here five anemones cling to one shell. (Banyuls, France. Ralph Buchsbaum)

16. The **proliferating anemone**, *Epiactis prolifera*, seems to be pinching off tiny anemones around its waist, but these young are not asexual buds. They first shelter within the body (¾ inch wide) of the parent, then emerge and complete their development on the outer surface. (San Francisco. John Tashjian at Steinhart)

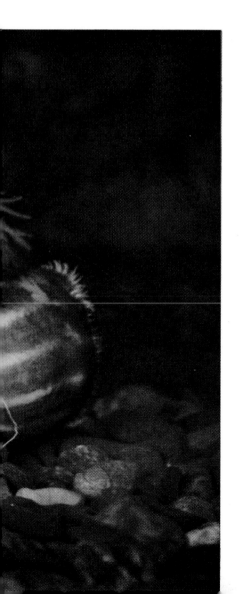

17. The **dahlia anemone**, *Tealia*, is often pale in color when found in deep water. (See shallow-water *Tealia* in Plate 20.) The column is covered with wartlike tubercles to which bits of stone and shell adhere. (Oregon. Ralph Buchsbaum)

18. The **plumose anemone**, *Metridium senile*, may in deep water grow as large as 8 inches tall and 5 inches broad; but those found in rock crevices at ordinary tides are usually small or young specimens. (Plymouth, England. D. P. Wilson)

19. The **opelet anemone** is another name for the snakelocks, *Anemonia sulcata* (Plate 14), which at low tide does not withdraw its tentacles but only shortens them as it droops in the sun. (Roscoff, France. Ralph Buchsbaum)

20. The **dahlia anemone**, *Tealia felina*, uses its robust tentacles to push rather large prey into its mouth. It feeds in great part on small crabs in rocky crevices. (England. D. P. Wilson)

21. The **gemmed anemone**, *Bunodactis verrucosa*, closes tightly at low tide, crowding a greenish disk and some fifty delicately banded tentacles into a contracted body measuring about 1 inch across. (Roscoff, France. Ralph Buchsbaum)

22. The **plumose anemone**, *Metridium dianthus*, is widely distributed and is one of the commonest anemones of the northern half of the American Atlantic coast. Young specimens have a simple disk which has not yet developed the deep lobes and frills typical of larger members. (New Jersey. David C. Stager)

23. A **solitary cup coral**, *Caryophyllia clavus*, dredged from the Bay of Biscay, abounds in the deeper waters off England, France, and Spain, and also in the coastal Mediterranean mud zone. If shell or gravel is lacking it is held in the mud by its pointed base. (D. P. Wilson)

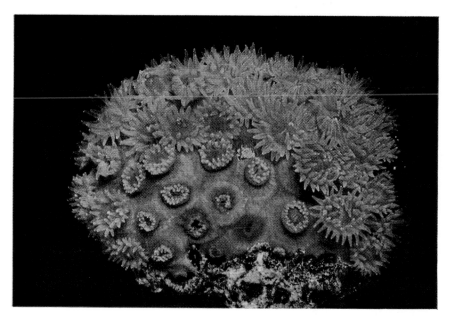

24. An **orange-colored coral**, *Astroides culy-cularis*, here shown at about natural size, carpets rocks along the coasts of Italy, often just below the water line. Only at the base of the colony, where some of the polyps have died, can one see the gray limestone skeleton, pocked with cavities that housed the polyps. (Naples Aquarium. D. P. Wilson)

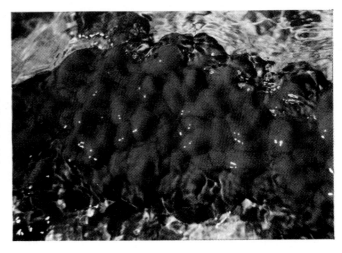

25. The smooth, gently lobated living edge of a *Porites* **coral platform** is dotted with minute polyps whose combined efforts produce coral platforms up to forty feet across. These support other corals on their exposed and eroded centers. (Great Barrier Reef. Allen Keast)

26. These **coral polyps**, here greatly enlarged, are part of a colony of *Phyllangia americana*, a reef-building West Indian stony coral. One polyp has just opened its mouth to receive a fragment of clam meat. In nature it captures living prey. (Jamaica. Thomas Goreau)

27. A large **brain coral**, *Lobophyllia*, originally dome-shaped, which has been killed at its center by exposure. (Green Island, Great Barrier Reef. Allen Keast)

28. Globose masses of **reef coral** with relatively large twelve-tentacled polyps appear green from the plantlike cells that live in their tissues. (Bimini. Fritz Goro: *Life* Magazine)

29. A prickly colony of **soft coral** from Micronesian waters. (Jerome M. and Dorothy H. Schweitzer)

30. A **zoanthid colony**, *Epizoanthus wrighti*, shown several times enlarged, resembles a cluster of the related sea anemones. Brought up by a free-swimming diver from a depth of eighty-four feet off the South Devon coast of England. (D. P. Wilson)

[continued from page 32]

what ruptures so many red blood cells all at one time and produces the periodic chills and fever of malaria. A loss of locomotor organs, and the development of complex life cycles with incredible numbers of offspring, are common to the parasitic way of life. So that sweeping all the odds and ends of protozoan parasitism into one big hodgepodge and calling it the Sporozoa does tidy up the rest of the protozoan classification, but it creates a group with members that really have very little in common and that do not represent a single branch of protozoan evolution. The several subclasses of Sporozoa include many important parasitic groups such as the myxosporidians of fish disease, the microsporidians that kill honeybees and silkworms and other higher invertebrates, and the haplosporidians that parasitize many groups from rotifers to fish. Even the sarcosporidians, which invade the muscle tissues of lizards, birds, and also mammals, especially sheep, used to be placed here. Now they are usually classed as fungi. Only one of the subclasses, the Telosporidia, seems to be a natural grouping of related orders, and as these include many animals of importance to man they will be briefly considered.

THE GREGARINES

The gregarines are mostly wormlike protozoans that infest the digestive tracts and body cavities of many invertebrates, but not of vertebrates. The young form usually lives within a host cell, but as it feeds and matures it protrudes from the cell, remaining attached only by the front end or leaving altogether and moving about in the intestinal cavity or one of the body spaces. Gregarines can be found by teasing out on a microscope slide, and then diluting with water, the content or the lining of the intestine of a cricket or a grasshopper. It is likely one will see the wormlike feeding stage gliding slowly by means that are not evident, perhaps by slow and inconspicuous muscular contractions. In this group of gregarines the body is divided by a partition into a small front segment by which it can attach to the host tissue, and a larger hind segment which contains the nucleus. One may also see two individuals attached end to end, the "gregarious" habit for which the group is named. It is an indication that sexual reproduction will ensue, with the front individual as the female, the one at the rear as the male.

THE COCCIDIANS

The coccidians excite little notice as human parasites, though species of the genus *Isospora* are commoner in human feces than one would suspect from the few cases of diarrhea actually reported. The bad reputation of the group rests mostly on the damage inflicted by Isospora, and more especially by the genus *Eimeria,* on domestic animals. Coccidiosis

takes a heavy toll of chicken flocks and other poultry; and rabbits and cattle may also be seriously affected, the latter having bloody feces, becoming emaciated, and often dying. Practically any farm animal may suffer from coccidian attacks, and so may dogs, cats, and even canaries. In addition to these vertebrate hosts, coccidians live in annelids, mollusks, and arthropods. The feeding stage usually resides within the lining cells of the intestine or of the organs that connect with it, often the liver. The virulence of many coccidial diseases is due to the tremendous numbers of parasites that result from the multiple fissions.

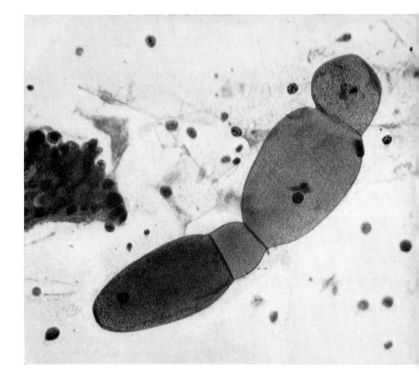

Gregarina is a parasitic sporozoan likely to be found in the intestine of a grasshopper, cricket or cockroach. Pairs of cells often remain together, each one subdivided into a small portion and a larger. In mating, the front individual will be the female, the rear one the male. (General Biological Supply House, Chicago)

THE HEMOSPORIDIANS

The hemosporidians live within the blood corpuscles or other cells of the blood system of vertebrates, and all of them require a blood-sucking intermediate host during part of their very complex life cycle. In human malaria, as everyone knows, the intermediate host is a mosquito of certain species of the genus *Anopheles.* For lack of this bit of knowl-

[49

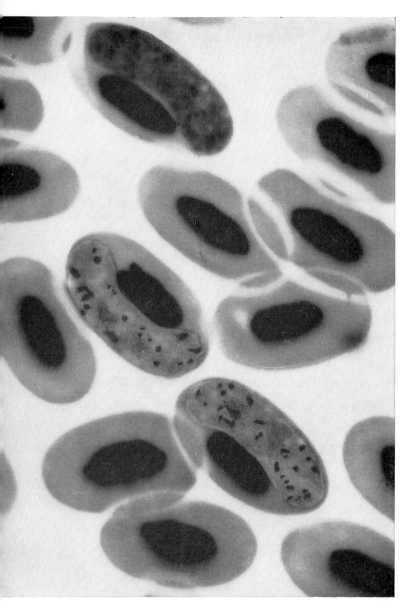

Three of these oval red blood cells contain a common sporozoan parasite of birds, *Haemoproteus*, here made more visible by use of a dye. The parasite is transferred from one bird host to another by a blood-sucking fly, in whose body the parasite goes through a sexual part of its life history. (General Biological Supply House, Chicago.)

edge, which was not finally established until 1898, the course of human culture was long deeply influenced by the sporozoan that we now call *Plasmodium*. No human tyrants, nor all the wars in human history, have taken the toll of misery and death exacted by the malarial parasite in those warm or temperate parts of the world where anopheline mosquitoes are infected with *Plasmodium*. Malaria was well known to the Greeks twenty-five hundred years ago,

but perhaps it was introduced, after they had already achieved their fine civilization, by soldiers returning from military triumphs or by slaves brought in to do their menial work. Whether malaria came to the New World with the Spaniards or was already here when they came, it was one of the major hazards, less mentioned but probably more important than either hunger or Indian attacks. Malaria may have been the disease that in 1607 killed half the settlers at Jamestown, and malaria epidemics are recorded for Massachusetts as early as 1647. It was one of the chief burdens of the pioneers who moved westward into the Mississippi Valley, and as late as the 1930's was still widespread in the southern part of that valley. If the history of man had not in the past been written to so great an extent by militarily and politically minded writers, it might tell a very different sort of story. The southern part of the United States has lost much of its strength to a disease that annually, until World War II, debilitated at least a million Americans and killed several thousand. During the war, when quinine ran out among the men at Bataan, 85 per cent of every regiment developed acute malaria. And in the South Pacific campaign there were five times as many casualties from malaria as from combat. Up to the end of the war there were in all the world some 350,000,000 cases of malaria annually, of which about 3,500,000 resulted in death each year.

Since that time a dramatic change has come. New therapeutic drugs, spraying of houses with DDT, better control of mosquito breeding places, and better organized health care have wiped out malaria in the United States and brought it completely under control in parts of Europe, especially Italy, where it was so long a heavy drain on the life of the people. A vast improvement has been made in a great many parts of Africa and of Asia. But to assume that man has necessarily consigned malaria to his unhappy past is naïve. Our control of malaria depends upon the proper functioning of a complex civilization that can break down as others have in the past, while the biological potential of mosquitoes and sporozoans is built firmly into the species. Long before there were men about, hemosporidians were living in lizards, birds, bats, small rodents, monkeys, apes, and others. Much of what we know about human malaria was first learned from studies in birds, whose malaria is transmitted by mosquitoes of the common genus *Culex* and certain related genera. There are four species of *Plasmodium* that cause malaria in man. *P. ovale* is rare but found in many separated parts of the world. *P. vivax, P. malariae,* and *P. falciparum* are common and widespread, and each causes a distinctive set of cyclic symptoms corresponding to forty-eight-hour, seventy-two-hour, and forty-hour cycles of development respectively.

The Ciliates (*Class Ciliata*)

The ciliates are mostly free-swimming forms that row themselves about by the beating of many cilia, so named for their resemblance to eyelashes. Abundant in all fresh and marine waters, ciliates flourish best where there is much decaying organic material, for most of them are bacteria feeders. Any water dipped up from the weed-grown edge of a stagnant pond, especially if it contains organic debris or fragments of vegetation, will on microscopic examination reveal a miniature community in which ciliates play many of the leading roles. Of all the protozoans they will be the most conspicuous, move the most rapidly (almost one-tenth of an inch per second, in some of the fastest species), and occupy the greatest variety of niches. They may be difficult to appraise at a glance, for they cross the field at all angles in a fast, powerful glide that can usually be slowed only by using anesthetics or such a barrier as cotton fibers.

The familiar *Paramecium* is often best seen when anchored to a bit of debris and quietly feeding on bacteria. This slipper-shaped animal has a conspicuous groove at one side of the body, and this is lined with cilia whose beating wafts bacteria and minute particles of organic material through the mouth opening into a funnel-shaped gullet. There special tracts of cilia compact the bacteria into a food ball, which is passed on, surrounded by a minute droplet of water, as a food vacuole. Successive vacuoles are launched into the fluid interior protoplasm and circulate in a regular path. One experimenter kept close watch on some individuals of *Tetrahymena,* a small relative of *Paramecium,* and estimated that each food ball was an accumulation of about a thousand bacteria and that a vacuole was sent out on its course once every six minutes. The spent vacuoles were eliminated some four hours later. A really large ciliate, *Stentor,* when placed in a rich suspension of euglenas, was observed to down these flagellated organisms at the remarkable rate of about a hundred per minute.

But not all ciliates feed by ciliary currents. Some are predatory, actively seeking out their prey and attacking it with a ferocity that matches anything seen in higher animals. *Didinium* feeds mostly on paramecia, devouring them whole, as many as eight in one day. It has no difficulty in opening its mouth wide enough to swallow any individual not too much larger than itself, but if greatly outclassed in size the didinium may have to struggle longer, and the victimized paramecium continues to swim about actively with the attacker grimly hanging on. In clearer waters, where oxygen content is high, bacteria feeders are few and carnivorous ciliates attack small herbivorous ciliates that feed on green or blue-green algae or on diatoms. Such carnivores may in turn be fed on by larger ciliated carnivores, and when the carnage is all over, fragments of dead plant and animal tissue will be cleaned up by scavenging ciliates. In this highly competitive microworld others have turned to exploiting both the external surfaces and internal cavities of invertebrates and vertebrates. Ciliates may themselves harbor smaller parasites or commensals, or they may live in a mutually beneficial relationship with alga-like flagellates that carry on photosynthesis within the ciliate body.

The firm shape of most ciliates is maintained by a stiff but flexible outer covering, the pellicle, and by the outer clear gelatinous layer of protoplasm that lies beneath the pellicle. Within the firm outer layer is a more fluid, granular protoplasm in which the nucleus floats, the food vacuoles circulate, and the contractile vacuoles work away at pumping out the excess water that accumulates more especially in the particle feeders. The cilia protrude through holes in the pellicle, which is handsomely marked with longitudinal or diagonal lines of ciliary attachment. At their bases, in the outer protoplasm, the cilia connect with the fibrils of the neuromotor system that coordinates ciliary movements. Much of the time the cilia beat so fast that all we can see is a flickering at the edge of the body. They move like the flexible arms of a swimmer doing the crawl, reaching forward in the relaxed part of the stroke and then striking backward through the water in a forceful sweep—not straight backward, but obliquely so that the animal rotates and describes a spiral path as it continues on a straight course. Aside from the ciliation of the body, which serves both locomotion and feeding, most members of this class share a unique nuclear situation that distinguishes them from other protozoans. The functions of the nucleus are divided between two separate bodies: a large nucleus concerned with the chemical processes of feeding and growth, and a small nucleus concerned with reproduction.

Asexual reproduction occurs, as in other groups, by a division of the protoplasm and each of the two nuclei between two daughter cells. But sexual reproduction usually takes place by a special kind of conjugation. The individuals become sticky and pair off, each couple adhering together by apposing their mouths and forming a protoplasmic bridge. This lasts for several hours, during which the nuclei undergo complex changes and a portion of each small nucleus migrates to the opposite member of the union. Thus the essential part of sexual reproduction is accomplished—the recombining of hereditary materials so as to produce offspring with new hereditary possibilities. In *Paramecium,* where it has been most studied, the two conjugants do not appear to our eyes to be visibly differentiated. But they are physiologically distinct, as it has been shown that pairing occurs only when the two members are from different strains.

Only a little of the behavior of ciliates is of the kind that we see in higher animals as they move directly toward some favorable object or situation in their environment. Ciliates secure very little warning of what surrounds them, beyond what current feeders can detect as they sample the water ahead, so that mostly they find the best conditions for existence by a kind of trial-and-error method, as we do when fumbling about in the dark. A paramecium does not react when entering a favorable situation but only when it starts to leave such an area. That is, on reaching a place where it can detect physical obstruction, too high or low a degree of acidity, or too high or low a temperature, it backs up by reversing the ciliary beat, and then changes its course slightly. If it meets the same unfavorable stimulus it backs up again and again shifts its course. We have named this the "avoiding reaction," and it can be repeated any number of times until the animal at last finds a free passageway or is turned back into the more favorable region in which it has been moving. Unlike those people who go about boasting that they know what they like, ciliates seem mostly to know only what they do not like. And they make their way about in life by getting "trapped" in those areas where they are best adapted to live.

As a group the ciliates are the most highly specialized of the protozoans, with a variety of feeding structures and of elaborate locomotory and coordinating systems that defy brief description. The ciliation of the body ranges from an even covering over the whole body, as in the holotrichs, to a few large cilia on the lower surface, as in the hypotrichs. On the basis of the distribution of the cilia, the class has been divided into a number of orders.

THE OPALINIDS

The opalinids, named for their beautiful opalescent appearance, are all mouthless parasites, mostly of the large intestines of amphibians. When removed from the rectum of the frog or toad, they will be seen swimming about by what appear to be short cilia that clothe the whole body. *Opalina* is oval, flattened, and has many similar nuclei. In the spring, at just about the time that frog eggs are hatching into tadpoles, *Opalina* produces cysts that pass out in the feces. Those that happen to be swallowed by a tadpole hatch and give rise by a sexual process (not the conjugation seen in other ciliates) to a new generation of opalescent adults that absorb food in the frog intestine. In spite of their superficial appearance they are often put with the flagellates, which they resemble in many ways, notably in the habit of dividing lengthwise—instead of crosswise, as the cili-

ates do. Moreover, their nuclei, which number from two to many, are all alike instead of being of two kinds, as in most ciliates.

THE HOLOTRICHS

The holotrichs typically have simple cilia, usually short and of equal length, that cover the whole body in lengthwise rows, as in *Paramecium*. Or the cilia may be restricted to certain areas of the body, as in the two or more ciliary girdles that encircle the barrel-shaped *Didinium,* and the rows of cilia that emerge between the plates of the armor that enclose its near relative *Coleps*. To follow the group tradition is to earn a living by bacteria feeding, and most have a ciliated groove or depression that funnels food into the always open mouth, reversing the ciliary beat if what comes in is undesirable. Some are predators, however, and *Didinium* and *Coleps* have at the front end a mouth that can be opened wide to swallow large prey. In *Didinium nasutum* the mouth is at the top of an extensible proboscis which is not fully protruded as the animal swims about, barging full on into anything that comes in its way. Didinia have been seen to strike the glass walls of aquaria, algae, euglenas, rotifers, the giant ciliates *Stentor* and *Spirostomum*—all without success. When, however, they happen to strike *Paramecium* or another common holotrich, *Colpoda,* the proboscis penetrates and fastens onto the victim, drawing it whole into the widely spread mouth. *Vorticella,* a bell-shaped ciliate, also gives way to the snout, as does frontonia, though this last is a very large holotrich and has to be eaten in installments. Mast, a leading American student of feeding in protozoans, saw one frontonia attacked in fifty-eight places by many didinia, but until it died after forty minutes it kept closing its wounds and swimming about actively, growing smaller and smaller all the time. Apparently the choice of food in didinia depends not on toughness of exterior or on size but on particular physical or chemical properties of the prey.

When a didinium attacks its usual food, a paramecium, the victim may shoot out a barrage of trichocysts, long, sticky threads extruded through pores in the outer covering. The undischarged trichocysts lie as a layer of carrot-shaped bodies in the outer protoplasm; and many physical or chemical stimuli, especially irritants, will cause their discharge. They may be defensive devices, but they make a didinium stand back only briefly. In the end the paramecium, enveloped in gelatinous threads, goes down the hatch. It takes more than trichocysts to discourage an animal like the didinium that was seen to devour two conjugating paramecia at one time. In a paramecium, at least, the trichocysts seem most useful as a means of anchoring the animal as it quietly feeds on bacteria. Though common in holotrichs, trichocysts are rare among other ciliates. Holotrich feeding habits also explore many other ways of getting along in the world. *Paramecium bursaria* harbors green flagellates, and it is said that the animal can survive on its green cells if bacteria are not available. The astomate (mouthless) holotrichs live in the digestive tracts of annelids, the livers of mollusks, the body cavities of annelids and crustaceans. Parasitic forms with mouths raise pustules in the skin of fishes or may be found on the gills of tadpoles. Many live as relatively harmless commensals, sharing the food of their hosts by taking up posts in the mantle cavities of bivalve mollusks or the intestinal tracts of sea urchins or mammals.

THE SPIROTRICHS

The spirotrichs have, leading to the mouth, a downward-curving zone of membranelles, large triangular plates of fused cilia that create powerful feeding currents. Spirotrichs may be divided up into heterotrichs, oligotrichs, and hypotrichs, according to their patterns of ciliation. The heterotrichs are covered all over with short cilia, and they include such well-known forms as the huge, trumpet-shaped stentors, named for the Greek herald in the Trojan War, who, according to Homer, had a loud trumpet-like voice. *Stentor* lives attached by the narrow end of the "trumpet," but may detach and swim about with the muscular body partly contracted. The large blue species, *Stentor coeruleus*, with the fully expanded body showing alternate stripes of white and blue from the white muscle fibers that underlie the blue-pigmented layer, and with the large membranelles of its feeding disk steadily wafting small flagellates and ciliates into the mouth, is one of the finest sights in the animal kingdom. It is quite impossible to leave the eyepiece of a microscope when such an animal is performing. Also in this group is the long, slender *Spirostomum,* about the length of a printed dash—and one of the largest of fresh-water protozoans. Often seen in dark, shady pools, it may when numerous whiten the surface of the water. *Balantidium coli* normally parasitizes pigs but may shift (when its cysts get into the food or drink of people who handle pigs) to the human intestinal wall, causing diarrhea.

The oligotrichs have the body cilia reduced or absent. Such are *Halteria,* familiar to those who examine pond water, as the minute form that seems to bounce like a ball across the field of the microscope; the marine tintinnids that secrete about themselves vase-shaped cases; and the many commensals of hoofed animals, including the astoundingly complex *Epidinium ecaudatum.*

The hypotrichs include many of the most common and most amusing ciliates that turn up in the fresh and salt waters usually examined. Oval and

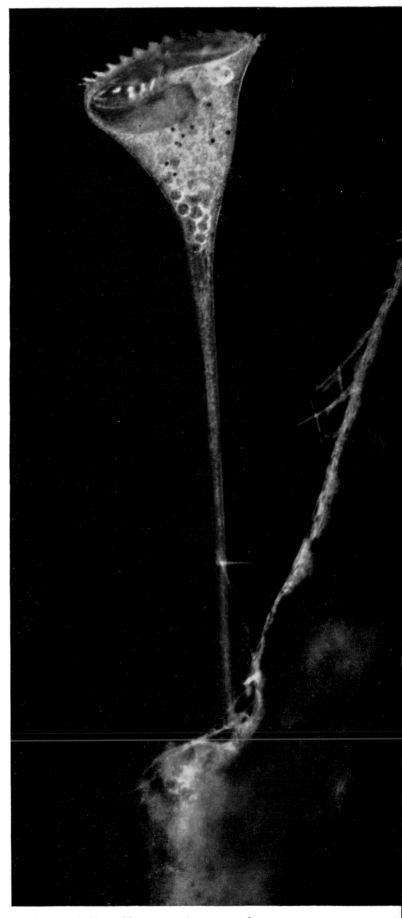

A fully expanded large blue stentor, *Stentor coeruleus,* with membranelles beating around the edge of the feeding disk. (P. S. Tice)

flattened, they have the cilia confined almost entirely to the flat undersurface, on which they creep about in a characteristic jerky manner. The cilia do not beat but are fused into a number of stout projections that act like little legs. The upper surface is convex and has only a few stiff sensory bristles. Well known are *Oxytricha, Stylonychia,* and *Euplotes,* as well as *Kerona,* a curious little commensal that crawls about on the outer surface of hydras.

THE PERITRICHS

The peritrichs typically are bell-shaped or vase-shaped forms that live attached by a long, spirally contractile stalk, and that have no cilia except those on the feeding disk that occupies the broad end of the bell. The cilia occur in circlets, and cling loosely to each other to form a kind of continuous undulating membrane that sweeps food particles into the mouth. When the animal is feeding the bell is held aloft, fully expanded, and the ciliary membrane sweeps in bacteria by creating a whirlpool or vortex, which suggested the name of the common genus, *Vorticella.* At the least alarm the stalk contracts like a coiled spring and the contractile bell folds its edge over the cilia. Any bell can develop a girdle of cilia, break loose, and swim away to a better neighborhood. When vorticellas conjugate, one of the members is of very different size. *Vorticella* grows singly or in dense clusters; and *Epistylis* is colonial, with stalks that are noncontractile. Both occur in marine waters but are most familiar from fresh waters everywhere, for they form whitish patches on submerged sticks and stones and in some streams are found springing from the body of almost every aquatic insect or crustacean. *Carchesium* colonies, in which the individuals contract their stalks independently, grow nearly ⅛ of an inch long on the underside of sticks and stones in fresh-water streams. *Zoothamnium* is like *Carchesium* except that there is a single branching system of contractile fibers, so that the whole colony contracts at one time. A freely moving peritrich is *Trichodina,* often seen moving about on the bodies of hydras by means of a posterior circlet of cilia. The round squat body has a concave undersurface bearing a horny ring, usually with curved hooks, by which it clings to the hydra and also to a variety of other aquatic hosts such as sponges, flatworms, frog tadpoles, other amphibians, and fish.

The Suctorians (*Class Suctoria*)

The suctorians have staked out a new claim in the protozoan world, and established a whole new class of animals, through their development of long, sucking tentacles that enable them to capture and feed on prey without either moving about or producing feeding currents. Though obviously derived from ciliates, the adult suctorians have been able to dispense with cilia altogether. Only the young are ciliated, and this helps them to move a little distance before settling down and competing for food with their parents, who live attached by a stalk to vegetation, to other animals, or to any solid object in fresh and salt waters everywhere. *Tokophrya* has a long, noncontractile stalk that holds aloft a club-shaped body. From the free end of the club it rigidly extends a number of very long and slender hollow tentacles, knobbed at their tips. When a ciliate sails unaware into one of these tentacles it is seized and held fast by a number of tentacles, while from three to ten of the hollow tubes in some way penetrate the surface covering and suck up the protoplasm. About fifteen minutes suffice for sucking dry a euplotes. The victim may thrash about and struggle mightily to escape, but it rarely does, even though held by only a few delicate-appearing tentacles. A specialist on suctorians watched many trapped paramecia in their death struggles without ever seeing one extrude trich-

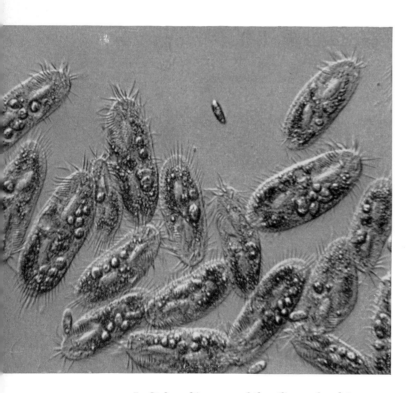

In *Stylonychia,* many of the cilia are fused in groups and are stout organs, easy to see as the animals move about on them. *Stylonychia* is flattened, with definite upper and lower surfaces. (General Biological Supply House, Chicago)

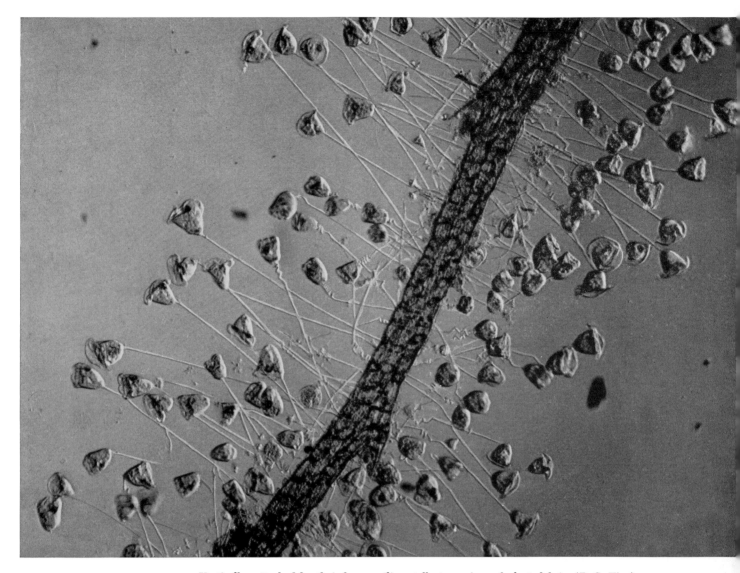

Vorticellas attached by their long, coiling stalks to a piece of plant debris. (P. S. Tice)

ocysts. During one of these uneven battles between suctorians and their victims, another observer once saw a stylonychia achieve a partial triumph. It underwent fission and one of the daughters escaped! *Dendrosoma* is a branching suctorian that has been found on many aquatic plants, rotifers, bryozoans, and crayfishes in fresh waters. When suctorians divide asexually they may split into two equal daughters or may bud off small individuals that swim about by cilia, then settle down, lose the cilia, and grow to full size. The process of sexual reproduction involves conjugation.

CHAPTER II

The Sponges

(Phylum Porifera)

Limy and glass sponges

SPONGES are more widely known from their cleaned and dried skeletons than they are as living creatures that flourish in all the seas of the world or encrust rocks and sticks in fresh waters. Familiarity with sponges through enjoying the luxury of a fine soft Mediterranean bath sponge or scrubbing a wall with a sturdy but elastic sheepswool sponge from Florida waters is hardly good preparation for recognizing such animals in the flesh. Peering over the edge of a boat in twenty feet of water, one sees on the clear, sunlit bottom an ugly black ball, somewhat larger than a grapefruit and with an uneven bumpy surface. If there is someone aboard who can manipulate a twenty-five-foot pole without being pulled overside, it becomes a simple matter to hook onto the sponge with the curved metal prongs that protrude from the far end of the pole and to pull the living animal from its firm mooring on the sea bottom, delivering it wet and glistening into the boat. Now it is seen to have a number of large openings through the jet-black leathery membrane that covers the surface. And if the sponge is sliced open the halves reveal cut surfaces that look like nothing so much as raw, slimy, dark-brown beef liver. What superficially resemble bile ducts are tangential sections of the main channels through which water is ejected out the large openings noted at the top of the sponge. Not apparent except on very close examina-

tion are the millions of microscopic pores that pierce the whole of the outer surface and through which water is sucked into the sponge when it is on the sea bottom and feeding by straining microscopic plants and animals out of the water. The steady stream that passes through the body into the many small pores and out the few large vents at the top also serves to bring oxygen to the internal cells of the sponge and to carry away their wastes.

The volume of water filtered by a good-sized sponge is tremendous. One estimate set the rate of active flow for a Bahaman wool sponge at about two quarts a minute, and perhaps several hundred gallons in twenty-four hours. To add one ounce to the weight of a growing sponge, as much as a ton of water may have to be filtered. The rate of flow can be diminished or stepped up, depending upon the condition of the water, by contraction of the vents or by opening them wide. The surface pores are less responsive than the vents and usually close only under injurious conditions.

The external pores, for which the phylum of sponges has been named the Porifera or "pore bearers," are represented in the dried bath sponge only by the few large vents, the small apertures having been stripped away with the removal of the flesh. And the extraordinary porosity of the skeletal network represents only the remnants of the complex system of internal channels and feeding chambers, for the bleaching of the skeleton has destroyed all the delicate fibers that supported the actual canals. In the simplest sponges the feeding cells completely line one vase-shaped internal cavity, while in complex sponges like the bath sponge they are restricted to innumerable little special feeding chambers interposed between the incurrent channels and the excurrent ones. In either case the cells that trap the food particles as they go by are also the cells that produce the food-bearing currents. These important and almost unique cells are called "collar cells" because they have, at the free end that projects into the cavity of the chamber, a single long, hairlike flagellum surrounded at its base by an erect and delicate protoplasmic collar. Food particles brought to the cell by the beating of the flagellum adhere to the sticky collar and slide down its outer surface to be engulfed by the cell. The many collar cells all feed quite independently, so that a sponge cannot digest any particle too large to be taken into a single cell. No matter how massive the sponge, its diet is restricted to minute organic particles, bacteria, microscopic algae, the smaller protozoans, and the many eggs and other single sex cells set free in the water by various plants and animals.

Sponges constitute the simplest of the well-defined groups of many-celled animals, and the only one in which the largest opening into the body is not a mouth and the feeding machinery has entrances that are less conspicuous than the exits. They are also alone among many-celled forms in having collar cells, though there are collared flagellates among the protozoans. For these reasons, and others besides, the phylum Porifera is removed from the ranks of the Metazoa (p. 15) and set aside in a separate subkingdom of animals, the Parazoa.

In quiet shallow seas one can sometimes detect a "boiling" of the water where the outgoing current issues in a jet from a large sponge. If the edge of a vent is struck sharply, it may be seen to close slowly, perhaps almost imperceptibly. There may even be, in some sponges, contraction of the whole body; and the early naturalists noted that these curious growths did "sometimes seem to shrink from the hand that tried to seize them." For the most part, though, the ceaseless inner turmoil of the steadily pumping sponge is masked by the deceptively quiet exterior. And to the casual observer sponges are as unresponsive as the rocks to which they grow firmly affixed. During various periods in the past, sponges were classed as plants, as plant-animals, and even as non-living secretions produced by the great variety of animals that take shelter in the numerous cavities of a sponge. Not until the middle of the nineteenth century were sponges finally assured of an unquestioned

Living horny sponge, *Hippospongia*, sliced in half on being brought up from the bottom off Batábano, Cuba. This is a commercial species; after the living tissue has been removed the horny skeleton is used for washing walls and automobiles. (Ralph Buchsbaum)

right to stand in the ranks of animals. This was after the last skeptics had been satisfied that sponges could feed like any animal without having to move about to gather their food. "The poor creatures," wrote one naturalist, "receive their nourishment from the wave that washes past them; they inhale and respire the bitter water all their lives." He could have saved his sympathy, because sponges were enjoying great prosperity at least half a billion years before man appeared on the scene. Vaselike fossil glass sponges and masses of fossil glass needles from the supporting framework of such sponges are found in the earliest fossil-bearing rocks we know.

An elaborate skeletal framework permeating the entire body is very important to an animal in which gelatinous material holds together loosely organized masses of delicate cells which must be firmly supported to keep the extensive network of canals and chambers from collapsing and so interfering with the vital circulation. Yet every group has its exceptions, and there are a few sponges without skeletons. The soft elastic framework of the bath sponge and its relatives makes these few aberrant forms useful to us, but such support without hard particles in addition is rare among all the thousands of kinds of sponges. Most are much too hard and scratchy, too brittle or friable, whether alive, dead, or skeletonized, to be of much use to man. Their bodies are usually thoroughly permeated with microscopic hard particles, or spicules, which either are simple needles or have a number of rays in a variety of configurations. In one class the spicules are calcareous, or chalky, but in most sponges the spicules are siliceous and like minute splinters of glass. If a fibrous network is present, it is usually combined with hard spicules. Those sponges in which long spicules protrude from the surface are quite bristly. As if to make doubly sure that no animal will be attracted to their flesh, many sponges have noxious odors. Little wonder, then, that sponges have so few enemies and that the bodies of the less compact forms give shelter to many hundreds of kinds of invertebrates, especially crustaceans and worms, and even to fishes. Among the few animals definitely known to feed on sponges are certain sea slugs (nudibranchs), limpets, and periwinkles—all of them mollusks. But perhaps there are others.

The known number of sponge species has been estimated as high as 4500, but of these only about 150 species, all members of the family Spongillidae, live in fresh waters. The rest are marine, and these grow most abundantly in warm shallow seas but are widely distributed also in temperate and cold waters and at all depths. During the *Galathea* expedition sponges were recorded from the sea bottom at nearly 21,000 feet below the surface. Fibrous sponges predominate in shallow tropical waters but give way to calcareous and siliceous sponges in cold water. The

glass sponges (p. 60) are deep-water forms. The favored substrate is rocky or hard bottom along the seashores or in coral-reef lagoons, though some sponges are found encrusting pilings, shells, or even the backs of certain crabs (Plate 2). A few forms lie free at the bottom, but all the rest are firmly secured in some way, either fastened to a solid object or on muddy bottom anchored by a long tuft of glassy spicules. An occasional hardy species, like *Tetilla mutabilis*, which lives in the mud flats of estuaries in southern California, can somehow manage to survive the temperature changes, pollution, and suspended sediments of such a habitat. But sponges as a group are especially vulnerable to suspended particles that could clog their labyrinthine channels; and they grow best in very clear waters, thriving on mud bottoms only in deep or very quiet waters where the mud is seldom or never in suspension.

The sizes and shapes of sponges vary from minute urns only a fraction of an inch long to erect vaselike or branching types 5 or 6 feet tall, or broad, squat, irregular or rounded masses big enough for several people to sit on. The simpler and smaller sponges are often radially symmetrical cylinders or vases, fastened at the lower end, with a single large opening at the top. But most sponges are colonial and have no special symmetry. They continue to spread out indefinitely in a plantlike manner and with little individuality. If a single vent with its contributory channels represents an individual in the diffuse colony, then it is difficult indeed to tell where one individual stops and the next one begins. Over long periods sponge colonies do change their patterns on rocks, almost as if they were moving about, by a constant reorganization of the cells around the periphery. As they meet other colonies of the same species they coalesce. The most common shapes are irregularly massive, encrusting, or branching, and the many large excurrent openings may be on the tips of branches or elevated cones, or sunk into craters. The same species may grow erect branches in quiet waters and cling matlike, molded to the substrate, where the surf is strong. In fresh waters and on temperate rocky shores encrusting sponges are most common. After a storm a beach may be strewn with decaying sponge fragments torn from the rocks, or with sponge-covered mollusk shells hurled in from offshore bottoms. On a beach in Panama we once saw hundreds of empty scallop shells cast up by a storm, and every one bore a finger-like sponge several inches tall. The finger-like, vaselike, and fanlike sponges are characteristic of warm, quiet seas or of the deep ocean bottom. In such quiet-water habitats many sponges have fairly regular growth forms, and in more elegant times than ours they were given common names like the fan, the trumpet, the bell, the lyre, the peacock's tail, Neptune's goblet, the sailor's nest, the feather, the mermaid's glove, the elephant's ear (p. 64), and Venus' flower basket (p. 61). Sponge coloration is extremely variable, even in the same species. Deep-water forms are likely to be drab grays or browns, sometimes white; but in shallow waters many of the encrusting sponges tend to take on brilliant hues: sulphur yellow, bright pink, scarlet, deep reds, all shades of purple, and beautiful greens. Both marine and fresh-water sponges often harbor algal cells, and a fresh-water species that appears green in full sunlight is colorless on the underside of the same rock. The horny sponges of commerce shade from light browns to jet black.

All sponges are capable of sexual reproduction, and though most produce eggs and sperms in the same body, they do so at different times, so that cross-fertilization occurs. The small motile sperms enter other sponges with the ingoing current, and the food-laden fertilized egg develops into a tiny flagellated larva that leaves with the outgoing jet. After swimming about for some time the larva attaches and grows into a young sponge. This serves to distribute the wholly sedentary sponges to new habitats and gives the young an opportunity to move over a bit before setting up shop in competition with their parents and relatives.

Animals as loosely put together as the sponges can be expected to have exceptional capacity for asexual reproduction and for the regeneration of injured or lost parts. Any part of a sponge can grow into a whole animal, though the process is slow and the attempts to raise commercial sponges from small pieces have met with only limited success (p. 66). When sponges with very high regenerative powers are squeezed through silk bolting cloth, the separated cells come together in small clumps, then in somewhat larger masses, and finally grow into complete sponges. All fresh-water sponges, and some marine ones too, regularly produce asexual reproductive bodies, called gemmules (p. 64). When conditions of life become unfavorable many sponges constrict off the tips of their branches or simply disintegrate and leave behind little masses of cells. These round up, remain dormant for a while, and with the return of better times regenerate into new sponges. Small sponges may not outlast a single year, but it is hard to believe that some of the largest sponges can attain their magnificent size without continuous growth over twenty-five or even fifty years or longer.

Most zoologists are repelled by the prospect of trying to identify sponges that fit their shape to the substrate on which they grow, vary in size according to the local prosperity of a spot they attached to when still a larva, and vary in color for reasons that are not always clear. Rare sponges dredged from deep waters are often easier to identify superficially than are the compact encrusting types found between tide marks. Sponge specialists have resolved the problem by basing the identification of species mainly on the chemical composition and geometrical configuration of the skeletal parts, which are consistent, highly distinctive, and readily preserved. It is relatively easy to set aside two of the classes: the simpler and mostly smaller forms, the calcareous sponges, and those siliceous sponges that we call glass sponges. All those siliceous and horny sponges left over are put into a third and much the largest class, which is less homogeneous and which has been divided up in somewhat different ways by the various specialists. The names of even the largest groupings are not yet stabilized.

The Calcareous Sponges
(Class Calcarea)

The calcareous sponges, as biologists call them— or the chalky or limy sponges, as they are popularly named on English-speaking shores—have spicules that are largely of crystalline calcium carbonate. They are all small marine sponges, ranging in length from about ⅛ of an inch to 5 inches at most. Usually white or of drab color, these inconspicuous little vases or tubes, often of bristly texture, grow singly, in clusters, or as branches of a bushy or compacted colony. Some of the genera are widely distributed about the world in shallow waters, except where the salt content is too markedly lowered by admixture of fresh water.

Whether or not a sponge has spicules of calcareous content can easily be determined by teasing apart a bit of sponge on a microscope slide, adding a drop of acid, and watching through the eyepiece to see if the spicules dissolve with the effervescence of carbon dioxide released from calcium carbonate.

Around the opening or vent at the top the cylindrical body is constricted a little, and often bears an erect fringe of especially long needle-like spicules. On the body, however, the most common type of spicule is three-rayed, with the rays at equal angles, T-shaped, or Y-shaped. Three-rayed and less numerous four-rayed spicules are distributed throughout in such a way as to strengthen and support the fragile structure of nonliving gelatinous matrix and delicate living cells. The surface may be strengthened by a special layer of spicules or by a parallel arrangement of the rays of many body spicules. Often long, hairlike spicules protrude through the body surface, giving it a hairy or bristly texture.

The simplest of shore sponges belong mostly to the genus *Leucosolenia,* a name that means "white pipes." But these sponges are so small and inconspicuous that they have never attracted much attention from fishermen and others who bestow common

A cluster of calcareous sponges, pulled from their attachment on wharf piling. Three vaselike ones at left are *Sycon coronatum*, about 1 inch long. Much-branched mass at right is *Leucosolenia complicata*. (England. D. P. Wilson)

species, in which the tubes are compacted into an encrusting meshwork of twisted tubes, may be yellowish, pink, red, brown, or bluish gray. The colonies are somewhat stiff, because the fragile structure of nonliving gelatinous matrix and delicate living cells is strengthened and supported throughout by both scattered and interlacing spicules.

The urn sponge, *Sycon*, is also called the crowned sponge, because the fringe of giant needles that rims the constricted opening at the top of the urn looks like a little crown. In one species from deeper waters the fringe is as long as the body itself. Crowned sponges have a more complex internal structure than do the little sacs of the *Leucosolenia* colony, but externally most species display a simpler growth form. The single cylindrical individuals, dull gray or yellowish, and usually about 1 inch in length, spring in small clusters from a single attachment. These are widely distributed, but they are best known on northern Atlantic shores. A colonial species with finger-like branches is an inhabitant of southern seas. They flourish where wave action is not too strong, and at low tide can be seen in tide pools, under stones, and hanging from wharf pilings or from the brown seaweed *Fucus* or the green eelgrass *Zostera*.

The purse sponge, *Grantia*, is named for R. E. Grant, who first really understood the structure and workings of sponges, gave them their phylum name, and cleared up the uncertainties about their status as animals. Now his work is recalled whenever we refer to the light gray or creamy white sponges that hang as little bags with the somewhat compressed opening down, and when the tide is out collapse to flattened purses. So abundant on certain English beaches as to occur by the tens of thousands in a few hundred yards, they hang in rocky crevices, or among the delicate red algae that droop from rock overhangs, or from the blades of eelgrass. Each is usually about 1 inch long; but D. P. Wilson, writing of *Grantia compressa* in *They Live in the Sea,* says that in English harbors where food is plentiful and wave action subdued the flattened sponges may be almost as large as one's hand. They are rarely the neat little bags drawn in books, but are much folded and twisted upon themselves. The manner in which they split along these folds, dropping fragments that attach and grow into new sponges, has been vividly described by Maurice Burton in *Margins of the Sea.*

The Glass Sponges

(Class Hexactinellida)

The possession of six-rayed spicules distinguishes the glass sponges from all others. Composed chiefly of silicon dioxide, the spicules show a variety and

names. Widely distributed on rocky shores near low-tide mark, they favor well-aerated spots where the water is in motion without being really surfy. *Leucosolenia* grows only in colonies of little vertical tubes connected by horizontal tubes or by a complex network of branching tubes. An upright branch encloses a single cavity, completely lined with flagellated, collared feeding cells, and opening at the top by a single vent. The colonies spread in tide pools or over the underside of stones as small fungus-like patches about ½ of an inch high. Or they hang as bushy growths, which have been compared to miniature bunches of bananas, from wooden wharf pilings or from the stems of the brown seaweed *Fucus*. One

60]

complexity far beyond anything seen in calcareous sponges. The rays may be covered with spines, their tips branched like brushes or feather dusters, or expanded into umbrellas or recurved anchors. They occur as separate particles, and in most members of this class are also hooked together into loose skeletal networks or firmly fused into rigid lattices of open structure that support delicate cellular complexes.

Most glass sponges are radially symmetrical and grow as solitary cylinders, vases, cups, or funnels, drab or white in color. Some are branching or have the branches fused into latticework. They are of moderate size, from 4 to 12 inches, but there are species 3 feet long; and a form like *Monoraphis* is much longer if we count its tremendously extended anchor (6 to 9 feet long and almost ½ of an inch thick).

The beachcomber will find no glass sponges. They are all deep-water forms, reaching their peak of abundance on bottoms three thousand feet or more below the surface, and then tapering off in numbers as they extend down into the great abyssal regions of the oceans. The glass sponges are among the finest rewards of dredging in the great deeps off the West Indies, the Philippines, the Molucca Islands, and Japan. N. B. Marshall, in *Aspects of Deep Sea Biology,* quotes from Alcock's recollection of trawling in the Indian Ocean: "As the trawbag came clear of the sea, it seemed at first sight as if it had fouled a sunken haystack, for there stuck out on all sides things that looked like bundles of hay, with here and there a bird's nest attached, which on closer inspection turned out to be great Hexactinellid sponges." In the deep waters to the west of the European coasts Le-Danois has found the cup-shaped *Asconema* and the vaselike *Pheronema* to be quite common, as are also species of the glass rope sponge *Hyalonema.* The name means "glassy thread," but the dried skeleton of a *Hyalonema* is better described as looking like an upturned bell-shaped wad of glass wool with a long, opalescent handle of spirally twisted spun-glass fibers. The tuft is a bundle of greatly elongated spicules that end in recurved hooks; and it splays out at the end, anchoring the living sponge firmly in the soft ocean floor. At its upper end this column of fibers protrudes into the body of the sponge and may even push up the perforated exhalant surface into a projecting cone, eliminating any sort of cavity in the upturned bell. Off the New England coast a species of *Hyalonema* is found in only thirty to forty-five feet of water, but even such forms have been, in the past at least, inaccessible as living sponges to anyone who could not manage to be on deck when a glass sponge was dredged up. To most professional zoologists, glass sponges are known only from preserved specimens or dried skeletons.

The unvarying climate and the slow, continuous current of deep waters are usually called upon to ex-

The beautiful skeletons of Venus' flower basket, *Euplectella,* are all that most of us ever see of glass sponges. (American Museum of Natural History)

plain the adaptations of glass sponges, and especially of such a form as Venus' flower basket, or *Euplectella,* which is brought up from depths of fifteen hundred to fifteen thousand feet off islands in the western Pacific, especially the Philippines and Japan. As displayed in the showcases of museums, the elegant skeleton of *Euplectella* is a foot-long curved tube of glistening siliceous open latticework. Strengthening the upper end is a perforated convex sieve plate; and bearding the lower end is a tuft of fibers that root the living sponge. From top to bottom the tubular lattice is wreathed with projecting ledges of fused siliceous spicules that strengthen the framework and add to its rigidity as well as to its loveliness. Within the closed cylinder there usually is to be found a pair of shrimps, male and female (of the genus *Spongicola*). These enter when very minute and then cannot escape because of the sieve plate over the exhalant opening. Such a glass sponge, with its pair of imprisoned dried shrimps, was long used in Japan as a wedding gift symbolizing the wish that the marriage would see the happy couple "together unto old age and into the same grave."

The Siliceous and Horny Sponges *(Class Demospongiae)*

There is more than one way to gain admission to this big and heterogeneous class, which includes four-fifths of all sponges. Members may have skeletons of siliceous spicules alone, of horny fibers alone, or of a combination of the two. A few genera without any skeleton at all have been slipped in, but they have the complex internal channels and the multiple, small, round, flagellated feeding chambers characteristic of the Demospongiae.

Sponges with skeletons composed entirely of siliceous spicules, or those which have in addition to such spicules a framework of fibers, are referred to as siliceous sponges (Plate 3). The ones with both

Fresh-water sponge, *Spongilla*, common in both running and standing waters. It may occur in either branching or encrusting form. (Vermont. William H. Amos)

spicules and fibers are the most numerous of all sponges. Those entirely devoid of spicules and supported by horny framework alone are called horny sponges. In either case the horny fibers are composed of spongin, a protein secretion chemically related to the connective-tissue fibers of human skin. The spongin is often impregnated with rock fragments and other minute foreign particles, so that most horny sponges are not soft enough to be of commercial use.

The siliceous sponges are divided into two main groupings. The Tetractinellida have no spongin but have four-rayed spicules. They are small to moderately sized, drably colored, rounded sponges which attract little attention. Among them is *Tetilla*, mentioned earlier. In the second grouping, the Monaxonida, members may or may not have spongin but they have one-rayed, needle-like spicules. Here are found most of the common and abundant marine sponges of shores and shallow waters, and the whole of the relatively small fresh-water fauna. A few marine monaxid sponges grow in deeper waters, some even at fifteen to eighteen thousand feet.

Among the monaxids are the largest of all sponges. Neptune's goblet, *Poterion,* and the cake-shaped loggerhead sponge, *Spheciospongia,* of the Gulf of Mexico, may be 2 to 6 feet tall or broad. In the cavities of one large (185,000 cu. cm.) loggerhead sponge at Tortugas, Florida, A. S. Pearse once found more than seventeen thousand animals, about sixteen thousand of them shrimps of the genus *Synalpheus.*

The breadcrumb sponge, *Halichondria panicea,* (Plate 1) is a cosmopolitan species, especially abundant on all English and other northern European shores and on the New England coast north to the Arctic Ocean, but somewhat spottier in occurrence on the American Pacific coast. It is reported also from places as far apart as Alaska, Ceylon, and Nova Zembla. Usually greenish in color, but also yellowish or orange, patches of different color may grow side by side. The fairly smooth surface is patterned with more or less regularly spaced miniature "volcanoes" through which the spent water issues. The colony grows as an encrusting sheet in rocky clefts, under rock overhangs, and under masses of brown seaweeds—in almost any firm spot that will not be exposed for long to the sun when the tide is out. In deeper water the sponge grows more massive, with higher, more slender "volcanoes." On the American Pacific coast it often encrusts beds of California mussels and gooseneck barnacles, along with the violet-colored *Haliclona,* which is common on some Australian shores. Also splashing color across shaded rocks on both sides of the Atlantic and on the Pacific coast are thin, shiny, brick-red or coral-red blotches of *Ophlitaspongia* (Plate 47). Usually more orange-red are patches of *Hymeniacidon,* with a rough surface that is puckered with grooves. On Atlantic beaches the red species is very abundant; the American Pacific coast species is yellow-green and grows in quieter waters, often on oyster shells. Encrusting practically all scallop shells in Puget Sound are yellowish brown growths of *Ectyodoryx parasitica,* less often of *Mycale adherens.* North of Puget Sound and into Alaska, mollusk shells, especially those of the rock oyster or jingle shell, may be honeycombed to the crumbling point with the tunnels of the yellow boring sponge, *Cliona celata,* a cosmopolitan species. Farther south, as in Monterey Bay, it bores in abalone shells but is not so generally widespread. In the Gulf of California Ricketts saw it growing, beyond tidal range, in its nonboring, massive form as reddish pink vases several feet in diameter. On the American east coast it is well known from South Carolina northward; and it is common in European waters. The yellow massive form with wartlike vents occurs offshore; the boring type tunnels in limestone pebbles and shells in shallow water. The activities of *Cliona* are important in disintegrating the empty shells that accumulate on the sea bottom, but we appreciate them less when the sponge weakens the shells of edible clams or scallops and becomes a pest in oyster beds by making oysters more vulnerable to their many enemies.

Finger sponge, with both spicules and horny matrix, from San Francisco Bay. Two tiny hermit crabs explore its surface. (Woody Williams)

Horny skeleton of the elephant's-ear sponge, from the Mediterranean, a fine-textured commercial sponge valued by potters. (Ralph Buchsbaum)

be lobed or branched. Most of the species that grow on the upper side of objects are greenish from the algal cells that they contain, but those on the undersides of rocks or in fairly deep water have no chlorophyll to mask their lack of color or their drab shades of tan, brown, or gray. Some species are not green even when growing in light. The colonies spread as small, thin patches perhaps an inch or two square, but in the best spots may be more than 1 inch thick and cover 40 square yards. They are most abundant in clear, quiet waters less than six feet deep, but some species tolerate deep water, or running water, or a small amount of pollution. Sexual reproduction occurs during the summer growing season; and in addition, fresh-water sponges characteristically produce asexual bodies, the gemmules, which lie dormant all winter and hatch into new sponges in the spring. They are easily seen in the fall as small balls of cells coated with a protective layer of anchor-shaped spicules. No predator is known to feed on fresh-water sponges, but the larvae of Spongilla flies (insects of the family Sisyridae) pierce the sponge cells and suck out their contents. Fresh-water sponges are of no economic importance except when they occasionally block water conduits or reservoir drains. The decay of sponges may give water what is known as "swamp taste." An excellent account of American forms may be found in Pennak's *Fresh-water Invertebrates of the United States*.

The horny sponges, the Keratosa, are typically shallow-water forms of tropical or subtropical seas, but some species extend even into polar waters. Though they all lack sharp spicules, the spongin fibers are usually impregnated with hard foreign materials, and only a dozen or so species are soft enough for commercial use.

The best commercial sponges were for centuries brought up by divers from the shores of the Mediterranean, so it is not surprising that the earliest uses of sponges known to us were among the ancient Greeks, and that in Greek mythology Glaucus of Anthedon was a sponge diver. In the Odyssey, before a dinner party for Ulysses, the maids were instructed to wipe off the tables with sponges. When Ulysses had finished with his wife's suitors, sponges were used to mop the blood from the floor. While Greek mothers sponged their houses clean and Greek fathers went off to the wars with sponge padding in their helmets and leg armor, Greek babies were bathed with sponges and pacified with bits of sponge dipped in honey. In Roman times sponges were used also as paintbrushes and were carried by soldiers as a substitute for a drinking cup, so it is understandable that Christ on the cross should have been offered vinegar in a soaked sponge. Today the sponge in the bathroom is more likely to be a marvel of modern chemistry, because overfishing of sponge grounds, in

The family Clionidae has other well-known borers, some of them busy in coral reefs. Most are sulphur yellow, a few green or purple. Some members of the family Suberitidae encrust the snail shells inhabited by various hermit crabs, and certain species are never found except on such shells, growing until they completely enclose the shell. When the shell disappears the crab continues to occupy the spiral cavity formed by the sponge, and it is presumed that both members benefit, the sponge by being carried about during its feeding, the crab by protection from predators (Plate 2).

The redbeard sponge, *Microciona,* is a bright red colony that grows as a low incrustation or, in deeper waters, as an erect mass of red branches perhaps 6 inches high. It is well known from South Carolina to Cape Cod, and has been much used in experiments on the dissociation and reintegration of sponge cells. A different species occurs in European waters.

The family Spongillidae comprises all of the fresh-water sponges. It consists of about 150 species, of which about 30 are known from ponds, lakes, and slow streams in the United States. Typically, they form inconspicuous matlike incrustations on rocks, logs, sticks, or leaves in the water, but they may also

Reef scene at Nassau. Many sea whips in foreground, two sea fans near center, and lobed masses of the coral *Montastrea annularis* dominating background. (Fritz Goro: *Life* Magazine)

a world in which people are multiplying faster than sponges, has made sponges more and more difficult to collect. Men must now use special diving equipment and go farther and farther from shore, so the price has risen accordingly. The more exacting professional users continue to buy the finest Mediterranean sponges for surgical and hygienical preparations, for dressing leather, for applying glaze to pottery, and for scouring and sponging cloth. Fine sponges are also used by jewelers, silversmiths, and lithographers. The great bulk of commercial sponges like the sheepswool, which are used for cleaning walls and automobiles and railroad cars, have in our century come mostly from the Gulf of Mexico and from the Caribbean grounds. Some sponge fishing is done in the Philippines, but it is of minor importance in the world market. An excellent and accessible account of commercial sponge fishing and sponge preparation, with a list of the chief commercial species and the areas from which they come, is P. Galtsoff's article in the *Encyclopaedia Britannica*.

The last "normal" year for sponge fishing was 1938, when more than two million tons of sponges were harvested, about 30 per cent of them from the United States fisheries in the Gulf of Mexico. In that year a disease struck at the 180,000 cultivated sponges that were being grown from sponge cuttings fastened down in artificial beds at Water Cay in the Bahamas. From there the disease rapidly spread to the natural beds of Cuba, northwest Florida, and British Honduras, where 700,000 sponge cuttings were killed. When the authors visited a Cuban fishery in June of 1939 the local fleet of sponge-fishing boats was tied up in the harbor, and the townspeople were desperately anxious for someone to minister to their dying source of livelihood. One old man brought us a sick sponge in a bucket of sea water and handed it over as tenderly as if it were an ailing child. When we went out with several fishermen to hook a few sponges from the sea bottom, we had difficulty in finding a healthy one. The disease was finally diagnosed by biologists as being due to a fungus, though some doubts remained. Useless sponges like the loggerhead were unaffected, but the valuable commercial species were all but wiped out. After reaching a mortality as high as 95 per cent in the worst areas, the disease began to subside. But the damage to the industry was long-lasting. Synthetic sponge competition was encouraged, and rising costs in overfished beds did the rest. In recent years sponge production in the United States has been as low as 6 per cent of the 1936 value.

CHAPTER III

Hydroids (at left) and jellyfish

Hydroids, Jellyfishes, Sea Anemones, and Corals

(Phylum Coelenterata or Cnidaria)

RADIALLY symmetrical, often gorgeously colored, and festooned with one or more circlets of graceful tentacles, coelenterates are indeed the "flowers of the animal kingdom," but they are animals nevertheless, and carnivorous at that. Their elegant symmetry is an effective design for snaring prey from any direction and passing it on to a centrally placed mouth.

Fleshy sea anemones hang tentacles downward in rocky grottoes or hold their delicate petaled disks upright in tide pools or on shaded rocks. Their coral allies rise, like minute anemones, from rigid cups of limestone, either singly or in massive colonies that in tropical waters form huge reefs. Feathery sprays of delicately colored hydroids soften rocky crevices and tide pools or are seen as bedraggled brown plumes in the beach flotsam.

In warm temperate waters the sea floor below low-tide mark is a colorful garden of foot-high sea fans, sea whips, and sea feathers, displaying plume-like or latticed branches of vivid reds, pinks, yellows, and purples. Soft corals thrust up spongy lobes like ghostly hands, and a little farther out the lovely sea pens anchor by their fleshy quills in the sand or mud. The deeper waters are a fairyland of tall and flexible gorgonians that sway with the currents. Through every opening and into every crevice of these coelenterate thickets dart fishes and invertebrates of all kinds, seeking food and taking shelter as do the animals in our woods. In the water above, jellyfishes pulse gently about or drift with the cur-

rents as minute little saucers or frighteningly large bowls of jelly.

At night the sea is lighted with new splendor by the many coelenterates that luminesce when stimulated. Millions of small jellyfishes flash with every wave, making the dark water sparkle. Now the submarine gardens reveal themselves as softly lighted, scintillating pathways that fade and then sparkle anew as the sea pens and other sessile coelenterates react to the touch of wandering fishes and bottom creatures.

Of more than nine thousand species of coelenterates, only a few small members, all belonging to the most primitive class, the Hydrozoa, have managed to invade fresh waters. These include the little hydras of ponds and streams, an uncommon hydroid, a tiny parasite in the eggs of the sturgeon, and two small jellyfishes that turn up sporadically. Some hydroids and sea anemones penetrate into brackish waters, where sea water is diluted by fresh, but the coelenterates as a group, and the reef corals in particular, flourish only in fully marine habitats and are noticeably absent near the mouths of rivers.

The great banks of reef-forming corals, and the luxuriant growth of other coelenterates that live on these reefs, are not found outside the tropics and subtropics. Yet many coelenterates, and even certain kinds of tall branching corals, are so abundant in temperate and cold waters that one can hardly think of this as a warm-water phylum.

Beyond the depths to which the aqualung or diving suits can take us, coelenterates are very much at home, even in the deepest trenches of the ocean floor. There they have been reached only by the instruments and dredges, and at lesser depths also by the cameras, of specially equipped oceanographic expeditions. The matchless English *Challenger* expedition (1872–1876) and the superbly equipped Danish *Galathea* expedition (1950–1952) dredged many lovely and bizarre coelenterates that were still alive and often still able to luminesce even after rough upward trips from fifteen thousand feet or more.

All of the attached and cylindrical coelenterates, whether they be large fleshy anemones or minute and glassily transparent members of a hydroid or coral colony, are called polyps, from the French word *poulpe,* for octopus. The term goes back to the Greek for "many-footed," and refers to the agile tentacles that capture and pass food to the mouth, but in a few species can be used for moving about. In the jellyfishes the tentacles have been pushed out, by a spreading of the body, to the rim of the umbrella. Where the handle of an umbrella would be, there hangs a tube with the mouth at its tip, directed downward, in contrast with the usually upright polyps. In either group, polyps or jellyfishes, some members may take up the opposite stance, and this is not surprising, for when we come to examine them closely we see that the two kinds are built on the same basic plan and that both fixed polyp and free-swimming jellyfish types may occur as stages in the life history of a single species. In both, the body is a sac with only one opening, which doubles as entrance for food and as exit for indigestible residues and body wastes. The main body cavity ("coel") is the intestine ("enteron"), and the saclike digestive cavity, or coelenteron, lends its name to the animals described in this chapter.

The digestive lining secretes juices that break down the food into a thick broth and the fluid food then circulates about the whole animal, or through branches to other members of a colony. Some cells lining the cavity engulf the small particles protozoan-fashion, and complete the digestion of what appears to be in most cases wholly animal food.

The phylum Coelenterata at one time included the sponges and the comb jellies. Then it was realized that the main cavity of sponges is a water passage, not a digestive cavity, and the sponges were removed. The coelenterates and the comb jellies still share the same phylum in many books, for they have the coelenteron in common. But they differ in several important ways, notably in the absence in comb jellies of the microscopic thread capsules, or nematocysts, which are characteristic of coelenterates and which they use to sting and to hold prey. More will be said of these later. In dividing the coe-

lenterates from the comb jellies it would be most logical to discard the old phylum name and to call the group the phylum Cnidaria (*cnidos* = "thread") to indicate the basis for distinction from the comb jellies, which (with one possible exception) have no thread capsules. Some leading students of coelenterates have already done this, but the name "coelenterate" is so well established and so widely used that it has seemed best not to change it here.

The outer surface of the coelenterate body is a protective epithelium, only one cell layer thick, so that the most fragile coelenterate bodies consist only of two microscopic layers of cells held together by a secretion of nonliving jelly. Jellyfishes acquire bulk and buoyancy by a tremendous increase in the amount of secreted jelly, and in the more advanced (scyphozoan) jellyfishes the jelly is invaded by cells and strengthening fibers. Even more cellular elements take over the gelatinous layer of sea anemones. Nevertheless, the extraordinary diversity in external form that we see in coelenterates consists only of superficial variations on one simple structural theme.

The phrase "spineless as a jellyfish" is meant to epitomize the flabby invertebrate way of life, and the animal it describes has little resemblance to the firm, muscular, and speedy fish. Zoologists prefer the name "medusa" for the jellyfish type. It was suggested by a fancied resemblance to the snaky tresses of the Gorgon Medusa, the mythological maiden whose hair was turned into serpents that petrified anyone who looked on them. Small animals are indeed paralyzed when they approach or are approached by coelenterates, for the heavy armature of stinging thread capsules, especially on the tentacles, makes them highly deserving of their reputation as "the stinging nettles of the sea." The oval capsules contain coiled hollow threads that can be discharged when properly stimulated. There are many kinds of such capsules in the group as a whole, and usually more than one kind in a species. Some are adhesive and used to attach the tentacles in certain modes of locomotion; others adhere to prey; still others wind like tiny lassos around the bristles of small animals and hold them fast. The largest and most important kind has a thread that penetrates small prey and injects a paralyzing poison. The discharged threads of the common anemones of temperate seashores have little effect on the relatively big, horny hands of human beings. At the most, one senses a sticky feeling as the tentacles adhere to a probing finger. Likewise many of the commonest jellyfishes of temperate seas either are quite harmless or only slightly annoy swimmers by producing strong prickling sensations. This is no comfort to those who tangle with cyaneas in Atlantic waters or with certain tropical jellyfishes for they are lucky to come away with no more than painful red welts. The real danger is pain or cramps so severe as to cause panic and prevent one from reaching shore, and this is especially true of encounters with one of the most dangerous coelenterates of all, the floating colony called the Portuguese man-of-war.

Isolated instances of the use of stinging capsules in certain species of flatworms and nudibranch mollusks have ceased to puzzle zoologists, since it has been shown that these are always obtained by feeding on coelenterates and then manipulating the captured capsules into positions on the surface where they can be used in the same manner as in the animals that produced them.

Coelenterates on the whole show little promise as a direct source of food for man. Sea anemones have long been eaten in France, Italy, and Greece, and in some of the Pacific islands. As late as the nineteenth century they were regularly sold in Mediterranean markets and brought a good price in Bordeaux. Some of the green anemones were especially popular, and after being boiled in sea water were said to acquire a firm and palatable consistency, excellent with any sauce. Wrote one early naturalist gourmet, "They are of an inviting appearance, of a light shivering texture, and of a soft white and reddish hue. Their smell is not unlike that of a warm crab or lobster." Some cooks prepared anemones as they would oysters, and often served the two together. Dahlia anemones are still eaten on the Continent but in England they are used only as bait with long fishing lines.

Certain jellyfishes are regularly eaten in Korea, Japan, and China. When these turn up in large shoals they are dried and cut into strips, which can be reconstituted with water whenever desired. The chief contribution of jellyfishes to the human diet, however, is indirect and is appreciated only by fisheries experts. Certain species of jellyfishes, says L. A. Walford in *Living Resources of the Sea,* are among the most valuable marine animals from man's viewpoint because they provide portable shelter for the young of commercially valuable fishes such as hake, haddock, cod, horse mackerel, and butterfish. The young fishes accompany their host in the floating surface plankton, feeding around it within a radius of several feet and darting quickly to safe harbor beneath its spreading umbrella whenever danger threatens. The relationship may even be an essential stage in the life cycle of some fishes, and the fingerling that fails to find a jellyfish host within a certain time may not long survive among the hungry predators of the sea. This is not to deny that some jellyfishes take a great toll of the juvenile fish population.

Red corals are fished from Italian and other Mediterranean coasts, and also in Japan, for manufacture into jewelry and various ornaments. Dried sea fans, sea whips, sea feathers, and especially

A common trachyline jellyfish of shore waters is *Gonionemus vertens,* shown here swimming actively. (England. D. P. Wilson)

dried and bleached coral skeletons, all of them highly decorative, are sold in the same shops that sell many tons of mollusk shells every year. Even the delicate, horny skeletons of sheathed hydroids have some economic value. In England, centering in the Thames estuary, there is a small "whiteweed industry." Boats drag iron rakes over shell-and-sand bottoms, pulling up feathery colonies of *Sertularia argentea,* sometimes other species or other genera. The processed hydroid plumes are dyed green or other colors and sold for decorative purposes, mainly in the United States, as "ever living house plants" or as "sea ferns."

Parasitism by coelenterates is rare, though even hydroids can parasitize fish; but the group as a whole has a notable talent for sitting down uninvited at the table of other invertebrates, or for living associated with snails, crabs, and a great variety of other creatures in a relationship which may possibly be of some benefit to the host as well as to the coelenterate guest. Playing the role of host, on the other hand, are the many jellyfishes and large tropical anemones that shelter fishes, all the large attached coelenterates that provide a place for myriads of tiny invertebrates to hang onto in a restless ocean, the coral crevices that shelter hundreds of kinds of fishes and crabs and worms, and—most important of all—the widespread mutualistic ties of coelenterates with green or yellowish brown algal cells. Certain hydras of fresh waters and many anemones of temperate and cold marine waters look green from the plantlike cells that live in their tissues. But in warm shallow seas such relationships are the rule rather than the exception. On coral reefs almost all coelenterates, jellyfishes included, harbor colored cells; and we believe that this contributes to their astounding success in warm waters.

Reproduction is both sexual and abundantly asexual. Like the sponges or any other group that readily reproduces by asexual means, coelenterates have extraordinary capacity to regenerate lost tentacles or branches, to grow by budding, or to reproduce by rupture of the body. Some species can regroup their cells and grow again even after the tissues have been dissociated experimentally by being passed through fine cloth, thus giving us answers to many problems dealing with the enviable adaptability of tissues less specialized than our own. When both polyps and jellyfishes appear in the life cycle, the reproductive chores are divided between a polyp that reproduces asexually by budding off medusas, and a medusa that reproduces sexually by shedding eggs or sperms into the water. The medusa may be free-swimming, or it may never be set loose, remaining always attached to the polyp or polyp colony. The fertilized egg of marine coelenterates develops into a little oval or elongate free-swimming larva, called a planula, which swims about for a time, then settles down, attaches to the bottom, and grows into a polyp or, by budding, into a polyp colony. Many modifications and short cuts occur in this typical scheme.

Of the three classes of coelenterates, the first or most primitive one is the Hydrozoa, in which many species have both polyps and medusas, often equally developed, in the life history. The Scyphozoa have minimized or dropped the polyp, staking their fortunes on larger and better jellyfishes. The Anthozoa have gone off in the other direction and have given up the medusa altogether, the sea anemones perfecting a larger and more muscular polyp, the corals specializing in great skeletal works.

Hydrozoan Polyps and Jellyfishes (Class Hydrozoa)

Hydrozoans are named from the resemblance of their polyps to the little solitary hydras of fresh water, but members of this class may also have a medusa stage. We are not always able to match the polyps we find attached on the bottom to the properly related little gelatinous medusas that swim and feed at the surface and reproduce sexually. Often polyps and medusas are separately described and named, and their relationship as stages of a single life cycle sometimes emerges only when we happen to see the medusa released, by an asexual process, from a polyp confined in an aquarium.

This is an important group, with close to three thousand species, and almost all are entirely marine; but it does include those few little polyps and medusas that live in fresh waters. The tentacled polyps of hydrozoans differ from those of the other classes in having a simple digestive cavity, undivided by ridges or partitions. The hydrozoan medusa can usually be readily told from the true or scyphozoan jellyfishes by its smaller size and by its possession of a velum, a transparent and muscular circular shelf that projects inward from the rim of the gelatinous umbrella (or saucer, or deep bowl, or bell, or whatever name best fits the variously shaped medusas).

Hydrozoans are notable in the animal kingdom for the many shapes that members of a hydroid colony assume. Aside from the division of reproductive chores between polyps and medusas, the polyps come in a variety of body forms, each specialized for its share of the colony housekeeping. Tentacled feeding polyps and club-shaped reproductive polyps are a frequent combination, but some colonies have one or more kinds of mouthless polyps that serve only for stinging prey or for protection. In other species there may be in addition a striking difference between the reproductive polyps that produce female medusoid individuals and those that produce male medusoids, both bearers of sex cells.

THE HYDROIDS

The hydroids are called "sea firs" in England and sometimes "sea plumes" in the United States. These names indicate the branching patterns of some common colonial forms, but they are rather misleadingly grand designations for most hydroids, which are

Feather hydroid, *Kirchenpaueria* (*Plumularia*) *pinnata*. About 2 to 3 inches high. (England. D. P. Wilson)

small and inconspicuous and seldom recognized as among the most abundant animals of the seashore. The plumelike colonies that rise to heights of 6 feet from their moorings on the sea bottom at depths of three thousand feet, and the equally tall solitary polyp, *Branchiocerianthus,* which has been dredged up from fifteen thousand feet below the surface, are conversation pieces. The vast majority range from a fraction of an inch high to several inches, with 8 to 12 inches as the upper extreme; and they are largely confined to the shores and to shallow waters, where they form delicate white, pink, violet, or brown tufts on rocks and wharf pilings, on seaweeds, and on many animal stalks and shells.

Hydroids are often mistaken for minute seaweeds because of their plantlike growth forms, though there the resemblance ends. The "flower heads" of solitary polyps or those at the free tips of branching colonies are voracious feeders on minute crustaceans and worms, eggs and larvae, or even on fishes. Few things are more beautiful than a microscope field filled with row upon row of elegantly shaped, glassy hydroid chalices, each with a circle of graceful transparent tentacles—or more potentially lethal. A small animal swimming through has as much chance of making it safely as a ship would have in sailing through waters so heavily mined that the detonating devices were almost touching. At the slightest alarm the outspread tentacles are whisked in with a liveliness that at once betrays their animal nature.

Favored and protected positions are acquired by hydroids that attach to the branches or stalks of sessile animals like sponges, sea whips, or sea pens—or that are constantly carried to new pastures on the shells inhabited by hermit crabs. Many hydroids share in the host's feeding currents by fastening to the outside of mollusk shells or worm tubes near the water intake. Some even live within the mantle cavity of certain oysters or other bivalves, and in the sievelike branchial cavity of certain tunicates.

There are two main types of hydroids, divided according to the extent of the transparent yet protective horny covering that the polyp or polyp colony secretes about itself. Most familiar of the fully sheathed hydroids is the cosmopolitan genus *Obelia,* with species on almost all shores. Some form delicate little white sprays that rise 1 or 2 inches above the creeping runners that attach to rocks, seaweeds, mussels, wharf pilings, or floating wood. In shallow waters below low-tide mark, yellowish species of *Obelia* grow 8 to 12 inches long. The various species are alternately branched or have stems that zigzag, with tentacled polyps arising at the angles and lodged in goblet-shaped transparent cups. From the axils formed by the stalks of these feeding polyps arise urn-shaped reproductive polyps enclosed in transparent containers of the same shape. At intervals

these bud off little medusas that swim away. Though they are barely visible to the naked eye, their jerky pulsations are familiar to those who examine plankton under the microscope. The muscular shelf that characterizes hydrozoan medusas is aborted during development, but otherwise the *Obelia* medusa is typical of the little flattened saucers allied to the sheathed hydroids. It has four digestive canals radiating from the central digestive cavity to the rim of the umbrella, and to these canals are attached the sex organs.

Besides the campanularian or bell-like hydroids, to which *Obelia* belongs, the many kinds of sheathed hydroids include such widespread families as the sertularians, in which the cups are not stalked but are set directly on long, graceful stems that branch to look mosslike or fernlike. A species of *Sertularia* was referred to earlier as the "whiteweed" of a small industry in England. In the plumularians the cups are also set directly on the stems, but the branches

Portion of a hydroid colony, magnified through a microscope, shows the many polyps with outspread stinging tentacles that lie in wait for small passing prey. (Bermuda. Ralph Buchsbaum)

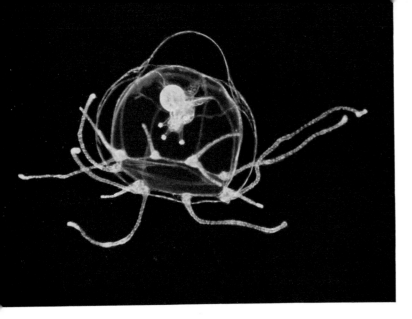

The minute jellyfish stage, *Lizzia blondina*, of a hydroid colony. (England. D. P. Wilson)

Of the medusas allied to the hydroids, few are as big or as cosmopolitan as *Aequorea,* or better known from their summer swarms. White or pale bluish green and somewhat flattened like the other medusas of sheathed hydroids, it has many radially spreading digestive branches, in some species more than a hundred. The tentacles are a short fringe when contracted, a long curtain of slender strands when fully extended. The polyp is minute and not known for all species. Stranded aequoreas, masses of jelly often about as big as one's hand, sometimes much bigger, are as well known to Japanese beachcombers as to those of American or European coasts. The luminescence for which they are noted can be rubbed off on the hands as luminescent grains, then dabbed on the

come out in only one plane, so that they resemble every kind of plumage from small feathers to long plumes, some growing up to 6 feet in very deep waters. The ostrich-plume hydroid, *Aglaophenia,* which looks like stout brown feathers, often about 3 inches long, is especially common, after storms have washed it loose, in the beach drift on the American Pacific coast. Other species are known from the Atlantic coast and European and many other shores as well. The podlike structures conspicuous among the branches are protective flaps covering the reproductive polyps.

In the naked hydroids, the horny covering is absent or scanty or extends only as tubes that stop at the bases of the feeding and reproductive polyps. These include a number of common genera that grow as rather large single polyps or as clumps or mats of vertical colonial polyps; they are mostly pink or rosy in color. *Corymorpha* is a solitary polyp up to 4 inches long that lives in mud flats. It is related to the solitary giant polyp, *Branchiocerianthus,* mentioned earlier as a deep-water form. *Clava* and *Tubularia* grow in long-stemmed clumps (Plates 4 and 5). *Hydractinia,* sometimes known as "hedgehog hydroid" because of the spininess of the encrusting mat formed by the basal stalks that unite the colony, is noted for the diversity of its several kinds of polyps, and also for its habit of encrusting shells adopted by hermit crabs. Whether it actually shares the host's food we do not really know; in any case it can live on rocks and wharf pilings, quite independent of the crabs.

Related to *Clava* and the other naked types is *Cordylophora lacustris,* the fresh-water colonial hydroid. In brackish inlets on marine coasts it is seen as white, bushy, treelike colonies, a few inches high, on stones, eelgrass, or wharf piles. When found in rivers and lakes it seldom exceeds 1 inch in height.

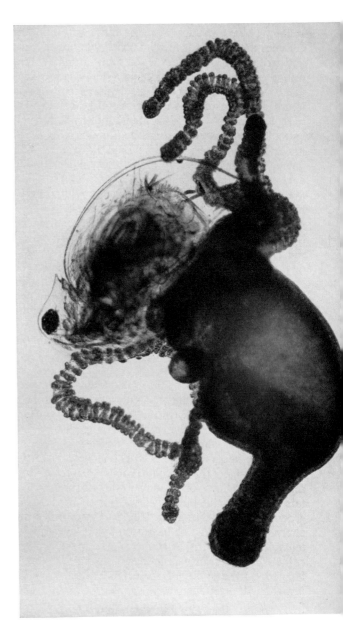

faces and hands of unsuspecting friends, creating weird effects in darkness. It may be added that all the hydroids mentioned earlier are also luminescent, though not so bright as *Aequorea.*

Medusas allied to the naked hydroids are usually deep-bodied little bells, like *Sarsia, Lizzia,* and *Podocoryne.* Many have never been matched to their polyps. The need of the larva to attach to some kind of solid substrate in those forms that have a fixed polyp stage keeps most hydrozoan jellyfishes tied to shore waters. Bigelow once observed that in the deep and open waters ten miles off Bermuda only 3 per cent of the jellyfishes he collected were of species with a fixed stage in the life cycle.

Hydras are naked little fresh-water polyps that

abound in unpolluted streams, ponds, or the shore waters of lakes, living attached to submerged stones, twigs, vegetation, or debris. Yet they rarely come to the attention of anyone who does not deliberately seek them out, for when disturbed they contract into all but invisible little knobs. Even when fully extended the cylindrical body is as fine as sewing thread, only ½ of an inch long or so, and has gossamer tentacles that barely match the body in length, or in some species are three or four times as long. Their regular occurrence in certain favored spots makes them the only living coelenterates readily and dependably accessible at great distances from the ocean. Though to the naked eye the hydra may appear as an insignificant little creature, under a hand lens or a microscope it becomes a spectacular beast that fully deserves to be named after the mythical monster slain by Hercules. Hydra had nine heads, and when Hercules cut one off, two grew in its place. Hydra's small namesakes are renowned for their ability to replace injured tentacles, grow a new "head" if beheaded, grow two heads on one body, or reproduce asexually by budding off new individuals from the sides of the body. In sexual reproduction the egg develops into a little embryo that may lie dormant during the winter but in spring develops directly into another polyp without any kind of free-swimming stage.

The green hydra, *Chlorohydra viridissima,* which harbors algal cells of the genus *Chlorella,* and the brown hydra, *Pelmatohydra oligactis,* in which the slender basal stalk is more obviously set off from the main part of the body than in other hydras, are cosmopolitan species, found on many continents. All the other species are limited to particular continents or continental regions. When green coloring occurs in *Pelmatohydra oligactis* it is always due to eating green food, such as green chironomid larvae. Starved animals lose their color, while well-fed ones on the usual diet are brownish or even black. *Hydra circumcincta* is a lovely orange-red if fed on ostracods or red copepods, and a rich color advertises the prosperity of its bearer.

Most large libraries have the original *Memoire* by Trembley on the behavior and regeneration of hydras. To read about his long romance with the little *"polypes d'eau douce en forme de cornes"* is to want to see the creatures feed, bud, and regenerate. For readers who prefer English, John Baker's book, also

Left. A hydra opens its mouth wide to swallow a water flea. The minute crustacean victim is already paralyzed by the stinging threads. *Right.* The daphnid has been swallowed and is in the hydra's digestive cavity; the body outline and the large eye can be seen through the body wall. (Eric Grave)

listed in the bibliography, tells of Trembley himself and of his work with hydras and other microscopic animals of fresh water. Hydras may be readily collected in nature or purchased from biological supply companies, and they can be cultured in the home if kept in pond water, maintained at temperatures below 75°F., and fed on small crustaceans such as daphnias. Detailed directions for rearing many kinds of invertebrates are given in the Galtsoff book listed in the bibliography.

THE TRACHYLINE MEDUSAS

A jellyfish in fresh water once seemed as anomalous as did a black swan to the ancients. Yet the black swan eventually turned up in Australia. And in 1880 a fresh-water jellyfish was discovered in the tank in Kew Botanical Gardens, near London, in which were kept the giant water lilies from the Amazon. It was named *Craspedacusta sowerbyi,* and afterward more were found in other botanical gardens in Europe, confirming the impression that it had been brought with water lilies from Brazil. During recent decades it has turned up on other continents, and is frequently but sporadically reported from all over the United States. Either it is becoming more widespread, or more people are aware of its existence and are keeping an eye out for it, especially in the most likely season, from July to October. It seems to favor

The commonest jellyfish encountered by amateur yachtsmen along the Atlantic coast of America is *Gonionemus murbachii,* whose tentacles and dark sense organs around the rim of the bell mark a circle as much as an inch in diameter. The cross-shaped marking in the dome of each bell is produced by the ruffled reproductive organs. (Massachusetts. Lorus and Margery Milne)

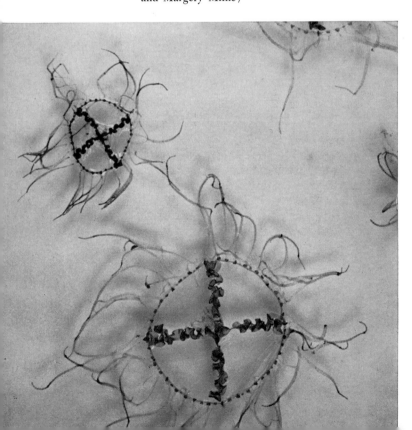

artificial bodies of water or those of limited size, such as aquaria, ditches, old flooded quarries, impounded streams, and small ponds, perhaps because it does best where plankton is very rich; but it has been found also in small lakes. No written account or colored plate of a beautiful or bizarre coelenterate from the ocean deeps can substitute for the thrill of looking over the edge of a rowboat, a thousand miles from the nearest salt water, and seeing little transparent hemispheres, 1 inch across at most and usually smaller, pulsating in the water. Removed to a large jar or an aquarium, where one can watch them at leisure, they are seen to have several sets of tentacles and to hold one group erect or obliquely upward, the others horizontal or extending downward. There is a shelflike velum extending in from the umbrella, and four radial digestive canals. From each of these hangs a baglike sex organ that looks like a little pistol holster. Though usually seen in small groups, all of one sex, they may occur by the thousands. They are known to feed on rotifers and various small crustaceans. The polyp stage, originally described and named as *Microhydra ryderi,* lives on the bottom as a minute ($\frac{1}{10}$ to $\frac{1}{3}$ of an inch) colony of several polyps lacking tentacles. A good account can be found in Pennak's *Fresh-Water Invertebrates of the United States. Limnocnida,* a similar jellyfish, is known from lakes and streams in Africa.

The fresh-water jellyfishes seem to be allied to the trachyline medusas, a marine group that differs from the hydrozoan medusas mentioned earlier in having a very minute polyp or none at all. It also differs in the nature of the sense organs found around the rim of the umbrella, which are thought to have a balancing function. A well-known marine member is *Gonionemus,* familiar to all students of biology from laboratory experience with preserved specimens. In nature it uses the adhesive pads near the tips of the tentacles to cling to the eelgrass among which it lives. When the light is not too bright or too low, *Gonionemus* fishes for its food by swimming in rapid pulsations to the surface, turning upside down, and then coasting slowly downward with its tentacles outspread in a wide net.

THE HYDROCORALS

The hydrocorals are a wholly marine group that includes the "stinging corals," likely to be long remembered by any inexperienced collector in warm waters who tries to break off what may look like an innocent and beautiful bouquet of light pink branching coral. They used to be lumped with the hydroids, which they resemble in many ways, but hydrocorals secrete massive skeletons of limestone, either erect and branching or leaflike, or low and encrusting. The millepores, which are white or of pale fleshy or yellowish tones, contribute a good share to the formation of many coral reefs and are very abundant in reefs of the western Atlantic. Another group of hydrocorals, mostly of deeper hues of pink, red, violet, or purple, also do best in warm waters but extend into temperate seas as branching species in deep water or encrusting ones in the more surfy shore waters. A lavender or purple encrusting form, *Allopora porphyra,* occurs as calcareous patches encrusting rocks at very low tide levels on the southern California coast. Its white polyps may be glimpsed in the small starlike craters that pock the surface of the massive colony.

THE SIPHONOPHORES

The siphonophores are floating hydrozoan colonies of great beauty, in which several kinds of polyplike individuals and a variety of medusa-like individuals are all combined into a single functioning complex that swims or drifts its way about, dangling drift nets of stinging tentacles to catch living prey. Most common in tropical and semitropical waters, they are to be found, especially in summer, drifting even in polar seas. On the Danish cruises of 1908 to 1910, an hour's tow in the Atlantic or Mediterranean brought in from six hundred to one thousand of these delicately transparent, milky, or subtly shaded colonies. Feeding polyps, contractile stinging tentacles, reproductive individuals, swimming bells, floating medusoids, protective flaps, and still other kinds of coelenterate units share the food netted from the rich animal plankton of surface waters. But many siphonophores can release gas from their floats in rough weather and sink below the surface, and some regularly live at greater depths, down to nine thousand feet. Even those at the surface are usually inconspicuous in the water and may escape notice despite their occurrence in immense swarms brought together by winds or currents. Around the globe, tropical and semitropical waters have much the same component of common siphonophores; those restricted to one ocean are the exception. In all warm seas *Hippopodius* trails delicate strings of polyps from a small cluster of swimming bells at the surface. A little more compact is *Physophora,* also circumglobal in warm waters but in summer carried northward by currents to southern Greenland, Iceland, and the Barents Sea. Superficially resembling little medusas are the tiny blue or greenish disks of *Porpita,* which from the deck of a liner in tropical waters can be seen by the thousands, dotting the ocean for many miles.

The only two siphonophores that are really well known, however, are the usually sky-blue "by-the-wind sailor," *Velella* (called the "purple sailor" in areas where it tends to be violet), and the even more vividly blue "Portuguese man-of-war," *Physalia,* which may also be tinted with bright pink or orange. In certain years both are carried northward in the Atlantic by steady winds and become stranded in great numbers on British, Belgian, French, and American Atlantic shores, far beyond their usual range, where their novelty attracts much attention. The same sort of thing happens in the southern hemisphere, Dakin says in *Australian Seashores.* There *Velella, Porpita,* and *Physalia* are stranded on the beaches of New South Wales, where the local name for the last is "bluebottle."

Velella looks like a single flat medusa, 1 to 3 inches long according to age or species, with a transparent iridescent sail set diagonally across the long axis of an oval float stiffened with horny material. From beneath the transparent gas-filled float is suspended the blue or pale purple body, with a single large-mouthed feeding tube at its center and this surrounded by rows of reproductive bodies and a circle of stinging bodies that look like tentacles. Their sting is innocuous to man. At intervals of several years countless numbers are washed up on the beaches of Florida, Oregon, California, Sicily, and many other mild parts of the world. Fleets of *Velella* are accompanied and fed on by certain mollusks such as the floating purple snail *Janthina janthina,* and by nudibranchs such as *Fiona.* Great shoals of *Velella* may at times furnish the main food of the giant sunfish, *Mola mola,* which is said to live entirely on floating coelenterates. As *Velella* is swept northward along the American Pacific coast, even sometimes to northern Washington, the big fish follows, far beyond its usual range.

Physalia (Plate 8) occurs in middle latitudes in the Atlantic, Pacific, and Indian oceans. For all the blue and pink iridescent beauty of the gas-filled float, the tentacles trailing downward for 40 to 60 feet, or perhaps even as much as 100 feet, pack a sting that can disable or kill a swimmer. Fatal injuries are said to be due to allergic shock in people who have become strongly sensitized by earlier experiences with the proteins of the large stinging threads. Nevertheless, all swimmers in warm waters should give this most dangerous of coelenterates a wide berth, and even those who examine *Physalia* from a boat or when the colony is stranded on a beach should use care. So many may accumulate on beaches as to turn the sand blue, and people suffer painful stings from the dead tentacles in beach sand or on fishing gear. We well remember the fiery welts on the arms of a laboratory helper in Bermuda who cleaned an aquarium that had housed a physalia weeks before and apparently still contained tentacle fragments that had dried on the walls. Oddly, there are animals that can exploit *Physalia* without suffering harm. A small fish, *Nomeus,* has never been found except in the company of *Physalia,* venturing away briefly, but always darting back to the safe harbor of the tentacles so deadly to other fishes, even those as big as the mackerel. A Japanese observer has seen *Nomeus* nibbling on the tentacles of its host, and perhaps it is in this way that it develops immunity to the stings. Whether *Nomeus* lures bigger fishes to the tentacles, as some say, we do not really know, but *Physalia* does feed on fishes—some accounts say mainly on flying fishes. This is not hard for us to believe, as our own first experience of *Physalia* was in the Caribbean, where for some eight or nine sunny hours our ship sailed through water seemingly alive with flying fishes and dotted to the horizon with a great flotilla of *Physalia*. Even from the deck of the small ship one could see the crest changing its shape and the float dipping from side to side in the quiet air. Douglas Wilson, who has studied physalias that occasionally come to Plymouth, in England, has suggested that this habit serves to keep the delicate float wet in hot, calm weather. A physalia kept in an aquarium will eat a proferred fish, first stinging and entangling it in the tentacles and then hauling it up under the float. There feeding polyps stretch down to spread their thin, transparent lips until they overlap, completely enveloping the fish as they pour out digestive juices and dissolve the flesh. The food particles are drawn up into the colony, further digested, and shared. Physalias fall prey to petrels and albatrosses, and fishes too, if we believe one old account that tells of an albacore swallowing a physalia and its accompanying little fishes. On tropical beaches ghost crabs nibble at stranded physalias from below, thus helpfully burying them.

The common jellyfish of all seas, *Aurelia aurita*. Here the saucer-like umbrella is seen from below. (England. D. P. Wilson)

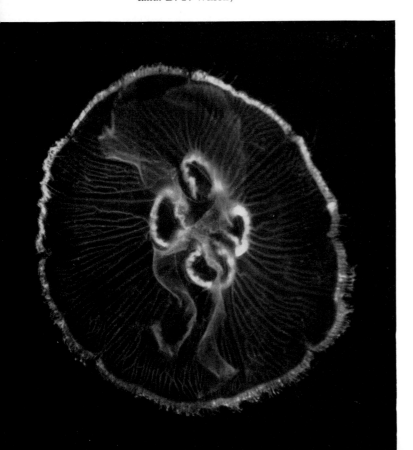

Vivid accounts of pelagic invertebrates, including *Physalia*, are to be found in D. P. Wilson's *Life of the Shore and Shallow Sea* and in Hardy's *The Open Sea*. The only place known to us where living siphonophores have been regularly displayed to the public is the Naples Aquarium. In the past, at least, *Physophora, Forskalia,* and *Hippopodius* were shown in the tanks whenever quiet weather made them available. Sea anemones, sea pens, and other sessile coelenterates are on display in many seaside public aquariums.

The True Jellyfishes

(*Class Scyphozoa*)

Almost all of the larger jellyfishes one sees in marine waters or washed up on the beaches as shapeless blobs of jelly are true or scyphozoan jellyfishes. Most familiar of these is the moon jelly, *Aurelia*, which can be seen in great shoals from the deck of an ocean liner. The milky saucers drift along together or swim slowly by rhythmic pulsations. The giant among jellyfishes is *Cyanea arctica*, sometimes 8 feet across, with long, trailing tentacles that extend downward for 200 feet. In the cold waters where these occur no swimmer could last long anyway, so we can only imagine what it would be like to be stung by such a monstrous coelenterate. Of more real concern are the 12-inch *Cyaneas* of temperate Atlantic waters, for these do turn up off beaches in summer, and they can cause painful red welts that remain discolored for many hours. Since some people also develop generalized symptoms or disabling muscular cramps, any swimmer stung by a jellyfish should promptly go ashore. There seems to be disagreement over whether there are any fatalities known to be due solely to *Cyanea* poisoning or to the painful stings of *Dactylometra quinquecirrha*, both common in the Atlantic. In tropical waters scyphozoan jellyfishes can be more dangerous. A sea wasp, *Chiropsalmus quadrigatus*, of the South Pacific and Indian oceans, is said to have caused deaths in from three to eight minutes. Such reports do not always rule out death from other possible causes, but the bad reputation of this cuboidal jellyfish is probably deserved. A swimmer or diver who feels uncertain about a mass of jelly coming his way should give it plenty of leeway, remembering that it is probably trailing long tentacles for some distance.

After a great storm, tropical waters or even beach sands may be filled with tentacle fragments still capable of dealing painful stings. Any jellyfish stranded at ebb tide should be examined with a stick or turned over with the toe of one's shoe, but not touched with bare skin unless readily recognized as of a harmless species. Having set down all these warnings, it is only fair to point out that of the two hundred or so

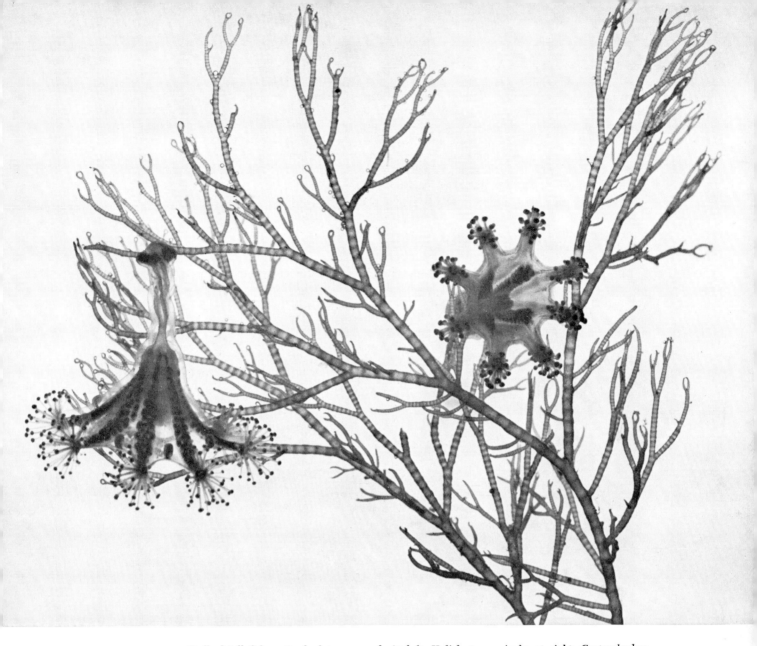

Stalked jellyfishes attached to seaweed. At left, *Haliclystus auricula;* at right, *Craterolophus convolvulus.* The bigger one is less than 1 inch across. (England. D. P. Wilson)

species of scyphozoan jellyfishes, some are harmless and many can cause only mildly annoying prickling or burning sensations. Moreover, there really is no poison that is not another man's meat, for in the Gilbert Islands sea wasps are considered a delicacy. The natives collect great shoals of them and scrape away the tentacles and umbrella, retaining little but the reproductive organs. Writing of this in *Margins of the Sea,* Maurice Burton says that boiled sea wasps taste like tripe—those first dried and then fried in deep fat, like pork cracklings. Jellyfishes are relished also by other peoples of the Pacific (p. 80); in Nagasaki one may buy the large *Rhopilema esculenta* in the market. Among the scyphozoans important in sheltering young commercial fishes is *Cyanea,* which gives cover to young whitings.

Scyphozoan jellyfishes are usually easy to tell from their tiny hydrozoan relatives because of their moderate to large size and because they lack the transparent shelf (velum) that projects inward from the margin of the umbrella in the hydrozoans. In addition, scyphozoans may have fringed mouth lobes, a scalloped rim, and a complex pattern of digestive canals that contrasts strongly with the four simple canals that radiate to the margin in the hydrozoan medusas.

A conspicuous four-sided symmetry shapes the external form and internal structure of most scyphozoans. The four stomach pouches and the four reproductive organs often show through the translucent body, and externally there are often four long, frilly mouth lobes that entangle food organisms and direct

[77

them into the mouth. Little sense organs may occur in four notches in the scalloped margin, or in eight notches, or in some higher multiple of four. Tentacles may also occur in marginal notches, alternating with the sense organs, or in other positions as well. Sometimes they form a fringe of indefinite number.

The jelly of scyphozoan medusas can be very bulky, and it contains many cells and strengthening fibers. Sometimes it is almost of a cartilaginous texture, so firm that one can jump on such an animal without crushing it. Even the firmest ones, however, are at least 94 per cent water.

The jellyfish is always the predominant stage in the scyphozoan life history. The polyp stage either is very small or is missing altogether. When present, it may transform directly into the adult; or it may elongate into a trumpet-shaped polyp with tentacles and then undergo a series of successive crosswise constrictions until it resembles a pile of saucers. One by one these little saucers are pinched off from the par-

ent polyp and swim away as little medusas, each growing into an adult jellyfish.

The true jellyfishes are usually divided into five orders, and the first of these is sometimes set off as a separate subclass because the members are not free-swimming like the rest but live attached.

THE SEDENTARY OR STALKED JELLYFISHES

These are the simplest scyphozoans, the stauromedusas or lucernids, which live attached by a sucker, usually at the tip of a stalk that springs from the center of the outer surface of a trumpet-shaped or goblet-shaped umbrella. They inhabit sheltered waters in the colder parts of the oceans, clinging to eelgrass in sheltered coves or bays, to algae in rock pools, or sometimes to rocks or shells. The margin of the umbrella may be circular, but typically it is drawn out into eight lobes, each tipped with a cluster of twenty or more short, knobbed tentacles. Such

The giant jellyfish, *Cyanea capillata*, stranded at low tide. (Maine. Ralph Buchsbaum)

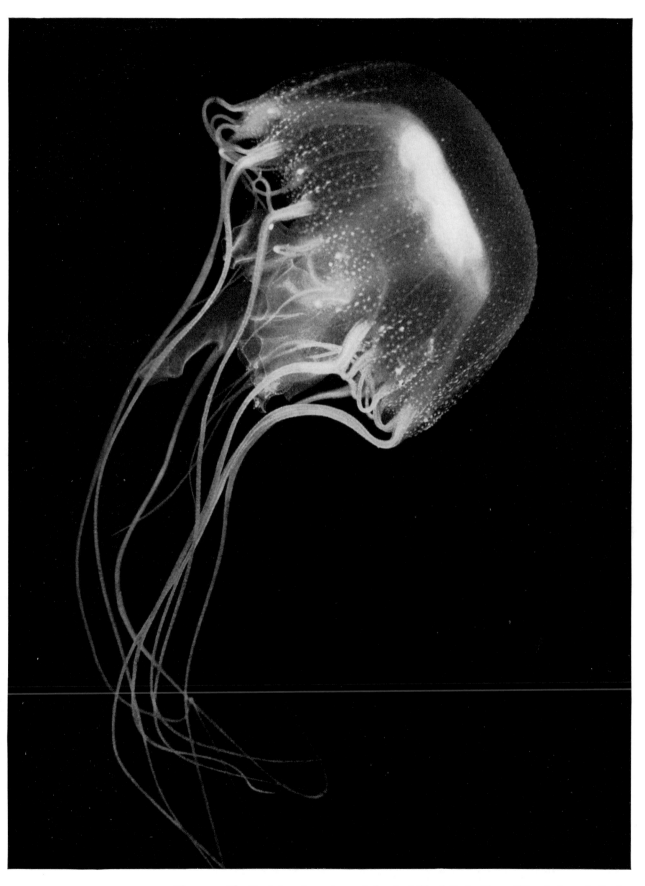

The sea nettle, *Dactylometra quinquecirrha*, is visibly dotted with wartlike clusters of stinging cells. Golden tentacles partially veil the pink flounces of the mouth lobes. Up to 8 inches across. (Delaware Bay. William H. Amos)

stalked medusas are only too easy to overlook, for most are only 1 inch or so across the open flaring end of the umbrella, and are the same brownish or greenish color as the seaweeds to which they cling. A few come in prettier shades of blue, violet, pink, or orange. The pendant mouth stalk is four-cornered, with little lobes, and ingests small animals that come its way. If the food supply runs low, some stalked jellyfishes can glide to new stations, adhering to solid support by the tentacles and by adhesive pads that alternate with the clusters of tentacles around the margin of the umbrella. They are said to breed at all seasons, and the egg develops into a stalked, trumpet-shaped adult without going through the splitting stage typical of many scyphozoans. Best known of the stalked jellyfishes are *Haliclystus* and *Lucernaria*.

THE CUBOIDAL JELLYFISHES OR SEA WASPS

In tropical or subtropical bays or harbors, or sometimes in the open sea, sea wasps had best be recognized by their cuboidal shape, not by testing their highly venomous sting. The colorless body has four flattened sides, and from each corner springs a tentacle or a group of tentacles, these often with some color. Feeding mostly on fish, they back up their voracious appetites by the strongest swimming habits known among jellyfishes. The cuboidal umbrella may contract up to 150 times a minute. Though many are only 1 or 2 inches high, some measure as much as 10 inches from margin to top of umbrella. The best-known genus of sea wasps, *Carybdea,* is luminescent. In spite of the evil reputation of *Carybdea alata* in the tropical Pacific, Atlantic, and Indian oceans, it is members of this genus that are relished in the Gilbert Islands (p. 77). The most fearsome genus of all is *Chiropsalmus,* especially in Philippine waters. Philippine and Japanese fishermen call this the "fire medusa" and keep their distance. *Chiropsalmus quadrigatus,* notorious for its rapidly fatal sting, is known from northern Australia, the Philippines, and the Indian Ocean. A related but less dangerous form occurs in the Atlantic from North Carolina to Brazil, and also in the Indian Ocean and northern Australia.

THE CORONATE JELLYFISHES

The coronate or crowned jellyfishes are recognized by a prominent horizontal groove that encircles the umbrella. Below this crowning groove the umbrella margin is furrowed by vertical grooves, each ending in the middle of one of the lobes of the often deeply scalloped edge. The beautiful sculpturing of these masses of jelly reminds one of some of the gelatin desserts that have been shaped in grooved, domelike metal molds. Coronate jellyfishes may measure 6 inches across, but most are under 2 inches. Though this is chiefly a deep-water group, some species, like the flattened *Nausithoë,* are common in all warm, shallow waters. *Nausithoë* is often seen in the Bahamas and in Florida, and is carried northward along the American Atlantic coast. It occurs also in more northern Atlantic waters. *Periphylla hyacinthina,* with a high, narrowly pointed umbrella and a beautiful purple color, is common in deep waters all over the world and is often seen at the surface.

THE DISK JELLIES

Not all the members of this group are as disklike as the common name suggests, but compared with other scyphozoans they do have flattened umbrellas when relaxed. They look hemispherical when contracted in swimming. Large and bulky kinds, especially *Cyanea,* are often called sea blubbers. The technical name, Semaeostomeae, makes a poor handle for these most typical of scyphozoan jellyfishes, which are the ones most likely to be seen in temperate waters. All are of moderate to large size, ranging from 2 inches to 2 feet across. The giant *Cyanea,* referred to on page 00, is exceptional. Disk jellies occur in all coastal waters, especially warm and temperate ones, often in great shoals of many thousands of individuals, usually at seasonal intervals. The umbrella margin is often scalloped into eight lappets, sometimes more. The four corners of the mouth are drawn out into four long, frilled lobes, each folded down the middle and forming a trough to direct food into the mouth.

Unfettered by a fixed stage, the lovely *Pelagia* is the only disk jelly free to roam the open seas. The purple-rose umbrella, shading into blue, is 2 inches or more across, and the scalloped margin has sixteen notches, eight tentacles, and eight sense organs; the tentacles and sense organs alternate in the notches. When *Pelagias* glide past a ship at night they glow like white balls of fire. Seen at a distance, they show as large winking spots instead of as the even glow caused by billions of luminescent protozoans. *Pelagia noctiluca* is abundant in the Mediterranean, and it is probably the same species that is swept up the American coast by the Gulf Stream and that delights Scottish observers whenever it arrives in the North Atlantic Current.

Also luminescent is the graceful compass jellyfish, *Chrysaora hysocella,* strongly marked on the umbrella with radiating V-shaped streaks. Toward the end of summer it appears in great numbers in European Atlantic waters.

Most widely distributed of the true jellyfishes is the moon jelly, *Aurelia aurita.* In all oceans, and from polar waters to the equator, it seems to vary little, though probably there are several subspecies that breed at different times and require different sea temperatures. When relaxed and drifting it is a shal-

[continued on page 97]

31. The **staghorn coral**, *Acropora,* abounds on reef flats but grows tallest and most branching in sheltered lagoons. At low tide, and in bright light, the delicate polyps draw back into the coral cups on the surface of the colony. (Great Barrier Reef. Allen Keast)

32. The **tube anemone**, *Cerianthus*, lives in a tube of hardened slime, down which it retreats when disturbed. It is common off European shores and has close relatives on other coasts. (Roscoff, France. Ralph Buchsbaum)

33. Lacelike patches of the **bryozoan sea mat**, *Membranipora membranacea*, grow over the broad fronds of seaweeds. The chambers of all the separate individuals stand out clearly long after the occupants have died. (Roscoff, France. Ralph Buchsbaum)

34. Delicate spirals of the **branching bryozoan**, *Bugula*, hang exposed in rocky crevices at low tide. (Brittany, France. Ralph Buchsbaum)

35. The **leaflike flatworm**, *Pseudoceros,* which has many drab-colored polyclad relatives in temperate marine waters, shows the gay coloring common in tropical animals. (Great Barrier Reef. Fritz Goro: *Life* Magazine)

36. A dense aggregation of minute **acoel flatworms**, *Convoluta roscoffensis,* shown much enlarged. When the worms rise to the surface sand at low tide, they expose to the sun the green algal cells that pack their bodies. (Roscoff, France. Ralph Buchsbaum)

37. A **marine ribbon worm**, *Tubulanus polymorphus,* exposed at low tide. Stretched out, it measured 6 feet. (Oregon. Ralph Buchsbaum)

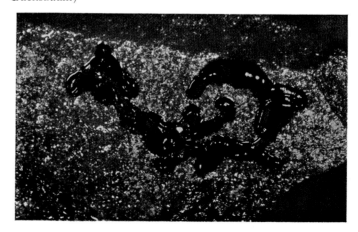

38. The **hairy chiton**, *Mopalia*, like many of its relatives, avoids light at low tide and must be sought under rocks on partially protected coasts. (Oregon. Ralph Buchsbaum)

39. The black tunic of *Katherina tunicata* overgrows the eight plates that are more fully exposed in other chitons. *Katherina* stands strong surf and does not retreat from sunlight. (Oregon. Ralph Buchsbaum)

40. The **common mussel**, *Mytilus*, grows in dense masses. Each mussel is attached by strong threads to rock or to other mussels. (Brittany, France. Ralph Buchsbaum)

41. The **queen scallop**, *Chlamys opercularis*, a common edible species of European Atlantic waters. It lies on the bottom with valves agape, and here displays along the lower mantle edge a row of black-pigmented eyes alternating with delicate tentacles. (Roscoff, France. Ralph Buchsbaum)

42. The **blue-eyed scallop**, *Pecten irradians*, the common edible scallop of the American east coast. Close-up view of shell gape shows its blue eyes and numerous tentacles, which screen incoming feeding and respiratory currents. (Woods Hole, Massachusetts. Roman Vishniac)

43. The **great scallop**, *Pecten maximus*, with convex valve below and flat valve above, is larger than the queen scallop and not so agile a swimmer. It is the most relished of European Atlantic scallops. (England. D. P. Wilson)

44. The **file shell**, *Lima,* has a rasplike covering of spiny ribs. The brightly colored sensory tentacles are contractile but cannot be withdrawn completely into the shell. (Marineland, Florida)

45. **File shells** are able to swim about slowly, clapping their valves, which are held vertically. (West Indies. Fritz Goro: *Life* Magazine)

46. **File shell** (West Indies. Fritz Goro: *Life* Magazine)

47. A **keyhole limpet**, *Diodora aspera*, 3 inches long, uncovered at a very low tide. By means of its muscular foot it clings to the rock, even in strong surf, from Alaska to Lower California. The ribbing of the shell is obscured by a calcareous growth. (Oregon. Ralph Buchsbaum)

48. In the **giant keyhole limpet**, *Megathura crenulata*, 7 inches long, the black, velvety mantle partly covers the oval shell. Found on the open coast, it is shown here in an aquarium. (Cy La Tour and Marineland of the Pacific)

49. This **giant land snail**, *Achatina fulica*, with a shell 5 inches long, was brought from Sierra Leone in Africa to the London Zoo. It was spread by man eastward from India to Hawaii. Freed of natural enemies, it is now a plant pest in the Pacific. (Ralph Buchsbaum)

50. The **garden snail**, *Cepaea hortensis*, native to Europe and introduced into eastern New England. Half an inch high and about as broad, it shows five dark bands. It lives in little colonies in moist places, and eats weeds but sometimes attacks vegetable gardens. (Bavaria. Otto Croy)

51. The **spider conch**, *Lambis lambis*, is a voracious carnivore fairly common on coral reefs. The sharp-edged operculum attached to the rear of the foot closes the shell like a door. (Great Barrier Reef. Jerome M. and Dorothy H. Schweitzer)

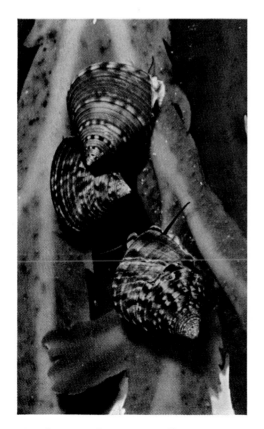

52. The **painted top shell**, *Calliostoma zizyphinum*, of European Atlantic shores, does not come above low-tide level except in favorable spots. (Roscoff, France. Ralph Buchsbaum)

53. A **Brazilian olive shell**, *Olivancillaria*, from the coast near Santos. When the snail is plowing through sand the lustrous shell is covered by two folds of the large mantle. (Othmar Danesch)

54. **Wrinkled purples**, *Thais lamellosa*, named for the purple dye they excrete, fasten their vase-shaped egg capsules to the undersides of rocks. They are the American west coast counterpart of the purples, or dog whelks, of Atlantic shores. (Oregon. Ralph Buchsbaum)

56. The **flat periwinkle**, *Littorina littoralis*, of temperate and cold Atlantic shores, depends on large seaweeds for food and for keeping moist when the tide is out. (England. Ralph Buchsbaum)

55. The largest **moon snail** of the American Pacific coast, *Polinices lewisii*, averages more than 4 inches long. The fleshy foot envelops most of the shell as the animal pushes through sand and feeds on other mollusks. (Cy La Tour and Marineland of the Pacific)

57. The **bubble shell**, *Hydatina physis,* is a snail with a shell only about 1 inch in length, but the mantle and head shield are voluminous. It lives on sandy and muddy bottoms, though here it is crawling on organ-pipe coral. (Australia. Jerome M. and Dorothy H. Schweitzer)

58. The **tiger cowrie**, *Cyprae tigris*, about 4 inches long, has a lustrous shell that has long made it the most sought after of South Pacific marine snails. (Great Barrier Reef. Jerome M. and Dorothy H. Schweitzer)

59. The **marbled cone**, *Conus marmoreus*, ranges from Polynesia west to the Indian Ocean. Despite its lovely shell, a favorite of collectors, it is one of the most dangerous of poisonous cone shells. The tube at the front (right) is the respiratory siphon; the proboscis that deals the sometimes fatal bite is retracted. (Great Barrier Reef. Jerome M. and Dorothy H. Schweitzer)

[continued from page 80]

low saucer, with extremes of size from 3 inches to 2 feet; but most are from 6 to 10 inches in diameter. The tentacles are short and extremely numerous, forming a fringe around the margin. Readily visible through the top of the milky white or bluish umbrella are four horseshoe-shaped reproductive organs, often colored violet or pink. From the underside hang four long, tapering, somewhat stiff mouth lobes. This is a relatively harmless jellyfish, and it feeds on minute organisms, chiefly copepods, which are collected in mucus on the umbrella surfaces and then licked off by the mouth lobes and carried by ciliary currents to the mouth.

Dactylometra quinquecirrha, with a long name and a bad reputation for painful stings, belongs to the same genus as certain dangerous jellyfishes of the tropical Pacific. (A Pacific species is shown in Plate 7.) It is seen from the Azores and New England to the tropics, and from West Africa, the Indian Ocean, the Malay Archipelago, and the Philippines to Japan.

The common sea blubber, *Cyanea capillata,* whose huge arctic variant has been referred to several times, is also called the pink jellyfish—probably by people who have not felt its fiery stings. In England it is "the hairy stinger" or "the lion's mane," the last name serving in the Sherlock Holmes story about a fatal case of *Cyanea* poisoning, "The Adventure of the Lion's Mane." Most individuals are not over 3 feet in diameter, with tentacles extending down for 75 feet, and 12-inch disks are most common. The color showing through the thick disk varies from a rosy pink to a brownish purple, and the yellow or reddish tentacles hang down in great bunches, the gaps between bunches revealing the frilled purplish mouth lobes. *Cyanea capillata* is abundant in the cool and cold waters of both the Atlantic and the Pacific oceans. Other stinging species are found in the tropical and temperate Pacific. This is another of the scyphozoans that are known to luminesce.

THE MANY-MOUTHED JELLYFISHES

There is no widely used common name for this group, and it helps little to say that the technical name, Rhizostomeae, means "root-mouthed." The rhizostomes have no single large mouth as do other jellyfishes, but feed through numberless small openings in the mouth lobes. Each of the four lobes is subdivided, elongated, lobed, and folded, so that in some members they suggested a bundle of eight long roots hanging from the lower surface. There are no tentacles around the margin, and these jellyfishes feed mostly on microscopic organisms drawn into the tiny mouths by ciliary currents. The 7-inch *Stomolophus* of the southeastern American coast and the larger *Rhizostoma* of European waters have a high, mushroom-shaped umbrella. Most interesting is *Cassiopeia,* common in quiet, shallow mangrove bays in

Florida and in the tropics. Thousands of them lie disk to disk, on their backs, the voluminous and branching mouth lobes exposed to the gentle food-bearing currents that sweep across. This relaxed feeding habit also displays to the sun the myriads of green cells that live in the tissues. Presumably the green guests utilize nitrogenous and gaseous wastes of the jellyfish and in return make it possible for *Cassiopeia* to live densely crowded in stagnant waters.

Sea Whips, Sea Fans, Anemones, Corals, and Others *(Class Anthozoa or Actinozoa)*

The anthozoans ("flower animals") are most familiar as the solitary sea anemones of temperate seashores, or as the corals, sea fans, and sea whips known to most people from their beautiful dried skeletons. This is by far the most conspicuous and most successful class of coelenterates, comprising more than six thousand species, all of them marine and most of them living in shore or shallow waters. All are cylindrical polyps, with no trace of a jellyfish stage in the life history. A little free-swimming planula larva serves to distribute many of those that live permanently attached. A few, like the sea anemones and sea pens, do move about at times. The free end

The many-mouthed jellyfish, *Rhizostoma,* feeds through countless small openings in the pendant mouth lobes. (Naples Aquarium. Ralph Buchsbaum)

The *Cassiopeia* at the left is swimming, and the one at the right is lying on its back in feeding position, with the branching many-mouthed lobes gathering food particles. (Lerner Marine Laboratory, Bimini. Fritz Goro: *Life* Magazine)

of the polyp is not conical, as in many hydrozoan polyps, but is expanded into a flat disk that has an oval or slitlike mouth at the center and bears one or more circlets of hollow tentacles. The external covering layer turns in at the mouth to form a tube, the gullet, which hangs into the digestive cavity. The gullet is lined with beating flagella and usually has one or two flagellated grooves that direct currents of water to the inside. Unlike the simple cavity of hydrozoans, that of anthozoans is divided by membranous partitions, all or some of which extend from the body wall to the hanging gullet.

The class Anthozoa is divided into two groups: the alcyonarians or octocorallians, in which all the parts are based on a plan of eight; and the zoantharians or hexacorallians, in which the body is based on a plan of six, or of a multiple of six, or on some

other number, but not on a plan of eight simple repeated parts.

THE ALCYONARIANS
(*Subclass Alcyonaria*)

Alcyonarians are all colonial growths, often colorful and luminescent, and they are especially conspicuous in warm seas. At a distance they show great variety of shape, most of them arising from the bottom as fleshy lobes or as slender branched feathers or fans. Except for the gorgonians, they are mostly rather insensitive to light, and they respond to touch only locally, though in a few forms the stimulus spreads for some distance over the colony. Those that are not permanently attached, like the sea pens, are the most responsive. Some that pay no heed to probing fingers will react to chemical or electrical stimulation. The stinging capsules are very small and cannot penetrate the human skin, so alcyonarians can be handled with impunity. If we examine them closely when the polyps are fully expanded we see that the feeding polyps are all remarkably alike and have a single circle of eight feathery tentacles. These are widest at the tips and somewhat flattened, and bear rows of side branchlets. The oval or elongate mouth may have one ciliated groove at most, and it opens into a gullet that has attached to it eight partitions readily visible in transparent polyps.

Many alcyonarians have a second kind of polyp without tentacles, and these may be concerned with circulation of water, which plays a large role in the expansion and contraction of the colonies as well as in respiration. Between the external covering layer and the thin digestive lining is a thick jelly layer that adds bulk to the body, and this is invaded by cells that secrete the skeleton of calcium carbonate or of horny material, either in little spicules of distinctive shape or as amorphous substance. Even when loosely scattered, the spicules give firmness to the flabby body; and those alcyonarians in which the spicules are densely packed or fused may contribute no small share to coral reefs. Also in the jelly are the digestive canals that unite the many polyps. The sex cells develop on the digestive partitions and are shed to the outside through the mouth.

THE SOFT CORALS

The soft corals, or alcyonaceans (Plate 9) with only scattered spicules stiffening the body, are best known in temperate waters from the flesh-colored, white, or orange-colored lobed masses called "dead men's fingers" in England and something less mentionable in France. *Alcyonium digitatum,* abundant in European waters, lifts its spongy, gelatinous lobes, like bloated fingers, as much as 8 inches high from gravelly bottoms below low-tide mark. In dull light the numerous and delicate transparent ends of the polyps form a white furriness over the surface as they project beyond the opaque lobes. At the slightest disturbance the little feeding disks are pulled in by special muscles, and the rest of the delicate columns follow, turning the formerly exposed parts of the polyps inside out, like the fingers of a glove, and

Dead men's fingers, *Alcyonium digitatum,* a fleshy colony of soft coral that extends delicate polyps. (England. D. P. Wilson)

into the safety of the digestive cavity imbedded in the main mass. In New England waters and northward, species of the related *Gersemia* have salmon-colored or reddish branches, or clusters of slender lobes. *Anthomastus,* which looks like a red mushroom with polyps strewn over the fleshy cap, is often dredged up by fishermen on the New England coast, and another species is known from deep waters off California. Though some soft corals extend into polar waters, this is largely a warm-water group with its great center the Indo-Pacific Ocean. There, in shallow waters, the flabby masses of what look like leathery seaweeds are alcyonacean colonies of moderate size and of drab shades of yellow, brown, or olive. Some run to dull reds or purples or other hues, and in deeper waters they grow more treelike and are stiffer (Plate 29).

THE ORGAN-PIPE CORAL

The organ-pipe coral, *Tubipora,* is a spectacular alcyonarian coral, with emerald-green polyps that emerge from brick-red limestone tubes. In some tropical waters it is an important reef-builder, though the massive layers of tubes, laid down over many generations, are not secreted as solid limestone as in true reef corals, but consist of fused spicules and lie within the living tissue of the coral. *Tubipora* belongs to the stoloniferans, a group with some small members in temperate waters that are the most primitive of alcyonarians. In these the polyps are not fused together but arise separately from a basal mat of runners. In the organ-pipe coral, however, the vertical limestone tubes that house the polyps are joined at intervals by horizontal platforms in which run connecting digestive canals. As the colony grows, the lower levels of the tubes are abandoned, and they become great tenements housing worms, small crabs, and innumerable other little animals (Plate 54).

THE BLUE CORAL

The blue coral, *Heliopora,* which does not look blue when the brown polyps are fully extended, is found on the coral reefs of the Indo-Pacific. The blue color of the broadly lobed calcareous skeleton is said to be due to iron salts, and the limestone mass is composed not of fused spicules as in other alcyonarian corals, but of fibers of crystalline calcium carbonate (aragonite) fused into sheets. The polyps live only in the surface portions of the cylindrical cavities.

THE GORGONIANS

The gorgonians or horny corals include the sea whips, sea fans, and sea plumes, which have a flexible skeletal core of a horny material called gorgonin. Of plantlike growth form, and colored vivid shades of yellow, red, orange, and purple, they furnish most of the "blossoming shrubbery" of Atlantic shores,

In the shallow waters of Indo-Pacific reefs the soft corals are mostly great flabby masses of what look like leathery brown seaweeds. (Great Barrier Reef. Fritz Goro: *Life* Magazine)

adding much to the invertebrate lure that brings so many skin divers to the shallow waters of Mediterranean, Caribbean, and Florida coasts. They are really most abundant in the tropical Indo-Pacific, but there they are inconspicuous in shore waters compared with the soft corals or the true reef corals.

Though mostly coastal or from waters no more than three thousand feet deep, gorgonians occur at all depths. Many are luminescent, and when the *Challenger* expedition in the 1870's was discovering so much that was new that everything since has been anticlimax, all the alcyonarians dredged from deep waters were seen to be brightly luminescent as they came on board, one shrublike gorgonian glowing with a soft pale lilac light. The larger deep-water colonies may reach 9 feet; and in the deep waters of Norwegian fjords the bright scarlet *Paragorgia* attains treelike growths. The shallow-water *Lophogorgia chilensis* is seen by aqualung divers on the rims of underwater canyons off La Jolla, California, as sparsely scattered, low-branching, coral-colored shrubs with white polyp "blossoms." Common in the same places is the reddish purple *Eugorgia rubens.* Typically, gorgonians have slender whiplike branches arising from a short main trunk that is firmly fastened to the bottom. When the stems have side branches

A deep-water soft coral, showing the lovely treelike form typical of alcyonaceans from the deeper waters of the Indo-Pacific region. (Aquarium of Nouméa, New Caledonia. René Catala)

Sea whips, a kind of flexible but horny gorgonian coral, are a dominant feature of the coral reefs of the western Atlantic. These were growing off the Virgin Islands at a depth of twenty-eight feet. (T. Parkinson: National Audubon)

the colonies may resemble feathers or great plumes. Having established a sure anchorage in the moving water, gorgonians are a standing invitation to settling larvae of invertebrates such as sponges, hydroids, bryozoans, and brachiopods, to hop on and take hold, later obscuring the host polyps or even, in the case of certain little crustaceans and worms, stimulating the host to pathological growth as it adjusts to the guests. Gorgonians are very sensitive to strong light, and they expand their polyps fully only at night or on dull days.

In shallow European waters, in many of the same places that support the fleshy hands of *Alcyonium,* we find the graceful little sea fan, *Eunicella verrucosa* (Plates 11 and 12), in which the treelike branches are flattened and grow all in one plane. It has a horny black branching skeletal core covered with orange, pink, or white fleshy tissue and innumerable little white polyps. The dried colony retains its lovely form, but the orange-pink color of the gayest specimens dries to a dull white, because the pigmentation is not in the spicules, as in most alcyonarians, but in carotenoid droplets in the living cells. Less disappointing when dried is the larger sea fan, *Gorgonia,* of semitropical waters, in which the flattened branches have cross-connections that convert the colony into a lattice of yellow, lavender, or purple "lace," with lasting color in the scattered spicules.

The red or precious coral, *Corallium,* has a different kind of skeleton, completely lacking the horny gorgonin. Highly prized since ancient times, the hard and entirely calcareous red or pink branching core lies hidden within the colonial tissue, which is fleshy and yielding though stiffened and colored by red, calcareous, evenly scattered spicules. The surface of the living colony is raised into little protuberances from which arise the pure white blossom-like polyps. Smaller elevations house a diminutive kind of polyp without tentacles.

Commercial fishing of coral was for centuries carried on off the coasts of Corsica, Sardinia, and Sicily, the south coast of France, the north coast of Africa from the Straits of Gibraltar to Tunis, and in the Atlantic from the Cape Verde Islands. A similar red coral, though inferior in beauty and texture, is also collected and worked in Japan. The coral colonies are strongly affixed to the rocky bottoms and slopes, and in the Mediterranean were collected by boats towing large wooden crosses dangling old nets and frayed rope mops that entangled and broke off the lovely red branches. The difficulties of coral fishing, especially with hand labor in past times, so enhanced the value of the coral that it was traded to the Indians and Chinese for emeralds, rubies, and pearls. The early Celts in Britain, before the Roman conquest, obtained coral by barter from the Gauls, and used it to decorate shields and other valuables. Its rarity and blood-red color inevitably suggested therapeutic powers, and to the end of the eighteenth century physicians made great use of powdered red coral in prescriptions. In our own century rural Europeans have continued to attribute special therapeutic value to coral necklaces and have given them to adults suffering from debilitating diseases or to children cutting teeth, for which they must serve as well as any other smooth, hard surface. Now the coral "trees" that once thickly covered whole areas of the Mediterranean are mostly smashed or gone. Only in specially protected areas or in recesses and grottoes do they survive in great numbers. In *The Silent World,* J.-Y. Cousteau presents colored photographs of red branches of *Corallium* hanging from the ceiling of a cave and "accumulating like stalactites." From such places it can be gathered only by divers, to whom the red coral branches, seen at depths below 120 feet, appear blue-black.

THE SEA PENS AND SEA PANSIES

The sea pens, or pennatulaceans, were named in the days when a pen still suggested the feathered quill of a bird. The fleshy, feather-shaped bodies add color to the same warm bottoms favored by their alcyonarian relatives, and also extend with them into temperate or cold waters. Sea pens, however, are restricted to soft bottoms, in which they anchor by means of the expansible bulbous tip of an elongate stalk. In size they range from a few inches to 3 feet or more. Their varied shades of yellow, orange, red, brown, and purple result mostly from the pigmentation of spicules scattered in the flesh, though many have dark pigments in the cells also. A horny central axis usually adds mechanical support. This group is noted for its bright luminescence, usually blue or violet, sometimes greenish or yellowish. The slime secreted by pennatulids contains luminescent granules; the dried slime will glow when water is added, but it cannot be stimulated in other ways. The intact animal, or pieces of a colony, luminesce only on stimulation. In the more primitive forms, like *Veretillum,* common in the coastal muds of the Mediterranean and also found in the Altantic, the upper part of the body is a stout fleshy club with flowerlike polyps strewn over the surface in no obvious order (Plate 10). More like a quill pen is *Pennatula phosphorea,* which lives somewhat farther from shore but often comes up in fishermen's nets. The stalk is yellow-orange, and the expanded upper part, which bears rows of polyps on each side as a feather bears its barbs, is purple. The polyps glow a bluish green, and when they are stimulated repeatedly, waves of light run the length of the region bearing the polyps. After this response the colony contracts and expels water. In the same Mediterranean and Atlantic habitats as *Pennatula,* and as far north as Norway, dredging brings up the related wandlike *Virgularia,* with a slender body up to 2 feet long and polyps closely packed in rows on either side at intervals along the stem. Pink, rose-colored, red, and purplish red varieties of *Pennatula* are widely distributed along the New England coast, growing more abundant as dredging proceeds to deeper and deeper water, even to six thousand feet. One species may be only 4 inches long, but the other, the great sea pen, well known to halibut fishermen, attains a length of 20 inches. Also present in these deeper waters are several tall wandlike forms related to *Virgularia.* They grow 3 feet high and may bend from the weight of sea anemones that live on the long basal stalk. On the American Pacific coast, in the mud of shallow bays from San Francisco to San Diego, are two common sea pens: *Stylatula* is rough to the touch and about 1 foot long; *Acanthoptilum* is smooth to the touch and up to 2 feet long. In *Between Pacific Tides,* Ricketts and Calvin tell of rowing in Newport Bay at low tide and looking into the shallow water at a pleasant meadow of waving green *Stylatula* pens "like a field of green wheat." When they reached down with an oar to unearth one, the feathery pens instantly snapped down into the sandy mud, leaving only their very tips to betray their presence. Entirely deep-water or abyssal are pennatulid families like the Umbellulidae. *Umbellula* has a very slender bare stem, perhaps 2 feet long, topped by a cluster of large orange-red or purplish flowerlike polyps. One that emitted a bluish light was hauled up from about fifteen thousand feet by the ship *Galathea.*

The sea pansy, *Renilla,* a very different kind of

A pale orange sea pen, *Leioptilus,* from deeper shore waters of the American Pacific coast. The stalk is partly imbedded in sand. Large specimens may be 2 feet long. (Ralph Buchsbaum)

pennatulid, is common in the West Indies and on warm American shores, extending northward to the Carolinas and to southern California. Related forms are known from the Red Sea and from Australian and other coasts. Though named for its kidney shape and violet color, it may be heart-shaped or of a rosy pink tint. It lies with the short stalk buried, and the flattened disklike body bears on its upper surface two kinds of polyps, arranged in a regular pattern. Sea pansies may occur in a muddy bay by the hundreds or even by the thousands, the lovely color obscured by a thin coating of sand or mud. Transferred to a dish of clean sea water and left undisturbed, the disk may expand to several times its contracted size and the polyps may open. If they are kept in the dark for several hours and then poked, a wave of soft bluish light spreads over the whole surface of the colony from the point touched. Renillas feed on small animals and larvae, stinging and swallowing them after the prey has become entangled in a mucous net secreted over the surface. They are themselves known to be eaten by nudibranch mollusks, one of the few animal groups with a taste for the coelenterates.

SEA ANEMONES AND CORALS
(Subclass Zoantharia)

This somewhat heterogeneous group includes the sea anemones, solitary and without a skeleton; the true or stony corals, with a skeleton and usually colonial; the black corals; the zoanthids; and the "tube anemones" or cerianthids. Not all fit the most common body pattern of parts repeated in multiples of six; but none fits the neat alcyonarian model of just eight feathery tentacles and eight internal partitions.

THE SEA ANEMONES

Though named for the lovely "windflowers" of mountains and woodlands, the familiar anemones of tide pools and rocky ledges more often suggest dahlias and chrysanthemums. There are about a thousand species of sea anemones, and most have a broad, flat, rayed disk crowning the free end of a stout muscular body. At the center of the rayed disk, which gives the group its order name, Actiniaria, is an elongate mouth, usually with a flagellated groove at each end for directing a current of water to the interior. Surrounding the mouth are one or more circles of tapering hollow tentacles that belie their harmless, petal-like appearance, wafting minute animals into the mouth or cramming it with worms, crabs, and fishes.

The common colorings in temperate waters are white, tan, salmon pink, orange, brown, olive, or green, but temperate-zone anemones may also be vividly red or striped and dotted in contrasting and breath-takingly beautiful geometric patterns of reds, blues, grays, greens, and purples. Even in tropical waters, where all groups put on a spectacular show, the anemones distinguish themselves by their brilliance of color.

Sea anemones unfold their disks in every sea, growing larger and more numerous from the poles to the equator, though any one species may not conform to the general trend. Mostly creatures of shore and shallow waters, they extend to all depths. Underwater photography has revealed an area 2100 feet deep, off the American Atlantic coast, where sea anemones are the most abundant form of life. On such mud bottoms they are anchored by a bulbous base, attached to manganese nodules on the floor, or cling to shrublike gorgonians or tall branching corals. The Danish Galathea expedition hauled up a hith-

erto unknown anemone from the Philippine trench, about 30,000 feet down, and very appropriately named it Galatheanthemum. From 15,000 feet the Galathea dredge yielded white anemones attached to the long stalks of Hyalonema-like glass sponges.

Entirely tropical are the floating minyads, many of them a lovely blue color like that so often seen in other floating coelenterates of warm surface waters. The giant stichodacytyline anemones are also exclusively tropical. These include Stoichactis, with a disk up to 3 feet across, a full complement of plant-like cells in its tissues, and an interesting set of small crustacean and fish friends. Best known of its animal commensals is the little pomacentrid "damsel fish," Amphiprion, that darts among the tentacles of Stoichactis in Indo-Pacific waters. Vividly banded in black and orange, with fins edged in black and white, it is very conspicuous as it plays about its anemone host; and it is said to lure other fishes to the host's disk or even to bring in offerings of food. At the least threat the fish darts quickly to the safety of the waving tentacles. The fish is apparently immune to the anemone's stings and perhaps becomes so by its habit of mouthing and nibbling the tentacles. In any case, a fish once acclimated to its host no longer incites the discharge of stinging cells on contact with the tentacles. Working at the Marineland of the Pacific, an exhibition aquarium in California, and using Stoichactis and Amphiprion imported from the Philippines, Davenport and Norris found that the protection of the fish seemed to reside in the mucous covering of its skin. The Dutch investigator Verwey, who studied this anemone from Djakarta Bay, off Java, has shown that at least in the conditions of an aquarium, the big anemone does not flourish without its small fish associate. Stoichactis is the upper limit of the size range. At the other extreme are minute polyps only a fraction of an inch long, some of them also tropical, like Gonactinia prolifera of the eastern Atlantic, which swims by waving its tentacles.

In temperate waters few anemones are as widespread as the plumose anemone, Metridium, which lives mostly below low-tide mark. The soft, rounded, feathery masses of tentacles, colored white, pink, orange, or brown, decorate wharf pilings and the underside of floating docks, or rise on broad muscular bodies, usually of the same color, in rocky caves or crevices where they can be seen at the very lowest tides. The large lobed and frilled feeding disk, covered with many hundreds of tentacles and with very little bare area around the mouth, is vaguely suggestive of the many-petaled chrysanthemum (Plate 18). Fine tentacles capture only minute plankton animals, which are swept toward the mouth by beating cilia on tentacles and disk. Metridium extends pretty well around the world in the northern hemisphere. It flourishes in cool European waters, and on the American Atlantic coast it is one of the largest and most familiar anemones from Labrador to New Jersey (Plate 22). On the Pacific coast it extends along the shallow shore from Alaska to Monterey, California. As far south as La Jolla it has been seen on the rims of underwater canyons by skin-diving, aqualung-equipped biologists, like Conrad Limbaugh of the Scripps Oceanographic Institute, who are learning to know the anemones and other invertebrates of deeper shore waters as we now know those of tide pools. In the Bay of Morlaix, in Brittany, where perhaps a third of the bay is difficult or impossible to dredge, Pierre Drach, of the Biological Station at nearby Roscoff, is diving with open rubber suit and aqualung on the steep rocky slopes. To the study of such slopes he is bringing the same careful methods of observation that we use so much more easily on land for studying exactly how animals are associated with each other. This is something we cannot learn from the jumbled masses brought up by the dredge from flat bottoms.

Favoring deeper waters and northern seas, around the globe, is the dahlia anemone, *Tealia,* which is large and stout and has short, somewhat blunt tentacles that taper from wide bases. In the variety of *Tealia felina* that is common on northern European shores the column is often red spotted with green, and the tentacles are strongly banded with reds, blues, grays, and olives. The deep-water variety, with a disk 1 foot or more across, is less strongly marked and likely to be buff, yellow, or orange. On American coasts the dahlia anemones are similarly bright red, and often also pink, and in Maine one has been called the thick-petaled rose anemone. They are common below low-tide mark as far south as Cape Cod on the Atlantic coast, and southward to California on the Pacific coast (Plates 17 and 20).

Rocky bottom is the favored substrate of anemones, and in protected areas every crevice is jammed, every tide pool carpeted, with anemones crowded disk to disk. Some burrow in sand or mud, then lie with the long, slender column completely buried and only the feeding disk outspread on the surface, as *Peachia* and *Milne-Edwardsia* on European shores, *Edwardsia* in New England, *Edwardsiella* and *Harenactis* on the southern California coast. Many anemones hang from wharf pilings or floating wood, cling to seaweeds or eelgrass, or attach to shells and stalks of sessile animals, especially if on soft bottoms. Others lead a mobile life affixed to jellyfishes and comb jellies, the backs of crabs, the shells of living marine snails, or the snail shells appropriated by hermit crabs.

The classical alliance between anemone and hermit crab is that of *Adamsia palliata* on the hermit crab *Eupagurus prideauxi* in European waters. The crab seeks out a young anemone and holds it until it

A group of plumose anemones, *Metridium,* from northern European waters. Some are expanded, spreading their great lobed and frilled disks. Two are contracted; the large one in the background, which has pulled in its disk, resembles a plump tomato. (Günter Senfft)

attaches to the shell just below the mouth parts of the crab. As the anemone grows, the base of its column extends upward in two lobes that meet and fuse, embracing the shell. The anemone secretes a horny membrane that roofs over any holes in the shell and extends beyond the shell margin, enlarging its capacity and so minimizing the number of times the growing crab must change houses. When it does move to a new shell, the crab transfers its associate, which submits readily instead of clinging stubbornly to the old shell as it does if we try to remove it. The anemone receives scraps of food from the crab's less-than-neat feeding, and the crab is protected by the stinging tentacles and also by the stinging filaments of the anemone. These last are long filaments that extend freely in the digestive cavity from the swollen glandular edges of the internal partitions. They are richly endowed with stinging capsules, and when the anemone contracts they are extruded through the mouth and through special holes in the body wall, the cinclides. Many anemones, including *Metridium,* extrude stinging filaments; but it is interesting that almost all the anemones that live on hermit crabs do have them. *Adamsia palliata* apparently cannot live without its crab host, but other anemones so associated are less dependent. *Calliactis parasitica* lives on *Eupagurus bernhardus* (Plate 15) in Europe, and *Calliactis tricolor* on hermit crabs along the American southeast coast and in the Gulf of Mexico. Other species of *Calliactis* and other anemones, however, are reported to have similar habits in all parts of the world, mostly in fairly warm waters, as of the Gulf of California, Chile, Hawaii, Japan, the Indo-Pacific, the Great Barrier Reef, East and South Africa. In the tropics certain reef crabs go about brandishing an anemone in each claw, presumably as defensive and food-catching devices, for the crabs are said to reach up and take food from the disks of the anemones.

Apparently contented anemones have been observed to hug the same crevice for more than thirty years. Others move occasionally, especially if their posts turn out to be too surfy or on the sunny side; and the more restless species walk about frequently by a slow kind of muscular gliding. The minyads, mentioned earlier, have the basal disk expanded into a rounded float. The tiny *Gonactinia* was mentioned earlier as one of the few anemones that can swim by stroking the water with its tentacles. Undulating the whole body produces brief swimming excursions for some bigger forms, and *Stomphia coccinea* in Puget Sound frees itself and swims about by muscular undulations whenever it is touched by certain starfishes. This may be a rapid-escape mechanism, as at least one of the starfishes involved has been seen to feed on anemones. For the most part, however, sea anemones have few predators besides those intrepid eaters —sea slugs and men.

Anemones expand their column and tentacles by taking in water, and they are very vulnerable to drying. Most live below low-tide mark where they never have to face this problem, but shore anemones usually pull in their tentacles and contract until the tide returns. The beadlet anemone, *Actinia equina,* of European waters, is bright red with a row of blue beads around the column just below the tentacles, but it occurs also in less common brown and green varieties. At Helgoland in the North Sea red and green *Actinias* literally carpet the rocks. On British and French shores one sees them on exposed spots where others cannot brave the surf and at high shore levels where more delicate anemones could not survive the long intervals of dryness. As the tide ebbs the beadlet contracts into a formless blob of red jelly

that in hot weather dries to a leathery knob before the water comes surging back to restore its elegant form, translucent coloring, and delicate texture. Actinias are the commonest of British shore anemones, and their habits of feeding on jellyfishes, small fishes, and other sizable prey are known to few people as to Douglas and Alison Wilson. They were surprised one day, however, to come upon a unique sight—a rocky ridge in a Devon bay that at low tide was covered with beadlets, each with a long, silvery sand eel protruding from its mouth. A shoal of fishes had run into the ridge, and there were the anemones, each striving to cope with prey much too long to be swallowed, while other animals were managing bites of the protruding bodies.

Suddenly contracting anemones often eject water from the mouth or through special holes in the body wall. At low tide one sees jets of water issuing unexpectedly from closing anemones, and hears the squshing sounds made by luckless ones that have been stepped on. Kneel beside a tide pool and poke almost any anemone, and it will hug your finger as the discharge of stinging threads makes the tentacles cling and as the folding disk pulls in. Then, as in a string pouch being closed by a tightening of the cord, the anemone may contract a ring of circular muscle around the opening and leave your intruding finger outside. One of the few anemones that does not close up and that rarely retracts its tentacles is the "opelet" or "snakelocks," *Anemonia sulcata,* a dull green or pinkish brown anemone common on European shores (Plate 14). In the sunny spots shunned by most anemones, it spreads its long, snaky tentacles, often tipped with mauve, where they best display to the light the green algal cells within the tissues. Perhaps it has little need to retreat, for its stinging capsules are especially large and numerous and it is often something of a feat to disentangle the clinging tentacles from one's fingers. Also green with contained algal cells are the two common anemones of the American Pacific coast, the solitary "big green anemone," *Anthopleura xanthogrammica,* and the "aggregated anemone," *Anthopleura elegantissima* (Plate 13). Like the snakelocks, they feed in full light. When darkness comes and most other anemones begin to unfold their disks and feed, the anthopleuras draw in their tentacles and rest.

The big green anemone is known from Japan, the North Pacific, and down the American Pacific coast from Alaska to Panama in the very low tide zone or in well-aerated tide pools. Flourishing specimens growing in brilliant sunlight are a beautiful emerald green, often marked with purple, and as much as 10 or even 16 inches across. In spite of their large size, their sting causes only a slight tingling. Under wharves, in caves, or in shaded spots they are pale green or even white, perhaps tinted with pink or lavender. The aggregated anemone, green with pink or lavender markings, is by far the more abundant of the two species, but it has a less extensive range and peters out south of San Luis Obispo and north of British Columbia. Aggregated anemones live in densely crowded beds higher up on the shore, often attached to rock in sand; they survive much sand deposition and scour. Perhaps they are helped by their patchy armor of adhering pieces of shell and gravel, which makes them look so much like the background that one often sits or walks on them unwittingly and then hears—or feels—their squashy wetness. Both species of *Anthopleura*, as well as many other anemones, have vertical rows of warts that cover the column. In some anemones these have no function we can discover, but in *Anthopleura, Tealia, Bunodactis* (Plate 21), and others the protuberances are glandular and sticky, and hold sand or shell fragments close about the column.

If green anemones that contain green algal cells are more deeply colored in full light than in shaded areas, we can see why this should be so, but what of other green anemones or the green varieties of *Actinia* that have no algae? These are also found to be more densely colored in brighter situations, and so are many red dahlia anemones. If we explain this by saying that the pigment acts as a screen against light too strong for the delicate tissues, this will not do for *Metridium senile*. The ones examined on British shores are, if anything, more likely to be white in the most lighted situations. This species of plumose anemone has an especially striking array of color varieties, even in those found living side by side. Fox and Pantin, working at Cambridge with specimens of *Metridium* from all over England and from Scotland, described the varieties as white, simple red, simple brown, brown with gray, simple gray, red with gray, red with brown, and red with brown with gray. The notation "simple red" covered red, orange, or salmon-pink hues, or even yellowish varieties, since these shades depend upon the intensity of the red pigment, or perhaps several pigments. The conclusion they drew was that the color varieties may be due to random variations in heredity and may be related to biological processes taking place within the animal. When the resulting colors are vivid, they may have no special value as coloration, but indicate only that bright color is no great handicap to an anemone and is therefore not eliminated by natural selection, as perhaps it is in drab-colored groups that match their surroundings. In some anemones the color is clearly related to the food supply. If the tentacles of a red *Actinia equina* are amputated and the animal eats the usual diet of red shrimp, the tentacles grow back red. If instead the anemone is fed on colorless

The aggregated anemone of the American Pacific coast, *Anthopleura elegantissima,* in the final stage of reproduction by body rupture. Only a thin strand of tissue still connects the two daughter anemones. (California. Woody Williams)

pieces of fish, the regenerated tentacles are colorless.

The responses of anemones are not always the ones we would make to the same kinds of stimulation, but they do seem suited to the life of an anemone. When taken into the laboratory by C. F. A. Pantin and his many students at Cambridge, *Calliactis parasitica* appears undisturbed by contact with an electrically heated wire that burns the skin of the column. Yet the tentacles twitch at the slightest tap on the walls of the aquarium or when waves are set up in the water by any object, whether or not it is an offering of food. To mechanical prodding the disk and tentacles are four thousand times as sensitive as the column.

Often it is impossible to pry an anemone loose without inflicting injury or leaving pieces behind. In nature there are species that treat themselves in this same way, either because of the roughness of the rock over which they move or because of incoordination. The plumose anemone is one of these, and it turns tragedy into triumph, because the fragments round up and regenerate into new anemones. *Diadumene luciae,* a small, slender, greenish anemone striped with yellow or orange, common on both American coasts, expands the basal disk and attaches it firmly, then pulls up the central portion, leaving behind a ring of small pieces that may regenerate into as many as a dozen or more anemones. It also has a more brutal approach to asexual reproduction—rupture of the whole body into halves that regenerate. This rapidly spreading anemone probably came originally from Japan, where it reproduces sexually as well.

Of the many genera that reproduce asexually, only *Gonactinia* is known to split across the body; all the others rend themselves lengthwise. This is an unsettling habit at best, and things do not always get divided neatly, so that anemones which divide asexually often have unconventional numbers of tentacles or mouth grooves or internal partitions. When matters really go astray, an anemone may end with ten or more mouth grooves instead of the more usual two.

The aggregated anemone, mentioned earlier, forms its colonies by asexual division of the body. The round anemone becomes elliptical and one end keeps moving outward until the stretched anemone is connected in the middle only by a narrow strand that finally breaks. Only uncrowded individuals divide, so that in a cluster only the ones around the

Brain coral in light, with polyps retracted. (Great Barrier Reef. Fritz Goro: *Life* Magazine)

edge pull apart, and small colonies spread out eventually into large, crowded beds.

Regeneration in anemones takes place most readily in primitive forms like *Harenactis,* the burrowing anemone, which can produce both disk and base from almost any slice of the body. When *Metridium* is cut across the column, the lower piece regenerates a new disk with tentacles; but the upper portion cannot readily produce a new base. Severed tentacles do not usually regenerate, but in *Boloceroides,* a Japanese anemone, the whole set of tentacles is shed and then replaced; and each cast-off tentacle becomes a new anemone.

It is a memorable day or sunset hour when one comes upon anemones spawning in a tide pool and sees the water turn cloudy with wave upon wave of ejected eggs, or in some species ejected larvae. The little free-swimming larva, oval or pear-shaped, often looks grooved along the attachments of the internal partitions. It develops a mouth but usually does not push out tentacles until after it settles down. Retaining the developing eggs in the digestive cavity to the larval stage or even beyond is only one method for prolonging maternal protection of the young. A small red sea anemone, *Epiactis prolifera,* common on eelgrass in Puget Sound but known all down the American Pacific coast, is frequently found with a complete circle of juvenile anemones in special brood pouches around the middle of the external surface of the column (Plate 16).

Usually we can only guess at the age of an anemone, for extended observations on particular anemones in nature are rare. The late W. K. Fisher, when he was director of the Hopkins Marine Laboratory at Pacific Grove, California, did observe some large green anemones that occupied the same crevice for at least thirty years. But the laurels for known longevity all go to captive anemones tended by methodical Scots. In *The Great Barrier Reef,* Dakin tells of Dalyell, a Scottish laird and fine naturalist, who about 1827 collected an *Actinia* from a rock pool at North Berwick and kept it in a little bowl, feeding it on bits of oyster or mussel and changing its water regularly. Finally known as Granny, it outlived Dalyell and three successive caretakers; and when things finally went wrong and it died, it was given a newspaper obituary notice half a column long. An even more famous batch of anemones, long identified as *Sagartia* and later as *Cereus,* were said to have been collected as full-grown anemones some time prior to 1862, and for many years lovingly tended by a lady who fed them fresh liver. They were finally given to the Department of Zoology at the University of Edinburgh, and there they thrived and budded until something went amiss and they were all simultaneously found dead in about 1940 or 1942. At that time they were at least eighty years old, more likely ninety, but they had undergone no obvious changes during all the years of observation.

THE TRUE OR STONY CORALS

The graceful sprig of white coral on the mantelpiece, rudely broken from its firm attachment on some coral reef, is little more than a brittle limestone cast of coralline symmetry. In life it was veiled with delicate flesh of pink, heliotrope, purple, red, yellow, green, or golden-brown hue; and it held blossom-like polyps secure in its sheltering craters. Though many tons of coral skeletons are every year distributed all over the world to ornament homes far from the tropics, the great economic importance of coral polyps lies in the serious hazards to navigation erected by their limestone-secreting habits. So rapid is reef growth in some parts of the South Seas that navigation charts more than twenty years old are said to be useless. Much modern research on living coral reefs is contributing toward a more successful approach to drilling for oil in fossil reefs left from earlier geologic periods when the extent of warm seas on our watery planet was far greater than it is in our time.

There are some twenty-five hundred species of true or stony corals (technically called scleractinian or madreporarian corals), and all have similar polyps that look like tiny and delicate anemones sitting in limestone cups. The polyps may be widely spaced, each occupying a separate cup; or the cups may be so close together as to have common walls; or the polyps may be joined together in rows and occupy grooves in a rounded skeletal mass. In the "brain corals" so common on coral reefs, sinuous skeletal grooves are fringed on each side by a continuous row of tentacles and have along their bottom a row of spaced mouths.

Relatively few corals are solitary, and these occupy isolated little cups or disklike skeletons several inches across. All the rest are colonial and join their small but numerous forces to secrete large coral tenements. The rounded boulder-like corals are hardier and predominate at the surf-beaten seaward face of most reefs. The branching antler-like corals (Plate 31) of shallow waters are more typical of the protected rear areas of a reef. Sometimes the same species of coral grows rounded or softly lobed in exposed situations and intricately branching farther back on the reef. Deep-water coral colonies have a treelike aspect, with narrow branches well suited to shed sediments that fall from above.

In the daytime coral polyps remain more or less contracted, then expand and feed at night, when plankton animals rise to the surface in greatest numbers. Corals with very small tentacles entangle minute crustaceans and other animals in strands of mucus and waft them to the mouth by beating cilia. The larger polyps with long tentacles grasp small prey, sometimes even tiny fishes, and drop the food onto the mouth or push it in (Plate 26).

The skeletons of stony corals are not laid down within the living substance, as in the alcyonarian corals described earlier, but are secreted by the outer layer of cells and lie completely outside the coral animals. Each polyp secretes about itself a limy cup filled with radiating ridges that alternate with the internal partitions. As the ridges grow by steady accretion, they push up the underside of the body into folds that conform to the hard ridges. Except for some of the orange-red or red solitary and deepwater forms, corals have no pigments in the skeleton itself, so that dried reef corals are various shades of off-white until they are bleached white by the sun or by those who prepare pieces of decorative coral for sale. Many reef-coral "heads" look red or green when broken open, but only because the old layers of porous colonial skeleton are thoroughly permeated by colored algae.

Corals live firmly cemented to the bottom, but some of the solitary forms, though attached when young, are freed later in life to shift about on sandy bottoms or to become imbedded in mud by a pointed base. The mushroom coral, *Fungia,* found mostly on tropical reefs, has a single large green or brownish polyp that may be 5 inches across or more. The fully extended tentacles stretch 2 or 3 inches beyond the disk. The young mushroom coral expands at the mouth end into a disk which is eventually set free. The original stalk then repeatedly produces and sheds disks until a number lie scattered about, and still growing, upon the bottom. The beautiful convex disk with its many large radiating ridges looks like the underside of the cap of a gilled mushroom; it is familiar to collectors of shells and corals. A free-living coral, *Heteropsammia,* provides shelter for a sipunculid worm; when the coral topples over, the worm sets it upright.

The subtle or gorgeous colorings of living corals, which make coral reefs as exquisitely beautiful as any flower garden, are provided in part by the golden-brown plantlike cells that live within colorless polyps, as well as by the many pastel tints lent by pigments in the flesh. The gayest contrasts often come from the other animals that throng all coral reefs, either attaching firmly to maintain a foothold on these biological oases in a vast, shifting ocean, or moving about freely from one coral crevice to another in the almost spongelike porosity of old coral layers. Gaily colored fishes dart in and out of coral thickets, and some of them browse on the coral to get at the worms in coral cavities. Little coral-gall crabs live within the branches of certain corals, the young female settling in the fork of a growing branch and becoming imprisoned as coral growth continues. In the perforated coral chamber it maintains respiratory and feeding currents, and when mature it is visited by a minute male able to make its way through the small openings in the coral.

Sediments would clog the delicate ciliary-mucus feeding apparatus of corals were they not constantly removed by reversing the ciliary feeding currents to carry foreign particles to the outer edge of the feeding disk and drop them off. Some polyps simply shake off sand by rising up in their little cups. Despite this steady grooming, rapidly settling sediments in shallow waters seriously limit the distribution of reef corals by smothering the little settling larvae and by making the water too turbid to admit sufficient light for the plantlike cells in adult tissues.

The classification of corals cuts across such differences as solitary and colonial habit, distribution over the seas, and whether or not the coral is an important reef-builder. It is based on the finer structure of the skeleton. Since it is not possible here to take up the many kinds of corals group by group, we shall consider them in two categories which are convenient for readers who live on temperate shores and which do have real significance in the mode of life of the corals.

Corals Extending into Temperate or Cold Waters

The solitary cup corals (Plate 23) and the tall branching colonies considered here belong to groups represented on tropical coral reefs and in deep tropical waters, but they are not restricted to such waters, and many do best in subtropical or cool seas all over the world. Nor are they limited to shallow waters, as reef corals are. Delicate branching forms that occur at great depths in the tropics, even to 24,000 feet or more, can be dredged at lesser and lesser depths as we move to cooler latitudes. Most of these corals do not harbor the plantlike cells that play so great a role in the life of reef corals, and they are quite negative to light. Where they do not keep to deep waters they grow in dim rock pools, on the undersides of stones, or in the shade of neighboring corals on a reef. The yellow, orange, red, brown, and black pigments which color the soft tissues of many may in bright situations help to screen the strong light.

The little orange-red solitary cup coral, *Balanophyllia elegans*, is abundant in shaded situations in Monterey Bay in California and northward to Puget Sound. When the delicate flesh is so tightly contracted that it forms a mere veil over the hollowed cup and its radiating ridges, it measures ¼ to ½ of an inch across. Fully expanded, the little polyp rises much higher than the cup and extends long, tapering transparent tentacles covered with wartlike batteries of stinging cells. On southwestern British shores *Balanophyllia regia*, with bright yellow warts on the tentacles, is called "the red and gold star coral." Close to shore it is rare, but in deeper waters its cups are found in great numbers.

The "Devonshire cup coral," *Caryophyllia smithi*, is found at low-tide mark in southwest England, and is often dredged from the continental shelf south of Ireland and at all depths in the English Channel, where it attaches to rocky outcrops on the soft bottom. The white or pinkish disk, about ¾ of an inch across, is ringed with chestnut brown around the mouth; the transparent tentacles have brown markings and silvery white knobbed tips. On the American Pacific coast *Caryophyllia* is a shore form in Puget Sound, and occurs deeper farther southward.

A larger fan-shaped solitary coral, *Flabellum*, is common on Mediterranean bottoms alongside *Balanophyllia*, and also on deep mud bottoms in the Atlantic. A salmon-colored species, about 4 inches across, comes up in dredges from Newfoundland to Florida. *Flabellum* is attached when young but later may lie loose on the bottom or with the tapering base imbedded in the mud.

The "star coral" of American coasts is *Astrangia*, which forms small encrusting colonies with closely spaced cups. The knobbed tentacles, dotted with warts of stinging cells, catch tiny crustaceans and even minute fishes. *Astrangia danae*, with colonies usually 2 or 3 inches across, has white or pinkish polyps less than ½ of an inch high. It encrusts rocks from Cape Cod to Florida. This is a hardy species, and when brought in to an aquarium, even after being shipped hundreds of miles from the sea, it can be maintained for some time on bits of raw meat. A species in southern California, once said to be common in pools near La Jolla, was described as orange or coral red, with lighter tentacles ending in white knobs.

In deep Atlantic waters the tall, branching colonial corals that dominate whole areas of the continental shelf, especially on its sloping edge, have large blossom-like polyps that are widely spaced on the shrublike or treelike branches. Dredging reveals slopes of the northeastern Atlantic, from six hundred to six thousand feet, where the bottom is covered with open or dense thickets of yellow *Madrepora* and *Lophelia*. A species of *Lophelia* is even better known from the deep Norwegian fjords, especially Trondheim Fjord, where at about six hundred feet the rocky bottoms support great banks of *Lophelia* and *Amphihelia*. These differ from typical coral reefs in that they never come to the surface. Also scattered over the continental shelves and slopes are great patches of *Dendrophyllia*.

All these deep-water branching colonies are encrusted with small solitary corals and with some three hundred species of other invertebrates that are fastened permanently and grasp their food out of the water that flows by, or that creep about on the branches safe above the smothering sediments of the soft sea floor.

Dendrophyllids are also well known in the Mediterranean for their lovely yellow or red polyps. *Astroides* (Plate 24) forms an orange-colored belt below the water line. A similar coral is *Tubastrea,* a bright red dendrophyllid that is widely distributed. On Jamaican reefs the red flesh of *Tubastrea* stands out in sharp contrast with the reef corals that take their soft green and golden-brown colorings from plantlike cells contained within the transparent and colorless tissues.

Corals Restricted to Shallow Tropical Seas

Nearly all shallow-water corals of warm waters— and this includes all the true reef corals—are abundantly filled with plantlike photosynthetic cells (called zooxanthellae and thought to be modified dinoflagellates). The chemical partnership that links animal and plantlike cells apparently makes possible the close spacing of the polyps of huge reef communities, in which millions upon millions of individuals are crowded together in great honeycombs of coral, further congested by myriads of hangers-on.

Reef corals do not digest their plantlike cells even though these always occur in the digestive lining. If starved or placed in the dark, the corals eject the little guests. Nor is oxygen usually in short supply on the wave-beaten surface of a reef. The most informed guess, that of C. M. Yonge, who during the Great Barrier Reef Expedition in 1928 performed many carefully controlled experiments on living reef corals, is that the corals benefit most from the rapid removal of their carbon dioxide, and especially of their nitrogenous and phosphate wastes—and that this rapid turnover of materials promotes the prolific growth of tropical reefs. This means that true reef corals are limited in their distribution to conditions under which the plant-animal bond remains intact.

Rate of growth varies with species, location, depth, and other factors. Some corals measured in the 1890's by Saville-Kent on Thursday Island, in the Great Barrier Reef area, were measured again twenty-three years later. A brain coral had increased from 30 to 74 inches in diameter, and a specimen of *Porites* (Plate 25), a very dense coral, from 19 feet to 22 feet 9½ inches. The East Indian reefs, below a depth of fifteen feet, grow upward as much as 4 inches a year.

A map of coral-reef distribution reveals that the reefs occur in a great warm belt that engirdles the middle of the globe, roughly between latitudes 30°N. and 30°S., so that the reefs of the western Atlantic extend for about the same distance north and south of the equator as do those of the Indo-Pacific. Within this belt temperatures average 21°C. (about 70°F.)

Each polyp of the coral colony (*Astrangia*) is about ⅜ inch high. It produces new individuals by budding, thus enlarging the colony. *Astrangia* tolerates the cold waters off Cape Cod, Massachusetts, but does not form reefs there. (American Museum of Natural History)

or higher, and never drop lower by more than a few degrees or for very brief periods. The most flourishing growth and the greatest variety of species is in waters that average 25° to 29°C. (77° to 84°F.), and most of the antler-like branching forms are in this narrower zone. Below an average temperature of 23.4°C. (74.3°F.), the species are dominated by the more resistant rounded forms.

A closer look at the map brings out great gaps in the distribution of corals where cold currents from the Antarctic stream north along the western coasts of continents. The western coasts of Africa and South America have almost no reef corals. Neither western Mexico nor California have any true reefs. Warm currents, on the other hand, make a small bulge in the reef belt at Bermuda, where the northward-flowing warm waters of the Gulf Stream support beautiful if not typical reefs at 32°N. The southernmost Atlantic reefs are those at the latitude of Rio de Janeiro (23°S.). In the Pacific the reefs extend northward to the southern shore of Japan, while in the southern hemisphere the reefs farthest from the equator are those of Queensland, Australia (about 24°S.). Other great gaps occur at the mouths of rivers, where fresh water and silt are fatal to the growth of reef corals.

Thus the lesser of the two great centers of reef-building, that of the Caribbean and adjacent waters, includes the reefs of Bermuda, the Bahamas, the West Indies, southeastern Florida, and parts of the coast of Brazil. Diving expeditions have found some reef growth on the western or Gulf coast of Florida, at depths of 50 to 150 feet. But only the southeastern shore of the peninsula of Florida has good reefs, and these can be seen a few miles south of Miami. Some

[111

Elkhorn coral formation off the Virgin Islands. This is the only stony coral listed among "venomous coelenterates." It is a menace to skin divers off the Florida keys and the West Indies. (T. Parkinson: National Audubon)

of the smaller coral species are accessible to anyone who wades out in many places along the Florida keys, even as far north as the shores of Elliot Key or on the bars south of Biscayne Key. F. G. Walton Smith's *Atlantic Reef Corals* will be helpful to anyone visiting the Florida shore, and it has brief suggestions on where to see the better-developed reefs of the Bahamas and Cuba. He lists nineteen species for Bermuda and forty species from Florida waters. Thomas Goreau has in recent years collected forty of the forty-one species recorded for Jamaica, and he reports that the density of growth is often comparable with that on the great Indo-Pacific reefs even though the number of species is far less. The Atlantic reefs are mostly bank reefs built on flat shallow platforms. They are farther from shore than true fringing reefs, but the lagoon channel that separates them from the shore is not nearly so deep as in the

barrier reefs of the South Seas. They are often some distance inward from the edge of the platform, so they do not slope off into very deep water as do atolls and barrier reefs.

The most densely crowded communities of animal species found anywhere on land or in the sea are those of the great coral reefs of the Indo-Pacific region, from the Red Sea and the east coast of Africa at one extreme to the islands of Hawaii, Tahiti, the Marquesas, etc. at the other. The reefs of the African east coast and of the island of Madagascar are fringing reefs, which lie close to shore in shallow water and continue to grow actively only on the wave-beaten seaward side, which slopes steeply downward into deep water. At low tide one can wade out to the partly exposed platform. Such fringing reefs are also well developed at Java, the Solomon Islands, and the Carolines, but grow less well at Hawaii and other islands that are near the outer edge of the Indo-Pacific coral region.

Barrier reefs consist of lines of reefs paralleling a mainland but separated from it by a lagoon channel deep enough to accommodate large ships. These are not well developed in the Indian Ocean but in the Pacific are found at the Society Islands, the Fiji Islands, New Caledonia, to the southeast of New Guinea, and at many other spots. The largest and best-known of barrier reefs is the Great Barrier Reef of northeastern Australia, which parallels the coast of Queensland for 1250 miles, though it is interrupted by many passages.

Atolls are the coral islands that romantic dreams are made of. These ring-shaped or horseshoe-shaped islands, surrounding a central lagoon with sheltering palm trees and mangroves, are dotted like oases over the vast Indian and Pacific oceans in waters thousands of feet deep.

Below the depths at which there is sufficient light for the photosynthesis carried on by their content of plantlike cells, reef corals cannot live. They grow best near the surface and are most abundant in the upper 60 feet of water, though many extend through the water layers down to 150 feet. Only a few manage to grow as low as 270 feet.

The best-developed reefs of the Bahamas, Jamaica, and Florida, according to Norman Newell, a leading student of Atlantic and other reefs, usually have three coral zones, which are determined by differences in depth and turbulence of water: an outer zone of massive corals, especially of yellow-brown *Montastrea annularis* lying at depths of thirty to sixty feet; a middle zone of brownish yellow staghorn corals, *Acropora palmata,* at five to thirty feet; and an inner rocky shoal rising to low-tide level. This last zone is characterized by the velvety yellow-orange or brown "stinging coral," *Millepora alcicornis* (not a true stony coral but a hydrozoan coral), encrusting coralline algae, sea fans, and small rounded corals. In the Indo-Pacific many reefs receive much greater contributions of limestone from the coral-secreting algae, and also in certain places from hydrozoan reef-builders like the organ-pipe coral and blue coral.

THE ZOANTHIDS

Without skeletons and with a marginal circlet of unbranched tentacles, zoanthids superficially resemble small anemones, except that most of them are colonial and are united at their bases. This is a small group, found in both shallow and deep waters and in cold and warm latitudes, but especially in warm shallow seas. Most zoanthids regularly grow on the surfaces of other animals, often on very specific hosts. Certain species of *Epizoanthus* occur only on particular glass sponges; others fasten to the shells

inhabited by hermit crabs, dissolving away the crab's shell and finally coming to enclose the crab directly. Other genera live on sponges, hydroids, gorgonians, corals, bryozoans, and worm tubes (Plate 30).

THE BLACK CORALS

The black or thorny corals, or antipatharians, are slender, branching, attached colonies of plantlike form ranging from an inch to several feet high. Most are known to biologists only as preserved specimens dredged from deep or abyssal waters, especially of the tropics and subtropics. The horny internal skeleton is black or brown and beset with thorns. According to Russel and Yonge, in the excellent account of products of the sea which concludes their book *The Seas,* the skeletons of certain black corals

The star coral, *Montastrea*, grows into yellow-brown boulder-like masses, 5 feet or more across, in Florida, the Bahamas, Bermuda, and the West Indies. The individual cups are only a fraction of an inch across and show the ridges supporting the internal partitions. (Fritz Goro: *Life* Magazine)

are used in China, Japan, the Malay Archipelago, and the Indian Ocean for making bracelets that are worn to ward off rheumatism, drowning, and other perils. Black corals occur also in the Mediterranean, the Red Sea, and the Persian Gulf, but having no decorative value they are no longer worked by Europeans as they were in ancient times.

THE TUBE ANEMONES

Like long, slender, muscular burrowing anemones are the tube anemones or cerianthids, which live buried in sand almost to the feeding disk. The slender tentacles arise in two distinct sets—an inner smaller set encircling the mouth, and a marginal set, each composed of one or more circlets. The body is surrounded by a tube formed of a hardened slimy secretion and lined with cast-off stinging capsules or imbedded with sand grains and other foreign particles. The feeding disk cannot be retracted into the column as in most anemones, but when disturbed it disappears down the protecting tube. The Mediterranean *Cerianthus* is well known to visitors to the Naples Aquarium, where fine specimens have been on display at least since the 1880's. In 1882 a small green individual was placed in a tank when it was only 1½ inches long and 2½ inches thick. In 1924, forty-two years later, it had increased ten times in size, and the crown of gracefully extended drooping tentacles had a diameter of 10 inches. Species of *Cerianthus* are also common in the English Channel (Plate 32) and along the American Atlantic coast. A brown species up to 6 inches long occurs from Cape Cod to Florida in shallow water. A larger northern species, with a rough tube up to 2 feet long, housing an anemone that stretches 18 inches, occurs in deep water from southern New England northward at least to the Bay of Fundy. On the American Pacific coast *Cerianthus estuari* is well known from sandy mud flats (alongside the burrowing and true anemone *Harenactis*) in Mission Bay. The outer set of transparent, delicately banded tentacles is spread out on the sand in a circle 4 or 5 inches across. A bigger species, which does not live intertidally north of southern California, may have a tube 6 feet long. Most cerianthids are tropical or subtropical.

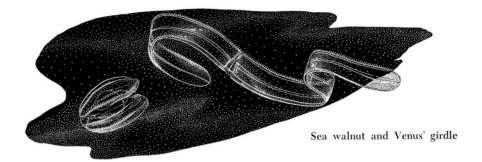

CHAPTER IV

Sea walnut and Venus' girdle

The Comb Jellies
(*Phylum Ctenophora*)

On a smooth stretch of wave-washed sandy beach one's attention is easily caught, even at some distance, by little oval balls of clear jelly that glisten in the sun like crystal beads. "Cat's eyes," fishermen on the American Pacific coast call them, and on many other shores such stranded comb jellies are known as "sea gooseberries" or, in the case of some of the slightly larger species, as "sea walnuts." If they are not too far gone the little sea gooseberries will revive in sea water, regain their gossamer loveliness, and swim about like paddle boats, propelled by the rapid beating of eight vertical rows of ciliary combs that radiate over the rounded body like the lines of longitude on a globe. The delicate transparency of comb jellies makes them all but invisible in the water, so that often they reveal themselves only in the rippling iridescence of the rows of beating combs as they diffract the light. Unless the water is smooth as glass they are likely to remain below the surface, and even when they come within one's reach they slip between the fingers or tear to shreds at the touch of an oar. Such diaphanous creatures are best gathered by towing a net behind a boat, but a few may be dipped up in a small net or container.

The daytime play of rainbow colors is replaced at night by luminescent waves of an intensity that is matched only by some of the deep-sea fishes. On summer nights the waters beneath a jutting wharf may shine with hundreds of languidly gliding comb jellies, which at the slightest disturbance light up along the eight comb rows. Dipped up and taken in a jar of sea water to a lighted room, they cease to glow. Then, if the room is darkened for at least twenty minutes, they shine again with a bluish or greenish light.

The phylum name, Ctenophora, means "comb-bearers," and the swimming paddles are made of large cilia that are fused at the attached end like the teeth of a comb. They are regulated and coordinated in their movements by a network of nerve cells that connect with a tiny sense organ housed in a glassy little dome atop the upper pole, the one opposite the mouth. Presumably the sense organ is concerned with balancing and helps to orient the animal as it swims.

The more primitive comb jellies, like the little sea gooseberries, have two long tentacles with which they fish for food. At times these are drawn up into knotted, stringlike masses, at other times stretched far out in graceful sweeping curves, the side branches that fringe one edge lending a plumelike elegance. The more advanced groups of comb jellies have only fringes of short tentacles or lack them altogether. When present, the tentacles or their side branches are thickly studded with special adhesive cells, unique to ctenophores and not to be confused with the thread capsules of coelenterates. The protruding heads of the adhesive cells are very sticky and cling to prey. At their inner ends they are attached to spirally coiled contractile filaments that yield to the pull of struggling prey but cannot be wrenched loose.

This is an exclusively marine group, though some do flourish in bays and estuaries with a salt content only one-third that of full oceanic salinity. Of more than eighty species, almost seventy can be found in warm seas, three live only in arctic and northern waters, three are deep-sea forms. Two species—the sea gooseberry, *Pleurobrachia pileus,* and the flattened thimble-like *Beroë cucumis*—are cosmopolitan and found from pole to pole. Distribution varies with temperature changes, and many comb jellies migrate from surface to deeper waters and back with the round of seasons, as *Pleurobrachia pileus* is known to do in the Black Sea. During the cool of spring it feeds at the surface, then descends gradually to about 110 feet as warm weather arrives, and remains below until winter weather returns, having followed water temperatures that remained always at about 52°F.

In stormy weather comb jellies sink below the surface; but their feeble swimming powers are of no avail against wind-whipped waters or strong currents and tides, so that they often accumulate in great swarms. Then they decimate the small animals that float near the surface, including the fry of commercially important fishes. Off the New England coast feeding comb jellies are a menace to cod eggs and young. And in England the fisheries experts have good reason to believe that swarms in certain

years wreak such havoc on small herrings as to be one of the important factors in determining the sizes of herring broods in the different years. The transparency of comb jellies readily reveals the truly formidable meals they make on copepods, tiny fishes, larvae, and eggs.

In warm seas ctenophores often have a yellowish cast from the yellow-brown, plantlike cells which they harbor. The relationship is apparently like that seen in many tropical protozoans, sponges, and coelenterates, which was discussed earlier.

The biradial symmetry of ctenophores is a two-sided modification of radial symmetry, and the basic body plan reminds us strongly of scyphozoan jellyfishes. The main cavity of the body is a digestive sac with branches. Though fine particles can be eliminated through two small pores near the upper pole, the main opening of the digestive sac is still the mouth, which serves also for ejecting fish heads and other sizable wastes. Between the fragile digestive lining and the delicate outer covering is a great bulk of secreted jelly which lends firmness and buoyancy, and in the jelly are various cells including long muscle fibers. Comb jellies do not pulsate like jellyfishes, but the elongated forms swim by gentle undulations of the whole body, and the aberrant flattened ones can creep about. When dropping vertically or actively moving along, the mouth end precedes. Resting or feeding comb jellies, however, often hang from the surface with the mouth up.

Both ovaries and testes occur in all individuals; they can usually be seen through the transparent body as they hang from the walls of the eight digestive canals that run below the rows of combs. The eggs and sperms are shed through the mouth, and the egg, fertilized in the open water, develops into a little free-swimming larva, the cydippid, which looks like a miniature of a sea gooseberry, with combs and two long tentacles. In the more highly developed ctenophores the cydippid must undergo reduction or loss of the tentacles, besides many other changes, before it achieves the adult form.

The ctenophores are usually divided into two classes, one with tentacles and one without.

Comb Jellies with Tentacles *(Class Tentaculata)*

THE CYDIPPIDS

The comb jellies that have departed least from the primitive ctenophore stock are the cydippids, the little globular, egg-shaped, or pear-shaped relatives of the sea gooseberry. *Pleurobrachia pileus,* referred to earlier as having a world-wide distribution, has an

Swimming sea gooseberries, *Pleurobrachia pileus.* In some the two long tentacles are extended, in others withdrawn. (England. D. P. Wilson)

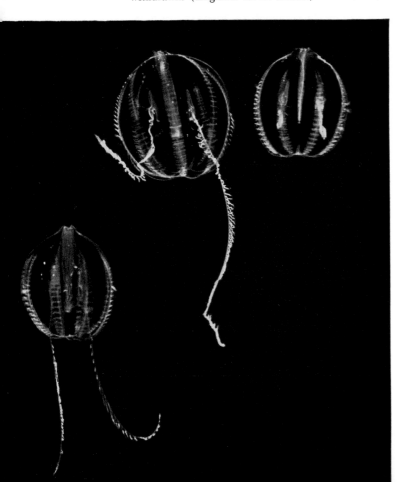

egg-shaped body less than 1 inch long and about ½ of an inch wide. It loops through the water sweeping two long tentacles, which can extend twenty times the length of the body or can be completely withdrawn into the two pouches from which they emerge. Each tentacle is fringed along one edge with short, sticky side branches that adhere to floating fish eggs, copepods, crab and oyster larvae, arrow worms, and tiny fishes. As the prey is caught the tentacle shortens and wipes the food off onto the rim of the narrow mouth, where beating cilia on the lips carry it swiftly inward to await its turn in the digestive sac—perhaps already crammed full with undigested little fishes.

During winter storms this comb jelly is driven southward along the eastern coast of America and can be seen in the waters of Long Island and New Jersey, but in early summer it is most abundant off southern New England, trailing orange-tinged tentacles. As the water warms it vanishes there and appears in great swarms, one individual almost touching another, over wide areas off Maine and Nova Scotia, the Arctic Sea, and northern Europe. Another species, *P. brunnea,* with purplish touches on the tentacles, abounds off the New Jersey coast in the fall. The little ovate spheres are also well known in the Pacific and the Antarctic. From San Diego northward along the whole of the Pacific coast the beaches are strewn with stranded *P. bachei;* but to see these little sea gooseberries maneuvering about in the water, with red-tinged tentacles sweeping every inch, there are few places that compare with Puget Sound, an arm of the Pacific Ocean that extends into northwestern Washington, offering protection to a great profusion of invertebrates.

A common "sea walnut" is *Mertensia ovum,* about 2 inches long and with the mouth at the more pointed end of the somewhat flattened but egg-shaped body. A delicate pink color tinges sense organ, tentacles, and comb rows. Though *Mertensia* can in winter wander as far southward as New Jersey, its southward extension in summer is Massachusetts Bay, for it cannot tolerate warm water. Great summer swarms are seen off Maine, but the center of distribution seems to be the Labrador coast, where it has been seen to feed on little sculpins. On the contrary, *Hormiphora plumosa,* a warm-water species of the Mediterranean and tropical Atlantic, is seen north of its normal habitat only as the warm flow of the Gulf Stream carries it up the American coast or to English waters. Species of *Hormiphora* and *Mertensia* occur also on the American Pacific coast.

THE LOBED COMB JELLIES

The lobed comb jellies have compressed bodies drawn out on two sides into large lobes. After starting in life as cydippid larvae that look like tiny sea gooseberries with two long tentacles, they transform into

The lobed comb jelly, *Mnemiopsis,* common along the American Atlantic coast, may be seen in great swarms in summer. When disturbed, as by the passing of a boat, it glows brightly along the eight rows of swimming plates. Large specimens are 4 inches long. (Massachusetts. George G. Lower)

adults without tentacle pouches and with tentacles reduced to short filaments and fringes close to the mouth. They can snare fishes longer than themselves, holding them fast with the short but powerful tentacles and closing them in, by means of the lobes, until they are safely inside the mouth. Usually they satisfy their voracious appetites on crustaceans and larvae small enough to be entangled in mucus and wafted into the mouth by ciliated grooves. *Mnemiopsis leidyi* is pear-shaped, slightly translucent, and up to 4 inches long. It feeds mostly on copepods and mollusk larvae, and when it is present in numbers bodes no good for the oyster industry, since it can down a hundred or more oyster larvae at a time. The summer swarms of lobed ctenophores are especially noted for lighting up New England waters with a greenish light of great intensity. From Cape Cod to South Carolina, *Mnemiopsis* readily adapts to marked changes in salinity and temperature. Individuals that in winter invade the coastal waters of New Jersey have been seen with combs continuing to beat until they finally freeze fast in the ice. Another species, often greenish amber in color, extends from South Carolina into the tropics and in summer is common around Jamaica. Its jelly is more rigid than in most, and it can be lifted by hand without injury, or readily maintained in an aquarium.

From north of Cape Cod into arctic waters the common lobed form is *Bolinopsis,* also well known from Scottish and northern European waters and from the cool waters of the American Pacific coast.

THE CESTIDS

The cestids ("girdle-like") are a somewhat surrealistic version of the lobed ctenophores. The body is a gelatinous ribbon, greatly flattened and elongated in the plane at right angles to that of the mouth and sense organ, so that these remain no farther apart than in lobed comb jellies. The tentacles are reduced to a tuft alongside the mouth and a row of short filaments along the edge bearing the mouth. They swim by graceful undulations of the body as well as by the beating of elongated comb rows. The well-known "Venus' girdle," *Cestum veneris,* shimmering with blue and green iridescence in the sunlight and sometimes reaching a length of 4½ feet, easily deserves the compliment of its name. The genus *Cestum* and the similar *Velamen,* both known from the Mediterranean and limited to warm waters, are represented by species that turn up around Florida.

THE FLATTENED CREEPING COMB JELLIES

The creeping ctenophores are an aberrant flattened group, often colored on the upper surface in dull reds or greens. Most are warm-water forms.

Ctenoplana, with combs and two tentacles, can creep on the bottom but usually floats at the surface off the shores of Sumatra, New Guinea, Indochina, and Japan. *Coeloplana,* leaflike and also with two tentacles but without combs in the adult, was discovered in the Red Sea, is abundant off Japan, and occurs also off Florida. It creeps about on particular alcyonarians. A curious cold-water form, *Tjalfiella,* also without combs, is found in Greenland waters creeping about on the deep-water pennatulid *Umbellula.* Recognizing a nearly sessile comb jelly that has no combs is a challenge even to the specialist. The affinities of *Tjalfiella* were revealed when little cydippid larvae were found in brood pouches on the upper surface.

Comb Jellies without Tentacles *(Class Nuda)*

The beroid ctenophores, so called from the name of the most important genus, *Beroë,* have no traces of tentacles, either in adult or larva. They are somewhat flattened, and are variously described as thimble-shaped, barrel-like, or mitre-shaped. The many fine branches of the digestive canals make a conspicuous and decorative pattern. At the open end is a very large mouth, and as the animal propels itself about by the beating of its combs, it sucks in sizable prey, often comb jellies nearly as large as itself. *Beroë* is thimble-shaped and up to 6 inches long. It is found in all seas, and in cold waters is of a delicate pink or lavender color.

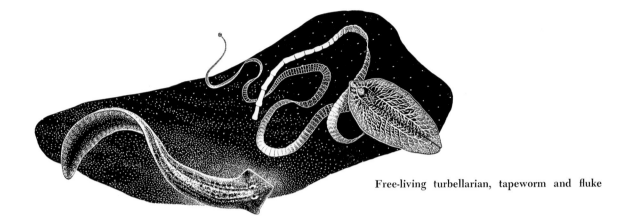

CHAPTER V

Free-living turbellarian, tapeworm and fluke

The Flatworms

(*Phylum Platyhelminthes*)

ONE may easily pass a lifetime without ever seeing a flatworm. The smallest ones are microscopic, and the largest ones, the ribbon-like tapeworms that may grow up to 50 feet or more in length, develop and pass their adult lives safely hidden within the bodies of their human or other vertebrate hosts. They are seen only when they die or are rudely removed by medical treatment. Best known, perhaps, are the ½-inch planarians used in classroom study and in zoological research. In nature these live unobtrusively in springs, streams, and ponds, crawling about on the vegetation or under stones. After gathering wild watercress one may have to rinse out little planarians. On marine shores the oval and leaflike polyclads, some of them 2 inches long and colorful or beautifully striped, may be seen by turning over boulders or peering into sheltered rock overhangs when the tide is out. Tantalizingly hard to find are the land planarians of moist temperate woods; by their nocturnal and retiring habits they elude even the serious students of flatworms. The occasional land planarian that turns up in temperate gardens or in greenhouses is usually an import from tropical lands, brought in with exotic plants.

Yet for all this, free-living flatworms are abundant and widespread; while the importance of the parasitic kinds in human history and in modern economic and political problems can hardly be exaggerated. One kind of parasitic flatworm, the blood fluke *Schistosoma,* lives in the blood vessels of more than a hundred million people. In World War II it helped to determine the outcome of many military actions in the South Pacific. Parasitic flatworms are still very much a part of the African and Asian pattern of disease, low productivity, and poverty. If the pattern is to be broken, the flatworm parasites that flourish especially—though by no means entirely—in tropical countries will have to be more widely understood and coped with. Some things that we think of as progress in many countries, such as the building of dams to supply irrigation canals, tend to increase the spread of blood flukes. To understand why, one needs to read the brief account that will be given of the life cycle of such flukes. In temperate latitudes Europeans and Americans, their pets, and their livestock, are still subject to infestation with flukes and tapeworms, though some of these have been brought under control. Many people who think of such parasites as occurring only under very unsanitary conditions have had "swimmers' itch" caused by the larval flukes that develop in numerous lovely lakes favored as summer resorts.

There are three classes of flatworms, roughly estimated to include almost nine thousand known species, only a fraction of the number that actually exist. The first consists almost entirely of free-living little worms. The other two classes, the flukes and the tapeworms, are exclusively parasitic and far more numerous. These are not attractive animals to the average layman, and when Aristotle became fascinated by the various worms that live in man, he felt obliged to justify his curiosity in these words: "In all natural objects there is some marvel, and if anyone despises the contemplation of lower animals, he must despise himself." From Aristotle's time to our own there have always been some minds that feel challenged by whatever is unknown, especially if it causes vast human suffering. The unraveling of the complexities of flatworm structure and habit is fortunately a very active field of modern research.

Soft-bodied animals that are several to many times as long as they are wide are inevitably tagged as worms, and this name has been applied to soft, elongated members of practically every large grouping of animals. Of all the kinds of worm-shaped creatures, the members of the phylum Platyhelminthes ("flat worms") are on the whole the most flattened and the most primitive. The digestive cavity, when present at all, has only one opening, as in the coelenterates. In place of the jelly that provides much of the coelenterate bulk, however, flatworms have a solidly cellular middle layer, which includes several sets of muscles and a variety of organs, especially of reproductive organs, a specialty of these animals.

With few exceptions, the flatworms are hermaphroditic—that is, each individual produces both eggs and sperms. This does not mean that self-fertilization is the rule. On the contrary, most flatworms are endowed with an amazingly complex set of organs for exchanging sperms with their neighbors or chance acquaintances and for storing the sperms toward the time when their eggs are to be fertilized. The fertilized eggs, enclosed in delicate capsules or in hardened shells, are shed to the exterior, and by means of adhesive secretions may be strung together in egg ribbons or masses or attached singly to stones or other objects. Some of the fresh-water flatworms are especially noted for their ability to multiply asexually by fragmentation or by crosswise rupture of the body. This has led to detailed studies of their ability to regenerate when experimentally cut into small pieces.

Beginning with the flatworms, all the groups of animals are two-sided or bilaterally symmetrical. Or they have some secondary modification of that kind of symmetry. Bilateral animals have a front end that goes first when the animal moves, and a rear or tail end that follows along. They also have differing upper and lower surfaces, and right and left sides that mirror each other. Organs that occur singly are usually in the mid-line, and paired organs occur on each side of the mid-line as in ourselves. This means that the flatworms are the first animals with a head. The major sense organs are concentrated on the head or front end, and most of the animal's wits are gathered into a brain, a concentration of nerve cells in the head. Speedier, more coordinated behavior is the result, with more rapid responses to prey or enemies than in the radial coelenterates.

The free-living flatworms have a highly developed talent for clinging to surfaces, and some fresh-water planarians even have well-developed muscular suckers for holding on. So it is not surprising that flatworms eventually took up parasitic habits and produced the formidable array of suckers and hooks by which the various flukes and tapeworms maintain their tenacious hold on the hosts that nurture them.

The Free-living Flatworms (*Class Turbellaria*)

The free-living flatworms are at least partially clothed with cilia that propel the smaller forms and the young stages of larger members. In water these cilia create the turbulence that suggested the name of the group. The larger turbellarians, whether aquatic or terrestrial, glide along primarily by muscular waves, though these may be invisible to the naked eye. To ease their way, land turbellarians must lay down a thick carpet of secreted mucus, over which they glide smoothly or sometimes hurry by a more energetic series of muscular contractions. Even the aquatic forms use a mucous bed, especially over rough surfaces.

Shapes vary from elongated cylindrical worms to extremely thin and flattened leaflike marine forms that are almost circular. Though a few have tail lobes, or little sensory lobes or tentacles on the head, these are for the most part streamlined little animals with no projections.

A very few turbellarians are parasitic, and some are internal or external commensals that share the food of their hosts while doing no serious harm. Most, however, are carnivorous, eating tiny animals of suitable size or working away, bit by bit, at large pieces of dead flesh or at living sessile animals, such as oysters or barnacles, that cannot flee. Land planarians can subdue insect larvae, snails, or even earthworms.

Turbellarians are divided into five orders based primarily on differences in the form of the digestive cavity; this internal distinction can often be readily seen through the transparent body wall.

THE ACOELS

The name "acoel" means "without a cavity," and these minute and delicate worms have no digestive cavity. The mouth, usually in the center of the under surface, directs the food into the inner mass of cells, where it is digested. Acoels are exclusively marine, and most of them are elongate or broadly oval and measure from $\frac{1}{25}$ to $\frac{1}{8}$ of an inch in length. They live so inconspicuously under stones, among algae, on muddy bottoms, and sometimes on sandy shores, that they are seldom seen by anyone not actively searching them out. Perhaps this is why almost all the known species of acoels have been described from temperate or arctic Atlantic waters close to the haunts of most biologists, or in the Mediterranean or other seas that connect with the Atlantic. That part of the Atlantic known as the Sargasso Sea is the home of *Amphiscolops sargassi,* which lives on the floating sargassum seaweed. Tropical or Pacific species are usually drifting forms picked up in nets towed from boats. Two shore species are known from Monterey Bay, California; but again, this is a base for sharp-eyed biologists.

Most acoels are white or drab in color, but one of the most celebrated species, *Convoluta roscoffensis,* is a beautiful rich green from the green algal cells that pack the elongated body (Plate 36). This species of *Convoluta* is named for Roscoff, France, the little lobster-fishing port where the University of Paris maintains the largest of its several marine stations. It occurs also on certain sandy beaches in Brittany and Normandy, always in dense concentrations of many thousands or millions of tiny worms. The patches look like splashes or streaks of fresh dark green paint on the wet sand laid bare by a receding tide. Concentrated only where they can be continuously wetted by rivulets of draining water throughout the low-tide period, the worms lie moist and glistening, displaying their green cells to the sun. Then as the tide returns and the first waves roll in, the green patches erase themselves in an instant. The worms sense the distant wave shock and dig rapidly below the surface. Twice in twenty-four hours, in rhythm with the tides, the worms rise to the surface and later sink below, keeping beyond the reach of pounding waves yet providing exposure to light for the green cells.

The young convolutas are white, like most acoels, but soon they become infected with green cells, which appear to be derived from little green flagellates that may also be found living free in the sand. At first the convolutas continue to feed voraciously on small organisms, and the plant-animal bond seems no different from what we saw earlier in protozoans and coelenterates. The photosynthetic cells utilize gaseous and especially nitrogenous animal wastes, and this benefits the animal also by speeding its chemical turnover. As the convolutas mature something happens that suggests the relationship has become unbalanced. The worms stop feeding and begin to digest the green cells, eventually dooming both partners, though not before the convolutas have laid eggs in the sand and ensured a new generation.

Many acoels have no eyes and depend on general sensitivity of the body to light; some have on the head two pigmented spots that overlie nervous tissue sensitive to light. *Convoluta roscoffensis* has two such orange-pigmented eyes, and between them lies an otocyst, a tiny balancing organ like those seen in many coelenterates. It shows as a golden dot in the center of the head on several of the worms in Plate 36.

THE RHABDOCOELS

A straight and unbranched digestive cavity distinguishes the little rhabdocoels ("rodlike cavity"), and it can be readily discerned through the transparent and usually colorless body wall. These are very small worms, microscopic or in most cases measuring less than ¼ of an inch. Of elongate shape, they may be plump or slender, and usually are clothed with short cilia. Most have a pair of pigmented eyes at the head end. Rhabdocoels are common in all fresh waters and on marine shores, especially on sandy or muddy bottoms. A few are restricted to caves or hot springs or manage to live in moist places on land. *Microstomum* occurs in both fresh and salt waters. A fresh-water species common in the eastern United States and in Europe is known for its armory of stinging cells, obtained from the hydras on which it feeds. When *Microstomum* undergoes asexual division of the body the parts do not separate at once, so that after several successive divisions there results a chain of connected subindividuals, each with its own mouth.

Formerly lumped with the rhabdocoels are the similar, though generally a little larger, alleocoels. These are now placed in a separate order.

THE TRICLADS OR PLANARIANS

Called triclads from their "three-branched" digestive cavity, or planarians because they are usually "level" or flattened, this group of flatworms is the most familiar because of the extensive use to which certain fresh-water species have been put in teaching and in research, as was mentioned earlier. Especially when the thin body wall is unpigmented, one may be able to see the three main branches of the digestive cavity, each with numerous side branches. From a point not far from the middle of the body, one main trunk extends forward into the head, and the other two extend backward on either side of the elongated body, which tapers to the rear. The mouth is on the under surface, near the middle of the body, and through the mouth triclads can protrude a long, muscular feeding tube or pharynx.

The fresh-water planarians, the marine ones, and those that live in moist places on land, belong to different suborders. Such correspondence between habitat and classification, were it more general, would greatly simplify the text of a book such as this one. Unfortunately it is very unusual among animals, as is pointed out by Libbie Hyman, the American authority on flatworms, in that volume of her *Treatise on Invertebrates* that deals exhaustively with the group.

Fresh-water planarians favor temperate waters

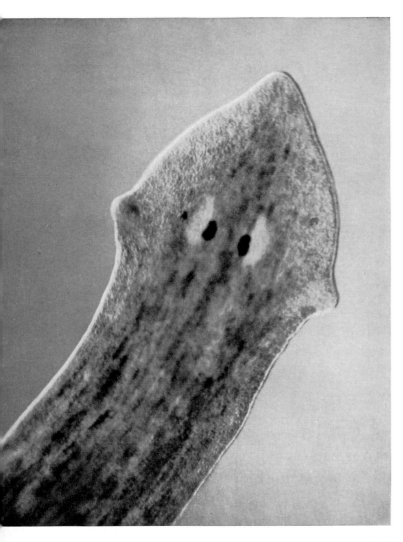

The head of the fresh-water planarian, *Dugesia ti-grina*, shows two pigment-cup eyes and a pair of sensory lobes. (P. S. Tice)

eye. A few planarians have two clusters of tiny eyes; and many are wanting in specialized eyes, though the bodies may be generally sensitive to light.

Planarians can be amusing and undemanding animals to keep and to watch. *Dugesia* (formerly *Euplanaria*), which has many species in Europe, Asia, and the Americas, can be collected in ponds or springs. Almost any spring or spring-fed marsh that supports watercress will have a lively population of worms moving about the vegetation or clinging to the underside of almost any stone one may overturn. A piece of raw meat, beef liver, or fish, strategically placed in such a spring, will bring worms from their hiding places by the hundreds, and they can be seen gliding smoothly upstream to the bait, guided by the meat juices in the current. A few worms can be easily maintained in a small bowl filled with bottled spring water or clear pond water. Tap water in most places is too toxic; and the worms will not flourish in an overheated room. They move about on the bottom and sides of the bowl in a slow glide, with the head bending from side to side as though testing what lies ahead. They will be seen to move toward the dark side of the bowl and to remain whenever possible in contact with some solid surface or film. Planarians do not swim freely through the water, but if they have been moving along the underside of the surface film they will leave the surface by gliding down attached to a strand of mucus. When the worms are not being observed the dish should be kept loosely covered to reduce evaporation and to protect the worms from strong light.

Bits of beef liver are most convenient for feeding many kinds of planarians; the food may be left with the worms for several hours, but then it must be removed, the bowl rinsed, and the water changed. When actively feeding, *Dugesia* extends its agile, tubular pharynx through the mouth opening, near the middle of the under surface. Sucking movements of this feeding tube break up the food into microscopic bits which can be swallowed along with the oozing juices. If unfed for weeks or even months the worms will not die but will use up their reserves and become smaller and smaller.

Dugesia, and several other common genera as well, are noted for multiplying by asexual rupture of the body, usually just behind the region which houses the feeding tube. *Dugesia tigrina,* the commonest species of the United States, breeds sexually only in early spring and summer, fastening its stalked egg capsules under stones. The rest of the year the worms reproduce only by asexual rupture; and in some places *Dugesia* seems to be permanently asexual. Those planarians that multiply by natural rupture have extraordinary powers of regeneration. Almost any piece of moderate size cut from a *Dugesia* will reorganize itself into a complete worm. If the worm

everywhere, and may also be found in cold mountain streams. In the warm waters of the tropics or subtropics they appear to be scarce. Though the usual size range of these worms is from ⅛ of an inch to 1 inch or so long, there are 4-inch planarian giants in Lake Baikal in East Siberia. Common colors are white, gray, brown, or black, sometimes spotted, streaked, or striped. In the most familiar genus, *Dugesia*, the head is triangular with two prominent little sensory lobes that detect chemicals, food, touch, and water currents. Most fresh-water planarians, however, have blunt heads which lack conspicuous lobes, though the sides of the head serve the same sensory functions. *Dugesia* and others have two eyes, each consisting of a pigment cup that shields light-sensitive cells in all directions but one, enabling the animal to respond to the direction of the light that strikes the is cut down the middle of the head and the gash renewed for several days so that the wound is not repaired, there will after a time be two complete heads on the single body.

The familiar white fresh-water planarian of the northeastern United States is *Procotyla fluviatilis,* which has a blunt head; also an adhesive organ, in the center of the front edge, which is used to capture prey. *Procotyla* belongs to the dendrocoelids, most of them white planarians, which are much more abundantly represented in the fresh waters of Europe and Asia.

The marine triclads are found mostly on gravelly or rocky shores in temperate or cold seas, and are known especially from the Mediterranean and Black Seas, though they occur also on other protected shores of the North Atlantic and of Japan. None is yet described from the Pacific coasts of the Americas or from Africa. A well-known marine triclad of the American Atlantic coast is *Bdelloura candida,* shaped something like a spearhead. It clings to the leg bases and gills of the horseshoe crab, feeding on small organisms brought in by the movements of the host. On English shores the commonest triclad is *Procerodes ulvae,* a tiny gray-banded or streaked worm with two eyes on the blunt head, and a broad rear end. It abounds under stones in places where fresh water trickles down a cliff or beach and is known for its ability to endure great changes in the salinity of water.

The land planarians have thoroughly exploited the use of slime as a means of overcoming the hazards of terrestrial life. Their invasion of the land is limited mostly to damp forest floors, where they hide during the heat of day under stones, fallen logs, or leaf mold, coming out only at night to find their prey. They seize, mount upon, and subdue small animals, often even snails or earthworms. Occasionally they turn up in well-watered gardens, where they hide in the daytime under boards or pots. Land triclads are often more brightly colored than their fresh-water relatives. When not uniformly gray, green, brown, or black, they may have black stripes on a yellow or orange ground, or light stripes on a dark ground. A few are blue or violet. Though there are hundreds of tropical and subtropical species, some of these a foot or two long, only a few species live in moist temperate woods or in temperate gardens. Those seen most often in the United States are not native planarians, but tropical ones shipped in with ornamental plants. Transplanted tropical planarians survive briefly in greenhouses or gardens, but usually die out, even in the kindest temperate climates, because they do not become sexually mature. The most successful tropical transplant, perhaps originally from the Indo-Malayan region, is *Bipalium kewense,* named for Kew Gardens near London, where it was first discovered.

Since it reproduces readily by asexual fragmentation, it has become permanently established in gardens in California, Louisiana, Florida, the West Indies, and other subtropical places. Large size (up to 14 inches long), striped pattern, and an expanded half-moon-shaped head edged with numerous minute eyes, make it easy to recognize.

THE POLYCLADS

The polyclads grace marine shores in every part of the world, most of them gliding about on the ocean bottom to seek their prey, or hiding under stones and in damp rocky grottoes when the tide is out. Some tolerate brackishness, but only one species, living in Borneo, is known from fresh water. Though they are named for the multiple branchings of the digestive cavity, most polyclads are instantly recognizable by their broadly oval, extremely flattened, leaflike bodies. Few follow the elongate fashion of triclads. On the whole these are turbellarians of fairly large size,

A planarian flatworm, *Sorocelis americana*, from a Missouri cave. This white dendrocoelid flatworm, with two rows of eyes, has many close relatives in Eurasia. (Ralph Buchsbaum)

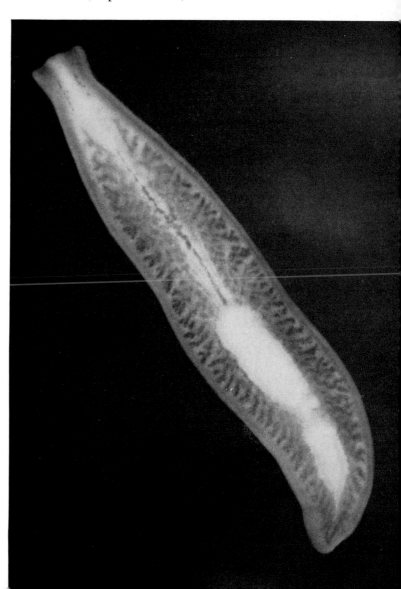

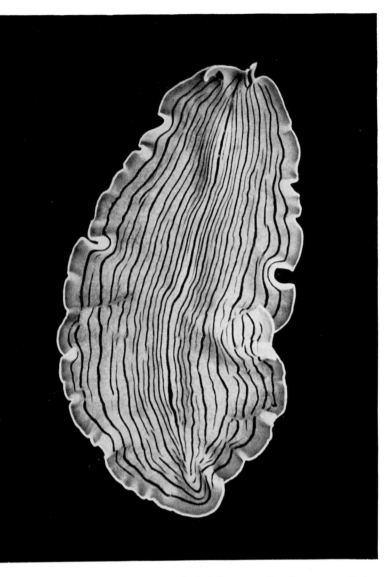

A striped polyclad flatworm, *Prostheceraeus vittatus,* about 1¼ inches long, glides over weeds or under stones on marine shores. The head, at top, bears sensory projections. (England. D. P. Wilson)

often 1 or 2 inches long. Many have a pair of sensory tentacles on the head, and two or more clusters of minute eyes. Numerous eyes may also be scattered over the front end or all or part of the body margin.

Warm-water polyclads, especially those of coral reefs, may be richly colored (Plate 35). Others are striped in strongly contrasting colors. Even many of the white, gray, or brown ones of temperate waters delight the eye with their translucency, their elegantly ruffled edges, and their graceful undulations when they take off on a brief swim through the water. Pelagic species, which drift or swim, are usually transparent or translucent and are found down to three thousand feet, as well as at the surface. Some

live in the open sea only by clinging to floating sargassum seaweed. None of the polyclads is a parasite, though a number are supposedly harmless commensals, like *Hoploplana inquilina,* which lives in the mantle chamber of the big marine snail *Busycon,* on the American Atlantic coast. The oyster leech, *Stylochus frontalis,* does serious damage to oyster beds in Florida, and it has close relatives that prey on oysters of both American coasts. Some members of its family are the largest American polyclads, broad worms over 2 inches long.

The Flukes *(Class Trematoda)*

The flukes take their Anglo-Saxon common name from their flat shape, and the technical name of the group comes from the Greek word *trema,* "a hole," which refers to the cavity of the suckers by which these small, often leaflike, exclusively parasitic worms attach to their human or other vertebrate hosts. Some have sharp hooks to supplement their suckers or other adhesive organs. The adults have lost the ciliated epidermis, the outer layer of cells that covers their turbellarian relatives. In its place is a thin cuticle secreted by underlying cells. Flukes, also called trematodes, are structurally simple in most respects, but the reproductive system, which occupies most of the animal's interior, is something else again. In complexity it equals any to be found in the higher animals, and its efficiency makes these lowly parasites truly formidable contenders for man's blood and other living tissues.

THE MONOGENETIC FLUKES

The monogenetic flukes are so labeled because they have a simple life history, with only one host. Of about seven hundred species described up to now, most are external parasites that live on the gills, or sometimes on the skin, of both fresh-water and marine fishes, feeding on the external covering layer or on oozing blood. In nature they seldom do much harm. But when man steps into the picture, providing special fish hatcheries where young fishes are raised in dense concentrations, these external flukes can cause serious losses of fish.

Hanging onto the outside of a fast-moving fish is not accomplished without a really tenacious hold, and *Gyrodactylus* fastens onto the gills of its hosts with a well-developed adhesive disk at the rear end. The center of the disk has two or four large hooks, and its periphery is bordered with small hooks. As they loop about on the surface of the host, external flukes inevitably stray occasionally into the cavities which connect with the exterior: the mouth, the nasal cavities, and the urinary bladder. In the course of much time, some of the monogenetic flukes have be-

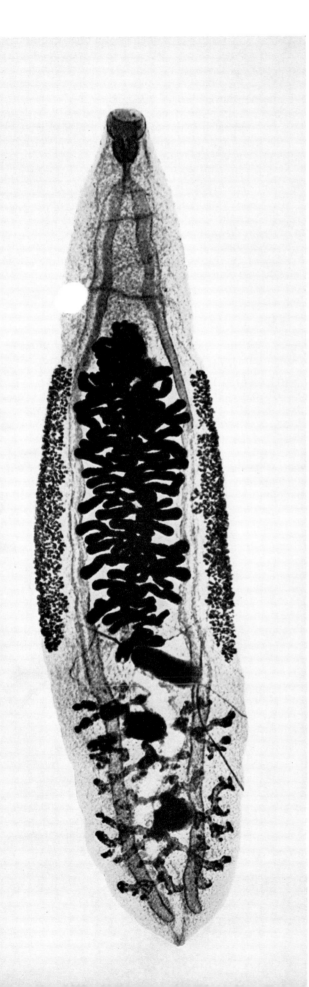

come adapted to living in the shelter of these cavities in fishes, amphibians, and aquatic reptiles. *Polystoma* hangs on with a rear disk equipped with six large suckers. The different species live, as larvae, on the gills of frog tadpoles; the adults of *Polystoma* are found in the urinary bladder of amphibians and also in the bladder, nose, and mouth of turtles.

THE DIGENETIC FLUKES

The digenetic flukes, as their name implies, have complex life histories involving two or more hosts. Typically they have four larval stages and live successively in three or even four hosts. As adults they are internal parasites of practically every kind of vertebrate—fresh-water, marine, and terrestrial. The larval worms live in snails, fishes, and other small animals. So large is this group of parasites, and so varied in structure and habit, that it can barely be touched on here. The five thousand or so known species are added to constantly. Details must be sought in zoological textbooks or in specialized books on parasitology suggested in the bibliography.

Adults of the digenetic flukes live mostly in the vertebrate intestine or in organs that connect with it, such as the liver. The Chinese liver fluke, *Opisthorchis (Clonorchis) sinensis,* occupies the bile passages of the human liver, causing serious anemia and liver disease from Japan and Korea through China to Indochina and India. The adult fluke is about ¾ of an inch long, and has two suckers, one at the front end surrounding the mouth, one a short distance back from the first. As in many flukes, the digestive tube rather promptly forks into two long digestive sacs with blind ends. The flattened baglike body is stuffed mostly with reproductive organs, and covered on the outside with a cuticle that resists digestion by the host. Hundreds or even thousands may obstruct the ducts of one host, shedding fertilized eggs that pass from the liver into the intestine and out with the feces. If it reaches fresh water, as is commonly the case, the egg may be eaten by an aquatic snail of a species favorable to the growth of the parasite. Within such a snail the egg hatches and the parasite develops through three larval stages, two of which multiply asexually. Finally a fourth stage, the cercaria, which has the two suckers and the forked intestine of the adult but has also a long tail, escapes from the snail in large numbers and swims about actively. On encountering fishes of certain species, the cercarias penetrate into the flesh and encyst there.

The Chinese human liver fluke, *Opisthorchis (Clonorchis) sinensis,* is about ½ inch long. The front sucker, the muscular sucking pharynx, the two-branched digestive tract, and both male and female sex organs show in this stained preparation. (General Biological Supply House)

[125

Since fish are commonly eaten raw in the countries where *Opisthorchis* occurs, the young flukes emerge unharmed into the human intestine, make their way up the bile duct to the smaller bile passages, there attach by their suckers, and feed on blood.

Another well-known liver fluke is *Fasciola hepatica,* whose cercarias leave the snail host and encyst on grasses and other vegetation in nearly all parts of the world. It thrives best in the dense concentrations of hosts provided by man's herding of cattle, sheep, and goats, and it may also be found in pigs, horses, and many wild animals. In some countries it finds its way into man by means of cercarias that cling to wild watercress.

Far more serious as a human problem is the blood fluke, *Schistosoma,* referred to in the introductory part of this chapter. A member of one of the several families of elongated flukes that live in the blood vessels of fishes, turtles, birds, and mammals, *Schistosoma* differs from the liver flukes not only in shape but in some other ways. For one thing, this fluke occurs as separate males and females, and the sides of the male fold over to form a groove in which the even longer and more slender female is held. Three widespread species debilitate an estimated 114,000,000 people. *Schistosoma haematobium* infects primarily the small veins of the urinary system and is found in much of Africa, the Middle East, and part of Portugal. *Schistosoma mansoni,* which occupies small intestinal veins, spreads misery in most of Africa, in South America from Brazil to Venezuela, and in some of the West Indies. *Schistosoma japonicum,* also a parasite of intestinal veins, accounts for an estimated 46,000,000 cases in Japan, China, the Celebes, and some of the Philippine islands.

For each of the three species of flukes there are particular species of fresh-water snails that serve as hosts to the larval stages. The fork-tailed cercarias that emerge from the snail burrow through human skin or are taken in with drinking water. Wherever schistosomes that infect man are prevalent it is hazardous to drink untreated water, or to bathe, wade in, or dip the arms in fresh waters. Millions of Chinese and Japanese become infected during the planting of rice as they stand bare-legged in flooded rice fields. In recent years the extension of irrigation systems in Africa and in the Near East has steadily multiplied the habitats for fresh-water snails, speeding the increase of this serious disease despite many control measures.

The temperate and more sanitary parts of the world are not free of blood flukes, for wherever suitable snail hosts occur, there may be swimming cercarias of some kind of schistosome. The adults often live in wild birds, especially ducks. Though the cercarias of bird schistosomes do not reach the human liver, their penetration of the skin causes a skin irritation known as "swimmer's itch." Repeated exposures may so sensitize an individual that he becomes prostrate and develops a severe rash. Swimmer's itch is especially serious in certain lakes in the north-central United States, but many other fresh-water and marine shores are affected. Chandler's *Introduction to Parasitology* lists as victims of swimmer's itch: vacationers in Quebec and New England west to Manitoba and Oregon, carp-breeders in Germany, rice-growers in Japan and Malaya, lake bathers in Australia and New Zealand—also sea bathers and clam-diggers on the American North Atlantic and Florida coasts, fishermen in San Salvador, and naturalists on the rocky shores of southern California and Mexico. Wherever bathers are aware of this annoyance they should wipe the skin dry immediately after leaving the water, and should avoid getting alternately wet and dry by playing in shallow water.

The Tapeworms (*Class Cestoda*)

The cestodes, named from the Greek word for "girdle" or "ribbon," are mostly long, flattened, opaque white or yellowish ribbon-like parasites. The adults live inside vertebrates, almost always in the intestine, but the larval stages develop in either vertebrate or invertebrate hosts. The life cycle is complex, involving one or two intermediate hosts in addition to the vertebrate "final host" that nurtures the adult.

Aside from the enormous length, 50 feet or more, attained by some tapeworms, their most notable feature is a complete lack of a mouth or any digestive apparatus. The body is covered with a protective cuticle, as in flukes, and the worms absorb much of their nutrition directly through the body wall from the intestinal contents of the host.

The scolex is a very small knob at the narrow or front end of the long body, and it bears the only organs of attachment. These may be suckers, hooks, or sometimes glandular adhesive areas. Behind the scolex there is usually a short, narrow, undivided neck region or growing region, and from this there is a constant budding off of body segments. Those closest to the neck are smallest and youngest, those farthest away the largest and most mature. Thus the chain of segments represents every stage of development, and widens gradually along the body's length.

Tapeworms have no specialized sense organs, not even the poor ones seen in turbellarians and in some flukes, though the body wall, especially that of the scolex, is well supplied with sensory cells. These worms are all business, and their energies are channeled into a prodigious reproductive effort which insures that a sufficient number of the young will find new hosts and keep the species going.

Not all tapeworms are divided into segments like the typical forms. There are undivided ones, which look more like flukes, but the distinction is not as fundamental as was once thought, and the two subclasses are based on other characters. The subclass Cestodaria includes forms with an undivided body and a ten-hooked larva, that live in the body cavity and intestine of lower fishes. The subclass Eucestoda, in which the larva has six hooks, comprises a few undivided forms and all the typical segmented tapeworms, including those few described here.

The beef tapeworm, *Taenia saginata,* maintains its place in the human intestine, despite the constant movement of materials in that active organ, by means of four suckers on the scolex. As in many other tapeworms, the male sex organs start to grow first and appear most prominent in the younger segments; both sets of organs are well developed in middle segments; and toward the most mature region the segments are nothing but little bags stuffed with eggs that have already begun to develop into embryos. The fully ripe segments, loaded with embryos, detach from the worm and pass out with the feces onto the ground or onto vegetation. As cattle graze they may ingest shelled embryos, and in the bovine intestine the eggshell is digested off and the six-hooked embryo is released to burrow its way through the intestinal wall and into a blood vessel. Carried by the blood to the muscles, the embryo remains there and grows into a sac or bladder which sprouts from its inner wall the inverted future head of the tapeworm. When man eats raw or undercooked beef the enclosing bladder is digested off, and the head everts and attaches to the human intestinal wall by means of the suckers.

Meat inspection has greatly reduced the incidence of beef tapeworms in Western countries; but though the bladders of this tapeworm are almost ½ of an inch long, they can easily be overlooked in the routine inspection of the jaw muscles and the heart, the parts of the cow usually examined by official meat inspectors. It is best to avoid raw or seriously underdone beef. Where sanitation is poor, as in Africa, or in countries where meat is broiled in large chunks, much of the population is infected. Among the Hindus of India, who have religious restrictions against eating beef, a diagnosis of beef tapeworm may be embarrassing to the patient; or when due to mistaken diagnosis through confusion with other tapeworm eggs that show six hooks, it can be deeply insulting to the patient as well as rather embarrassing to the physician.

The pork tapeworm, *Taenia solium,* which has a crown of hooks on the scolex in addition to the suckers, is likewise rare among Jews and Moslems. Though the bladderworms are common in pigs, the adult in humans is rare in the United States, more common in parts of Europe where pork is eaten without thorough cooking.

The largest and most injurious tapeworm that parasitizes man is the broad fish tapeworm, *Dibothriocephalus latus* (formerly *Diphyllobothrium latum*), a monster up to 55 feet long, with three to four thousand segments. In man it usually averages from 15 to 20 feet long. For centuries it has infected central Europe, and now occurs in 20 per cent of Finns and almost 100 per cent of the population of certain Baltic

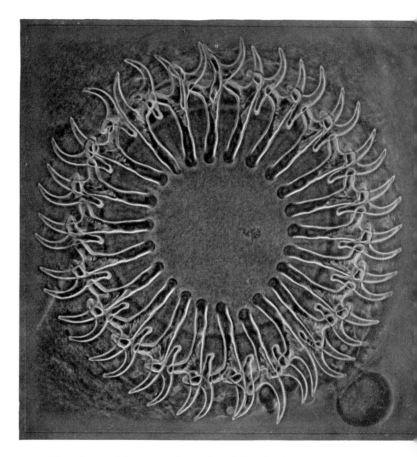

The circlet of hooks on the scolex of the dog tapeworm, *Taenia pisiformis,* as seen by darkfield photomicrography. (Montana. W. C. Marquardt)

areas. It may be found also in such places as Ireland, Palestine, Uganda in Africa, Siberia, Japan, and Chile. In North America it is known from Michigan, Minnesota, Wyoming, Manitoba, Alaska, and even Florida. Long thought to have been brought to the Great Lakes region by lumbermen from northern Europe, this tapeworm may also have come with Asians over the Bering Straits; or it may have been well established in fish-eating wild carnivores, like the brown bear, before man's arrival. In addition to man and the bear, it has been reported also in the dog, cat, fox, and others. The life history involves two intermediate hosts. The eggs must reach water and must be eaten by copepods (tiny crustaceans), which in turn must be eaten by one of a variety of fishes. In the Great Lakes region northern pike and pickerel are most commonly infected, as are also the sauger and yellow perch. Since this region ships great quantities of fish to other localities, the tapeworm has been widely spread. One should therefore not taste raw lake fish during food preparations, or eat smoked fish from infected regions unless it is known to be adequately treated.

Common in the great cattle- and sheep-raising regions of the world, especially in Africa, the Middle East, Australia, and South America, is *Echinococcus granulosus,* which passes its adult life in dogs and doglike animals but usually develops as a larva in herbivorous animals. The eggs may be passed by the lickings of a friendly dog to the hands and face of man, from where they can reach his mouth. Though the adult is minute in this case, the larva (developing into what is called a hydatid cyst) can grow, in the human liver, to the size of a grapefruit or larger. When one or more of these cysts develops in the human brain, the results can be very serious or fatal.

The dwarf mouse tapeworm, *Hymenolepis nana,* is the smallest adult tapeworm found in man, but it makes up for its small size by large numbers, perhaps hundreds or thousands in one person. The greater the number present, however, the smaller they grow, so that in heavy infestations they are only about 1 inch long. World-wide in distribution, this is the commonest tapeworm of the southern United States, where it infects from 1 to 2 per cent of the population, especially children. Though different from almost all other tapeworms in being able to complete its life cycle in a single host, such as man, the rat, or the mouse, it can revert to ancestral habits and use fleas or flour beetles as intermediate hosts. Usually people ingest the eggs by contamination with human feces or in food containing mouse droppings.

CHAPTER VI

The Ribbon Worms

(Phylum Nemertea)

THE smallest of these soft, elongated, mostly marine worms may be threadlike and only a fraction of an inch long. The giants of the group, however, are the longest, though certainly not among the largest, of invertebrates. Exactly how long it is difficult to say, for all the ribbon worms are highly elastic, and the really long ones stretch out, threadlike, for yards and yards—some say much more than 30 yards in *Lineus longissimus,* the blackish brown worm of the North Sea. The English call it the "bootlace worm." Modest length, not more than about 8 inches, is more usual. The body may be cylindrical, as in *Lineus,* though more often flattened on both sides or flattened below and convex above.

Bright colorings of orange, red, purple, or green, these mostly on the upper surfaces, may betray the worms to the eyes of naturalists scanning rocky crevices or overturned stones at low tide. More often the colors blend with red or green algae or other colorful growths among which the worms live. To find small nemerteans, collectors place masses of seaweed or of bryozoan colonies that resemble delicate seaweed in dishes of sea water and let the small worms creep out on the walls of the dishes, where they can easily be seen. Some worms are white or yellowish, others somber grays or browns, but many are handsomely patterned with strongly contrasting rings or longitudinal stripes or both. The front end is not set off as

a distinct head, though the tip may be expanded and have colored markings, several or numerous eyes, and sensory grooves, which make it look superficially like a head. The rear end is more or less pointed.

Another common name, proboscis worm, less widely used, calls attention to the most distinctive feature of nemerteans. This is a long, extensible, tubular proboscis that can be shot out the front end with explosive force to grasp prey or discourage enemies. The proboscis coils about the prey, holding it firmly and entangling it in sticky mucus which may be irritating or even poisonous. The proboscis is also everted as a device for burrowing in sand or mud or for attaching to objects as an aid in creeping about. It can be made to evert by irritating the animal, by plunging it into fresh water, or by placing it in a small dish of sea water and cautiously adding alcohol, drop by drop. The accurate aim of the proboscis receives recognition in the technical name of the phylum, Nemertea, from a Greek word that means "unerring." In some of the commonest worms the tip of the proboscis is armed with a sharp spike or stylet, which pierces the prey, sometimes several times, before a toxic secretion is poured on. Worms may have two or more pouches with a reserve supply of stylets, so that replacement can be made quickly if the main one is damaged. When not in use the proboscis is

The bootlace worm, *Lineus longissimus,* a fragile nemertean that is often many yards long. At low tide it hides under rocks or in the holdfasts of kelps. (England. M. A. Wilson)

sheathed in a muscular tube that lies above the digestive tract.

As it goes on mostly at night, feeding is not often observed. The favored food seems to be annelids, and these have been seen to be swallowed whole, making a prominent bulge in the thin, elastic body of the nemertean. Mollusks, crustaceans, and fishes are also eaten, though bigger prey may be sucked at, not downed in one piece. Undigested residues do not have to be cast out the mouth, for the nemerteans are the lowest animals that have an anus, a second opening to the digestive tract, which voids materials from the rear end of the animal. The ribbon worms are built much like flatworms, but aside from the anus they can boast another important improvement. They

have contractile blood vessels. Waves of contraction in the strong muscles of the body wall also help to push blood and food along their respective tubes, and in a worm at rest it is these powerful muscular waves that are seen to pass along the body.

A few ribbon worms swim by undulations of the long body. The young and the smaller forms glide along, by means of beating cilia on the body surface, over a lubricating bed of secreted slime. In larger worms more use is made of muscular contractions for creeping. Some even spiral ahead at times by agile body contortions.

One may grasp several inches of a delicate, slimy nemertean and pull cautiously lest it break, yet have it slip from one's fingers and disappear down a crack in the rock. Worms that do break in escaping from would-be captors, human or animal, almost always replace a missing rear end; and certain species can regenerate a whole worm from any fragment that contains a portion of one of the lateral nerve cords. As in flatworms, the capacity for regeneration goes with the natural capacity of certain species for reproducing asexually by fragmentation of the body, especially during warm months. A large specimen of *Lineus socialis,* which lives gregariously under stones on the American Atlantic coast (or of *Lineus vegetus* on the west coast), may fragment into six to twenty or more pieces. After transforming into complete worms of smaller size, these grow again and later reproduce sexually. Most though not all ribbon worms are of separate sexes. The eggs are usually laid in gelatinous strings or masses, and the young hatch as juvenile worms. In some species of *Lineus,* in *Cerebratulus,* and in some of their relatives, the egg hatches as a gelatinous, helmet-shaped, free-swimming little larva, called a pilidium. It must feed on microscopic organisms and develop further before it takes on the structure of the adult.

For the most part, ribbon worms are bottom dwellers on temperate marine shores, where they burrow in mud or sand or creep about among rocks and seaweeds between tide marks or in shallow waters. Only a few burrow into the deep-sea bottom, sometimes at depths of forty-five hundred feet or more. Of some 570 described species, nearly 200 are found along the Atlantic or Mediterranean shores of Europe. About 100 live on the Pacific coast of North America, at least 18 of them identical or very similar to European species. The Atlantic coast of North America has few more than 50 known species, and W. R. Coe, the American authority on nemerteans, thought this was due to the cold arctic current that comes close to the coast as far south as Cape Hatteras, for many of the missing genera are warm-temperate forms. Almost 30 species are described from Japanese shores. In the open seas, chiefly the southern parts of the North Atlantic, there are nearly 60 gelatinous species that drift or swim slowly far below the surface. They have been brought up from depths ranging from six hundred to nine thousand feet, most from below three thousand feet. Nemerteans are less common in tropical or subtropical seas, but well represented in arctic and antarctic waters, often by the familiar temperate genera: *Lineus, Amphiporus, Cerebratulus,* and *Tetrastemma.*

Perhaps the most cosmopolitan species is *Lineus ruber,* found from Siberia to South Africa. The slender, rounded body is 3 to 9 inches long; and different varieties are colored red, green, or brown, any of them difficult to see in natural surroundings, even when one has lifted the stone under which the worm lives.

Fresh waters, especially in northern latitudes, harbor species of the genus *Prostoma.* What seems to be a single species, *Prostoma rubrum,* a slender reddish worm less than 1 inch long, can be found in pools and quiet streams in nearly all parts of the United States. It clings to the leaves of aquatic plants and feeds on minute crustaceans, nematodes, and turbellarians. In Europe this genus has also an eyeless variant that lives in caves.

Land nemerteans are all of the genus *Geonemertes.* The two best-known species are slender, pale in color, and not more than 2 inches long. By exploiting the nemertean talent for copious secretion of slime, land nemerteans manage to live along marine shores, in moist earth, or under foliage and fallen logs, in such places as Bermuda, Australia, New Zealand, and many South Pacific islands. In the Seychelles, *Geonemertes arboricola* occupies the leaf bases of a screw pine (*Pandanus*) tree, often living high in the tree.

A common nemertean of the American Pacific coast, *Amphiporus bimaculatus,* that has many relatives on other shores. It is short (up to 6 inches) and broad for a ribbon worm. (Ralph Buchsbaum)

Only *Carcinonemertes* has been classed as a parasite. It lives on the gills of various crabs when it is young, and then moves to the egg masses, both feeding on the eggs and living as a commensal by eating any small animals it can find as it clings to its host. Adults of *Carcinonemertes carcinophila* are about 1 inch long and orange- or brick-red.

Commensal nemerteans live mostly in tunicates, sponges, or bivalves, sharing the food in the host's feeding currents. Common in the mantle cavity of various clams on European and both American coasts is *Malacobdella grossa,* a short, white, thick worm, with an adhesive disk at the rear. It creeps in leechlike fashion. The genus to which it belongs constitutes a separate order of nemerteans.

The other three orders contain all the more typical elongated worms; they are distinguished from each other mostly by internal characters, such as the arrangement of the muscle layers. The paleonemerteans, with an unarmed proboscis, include such forms as *Tubulanus,* species of which are shown in Plate 37 and below. Also with unarmed proboscis are the heteronemerteans, among them *Lineus* and *Cerebratulus.* The latter is a very large, firm, and flattened worm which lives in burrows in sand or mud and swims actively through the water. The hoplonemerteans, with an armed proboscis, are divided into two suborders. In one the members have at the tip of the proboscis a single stylet, a straight or curved thorn which pierces and holds prey. These include many quite common shore forms such as *Amphiporus;* the very slender *Emplectonema,* found among mussels and barnacles on pilings; and *Paranemertes peregrina* of the American west coast, often a rich purple on the upper surface. The parasitic or commensal *Carcinonemertes* belongs here, as do various commensal species, the fresh-water forms, and also the land nemerteans. In the second suborder, members have on the tip of the proboscis not one large stylet but a large number of minute ones. These worms include some shore species, but most float or swim in the open sea far below the surface. Many are broad, flattened worms, of yellow, orange, pink, or red hues. The drifting types are quite gelatinous, the swimming ones equipped with tail and sometimes also with side fins.

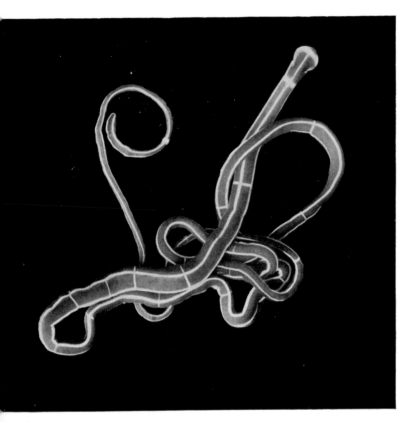

Tubulanus annulatus, a long, slender ribbon worm common on European shores, may be several feet long. It lives in a mucous tube under stones or in crevices at low shore levels. (Rupert Riedl and Encyclopaedia Britannica Films)

CHAPTER VII

A Variety of Animal Groups

In the animal kingdom are a number of small groups whose members have charms for people with the most observant eyes or a special curiosity and persistence for seeking out animals of small size, few species, or unobtrusive habits.

All of these descriptions apply to members of the phylum Mesozoa. They are minute ciliated worms found living as parasites in the kidneys of squids and octopuses, clinging to the walls of tubes while their elongate bodies float freely in the urine. Mesozoans parasitize many other invertebrates, finding homes in the tissues and body cavities. Their habits remind us of protozoans, but their bodies are multicellular—more like the two-layered little planula larvae of coelenterates. It is tempting to think of mesozoans as being transitional between these groups, and this temptation has led to the phylum name. Probably they are degenerate in their simplicity, degraded by parasitism, but they still appear to be the simplest of multicellular animals—simpler than any flatworm or coelenterate.

Quite another kind of group is the Phylum Nematoda, enormously abundant, and with great numbers of species, and boasting among its members some of man's most loyal companions, though they can hardly be called friends. Nematodes are included here only because they are thought to be related to five of the small groups that follow them immediately in this chapter. The six groups are often lumped together as six classes of a superphylum, Aschelminthes, but the evidences for doing this, or for separating the six from certain other phyla in this chapter, are too technical to be given here. Instead, each group is awarded separate status as a phylum with a distinct body plan.

The Roundworms

(Phylum Nematoda)

The cost of minimizing one's enemies always runs high, and we are now paying dearly for having so long underestimated the prevalence and powers of roundworms. The big ascarids that live in the human intestine were well known to the ancient Egyptians, as one can hardly ignore a foot-long worm that slips out with excrement when it dies, or one that may go astray and suddenly emerge from a nostril. In our own day ascarids are widespread in the world, including Europe and the Americas, especially in warm, moist areas. In the mountainous parts of the southeastern United States, clay soil, a mild, rainy climate, dense shade, and the habits of small children, dogs, and pigs combine to spread and protect *Ascaris* eggs in the dooryards where children play, and from where they carry the eggs into their homes. In hot, dry climates, especially from Arabia to India, the 4-foot guinea worms that lie coiled under the surface of the skin are even harder to overlook. Very likely these are the same as the "fiery serpents" that plagued the Israelites in biblical times.

Every species of vertebrate that is examined turns out to harbor nematode parasites, and there are two billion estimated cases of human infection, not much less than the total number of people in the world. Roundworms as huge as ascarids and guinea worms are very exceptional, but parasitic forms are generally larger than the free-living ones. These last are much more numerous and barely visible to the naked eye. Magnified, they look like animated bits of fine sewing thread, hence the phylum name, Nematoda, which means "threadlike." Free-living roundworms are inconceivably abundant in moist soils, present even in deserts and on mountain tops, common in all fresh waters, found in hot springs and arctic ice pools, living in every sea from pole to pole. Yet small size and transparency kept them unseen until after the discovery of the microscope. They find their own food, steadily devouring bacteria or small animals and plants of soil and water. Their teeming numbers and their versatility were noted by nineteenth-century zoologists.

In 1881 a German investigator, seeking to find out why sugar beets, a mainstay of German agriculture, seemed suddenly "to tire" of any soil in which they had grown for many successive years, traced the trouble to parasitic "eelworms." At first the study of soil nematodes parasitic in plants grew very slowly. Beginning in the 1940's, however, Western countries have been greatly stepping up their efforts at nematode research, having suddenly begun to appreciate the ways in which modern farming methods have intensified the competition between man and the nematodes for large agricultural crops. Parasites are usually highly specialized, able to live on only one or a few closely related species of host, so that originally soil nematodes found their wild plant host sparse and widely scattered. Then man discovered agriculture —how to grow edible plants in such dense concentrations as to make it worth while for the big human animal to feed on even the smallest grains.

Nematode head with hooks (top) and whole worm

The nematode threat must have grown slowly through the centuries, until recent methods for planting vast acreages to the same crop, and the explosive expansion of the human species, created unlimited horizons for nematode hangers-on. Though roundworms parasitic in man share only a small part of his food after he digests it, the soil nematodes parasitic in plants take more than a tenth of the crops grown by American farmers, for example, even before the harvest. The damage in the United States is estimated at $500,000,000 each year; in Great Britain the annual loss of potatoes alone is judged to cost about £2,000,000. Since the worms increase with the years and with crop size, the best remedy is crop rotation to deny the nematodes access to their host. Much of what was in the past attributed to soil exhaustion, to be cured by crop rotation, was in reality nematode damage, especially by those nematodes that pierce plant roots and suck the juices. The plant symptoms are wilting, stunted growth, leaf discoloration, and root swellings or galls—none of these specific to nematode infestation or always easy to tell from losses due to drought or a lack of soil nutrients. Our concentration on methods for treating these last problems has delayed appreciation of the role of parasitic worms.

Lists of animal numbers usually credit the nematodes with about ten thousand known species. The true number of existing species is estimated to be about five hundred thousand—second only to the insects. The discrepancy is easily explained. The larger number takes into account all the as yet unexamined but highly specialized parasites of many thousands of vertebrates, invertebrates, and plants, plus all the free-living forms, judged to outnumber the parasites. Nematodes are typically minute, cylindrical, tapered at both ends, covered with a tough cuticle that is transparent or translucent; they usually thrash about in a way that immediately identifies them to the eye, and they look so much alike, even under the microscope, that the job of distinguishing and naming so many superficially similar species makes even the experts stand back.

Nematodes used to be studied either as parasites or as free-living worms, and students of one group often paid scant attention to the other. Since the habits of nematodes, like those of most animals, do not necessarily correspond to the evolutionary relationships on which classification must rest, the grouping of these worms has had recently to undergo extensive repairs in order to combine the two kinds of worms. For details one may refer to Volume III of the treatise by Hyman, to the specialized volumes on nematodes by the Chitwoods, or to Chandler's very readable text on parasitology. Here we shall merely present some points about roundworms in general and then go on to discuss a few kinds of worms of special interest.

Nematodes occur in two general forms. The really long, threadlike ones, that have hardly any taper, are greatly outnumbered by the shorter spindle-shaped forms, which taper markedly to blunt or slender tips, the rear end often the more tapering and pointed. Especially in the minute forms, the animal is colorless and the cuticle is transparent, putting the internal organs on full display. Or the cuticle is translucent and lends a whitish or yellowish cast. There are no cilia, outside or in, and in parasitic forms the cuticle is often very smooth; but it may be finely striated, or bear bristles, spines, ridges, or other markings and expansions. The mouth is at the front tip, surrounded by little sensory lips, which may also be muscular and used in sucking. Just inside the mouth there may be cutting ridges, teeth, or piercing stylets for puncturing plant or animal prey. Beyond these there is usually a short muscular pharynx that sucks food into the intestine. The sexes are almost always separate; and the smaller male bears special equipment at his slightly curved rear end. The stiff cuticle and the lack of any but lengthwise muscles permit only serpentine undulations for swimming or gliding, crawling when assisted by body bristles or other devices, and in microscopic worms a kind of thrashing about, which in open water leads nowhere. Among aquatic plant debris, in sand or mud, in soil, or in the fluids or tissues of a host, friction against solid particles may help the whiplike contortions to move minute worms along or enable them to explore their surroundings.

Marine nematodes are on the whole the largest of the free-living forms; some are nearly 2 inches long. They turn up in any sample of shore sand or mud, but especially in soft muds full of the microscopic plants and organic debris on which they feed. On such bottoms they are the most numerous of all multicellular animals. A handful of muck could easily contain many thousands of individuals of fifty or more species. Even in antarctic waters a thimbleful of bottom material will teem with hundreds of nematodes of species common almost anywhere. The record depth for bottom-living nematodes is more than 21,000 feet.

Fresh-water forms are also widely distributed, being carried about by currents, by wading birds and other animals, or by drifting plants. They occur in still or running water, but are most abundant on the shores of lakes, where they favor stony or muddy or plant-invaded bottoms. Some have hollow stylets and suck plant juices; others are feeders on decaying particles; many are voracious feeders on protozoans, on other nematodes, or on their little relatives, the rotifers and gastrotrichs, discussed later in this chapter. Nematodes able to survive in hot and sulphur springs in Germany are of the same or closely related genera as those found in Yellowstone Park in the United States or in hot springs in China. Those of swift or tumbling mountain streams are able to fasten by sticky secretions from glands at the tail tip, and such adhesive glands occur in most free-living nematodes, though not in the parasitic ones.

Land nematodes are spread about by winds and plants and other animals, almost like protozoans, and indeed they are similarly suited for wide dispersal of the same common species by their small size and habit of resisting drying when in an inert state. Some species, however, have very specific niches, and the one most often pointed out is *Turbatrix silusiae,* described from the felt mats on which beer-drinkers set their mugs in Silesia, in Germany. A relative, *Turbatrix aceti,* long called the vinegar eel, feeds on the organisms that form the "mother" of naturally fermenting vinegar.

The mermithid nematodes, such as *Mermis* above, are long, threadlike worms that taper less than typical members and are often mistaken for the hairworms described later in this chapter. They do, however, taper more than the hairworms. The adults are from a few to 20 inches long, and are found in soil,

sometimes in water, but do not feed. The juvenile stages are parasitic in insects, often in grasshoppers or crickets, feeding on all the organs as they grow to adult worms and then emerge. Mermithid damage to insects should be of some consolation to farmers, beset as they are with nematodes harmful to crops.

The free-living soil nematodes have been carefully estimated in Danish soils, where grassland may teem with almost 2,000,000 worms per square foot, and cultivated soils with up to 200,000 worms in the same area. For most species 90 per cent of them can

Mermis, a mermithid nematode worm. (Pennsylvania. Ralph Buchsbaum)

be found in the top two inches of soil, and none below four inches. Some soil nematodes have been reported, however, down to a depth of twenty-five feet. The smaller ones, perhaps only $\frac{1}{50}$ of an inch in length, feed on bacteria and small algae. The larger ones with teeth or grinding devices feed on protozoans, rotifers, and other nematodes. To gather them for microscopic examination one needs to put fresh garden soil in a piece of cheesecloth and set it in a funnel stopped by rubber tubing and a clamp. When the funnel is filled with water, the nematodes wriggle downward into the stem and collect there. After some hours the water in the stem can be run into a glass dish.

The parasitic soil nematodes, referred to near the beginning of this chapter, spend the active part of their lives in plant hosts, but many have inert cysts that have been known to survive in soil for many years, one as long as thirty-nine years. Attempts to control their depredations range from crop rotation to chemical fumigation, flooding of the soil, or encouraging the growth of fungi that trap nematodes. None of these methods is completely successful. The sugar beet eelworm, *Heterodera schachtii,* referred to earlier as the first nematode known to infest crops, is restricted to the roots of a few plant species. The potato-root eelworm, *Heterodera rostochiensis,* also attacks tomatoes, and it causes great losses from Ireland and Great Britain to Germany and most of western Europe except Norway. The root-knot nematodes, said to be a number of distinct species of the genus *Meloidogyne,* infect nearly a thousand varieties of plants, at least seventy-five of them garden and field crops, fruit and shade trees. These are mostly warm-climate nematodes, but under glass they flourish anywhere. In England they do great damage to tomatoes and cucumbers in commercial greenhouses unless controlled by steam sterilization, an effective method where the soil used is limited in quantity.

Man's struggle with parasitic roundworms was recorded about 1550 B.C. in the Ebers Papyrus, named for the archaeologist who made the first translation. Found in 1872 in a tomb in the Nile valley near Thebes, the papyrus is a collection of remedies against the various diseases that harassed the ancient Egyptians. To "expel the roundworm in his belly," it advises the physician to try thirty-two different recipes, with ingredients ranging from pomegranate roots and red ochre to turpentine and goose fat. Old Chinese writings, one from 217 A.D., speak of "the long worm," 5 to 6 inches or up to 1 foot in length. The size and symptoms are those of *Ascaris lumbricoides,* which may even reach 14 inches. It is thought that man picked up this long-time companion when he started to domesticate pigs, and in the process also domesticated his own human strain of worms. The ones that attack man and pig look identical, but they do not readily exchange hosts. Nevertheless, both pigs and dogs ingest the eggs of the human parasite and help to spread them about to small children playing outdoors. Prevention of infection with *Ascaris* eggs must begin with sanitary disposal of human feces and with teaching young children to wash their hands before eating. Even in parts of the world where human feces are used as fertilizer to grow leafy vegetables, the most important source of infection is direct contamination through the hands. Though a female *Ascaris* may lay 200,000 eggs daily, many hazards beset the eggs: drying, too high or too low temperatures, and the sanitary plumbing or

sometimes cleanly habits of men. When the shelled eggs do find their way back to the mouth, they already contain young larvae, and these hatch in the intestine, burrow into blood vessels, and are carried to liver, heart, and lungs. In the lungs they take hold, make their way back to the trachea and throat, and down to the intestine again, this time arriving with size and health improved by travel. They bite the intestinal wall, sucking in tissue juices, and also taking the digested food of the host. Most of the really serious damage is done by the young worms as they travel, but even the adult is a very unreliable parasite. It may puncture the intestinal wall or wander up the bile duct, with fatal results.

The trichina worm, *Trichinella spiralis,* is much less widespread in the world, and almost entirely absent from the tropical regions that have more than their share of other parasitic worms. In arctic regions it is common among Eskimos, and it does occur to some extent in Mexico and temperate South America. But chiefly it is a parasite of Europe and the United States, where it is encouraged in its efforts to keep going by the habit of feeding garbage, which usually contains pork scraps, to pigs. Wherever garbage is fed to pigs as a method of disposal in larger American cities, the incidence of trichinosis is high. In the United States this applies chiefly to the North Atlantic seaboard and to California. Many of the most serious cases are concentrated among people who enjoy various kinds of raw sausage and who make it themselves from a single but highly infected hog. Most infections are due to eating raw or underdone pork, occasionally bear or walrus meat. In the United States fewer than six hundred clinical cases a year are clearly diagnosed, and of these less than 5 per cent are fatal. But many serious infections are mistakenly said to be intestinal flu, food poisoning, or typhoid fever. Since the estimated incidence in the United States, as determined from examination of the diaphragm at autopsy, ranges from 5 per cent in New Orleans to more than 27 per cent of the people in some northern and western cities, the vast majority of cases must go undetected or end in medical statistics as "psychosomatic" or other illness. Perhaps the milder symptoms of trichina worm infection are simply less severe than the weakness, diarrhea, abdominal pains, nausea, fever, puffy eyes, and extreme muscular pains that characterize fatal attacks. The adult trichina worm is a tiny intestinal parasite, but serious or fatal results are attributable to the even smaller larval worms as they burrow through the intestinal wall and enter lymph or blood vessels, become distributed about the body, then burrow through every tissue or organ to settle down in striated muscle tissue. There they grow to be $\frac{1}{25}$ of an inch long, ten times their larval burrowing size. They become sexually differentiated, roll into a spiral, and become enclosed in a walled cyst developed by the host. They do not develop further unless host muscle is eaten by another susceptible host and the cyst wall is digested away in the host's stomach or intestine. An ounce of infected sausage may contain more than 100,000 encysted little worms; and the person who eats it may become the sole support of 1500 offspring from each female that hatches in the stomach or intestine, so that the body tissues become riddled by more than 100,000,000 larval worms. Since the cysts are microscopic, gross meat inspection does not reveal trichina worm infection. Prevention could be greatly aided by careful inspection of pork, as in Chile, or by prohibiting the feeding of garbage to hogs, as in Canada or England. Until better measures are adopted in the United States, each individual should take care never to eat pork that is not thoroughly cooked.

Hookworms are tiny worms, only about ½ of an inch long, that live in the human intestine, holding on by clamping the mouth on a bit of intestinal wall, and feeding by sucking in blood and tissue juices. Only recently have these worms been brought under enough control to cede first place to the schistosomes (discussed in the chapter on flatworms) as the most damaging wormlike parasites of man. *Necator americanus,* whose name means "the American killer," probably came to the United States from Africa and is primarily a tropical worm, abundant in middle latitudes around the world wherever moderately warm temperatures, moisture, and soil conditions are favorable. Its dependence on warmth and moisture keeps it confined in the United States to the southeastern states—from Virginia west and southwest to Arkansas and Texas.

Somewhat more injurious to its hosts is *Ancylostoma duodenale,* chiefly a northern species and the dominant one in Europe, North Africa, western Asia, northern China, and Japan. In most countries farming and mining are the main occupations of hookworm victims; and in western Europe the worms first attracted attention during the building of the Saint Gotthard tunnel through the Swiss Alps. Afterwards the worms were spread to many European mines. Other species of hookworms occur in cats and dogs and occasionally also in man. The life history has some similarities to that of *Ascaris,* but the eggs hatch in the soil and it is the active larval worms that enter the human body, usually burrowing through the skin of bare feet, but also sometimes taking advantage of any other means to penetrate the human skin or enter the mouth. Once inside the skin, they enter lymph or blood vessels, are carried to the lungs, coughed up and swallowed, arriving finally in the intestine. There they sap vitality, chiefly through blood loss, of individuals who are malnourished to begin with. The effects of hookworms are not dramatic, but they under-

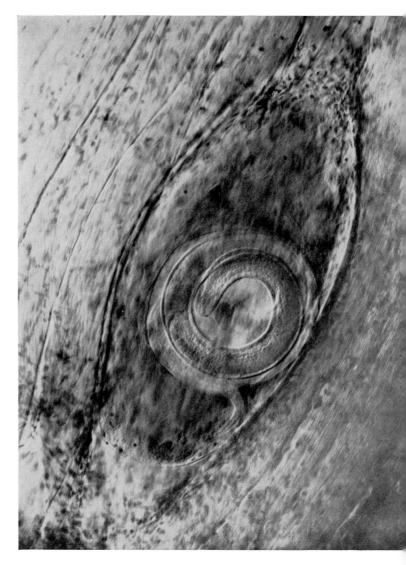

Trichina cyst in hog muscle. The dormant curled-up larva of *Trichinella spiralis* is about 1/25 inch long and is enclosed in a wall formed by the host. Stained preparation. (P. S. Tice)

mine whole communities, generation after generation. The wearing of shoes is an important means of protection against ground polluted with hookworms; even light sandals help.

The guinea worm, *Dracunculis medinensis,* was referred to earlier. In central Africa, Egypt, the East Indies, and especially from Arabia to India, it is one of the really serious penalties for a way of life in which the same sources of water serve for drinking, bathing, and laundering. The large female worm, only 1/25 of an inch wide but up to 4 feet long, lives in the deeper skin layers but comes close to the surface to produce a skin ulcer and discharge larval worms whenever an infected arm or leg is suddenly plunged into cold water, as in laundering or in dipping up water from wells or village ponds. The tiny worms swim about until they perish or are swallowed by a second host, a species of *Cyclops,* a tiny crustacean. When drinking water is dipped up (often by the same individuals who infect the water by standing in it as they lower their buckets) it contains infected crustaceans that harbor larval worms. Redesigning wells and filtering water could eliminate this disease, but in India religious traditions that surround the ways of obtaining and using water have made change slow.

More than fifty species of roundworms parasitize man occasionally, but only about a dozen are important human parasites. Five have already been mentioned. Some others are the subtropical and tropical filarial worms that cause elephantiasis; the African eye worm, *Loa loa;* and the world-wide whipworm, *Trichuris trichiura,* which usually lives in the large intestine, causing symptoms ranging from abdominal pain to severe emaciation and prolapse of the rectum.

The one roundworm most likely to have parasitized readers of this book is the pinworm (seatworm or threadworm) *Enterobius vermicularis,* found all over the world, but rare in the tropics. It flourishes in Europe, where even the cleanly Dutch children are said to be 100 per cent infected, and in North America, where sample surveys show that 30 to 60 per cent of white children in Canadian and American cities have pinworms. Negroes are less susceptible, and in Washington, D.C., Negro children have an incidence of only 16 per cent, compared with 40 per cent for white children. These are little white worms, the females up to ½ of an inch long, that live in the cecum, appendix, and adjacent parts of the large intestine. When the females are full of eggs they migrate to the rectum and lay their eggs around the anal opening. Their movements cause intense itching, often sleeplessness and nervousness. Scratching of the anus, and liberation of the eggs into the air and onto sheets and clothing, spreads the eggs about so effectively that in some households and institutions eggs can be taken from almost any surface or object. It is easy to imagine how the eggs reach the mouths of adults, but more especially of children, in such places. For this worm, treatment is easier than prevention.

The Rotifers (*Phylum Rotifera*)

One of the most fascinating, and busiest, of sights is a drop of pond water magnified to reveal a field of feeding, crawling, and swimming rotifers. These intensely animated microscopic creatures occur in a great variety of fantastic shapes and handsome surface sculpturings. Their greatest attractions, however, are their incessant external activity and a transparency that displays the lively inside workings as might a glass model.

After the bewilderment induced by a first glimpse of a vivacious rotifer, attention centers on an eye-catching piece of gadgetry at the front end, the corona or "crown," used for both feeding and swimming. It includes the mouth and the more or less expanded area of delicate ciliated skin surrounding or close to the mouth. In the hunting rotifers, which go forth in search of food, swimming or gliding through food-laden water, the corona is external and often convex. In many species which live permanently fixed by a long stalk, or in those which attach temporarily while feeding, the coronal lobes may be protruded from the mouth during feeding, then retracted. Some of the large and beautiful stationary rotifers have a lobed and funnel-shaped corona with long bristles that prevent escape of the prey when the lobes of the funnel close down on some small animal that happens to enter.

The most familiar rotifers of fresh waters are the bdelloid ("leechlike") rotifers, elongate little animals that creep in leechlike or inch-worm fashion on the bottom or on plants. Bdelloids typically have a corona consisting of two elevated disks, and these propel the animals on brief excursions through the water. The large fused cilia that fringe the two coronal disks beat in such a way as to create the illusion of two rotating cogged wheels. These were the first rotifers discovered by the early microscopists, so that long before the illusory matter was finally cleared up, all the microscopic creatures with expanded crowns of cilia at the front end had been named "wheel animalcules." The formal name of the phylum, Rotifera, means "wheel-bearers."

Rotifer shapes may be wormlike, as in bdelloid rotifers; flower-like, as in the sessile forms that have great expanded coronas; or rotund, as in the rotifers that float freely in open water. The common freshwater bdelloid rotifer, *Philodina,* has an elongate body distinguishable into a corona-bearing head, a central region or trunk, and a tapering foot region. At the end of the foot are two pointed projections called "toes," and from each of these open cement glands that secrete a sticky substance by which the animal anchors temporarily while feeding. The toes are also of use in creeping about, as the flexible body alternately lengthens and takes hold by the front end, then contracts and fastens by the toes. The whole body is enclosed in a flexible cuticle which is folded into sections that telescope into each other when the animal contracts. In some rotifers the cuticle of the trunk region is hardened into an armored case or lorica, either smooth or ornamented with grooves or spines. One or more eyes may be seen on the front end as red flecks.

From the mouth the digestive tube leads promptly to a gizzard-like swelling, the mastax, which has powerfully muscled hard jaws. Through the transparent wall the toothed jaws of the mastax can be seen grinding away at the food that is swept down the mouth. In some species the jaws are long and slender, forming a kind of forceps that can be extended through the mouth to grasp prey.

The tiniest rotifers are not nearly as small as the smallest protozoans, but members of both groups are generally of comparable size, and the largest rotifers are only about 1/50 of an inch long, not as long as the giant fresh-water protozoan, *Spirostomum*. Little wonder, then, that the early microscopists confused the many-celled rotifers with ciliated protozoans, for the two groups are similar in many superficial ways and resemble each other even more in habits. Like ciliated protozoans, the rotifers swim in spiral fashion, attach to vegetation and feed by ciliary currents, often live in cases attached to water plants, and have a cosmopolitan distribution. Geography means nothing to animals so small that they can be swept along in the feeblest movements of water—and so resistant to drying, either as dormant eggs or as desiccated adults, that they can be carried about by winds and on the feet of birds. After months or even years in the inert state, some rotifers can again spring into activity at the first wetting. If conditions are the same, a lake in Germany, or for that matter one in China or in South Africa, will have the same species of rotifers as one in the United States. Relatively few species are restricted to special conditions, as are those found only in highly alkaline lakes in the western United States, or those that live attached to particular species of aquatic plants.

Basically, however, protozoans and rotifers are very different, for the latter are composed of the equivalent of a large number of extremely small cells. The cell membranes present in the embryo mostly disappear in the adult, leaving tissues that are protoplasmic masses with numbers of nuclei. Each of the nuclei occupies a definite position, and through the transparent body wall they can be seen and counted. The number of cells of a late embryo, or the number of nuclei of an adult, is constant for any species—usually between nine hundred and one thousand. In their cell or nuclear constancy rotifers are almost unique among multicellular animals, though this phenomenon does occur to a lesser extent in a few other phyla. The rotifer body is of a structural grade that includes several complete systems of organs, some of them more complex than those of the flatworms, some less so.

No large grouping of animals is more partial to fresh waters than are the rotifers. Of some seventeen

hundred described species, only about fifty are said to occur solely or mostly in the sea, though common fresh-water species are often carried into brackish or salt waters and manage to survive there. Of the marine forms nearly all live on shore bottoms. Only two species have been seen afloat in mid-Atlantic. The fresh-water rotifers also stay close to shore, about 75 per cent of them living on the bottom or on plants at the edges of lakes and ponds. Not more than about a hundred species are freely floating types, completely independent of any firm substrate.

A few rotifers live on the external surfaces of other animals, as on the gills of crustaceans. Among the parasitic species are *Proales parasita* and *Ascomorpha volvocicola,* which enter colonies of the colonial protozoan *Volvox,* living and breeding within the spherical colonies and feeding on the members. *Drilophaga* parasitizes fresh-water annelids, and there are rotifers parasitic on protozoans, hydroids, pond snails, and plants.

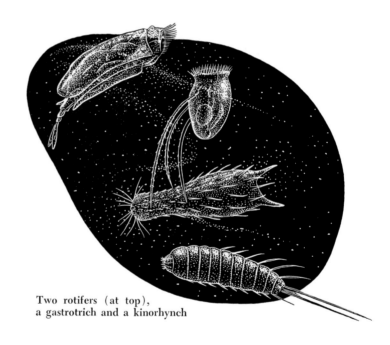

Two rotifers (at top),
a gastrotrich and a kinorhynch

Though many bdelloid rotifers are fully aquatic, this group is the one most characteristic of lichens and mosses. Their almost incredible capacity to survive when seemingly as dry as dust particles enables them to live even in such intermittently wet places as rain gutters and cemetery urns, moss-covered walls or roofs, glaciers, rocks, and the bark of trees. Drying must occur gradually, as it does in the crevices of moss, and the rotifer withdraws into the central trunk region, puckering the two ends shut. The body shrinks by loss of water and becomes more and more wrinkled. In the desiccated state rotifers in moss usually survive three or four years, in one presumably reliable case as long as twenty-seven years. When wet again they return to normal activity in from ten minutes to a day.

Reproduction in rotifers can be sexual, and the sexes are separate. But much of the time the females are fully in charge, producing young without having to bother with males. In one small group of primitive marine rotifers, so far known only from European waters, males and females are nearly similar in structure, though the males are slightly smaller and less abundant. The eggs must be fertilized, and they hatch into animals of either sex. Among bdelloid rotifers no males have ever been seen, and the eggs laid by the females always develop, without fertilization, into more females. About 90 per cent of all rotifers are members of a third group, the Monogononta, in which males are produced only during a few weeks of the year, at which time they are fairly abundant but live for only a few hours to a few days. They usually impregnate the females by hypodermic injection through the body wall, rarely by copulation. These males are often about one-third the length of the female, sometimes much smaller. They are also degenerate, lacking mouth and mastax, or other organs as well. There are two kinds of females, indistinguishable externally. During most of the year one type prevails, laying eggs that develop without fertilization into females of the same type. At critical times in the year, when the environment is undergoing some marked change, another kind of female hatches from the eggs. These are capable of being impregnated by males, but if they are not, their eggs hatch into males. When males do impregnate this second type of female, the eggs that are laid have thick, hard, and often ornamented shells and can withstand drying, freezing, or other hazards. Such "resting eggs" or "winter eggs" can tide the species over unfavorable seasons or events; they later hatch into the type of female that carries on without males.

The Gastrotrichs

(*Phylum Gastrotricha*)

Anyone who examines old protozoan cultures or pond debris under the microscope, looking for protozoans or rotifers, will sooner or later see gastrotrichs, elongate transparent creatures usually less than $\frac{1}{50}$ of an inch long, and colorless except for any colored food they have ingested. Most observers pass them by as just another kind of ciliated protozoan, but the cilia by which they swim or glide are restricted to the under surface, and there are some on the head.

The upper surface of the cuticle of the trunk is usually clothed with overlapping scales, with bristles or spines, or with spined scales. Those most often seen in fresh waters are bristly, have a slightly constricted neck that sets off head from trunk, and end in a forked tail that has at each tip a cement gland serving the same function as in rotifers. They browse on the bottom or on vegetation, and swim only briefly. About the size of rotifers, the gastrotrichs also resemble them in many details and feed on the same small organisms or organic debris. They have no spreading feeding disk, and food particles are sucked in by a muscular throat (pharynx) like that of nematodes, the group to which they seem to show most affinity.

About 60 per cent of known gastrotrichs live in fresh waters, but one group is exclusively marine. So far it is known only from European shores, where the most devoted observers have worked. The animals glide, crawl in leech fashion, or remain attached for long periods. They are hermaphroditic, producing both eggs and sperms.

The group which includes most of the common gastrotrichs of fresh waters has many marine members also. The fresh-water forms are seldom found in running water, for they favor habitats with much decay, such as vegetation-choked shores of ponds and lakes, mossy pools, and bogs. Surprisingly, they also occur in large numbers in the damp sand near the water's edge on sandy beaches. In all these gastrotrichs the male organs seem to have degenerated; all individuals are females and lay eggs that develop without fertilization.

The Kinorhynchs

(*Phylum Kinorhyncha*)

A little more than a century ago, the ardent French microscopist Felix Dujardin turned his attention to some seaweeds collected along the coast of the English Channel. Upon these marine plants he discovered a strange creeping animal less than $\frac{1}{16}$ of an inch long. It resembled nothing he had ever seen before, and it had spines around the region he regarded as its neck. For this reason he named it an "echinodere." Thirty years later, a German zoologist concluded that the echinodere and several similar creatures that had been discovered should be regarded as belonging to a special group, the Kinorhyncha, using this term to show that all of them pull themselves along by a sort of snout. Some people would have preferred the group to be called the Echinodera.

These are exclusively marine and microscopic, with elongate bodies covered by a jointed cuticle that suggests segmentation. Most of what is known about kinorhynchs has been learned from those along European shores. Yet these animals have been found on northern American coasts, Japan, Zanzibar, and the Antarctic. They must be widely distributed.

Kinorhynchs have no cilia and cannot swim, but crawl about on muddy or slimy bottoms, swallowing fine debris. Some live on seaweeds, browsing on microscopic algae. To feed, the animal extends the spiny, retractile head and protrudes a mouth cone with a circlet of spines. Then it sucks in the food by means of a muscular throat. Externally the males and females cannot usually be told apart, but sexual reproduction occurs at all seasons. The eggs hatch into a larval stage.

The Priapulids

(Phylum Priapulida)

This small phylum has, so far, only six species of marine wormlike animals of dull color and moderate size, the largest about 3 inches long. The cylindrical and superficially ringed body, so warty that the animal was once classed with the sea-cucumbers, has a shorter front region which can be inverted and withdrawn into the longer trunk region. The front is well armed with rows of spiny teeth, for capturing

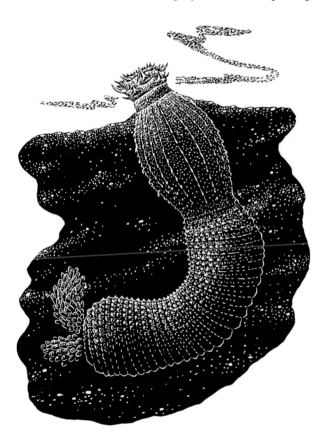

prey as the worm plows through muddy bottoms. Three species have long been known from northern seas around the globe, down to 1500 feet (500 m.), and as far south as Massachusetts and Belgium. One of these, *Priapulus caudatus,* or a form almost like it, is found also in antarctic seas, as is another species of the same genus. Until 1959 no priapulids were known from middle latitudes; then a new species was brought up from the cold bottom of the mid-American trench, at a depth of nearly 17,000 feet, off the western coast of Costa Rica.

The Horsehair Worms

(Phylum Nematomorpha)

The horsehair worms have been known for many centuries, and almost from the beginning have been associated with the myth that they were animated horse hairs, transformed after being dropped from horses into bodies of fresh water or into drinking troughs. The resemblance is not too far-fetched, for these long, fine worms are often about 6 inches long and black or brown in color, though the color may be yellow or gray and the length may approach 3 feet. The diameter of the body ($\frac{1}{10}$ of an inch at most) is almost the same throughout, though it tapers very slightly at the rear and a little more at the front end. Males are shorter than females and usually slightly curved at the rear.

We no longer need a fanciful explanation for why horsehair worms suddenly turn up, full-grown, in a body of water that had none the day before. The larval worms develop within the bodies of insects, usually land beetles, crickets, and grasshoppers. The adults emerge full grown and make their way to water. They have a degenerate digestive tract and never feed. Though the males can swim slowly, the females do little more than writhe about.

In the springtime one may find writhing masses of as many as twenty tangled worms, and this has given rise to another common name, gordian worms, referring to the Gordian knot of the ancient Greek myth. Only one pair of worms is involved in a copulation, however, and the fertilized eggs are laid in long, gelatinous strings. After hatching, the larva swims about for a short time, then presumably encysts on vegetation at or near the water's edge. Thus larval cysts can be ingested by water beetles, and perhaps a falling water level exposes some of the vegetation, making the cysts available to crickets and grasshoppers feeding near the water's edge. The genus *Gordius* is known from ponds and ditches all over the world. Other genera are less cosmopolitan, but horsehair worms occur from the tropics to cold-temperate regions, even above timber line on mountains. There are about eighty species, only one of them marine.

The Spiny-headed Worms   *(Phylum Acanthocephala)*

Only when they are tucked away in someone else's intestine can these worms be looked on as animals of unobtrusive habits, though it is true that few people ever see any of the four hundred known species or are even aware of their existence. The spiny head referred to in both common and technical names is a burrlike and retractile proboscis by which the worm clings to the intestine of fresh-water, marine, or land

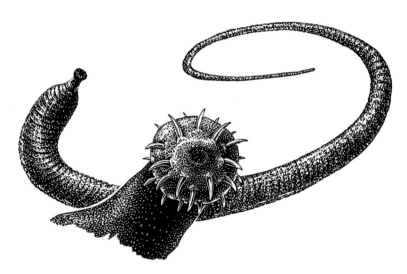

vertebrates. Fishes and birds are favored hosts, but many mammals receive their share of attention, and occasionally also man. Like the tapeworms, which they resemble in many respects, these spiny-headed parasites have no mouth or digestive tract at any time in life, risking all on finding hosts to support them. They have few internal organs that are not directed toward a prodigious production of offspring, and the success of the species rests on enough of these surviving all hazards and eventually making their

way back to the vertebrate host to reproduce again.

The adult lives a life of ease, absorbing food through the body wall and resisting digestion by means of the thin cuticle that covers the body. The chief damage to the host is local injury at the point where the proboscis is attached, but if the proboscis perforates the wall, it may cause a fatal peritonitis. In really heavy infestation the worms may interfere with digestion and cause loss of appetite.

The spiny proboscis, armed with rows of stout recurved hooks, can be turned inside out on retraction. And the knoblike or slender forepart of the body, made up of the proboscis and an unarmed neck at the base of the proboscis, can be withdrawn into the much larger trunk region. The trunk may be short and plumpish or long and cylindrical, but only in certain worms is it curved or coiled or beset with spines.

Most acanthocephalids are under 1 inch long, some only a small fraction of an inch, but the common species that lives in pigs all over the world reaches a length of more than 2 feet and looks as formidable as its name, *Macracanthorhynchus hirudinaceus.* This giant parasite has, in the past at least, been reported in people of the Volga valley in southern Russia. The knoblike proboscis is armed with five or six rows of very stout thorns, and the long, pinkish, wrinkled trunk tapers from front to rear. As in nearly all spiny-headed worms, the male is much smaller than the female. The eggs develop, within the mother, into a young larval stage that is enclosed in a hard spiny embryonic shell. Shed with the host's feces, the shelled embryos can survive in soil for up to three and a half years. When swallowed by grubs of June beetles or similar insects, they develop within the insect body. Pigs become infected when they eat either grubs or beetles as they root about in pastures.

The only other species that has been found at times in man is *Moniliformis dubius,* a common parasite of house rats. In the United States and in South America it spends its larval life in cockroaches, and these infect rats that feed on them. In Europe a beetle (*Blaps*) has been implicated as a larval host. The adult worm may reach 1 foot in length and has a really wicked-looking proboscis, cylindrical and covered with twelve to fifteen rows of thornlike hooks.

People sometimes unwittingly eat cockroaches or beetles, and there are other possibilities for getting infected with these resourceful parasites, but fortunately human infections are quite rare. The habits of dogs provide more opportunities for such worms, and dogs or coyotes in North America sometimes harbor *Oncicola canis* and may display rabies-like symptoms. In Texas, where most of the known cases occur, the armadillo may act as a transport host between the dog and the arthropod that first harbors the larva.

The Entoprocts

(Phylum Entoprocta)

These are tiny (less than ¼ of an inch high) aquatic animals that live as solitary individuals or little colonies, superficially resembling hydroids because the round or bell-shaped, flower-like body supported on a stalk is crowned by an oval circlet of tentacles.

Under the microscope, an entoproct's tentacles are seen to be ciliated on their inner surfaces and to create ciliary feeding currents that gather microscopic organisms and particles. The intestine is U-shaped; and this, together with the tentacular crown and the habit of growing attached to various objects or on other animals, reminds us of the familiar moss ani-

mals (bryozoans). For many years, in fact, the entoprocts were included within the phylum Bryozoa. But the body of an entoproct differs from that of a moss animal in so many ways that a separate phylum became necessary for them. It is named for the position of the anus—within the circlet of tentacles. In moss animals the anus opens outside the tentacular crown. In hydroids, of course, there is no anus.

Entoprocts are almost entirely a marine group. So far the only fresh-water genus (*Urnatella*) has been found in India and the eastern part of the United States. The remainder of the sixty-odd known species of entoprocts have been collected widely on marine shores or in shallow waters around the world. Finding these inconspicuous animals is an exciting challenge to anyone who likes to see at first hand a small group known to most people only from books.

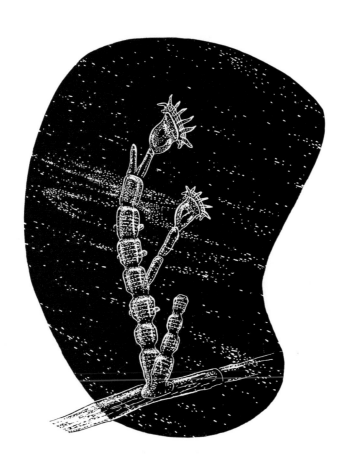

CHAPTER VIII

The Arrow Worms

(*Phylum Chaetognatha*)

ALMOST any bucketful of sea water, whether from the surface close to shore or from the depths, is likely to contain a few pencil-slender arrow worms, so transparent as to be overlooked. Even hundreds of them may draw no attention to themselves unless the water in which they swim is poured into a shallow dish with a black bottom. Then the arrow worms show as ghostly, darting creatures from ¾ to 4 inches in length.

All of the thirty-odd species of arrow worms are free-living. Most of them are pelagic and cosmopolitan. Sometimes they become extremely abundant, swimming in great masses that can cloud the water with a grayish tint, particularly at certain times of the day and year. Usually this matches occasions when the sea is locally rich in the favorite foods of arrow worms: microscopic diatoms and other algae, protozoans, copepod crustaceans, and larvae of many other animals, including fish. Toward all of these an arrow worm is a formidable predator, but to jellyfishes, ctenophores, small fish, whale sharks, and whalebone whales, it is merely part of the nourishing plankton.

As an arrow worm rests quietly in the water, its body ordinarily is straight and horizontal. Folded compactly under a thin rounded hood at the anterior end is a pair of sickle-shaped hooks set with movable spines. These serve as jaws when the hood is turned back and the arrow worm darts for about its own length after prey. Between the hooks and surrounding the slitlike mouth are dozens of short bristles.

The *chaetae* from which the phylum Chaetognatha takes its name ("bristle-jaws") are the spines on the prehensile hooks which, when spread and held out stiffly, form the most conspicuous feature of an arrow worm's head. Closer inspection, however, soon leads to discovery of two widely spaced clusters of simple eyes (ocelli), each cluster roofed by a three-part, light-collecting lens. The largest part faces somewhat to the side. A diminutive brain may be visible, connected by very fine nerves to the eye clusters, to the muscles controlling the grasping hooks, and to a narrow organ on the midline believed to apprise the animal of chemical substances in the water—the aquatic equivalent of the senses of taste and smell.

Fully half of an arrow worm's body is trunk, set off from the head by a slightly narrowed neck and from the tail by another change in body diameter. The sides of trunk and tail bear thin, streamlined fins suggesting the feather vanes on an arrow. From these the principal genus gains its name (*Sagitta*) and chaetognaths receive the familiar term arrow worms. The tip of the tail also bears a transverse fin.

Each of the fins is supported firmly by hair-thin rays, but no special muscles permit separate movements of these extensions of the body. Instead, they serve in maintaining balance and in making more effective any movements of the body as a whole in the water.

Except for the fin rays, no structure resembling a skeleton ever develops in an arrow worm. The muscles are chiefly longitudinal ones, used in bending the body in locomotion. They are supplemented in the head by other muscles serving to move the grasping hooks.

An arrow worm's digestive tract is a straight tube from mouth to anus. Often it is the most conspicuous part of the animal simply because the small creatures being digested in it have not yet achieved the degree of transparency of the predator surrounding them.

Arrow worms resemble chordates in having a skin that is several cells thick in some areas and in possessing a tail posterior to the anus. The body cavity, moreover, arises during embryonic development in the manner characteristic of echinoderms and chordates but no other phyla. Yet the chaetognaths have no separate circulatory system nor respiratory or excretory mechanisms. Instead, the fluid in the body cavity is propelled by cilia and by movements of the body as a whole, and serves to transport food and wastes from the digestive tract to the body wall, and oxygen absorbed from the sea in the other direction.

Actually, the body cavity is cut into a head portion, a trunk portion, and a tail portion by transverse partitions, and is separated incompletely into a right side and a left by a perforated longitudinal sheet of tissue (mesentery) holding the digestive tube in place.

The tail cavity contains a pair of testes, from which the sperm cells escape through ruptures after being coated with mucus to form spermatophores. The trunk cavity, on the other hand, contains a pair of slender ovaries, with ciliated oviducts opening to the outside of the body. Hence an arrow worm is a hermaphrodite, with a male tail and a female trunk. The fertilized eggs are discharged and develop while floating in the water. In many features the embryos resemble those of echinoderms and chordates.

Probably the planktonic genera *Sagitta, Eukrohnia,* and *Pterosagitta* include only species depending upon self-fertilization. *Sagitta* is easy to recognize from the two pairs of lateral fins, *Eukrohnia* by the long, slender neck region and single elongated pair of lateral fins, and *Pterosagitta* from the thick-necked appearance given by a massive collarette extending back to the single pair of small lateral fins.

Spadella is a very different arrow worm, associating with the bottom and clinging to objects there by means of adhesive papillae. In *S. cephaloptera* these are located on the ventral surface of the tail; other species wear the miniature suckers on finger-like projections situated just in front of the tail fin.

In all members of *Spadella,* the body is more stocky, and the animal spends much of its time holding to a rock or an alga, waiting for food to come within darting distance. Often it seizes victims without even letting go of its support. Cross-fertilization is the rule in *Spadella,* and the eggs are cemented to the bottom.

Temperature of surrounding water seems important to many arrow worms at the time of reproduction. The pelagic kinds that migrate vertically in the tropics are exposed to a large range of temperature every day, since at one thousand feet below the surface the water is close to the normal freezing point whereas surface layers may be quite warm. Apparently they become dependent upon access to temperatures higher than those in the depths, for, if currents carry them into colder water, they fail to reproduce even though they may grow to twice their normal size.

The arrow worm, *Sagitta setosa,* occurs in surface waters in incredible numbers at certain seasons. At such times it is an important food for fishes. (England. D. P. Wilson)

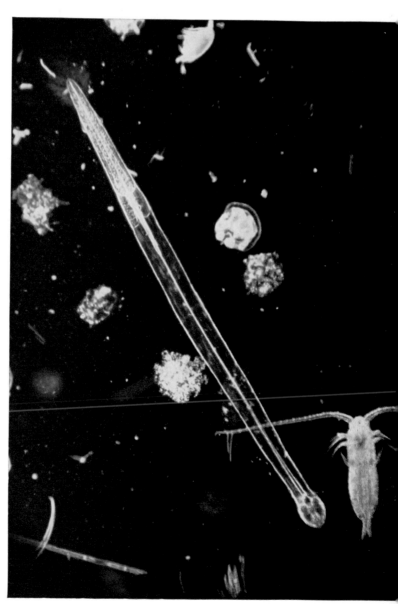

CHAPTER IX

The Acorn Worms
and Their Kin

(Phylum Hemichordata)

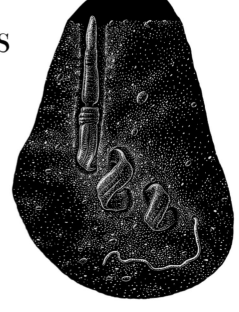

An acorn worm in its
burrow in the sea bottom

AMONG the treasures to be found in sand and sandy mud along the world's seashores are fragile, pinkish tan animals called acorn worms. At first glance each might be thought to be a pale, soft-bodied earthworm. The 5- to 6-inch body even wears a swelling near the anterior end, suggesting the clitellum of an earthworm. But the body of an acorn worm is not segmented, and the enlarged region is a collar that extends completely around it.

Sometimes an acorn worm is exposed when a stone, half-sunken in the bottom, is lifted. One wall of the worm's burrow is taken away. These creatures build branching U-shaped or Y-shaped tunnels in the bottom sediments, lining them with mucus. At night an acorn worm may emerge from its burrow and creep over the bottom among eelgrass or other plant tangles, but by day it is almost sure to be out of sight.

In spite of the wormlike body, acorn worms possess a feature that, until recently, was regarded as earning them a place in phylum Chordata, as degenerate relatives of the vertebrates. Between the pharynx region of the digestive tract and the outside of the body, acorn worms and some of their close kin show a series of paired openings. Clefts of this kind are known otherwise only among the chordates and, possibly, one extinct genus of echinoderms.

Today the phylum name Hemichordata is regarded as suggesting a sort of halfway station, not really eligible for inclusion among primitive chordates but rather worthy of a phylum by itself. Similarities between embryonic stages of hemichordates and echinoderms may indicate a closer link with sea stars and their kin.

The first part of an acorn worm, anterior to the collar region, contains a contractile chamber serving as a heart. It draws blood from a dorsal longitudinal vessel, pumps it through an organ assumed to serve in excretion, thence around the digestive tract on each side, to join into a ventral longitudinal vessel. This first part of the body is used also in burrow-making and in pulling the body along when the animal is exposed on the surface. Cilia, which cover the body, help in a slower, gliding kind of locomotion.

The mouth opens below the forward end of the collar and leads into a long, straight digestive tract. The anus is at the posterior end of the body, and there is no postanal tail as in chordates. Just behind the collar, the gill openings from the pharynx discharge water taken in through the mouth. This copious flow is directed from the dorsal surface into the worm's tunnel or the surrounding sea.

In some species of the genus *Balanoglossus,* the first part of the body and the collar together might suggest an acorn in its cup; from this the most familiar of the hemichordates receives a common name. In *Saccoglossus* the first part of the body is greatly extended. The twenty-odd species of *Balanoglossus* include *B. clavigerus* from the Mediterranean and *B. aurantiacus* from the coast of the Carolinas. *Saccoglossus kowalevskii* is found on both sides of the North Atlantic and is probably the acorn worm most frequently encountered.

Members of the genus *Ptychodera* resemble *Ba-*

lanoglossus but have large, conspicuous gill pores. *P. flava* is a denizen of the Indian and Pacific oceans, and *P. bahamensis* of the Bahamas and West Indies.

In addition to nearly one hundred different kinds of acorn worms, the phylum Hemichordata includes a few diminutive colonial members which bear tentacle-studded arms on the second region of the body but lack gill slits. These animals secrete a covering for themselves and live within deep cupshaped cavities in a manner reminiscent of moss animals (bryozoans). Related to this life in a blind tube, each has the anus far forward, just posterior to the arm-bearing collar region, and hence over the edge of the tube opening while the animal is feeding, its ciliated tentacles exposed, creating a current in the water that brings food particles and oxygen.

Each individual of *Cephalodiscus* may be ¼ of an inch long, not counting the slender stalk extending down into the depths of the community shelter, there making contact with other neighboring individuals. From the dorsal surface of the second region of the body, *Cephalodiscus* has two rows of from five to nine arms each, every arm fringed with from twenty-five to fifty tentacles.

Individuals of *Rhabdopleura* are less than ¹⁄₁₆ of an inch long, not counting the stalk. Each bears two comparatively huge, gracefully curved arms with ciliated tentacles, again on the middle region of the body.

Both of these colonial hemichordates reproduce by budding and also sexually. Ordinarily a colony consists of the matured buds from a single individual. The buds are formed low on the stalk and begin as an extension of the previous animal. The first body division of the new individual proceeds to secrete a new addition to the community shelter, and later matures in it—still with the possibility of producing further buds either in the same line or as branches of the colony.

Rhabdopleura normani has been collected from west Greenland to the Azores, usually attached to old dead parts of corals. *Cephalodiscus* is a larger genus, with representatives from the Arctic to the Antarctic, most of them obtained by dredging. They grow on rocks, clamshells, and other firm surfaces. Often, in turn, they are overgrown by hydroids and moss animals, adding to the complexity encountered among the living things on a shell or a stone.

The acorn worm *Ptychodera bahamensis* of the Bahamas and West Indies uses its acorn-shaped proboscis as a burrowing organ and makes branching U- or Y-shaped tunnels in bottom sediments. (Bermuda. Ralph Buchsbaum)

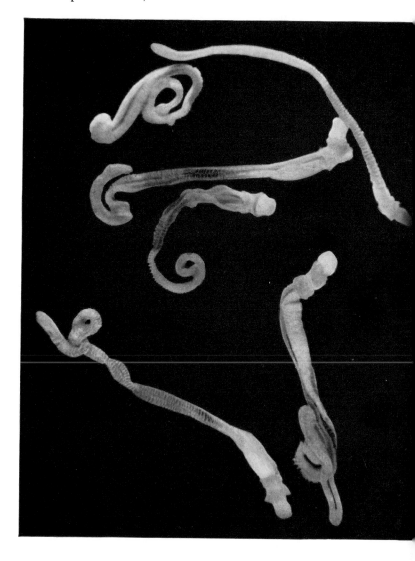

CHAPTER X

The Beard Worms

(Phylum Pogonophora)

AMONG the most astonishing discoveries made with deep-sea dredges in the twentieth century was the finding of this assemblage of tube-building, wormlike creatures, for they live their solitary lives and reach a length of as much as 13 inches, a diameter to $\frac{1}{10}$ of an inch, with no trace whatever of a digestive system—a condition unique among free-living many-celled animals.

The body of one of these long and exceedingly slender worms shows a subdivision into three regions: a proboscis bearing from one to more than two hundred tentacles on its underside; a collar-like enlargement; and a long posterior body whose final third may be marked off into a large number of successive rings by rows of raised adhesive areas. With these a beard worm clings to the slender, close-fitting tube it has secreted in the bottom mud. The tube consists of a series of rings or slightly funnel-shaped pieces

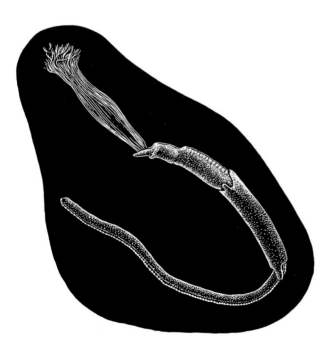

composed of animal cellulose—the material found in the tunic of a sea squirt.

Enough is known about the embryos of beard worms to show that they too lack a digestive tract and consequently cannot be assumed to store enough food to last for the lifetime of the worm. Instead, a beard worm seemingly must depend upon decomposition products diffusing to it from bacterial action in the surrounding abyssal water, or must be able to control digestion outside its body in an enclosed space of some kind.

In searching for an enclosed space of this description, scientists have looked suspiciously at the slender cavity within the spiral of the single tentacle in species of *Siboglinum,* or between the outstretched parallel tentacles of worms in other genera.

In *Galathealinum* somewhat more than one hundred tentacles lie side by side, anterior to the worm in its tube. In *Spirobrachia* the number may be more than two hundred. In *Lamellisabella* the tentacles form a watertight cylinder for most of their length, and only the tips are free. Into this cylinder extend short lateral projections comparable to those found on one or both sides of the tentacles in all other beard worms.

The tentacles do have thin walls and an extension of the closed circulatory system. But so far, no gland cells have been discovered that could secrete digestive ferments, and the secret of the beard worms' nourishment remains an intriguing enigma.

Of the twenty-four known species of beard worms, thirteen have been found only at great depths between Kamchatka and the islands just north of Japan. Four more appear to be limited to somewhat shallower waters in the same general region. *Siboglinum* has been dredged from the Skagerak off the Norwegian coast at depths from 500 to 2000 feet, from British waters, and from tropical western parts of the Pacific. The last is the only known home of *Galathealinum. Lamellisabella* has been recovered from close to ten thousand feet below the surface in both the Okhotsk Sea and the Gulf of Panama.

CHAPTER XI

The Phoronids

(Phylum Phoronida)

BELOW the level of low tide, pier pilings in the Bay of Naples wear a feltwork of interlacing membranous tubes two or three inches thick. Each tube is the individual home of a wormlike animal, *Phoronis kowalevskii*. Like the fourteen other species comprising this phylum, these tube-dwellers wear a horseshoe-shaped crown of ciliated tentacles with which they entrap food particles in a mucous film carried to the mouth at the bottom of the horseshoe.

Most phoronids are less than 8 inches long, some as short as $\frac{1}{40}$ of an inch. A giant is *Phoronopsis californica,* which lives singly in the estuaries along the California coast in blind tubes as much as 18 inches long and $\frac{5}{16}$ of an inch in diameter. The entire 12-inch body of this phoronid is orange, its tentacles an even brighter shade of the same color. Some-

times it leaves the $\frac{3}{4}$-inch plume of orange tentacles exposed at the end of its sand-impregnated tube, and draws attention in this way.

On the Atlantic coast of North America, 5-inch *Phoronis architecta* is common in the sand flats of North Carolina and as far north as Chesapeake Bay. It also builds isolated tubes.

In Australia, a different reddish-colored phoronid as much as 6 inches long builds a home for itself in the wall of another tubedweller, the tube anemone *Cerianthus.*

Phoronids have red blood in a closed system of vessels. Most are hermaphroditic, and the fertilized eggs develop into swimming larvae. Eventually the young settle down to build a tube and grow by metamorphosis into adult form.

CHAPTER XII

The Moss Animals

(Phylum Bryozoa or Ectoprocta)

Anyone curious about animal life in water is almost sure to meet moss animals (bryozoans) in many guises. A piece of seaweed is cast upon the beach: over some of the floats and leaflike areas is a limy coating with a pattern of minute pores. This encrustation is a "lace coral," the work of one type of bryozoan (Plate 33). Or the spire of a whelk shell is rough with a different limy coating: the colony of another moss animal.

The nautically minded often meet bryozoans. A skiff, pulled ashore after a summer at its mooring in salt water, must be examined underneath for barnacles and other fouling organisms. Some of the shrubby and fuzzy growths are almost certain to be bryozoans. Even in fresh water toward autumn, the piers of a boat dock may develop enormous masses of gelatinous material patterned in a mosaic of brown markings over the surface. This too is a colonial moss animal, not the egg mass of a giant frog.

Moss animals are all colony builders, and never live alone. Each individual is of microscopic dimensions, seldom more than $\frac{1}{64}$ inch in length. It lives a few weeks attached to the walls of a chamber formed of its own secretion while capturing still more minute particles of food in a current of water created by cilia on its many tentacles. The presence of cilia on the tentacles distinguishes a moss animal from any coelenterate hydroid.

Bryozoans have a U-shaped digestive tract in which the mouth is centrally placed in a ring or horseshoe-shaped group of tentacles and the anus lies near the mouth but is not encircled by the tentacles. The anus is exposed when the tentacles are fully extended from the chamber housing the animal. Otherwise the body of each individual is astonishingly simple. It contains no respiratory, circulatory, or excretory system. Nor do the reproductive organs open to the outside by organized passageways.

The brevity of life span for individual moss animals could be suspected from examining a healthy colony with a hand lens. Each community begins as a sexually produced single individual maturing from a newly attached juvenile which has just gone through marked changes from the embryonic swimming stage. The first individual produces asexual buds, each of which adds another chamber and another zooid—and more buds. Consequently the periphery of a growing incrusted colony or the tips of the branches of a feathery clump of bryozoans is always the youngest part.

Back from the edge or the tips, the hand lens usually reveals chambers empty except for minute brown lumps, the "brown bodies" which remain from a degenerated individual zooid. Still older parts of the colony are likely to be inhabited again by feeding individuals, for into the chamber of a dead zooid the colonial cross-connecting strands send a new bud to provide a replacement. Often the first meal of the new zooid is the brown body representing its predecessor.

No one is sure why each zooid dies so young. Possibly it is poisoned by nitrogenous wastes, with no excretory system to discharge them to the outside world. This seems improbable, since oxygen is exchanged for carbon dioxide with no respiratory system, merely by absorption and release through thin areas of the body wall, including the crown of tentacles. Perhaps the zooid dies by rupture in freeing its sexually produced offspring. The timing would correspond well. And a habit of this kind would not be without precedent, whether in the clamworms or the sea lamprey or Pacific salmon.

Each active zooid is a sort of jack-in-a-box, often concealed by a little trap door. Contraction of certain body muscles causes an increase in the hydraulic pressure inside the body cavity. This pressure is relieved when the crown of tentacles moves through the doorway into the surrounding water. Additional muscles may even widen the opening, as though to speed the tentacle crown on its way. Yet the first disturbance is enough to cause still other muscles to drag the everted crown back into the safety of the chamber. If it has a lid, the door snaps shut.

In order to use this hydraulic method in extending the crown of tentacles, each zooid must fill its chamber. It must also retain space to accommodate the tentacle crown whenever this feeding organ is endangered. These conflicting requirements leave no space for growth. Nor does the organization of the colony provide for the general expansion of individuals. The colony grows by addition of new chambers and new zooids.

The permanence of a bryozoan colony is improved if the chambers have thickened walls. The zooids are also better supported, and can reach more successfully into the water for particles of food. Yet allowance must still be made for the out-and-in movements of the tentacle crown. Several solutions to this problem are possible, and different bryozoans have become adapted in one way or another.

Some moss animals with armored chambers leave one wall—usually an end one, overhung by protective spines—thin and membranous, flexible enough to be pulled in while extending the tentacles, and to bulge out again when the feeding organ is retracted. Other bryozoans possess a second, special "compensation cavity" within the chamber, with its own small opening to the outside world. Muscles that dilate the compensation cavity squeeze the zooid and cause the tentacle crown to pop out. Retraction of the crown forces water from the compensation cavity, giving the zooid space within its box.

A third method seems still simpler: the contraction of muscles dilating the opening of the chamber compresses the fluid in the zooid's body cavity and ejects the tentacle crown. Retraction is at the expense of space in the chamber opening through which the feeding organ is withdrawn.

So many different forms of life compete for space on rocks and shells, pilings and boat bottoms, that bryozoans are ever in danger of being overgrown. In many places, suffocation under inedible sediments is another hazard for all attached animals. Seemingly to deal with this dual jeopardy, most colonies of bryozoans in the larger of the two marine orders support non-feeding zooids serving to police the immediate world of the feeding individuals. That this should also be the order in which hinged doors is usual is no coincidence. The defending zooids are merely ones whose trap doors are modified as tools.

One type of policing zooid is the avicularium, in which the movable door has become the jaw of a snapping individual resembling a beaked bird's head, and named from the Latin *avicula,* a little bird. The other type has the door modified into a long, whip-like organ that can be swept over the surface of the colony. Avicularia seize and hold small invaders of

A large colony of a fresh-water bryozoan, *Pectinatella magnifica,* found growing on submerged wood in quiet water. This massive species is common east of the Mississippi valley. (Pennsylvania. Ralph Buchsbaum)

all kinds, preventing them from settling among the feeding zooids. Usually the little jaws continue to clamp on victims until they die and decompose. Bacteria and other microorganisms from the decay processes may well augment the diet of the feeding members of the bryozoan colony.

Under the microscope the gelatinous matrix of a *Pectinatella* colony is seen to be studded with delicate flower-like individuals, each with a crown of ciliated tentacles that gather food. (Pennsylvania. Ralph Buchsbaum)

About 6000 different species of living moss animals have been discovered, distinguished primarily upon differences in the chambers they construct. One small class is confined to fresh water. With rare exceptions, all members of the other, larger class live where the sea has its full salinity. Most are shore or shallow-water forms. They occur in all latitudes. Some are known from depths of 19,500 feet.

Fresh-water Bryozoans

(Class Phylactolaemata)

A microscope is needed to see that in this class a little flap of body wall projects over the mouth as though guarding the gullet. Yet this detail has given the name of the class, from the Greek *phylacterion,* a guard, and *laimos,* the gullet. Far more obvious is the fact that the tentacle crown is horseshoe-shaped or at least kidney-shaped, rather than circular. The body wall of each zooid contains a layer of muscles and the body cavity (coelom) is a colonial affair, continuous from one zooid to the next.

Fresh-water bryozoans are widely distributed, often cosmopolitan. During warm weather they reproduce sexually, but when winter comes they bridge it in the form of asexually produced armored balls of cells called statoblasts. These latter tolerate freezing in the ice, and can be carried from pond to pond on the muddy feet of birds and muskrats. The statoblasts are released in autumn when the parent colony dies and disintegrates.

On the undersides of stones and sticks in ponds and streams, particularly in shady places, fine-branching, vinelike growths or bushy clumps with a zooid in each end chamber are usually either *Fredericella* or *Plumatella.* The former has oval or kidney-shaped crowns of tentacles, the latter strictly horseshoe-shaped food-capturing organs.

Another type of moss animal in fresh waters produces masses of gelatinous material as a base. *Pectinatella* individuals form a thin crust over the common jelly secretion, organized into a mosaic of brown-streaked areas each half an inch across, on a mass reaching two feet or more in diameter. The brown streaks radiate from a center, yet each streak is itself a complex colony—a radial line of zooids. Each area in the mosaic may include twelve to eighteen zooids, all reaching out their feeding tentacles, yet able to snap back into the protection of the jelly.

Pectinatella's central jelly becomes the repository for the innumerable statoblasts. These are armed with a belt of hooks around an encircling air-filled cushion suggesting a life preserver. Empty shells of germinated statoblasts and dead ones sometimes drift to shore in windrows, speckling a beach to a width of one to four feet from the water.

Pectinatella forms fixed masses on underwater objects. *Cristatella* remains oval or elongate, as a creeping ruglike colony often encountered on the underside of a water-lily leaf. These colonies glide very slowly over plant stems, apparently through concerted movement of the muscles in the body walls of the zooids that secrete the underlying jelly. Half an inch to an inch a day are respectable speeds for this bryozoan. At intervals a colony of *Cristatella* pinches itself into two or more pieces, and each goes off on its own, elongating as new zooids are added. By late autumn, a lily pad floating on a pond particularly rich in food for bryozoans may wear a whole mesh of *Cristatella,* where separate colonies have fused together.

Marine Bryozoans

(*Class Gymnolaemata*)

The zooids of marine moss animals have no little flap of body wall projecting over the mouth, and hence the gullet is exposed, as is indicated by the name of the class (from Greek *gymno,* naked, and *laimos,* the gullet). In these bryozoans the tentacle crown is circular. The body wall contains no muscle layer, and each zooid has a separate body cavity (coelom).

A great many marine moss animals are cosmopolitan, apparently having been carried throughout the world on floating seaweeds, drifting wood, and the bottoms of ships. Consequently a remarkable variety can be found on almost any rock covered by water at low tide, on any wharf piling that has stood for a season, or among the fouling organisms on a boat bottom.

Each of the three methods by which moss animals provide for hydraulic extrusion of the tentacle crown is characteristic of an order. Those retaining at least one wall of the chamber as a thin, flexible membrane may thicken the other walls but not impregnate them with lime. These bryozoans wear around the extruded feeding organ a pleated collar with stiffening rods, suggesting a circular comb. They use this device to close the opening of the chamber after the tentacles have been withdrawn, and are the "comb-mouths" of order Ctenostomata. One of the strangest of them is *Victorella pavida,* whose long, slender, vaselike chambers arise from a branched, vinelike growth attached to underwater objects. It was discovered first on docks in the Thames River at London, and not only tolerates brackish water to a degree unusual among bryozoans but seemingly lives also in the fresh waters of Lake Tanganyika in Africa, on stones and shells and in cavities of fresh-water sponges there.

Members of several ctenostome families specialize in dissolving their way into the limy shells of conchs and other heavy marine mollusks, replacing the material removed by thin-walled chambers of their own.

Bryozoans whose chamber walls are all calcified have circular openings, and exchange space in the narrow vestibule opening to the sea for space in the body cavity when the tentacle-bearing crown is pushed out or pulled in. These are the "narrow-mouths" of order Stenostomata. None of them possesses avicularia or the whip-wielding vibracula, but reproduction may include a technique found nowhere else among bryozoans: they produce a number of embryos from each fertilized egg—like identical quintuplets, except still more numerous. The largest genus (*Tubulipora*) includes many kinds forming prone or erect colonies, often expanded into fanlike clusters from which the reproductive zooids project as clearly specialized members of the population.

The remaining marine bryozoans either retain one membranous wall in the calcified chamber or produce a compensation cavity. The opening of the chamber is usually protected by a movable door, as the "lip" referred to in the name of the order Cheilostomata, the "lip-mouths." This order is the only one in which some zooids are modified into avicularia or vibracula, serving to keep the colony immaculate and uninvaded. Most marine bryozoans are cheilostomes.

One of the most striking and largest of the cheilostomes is the barely calcified *Bugula turrita,* colonies of which are treelike, with branches each a spiral tuft of flat, fan-shaped groups of branchlets. Double rows of zooids on each branchlet have the openings facing in a single direction, the surface over which the avicularia patrol. These guardians swing on slender, flexible necks, back and forth with beaks wide open.

Fully developed *Bugula* colonies may protrude from wharf pilings and sea walls to a distance of 12 inches, the bright yellow or orange tentacles contrasting with the dark water anywhere from Maine to Brazil. Other species of *Bugula* are widely distributed in the northern and eastern Atlantic (Plate 34).

A very different type of cheilostome is the sea mat *Flustra foliacea,* so abundant on the shores of western Europe. Often it is mistaken for a seaweed, for it forms erect, leafy colonies. Each surface of the broad, bladelike branches is densely fitted with zooid-containing chambers, each with two little horns. Among the zooids are scattered, smaller, rounded avicularia with broad lips suggesting the distorted mouths of Ubangi women in the Belgian Congo.

CHAPTER XIII

The Lamp Shells

(*Phylum Brachiopoda*)

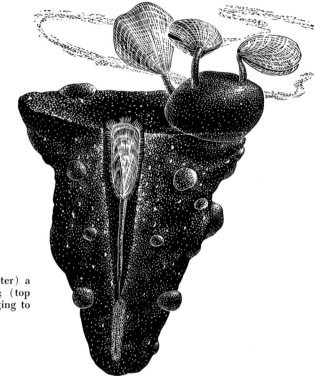

A variety of lamp shells: (center) a lingula with its stalk in mud; (top right) hinged lamp shells clinging to a rock

THE two parts of a brachiopod shell fit together like saucers facing one another. But instead of these being a right valve and a left, as in clams, one brachiopod valve is dorsal, the other ventral.

In most brachiopods, the ventral valve is somewhat larger and more convex, and extends beyond the dorsal valve around a definite opening. This gives the shell a general form like that of the oil lamps of Greek and Roman times, so often represented symbolically as the "lamp of wisdom." The classic lamp was lit through a hole corresponding in position to the one through which a living brachiopod has a short stalk serving to anchor the animal to some support. Usually the stalk holds the larger valve uppermost.

The 260 or so existing species of lamp shells are all marine. They represent today a slowly dwindling line whose ancestors can be traced clearly in the fossil record for 500 million years. During four-fifths of that time, they have been in slow decline. About 3000 different extinct species of brachiopods are known.

Two genera of brachiopods hold the record for surviving longer than any other group of animals. *Lingula,* found first in the early strata of Ordovician age, goes back at least 350 million years, although none of its existing species is particularly ancient. The other genus, *Crania,* dates from late Ordovician to the present, and is still millions of years older than the next competitor. During Ordovician times, lamp shells were more abundant than any other fossil-producing type of animal.

Inside its shell, each brachiopod shows a relationship to bryozoans and phoronids in possessing a pair of curled, tentacle-bearing arms, one on each side of the mouth. Cilia on the tentacle surfaces create water currents which enter at the sides of the shell, bringing minute food particles and oxygen. Glands on the tentacles secrete a mucus film in which food becomes trapped. The loaded mucus is then swallowed. The water leaves on the animal's midline, where the shell valves gape most broadly when the muscles controlling them relax.

Modern brachiopods include a few with shell valves as much as 3 inches in greatest dimension. Some fossil forms exceeded 1 foot across. Existing lamp shells inhabit all seas at all latitudes, and find places at all depths, from the intertidal sand flats to the great abysses. Many of them are abundant locally. Some are widespread, either geographically or in the depths they tolerate.

The shells of brachiopods provide easy cues for identification. Those of *Lingula* are elongate, oval, suggesting a finger nail, and the two valves of a pair have almost identical dimensions and shape. The stalk emerges between them instead of through a hole in one valve. *Lingula* and *Crania* both represent the smaller class Inarticulata, in which the shells lack an interlocking hinge mechanism. Both valves are movable, and sometimes they are twisted in relation to one another while the animal is feeding.

Crania lacks a stalk, and is found cemented by the ventral valve of its almost circular shell to rocks along north European coasts and in the West Indies. By contrast, *Lingula* and the similar animals of genus *Glottidia* have a long, slender, flexible stalk, and use it to anchor themselves temporarily at the bottom of vertical, mucus-lined burrows in sand flats below low-tide mark. If the waves wash the sand away, these brachiopods can dig in again. *Lingula* has many species in the Indian and Pacific Oceans. It is one of the commonest lamp shells around Japan. There, and around islands in the South Pacific, they are sometimes gathered as shellfish for human consumption.

Glottidia is found on both coasts of America, from the Carolinas to the Gulf of Mexico and from California to Peru. The shell valves may be 1 inch in length, $\frac{2}{5}$ inch across, with a stalk extending about $\frac{3}{4}$ inch.

Most modern brachiopods have limy teeth on each shell valve, serving to lock them in alignment at the hinge on the posterior edge. As such they are members of class Articulata. They differ also from the inarticulates in that the intestine ends blindly, with no anus, and residual wastes must be discharged as pellets through the mouth. The supporting stalk extends through a hole in the ventral shell valve, and customarily is used to hold the animal in a horizontal position like a little bracket from some vertical rock surface.

The hinged lamp shells are identified according to the form of the shell and the degree of development of a symmetrical pair of limy loops inside the smaller valve, serving to support the food-collecting, tentacle-bearing arms (lophophores). The one common brachiopod along the New England coast (*Terebratulina septentrionalis*), for example, has a pear-shaped shell about ½ inch long, ⅓ inch wide, within which the skeletal loops have fused into a single ring resembling a small stirrup with a hole the shape of an inverted heart. This same species is found also on coasts of Norway and Scotland. Others of the same large genus occur from the Antarctic to the Arctic in essentially all oceans.

In *Neothyris lenticularia* of New Zealand waters, the support for the tentacle-bearing lophophore has become a tremendous loop suggesting the newspaper holder below a metal letterbox, except that the center of the delicate skeleton is fixed by a median, blade-like extension from the region of the shell's hinge teeth. Even more crossbars bolster the lophophore skeleton in *Laqueus californianus,* whose barely ridged and highly convex shells reach a length of 2 inches on animals affixed to rocks along the Pacific coast of North America.

Lamp shells of the genus *Argyrotheca,* from the West Indies and western South Atlantic, are hermaphroditic. Otherwise brachiopods are either male or female. Their eggs and sperms are released into the body cavity and discharged from the excretory tubules (nephridia).

Most brachiopods retain their eggs within the shell valves until fertilization has been followed by some embryonic development. A few possess special brood pouches, either in the vicinity of the tentacle-bearing lophophore or, as in *Argyrotheca,* as enlargements of the excretory tubules.

When the swimming larvae are released, they move slowly through the water, propelled by cilia over at least the anterior lobe of the three-lobed body. A few days later, the larva metamorphoses, sinking to the bottom. Its posterior lobe elongates as the supporting stalk. The middle lobe enlarges to envelop the rest of the body and becomes modified into the two layers of tissue (mantle) secreting the shell valves and the food-gathering lophophore.

Irregularities in the rate of shell secretion usually provide eccentric rings comparable to those that have been used in estimating the age of clams. Apparently four years is a common life span for a lamp shell.

Three brachiopods attached to a piece of rock and to each other. Preserved. (P. S. Tice)

CHAPTER XIV

The Peanut Worms

(*Phylum Sipunculoidea*)

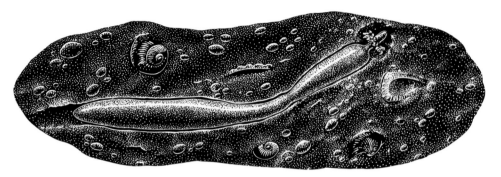

To a group of about 250 different species of sedentary marine worms the name "peanut worm" has been applied, although the extended animal resembles more a baseball bat with a crown of food-collecting tentacles at the small head end. Yet, if disturbed, the worm suddenly shortens, pulling in the anterior

half or third of its body, and rounding out to an appearance remarkably like that of the edible part (seed) of a peanut.

The most striking feature of these worms is the slender anterior part of the body (the introvert), which rapidly and smoothly runs in and out of the larger, cylindrical, posterior part. Actually the introvert turns in like the finger of a glove or the wall of a slender balloon pressed at the end by a lead pencil.

An undisturbed peanut worm extends its introvert from the opening of the burrow and sweeps the mucus-covered tentacles over the sea bottom, collecting microscopic plants and other bits of nourishment. These are digested in a long intestine which is both looped upon itself to open at an anus well forward on the animal's ventral surface and also spirally twisted within the body cavity.

Most sipunculoids live in shallow water, but some have been found in depths greater than fifteen thousand feet. Many peanut worms live in holes in submerged rocks. *Sipunculus nudus* reaches a length of about 8 inches and a diameter of ½ of an inch along sandy coasts of southern California, Japan, Europe, and Florida. *Golfingia* (*Phascolosoma*) *margaritacea* of more northern shores in both the Atlantic and the Pacific is more slender but may be 14 to 18 inches long. All peanut worms develop from an active swimming larva (trochophore) and discharge their eggs or sperms through their excretory tubules (nephridia) from the body cavity into the sea, where fertilization takes place.

The peanut worm *Golfingia* (*Phascolosoma*) loses its similarity to a peanut as soon as it extends from the contracted position. Here the smaller front end is being everted into the sand, turning inside out like a finger of a glove. (Oregon. Ralph Buchsbaum)

CHAPTER XV

The Echiuroids

(Phylum Echiuroidea)

AMONG the marine animals for which none of the scientific pigeonholes seems adequate are some sixty-odd whose general sausage shape as adults conceals the fact that they originate, as do so many mollusks and annelid worms, from a swimming trochophore larva. The echiuroid proceeds, in fact, as though to become an annelid, developing exactly fifteen segments to the body. Then it loses almost all evidence of these features, and takes up life either buried in the mud or protected within the cavity of some shell or coral rock.

Echiuroids ordinarily hold their mouths at the doorway of the burrow or hiding place. Beyond it, into the sea, the animal extends a long, troughlike or spoon-shaped prostomium and moves this about while cilia on the concave surface gather detritus from the bottom and pass it to the mouth.

On both sides of the Atlantic Ocean and along the Pacific coast of America from California northward, *Echiurus pallasii* reaches a length of 12 inches plus the 4-inch prostomium. *Echiurus echiurus* of Europe is found in the same mud flats but makes a U-shaped burrow and enlarges this as it grows.

In *Bonellia* the prostomium is as much as 3 feet long and forked toward the tip, but the living habits and food-gathering procedure of the female are almost identical with those of *Echiurus*. Larval *Bonellia* appear able to develop into either sex, but all of those that settle on the bottom become females. A larva that chances to settle on the extended prostomium of a female *Bonellia* becomes, instead, a male.

The female echiuroid *Bonellia viridis* has a green-colored oval body with a long, extensible proboscis, forked at the tip. The minute male lives within her body. (France. Ralph Buchsbaum)

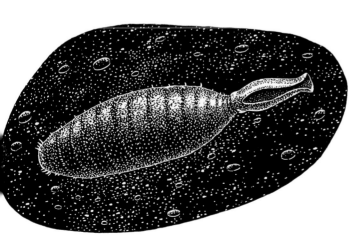

He remains microscopic in size and lives as a parasite upon his mate, in her mouth or excretory organs or reproductive tract.

Urechis, an echiuroid of the intertidal zone, has a different method of feeding. It uses its burrow as the support for a finger-shaped tube of mucus cemented to the rim of the burrow opening. Body movements of the worm in the U-shaped burrow draw water through the mucus filter, which strains out food particles. After the mucus tube becomes loaded, pumping is more difficult. *Urechis* then swallows the tube with its enclosed meal, moves to the burrow opening, and attaches the rim of a new mucus filter. When the water is charged with microscopic particles, *Urechis* may swallow and replace its filter every two or three minutes. But if the water is clear, a whole hour may be needed to load a single mucus tube.

[157

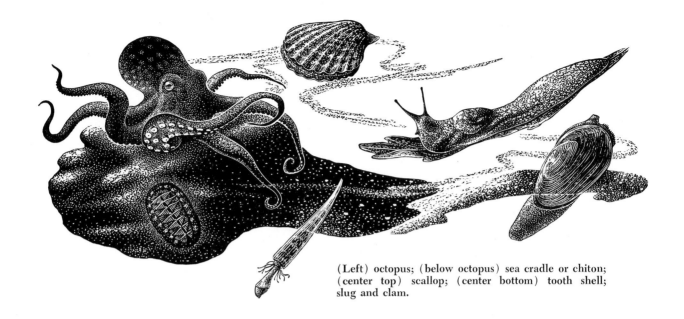

CHAPTER XVI

(Left) octopus; (below octopus) sea cradle or chiton;
(center top) scallop; (center bottom) tooth shell;
slug and clam.

The Mollusks

(*Phylum Mollusca*)

To many people the mollusks are "shellfish." Clams and oysters, perhaps snails and squids, are the most familiar kinds. Yet squids have no obvious shell, and no one seriously would consider a plate of cooked snails as fish except on "fish day." Nor did those who gave the phylum Mollusca its name (from the Latin *mollis,* soft) have in mind the giant squids of the open oceans, creatures that wrestle—sometimes successfully—with the great sperm whales.

Better than forty thousand different kinds of living mollusks are known, a total exceeded among invertebrate phyla only by the arthropods. These mollusks include representatives above the snow line in the Himalayas at an altitude of 16,400 feet, and deep blue sea slugs creeping on the underside of the surface film in the open ocean, and clams plowing the sea bottom at a depth of at least 17,400 feet where the hydrostatic pressure is almost four tons to the square inch. Some snails manage to survive freezing in the ice over ponds, and others tolerate thermal springs at a temperature of 112 degrees Fahrenheit. A few desert snails live where the air above them at noon is in the same temperature range.

All of this versatility demonstrates the possibilities

in an unsegmented body whose dorsal and lateral surfaces bear a fleshy tissue (the mantle) capable of secreting an external limy shell. Ordinarily the ventral surface is a flat, creeping foot. Features of the foot, mantle, and shell are particularly helpful in identifying each different kind of mollusk.

Some features of mollusk anatomy are peculiar to this phylum. A rasping organ (radula) is found in the mouth of most mollusks as a ribbon-shaped tool that can be slid back and forth while its sharp teeth act like those on a file, scraping free small particles of food. All mollusks, even the largest and most active, have a nervous system consisting of only three paired ganglia. One lies above or beside the mouth, a second below the gullet as a center for nerves to the foot region, and a third still more ventrally with connections to mantle, gills, heart, and other visceral organs.

This way of life is very old. Clams appear early in the fossil record, along with uncoiled snails and the ancestors of today's splendid pearly nautilus. Altogether, more than forty thousand extinct kinds of mollusks have been found, showing that modern shelled types are but the living heirs to a spectacularly diverse heritage.

The Mollusk Aborigines

(Class Monoplacophora)

Until 1957 no mollusk had been found giving more than token support to the scientists' hunch that, in the remote past, a limpet and a clamworm had shared a common ancestor. All known mollusks had gone ahead with their evolution in ways that placed no premium on a segmented body, whereas the annelids had found special advantages in partitions isolating a series of chambers—each a part of the body cavity.

Then, among a collection of bottom animals brought aboard the Danish research ship *Galathea* in 1956, from nearly twelve thousand feet below the surface of the Pacific Ocean some three hundred miles from the nearest shore (Nicaragua), biologists found some "living fossils"—ten complete, preserved specimens and three empty shells of a kind of creature no one had ever seen before. They named it *Neopilina galatheae,* and recognized it from its shell as representing a type of life believed extinct since the Devonian period of geological time, four hundred million years ago. No animal discovered in recent years has meant so much in scientific understanding.

The deeps of the sea must hide many such treasures. In December of 1958, four more specimens of *Neopilina* were hauled up to daylight from more than nineteen thousand feet below the surface. Until the dredge of the American research vessel *Vema* arrived, these mollusks had been living on the bottom of an ocean valley known as the Peru-Chile Trench, about one hundred miles from the coast of northern Peru. This was more than thirteen hundred miles from and seven thousand feet deeper than the earlier find. The species collected aboard the *Vema* received the name *N. ewingi,* to honor Dr. Maurice Ewing of Columbia University, who had arranged the expedition as part of a long-term enthusiasm for deep-sea biological exploration.

Both kinds of *Neopilina* could easily be mistaken for some kind of limpet with a small flat foot. The largest of the thin, almost circular shells is about ¾ of an inch long and about ³⁄₁₆ of an inch high, like a short stocking cap with the extra material drawn to a low point in the middle at the front.

Shells of this general style are known from the early Paleozoic sedimentary rocks, and the only strange thing about them is the pairs of little scars on the inner surface, showing where muscles held the animal to its armor. That these scars were (and are) paired attracted no special attention until a preserved *Neopilina* became available for study. Then the creature was seen to have a pair of gills on each side of the foot under the mantle to correspond to each pair of muscle attachments. And between the gills, paired excretory tubules open—tubules (nephridia) far more like those of marine annelid worms than those of any mollusk known.

Neopilina cannot be said to be segmented, for its body contains no crosswise partitions—but, in this sense, neither can an adult leech. And no one has yet seen the young of these mollusk aborigines. The duplication of parts, whether gills or excretory tubules (nephridia) or shell-holding muscle bands, all show a similarity to annelid worms. At the same time, a pair of fleshy flaps on each side of the mouth suggest the food-manipulating organs of a clam. A series of short tentacles just posterior to the mouth, in front of the foot, could well represent on a diminutive scale the "arms" of an octopus or squid.

Whether *Neopilina* creeps over the oozy bottom on a thin cushion of secreted mucus or lies on its back and uses the mucus film as a trap for food may eventually be learned. Its one-piece shell provides the basis for the name devised in 1957 for the new class Monoplacophora ("one-plate-bearer"). No doubt other "living fossils" will come to light as explorations continue in the dark depths of the sea.

The Sea Cradles

(Class Amphineura)

If an animal clinging to a rock at the seashore wears a shell consisting of eight transverse limy plates, it is a sea cradle (chiton). The natives of the West Indies call these exclusively marine animals "sea beef," and sometimes collect them to cook as food. American Indians on the Pacific coast used them in this way too, and had available the largest sea cradle in the world—as much as 13 inches long.

The broadly oval foot of a sea cradle provides the animal with a suction cup for clinging to rocks and a means for slowly moving from place to place while rasping algae from the rock face by repeated strokes of the filelike radula. The edge of a sea cradle's mantle comes down around the foot, and wears an encircling girdle of minute limy plates suggesting a coat of mail.

Above the girdle, the mantle secretes the eight valves of the shell proper, each fitted to its neighbor in such a way that the animal can curl up into a ball if detached from its support. While partly curled, the inverted chiton may rock gently like a cradle.

Sometimes the hard, whitened valves from a dead sea cradle wash ashore separately and are called "sea butterflies" because of the limy wings that provide the hinge action between one plate and the next. In some localities the chiton itself is known as the "butterfly fish." The series of shell valves might be assumed to indicate segmentation. But it does not correspond to the arrangement of bushy gills (six to eighty pairs) along the sides of the sea cradle's foot, or to the ladder-like cross connections between the two separate but parallel nerve cords from which the class Amphineura takes its name (Greek *amphi,* on each side, and *neura,* a nerve). None of the other internal organs shows a pattern suggesting repetition.

Although they lack eyes, most chitons are sensitive to light and feed only in hours of darkness. Many of them return to the same site whenever not actually foraging. Others apparently never leave the "home spot." The commonest sea cradle of exposed coralline- and mussel-covered rocks along the Pacific coast of America (*Nuttallina californica*) remains fixed in this voluntary way. Repeated pounding by the waves and erosion aided by this 1½-inch mollusk produce depressions the size and shape of its spiny girdle and create little eddies with the ebb and flow of each wave. The eddies deposit seaweed debris in the depressions, bringing food to the animals in this way. *Nuttallina* is believed to survive for more than twenty-five years in this sedentary life, and the depressions are used by generation after generation of this mollusk, probably for thousands of years.

The giant of all sea cradles is *Cryptochiton stelleri,* whose brick-red girdle completely covers the shell valves. It is called the sea boot or gumboot, and inhabits rocks from Bering Strait to California and to Japan. A 13-inch specimen may be 6 inches wide.

On the intertidal coasts of Alaska, the most abundant sea cradle is the large, dead-black *Katharina tunicata* (Plate 39), whose valves barely show where the expanded girdle leaves little heart-shaped gaps along the back. It is common on both sides of the North Pacific, seeming to prefer rocks that form ledges about halfway between mid-tide and low. It tolerates full sunlight longer than most chitons.

Along Atlantic coasts the sea cradles are smaller in high latitudes, and the ¾-inch species of *Lepidochiton* tend to be the chief ones found with a clean-appearing zone of girdle platelets. *Chaetopleura apiculata,* of about the same size, is common below low-tide mark from Cape Cod to Florida; it has a hairy girdle and a keel down the middle of the shell valves. In tropical waters, far larger chitons tolerate intense sunlight for hours while exposed by the tide.

Each sea cradle is either a male or a female. Many of them congregate in springtime, which is spawning time, and the females may each lay two long, spiral strings of eggs in jelly. The egg strings of *Ischnochiton magdalensis* on the California coast average 31 inches in length, and have been found to contain between them from 100,000 to 200,000 eggs. The young emerge as swimming larvae, but within a couple of hours they settle and transform to the shell-bearing adult.

In addition to the sea cradles or chitons with plates (the "loricates" of order Polyplacophora), the class Amphineura includes some seemingly degenerate, shell-less animals (order Aplacophora). These are the 1-inch, wormlike solenogasters, which live in the sea at depths greater than ninety feet, creeping over hydroids and corals upon which they feed.

Each solenogaster has a cylindrical body with a mouth at one end and an anus between two projecting gills at the other. If a foot is present, it consists only of a narrow ventral groove. Apparently all solenogasters begin as a larva with seven transverse limy plates on the back and a radula in the mouth. But the plates, and in some cases the radula as well, are lost at maturity. The body is then clothed in limy spicules that project from the enveloping mantle.

The Snails and Slugs

(Class Gastropoda)

When a person describes something as being a flat spiral, he usually compares it with a watch spring, a butterfly's tongue, or a snail shell. All snail shells today do have a spiral origin, even when (as among the limpets) no outward trace of this may remain. Back at the beginning of the fossil record, however, the earliest known snails had straight shells or long, curved, conical ones suggesting today's tusk shells, except that they were closed at the small end. Through adoption of a spiral shape, a snail can carry within the armor of the shell a long, pointed mound of body and manage it in a neatly portable form.

Most snails glide about on the large, flat, foot portion of the body and show a definite head end, often with eyes and sensitive projections (tentacles). Usually, when danger threatens, the snail can withdraw into the safety of the shell, pulling in first the tentacles and head, then the complete foot. A good many snails even carry on the side of the foot a flat plate which forms a hard door (operculum), closing the shell completely after the animal is inside.

That snails and slugs appear to creep on their belly surfaces is recognized in the class name (from *gaster,* the belly, and *pes, podos,* a foot). The gastropod combines a skidding action of the rim of the foot along a sheet of mucus secreted at the anterior end, with movement of the sole proper in a series of waves. Transverse bands of the sole alternately support the weight of the animal and are moved backward in a stretching action, and then are lifted clear to shift forward again, ready to take part in the next downward cycle.

The ⅓-inch chink shells (*Lacuna*), which superficially resemble periwinkles, creep about on seaweeds and eelgrass with a different gait. The foot is grooved lengthwise, and the snail waddles—advancing one side of the foot and then the other, swaying

[continued on page 177]

60. The **spotted sea hare**, *Aplysia dactylomela*, ejecting a cloud of purple secretion on being disturbed. The two fleshy lobes that form the sides of the body cover a thin horny shell that lies buried under the skin. From the southern half of Florida to the West Indies it may be seen in shallow water during the breeding season. (West Indies. Fritz Goro: *Life* Magazine)

61. A **sea slug**, *Okenia quadricornis*, with a tuft of gills near the rear end. Like other sea slugs, it has a larval shell, which later disappears. (England. D. P. Wilson)

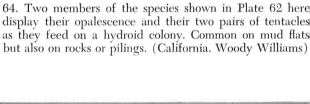

64. Two members of the species shown in Plate 62 here display their opalescence and their two pairs of tentacles as they feed on a hydroid colony. Common on mud flats but also on rocks or pilings. (California. Woody Williams)

62. One of the commonest **sea slugs** on the American Pacific coast is *Hermissenda crassicornis*, with tufts of gill-like extensions on the back. It is usually colored as shown here, but the color may vary. (Oregon. Ralph Buchsbaum)

63. Its coloring and the branching processes make *Dendronotus frondosus*, a **sea slug** 2 to 3 inches long, hard to detect when it crawls among seaweeds. It often feeds on *Tubularia* (Plate 5). Distributed on northern shores around the world. (England. D. P. Wilson)

65. A **tropical sea slug**, *Ceratosoma*, with a retractile tuft of gill-like plumes surrounding the anus. Except in coloring, it resembles many white or yellow sea slugs that live in temperate waters. (New Caledonia. René Catala)

66. A bizarre **tropical sea slug**, very firm in texture and about 3 inches long, crawling about on the branches of a gorgonian colony. (Great Barrier Reef. Jerome M. and Dorothy H. Schweitzer)

67. The **clown sea slug**, *Triopha carpenteri*, about 2½ inches long, lives on seaweeds and in tide pools but seems to be avoided by tide-pool fishes. (California. Woody Williams)

→

68. **Sargassum sea slugs,** *Scyllaea pelagica,* live attached to floating sargassum sea-weed. One of the sea slugs, freed from the seaweed, shows two pairs of leaflike extensions from the back that serve as gills. Two still cling to the seaweed, which is covered with delicate little branching colonies of a hydroid. (Marineland, Florida)

69. The **sea slug** shown in Plates 62 and 64 is here shown laying a spiral ribbon of eggs against the glass of an aquarium. (California. Woody Williams)

70. A **common garden slug**, *Limax*, often feeds on tomatoes. It seldom faces such bright light, as it lives in gardens and woods and comes out to feed only at night. The mantle covers less than half of the body and hides a rudimentary shell. Native to Europe and introduced into the United States. (Hal H. Harrison: National Audubon)

71. The **black slug**, *Arion ater*, grows to 6 inches in length. It lives in coarse grass in meadows or gardens. (England. John Markham)

72. A group of swimming **European squids**, *Loligo vulgaris,* seen head-on through glass at the Naples Aquarium. Squids are greatly relished as food in Italy and in many Asian coastal communities. (D. P. Wilson)

73. A group of **American squids**, *Loligo pealii,* about 8 inches long, seen in side view. Living in great schools from Massachusetts Bay to Cape Hatteras, these squids serve as food for fishes and as bait for fishermen. (N. J. Berrill)

74. A **pearly**, or **chambered**, **nautilus**, *Nautilus macromphalus*, that lived for fifty-nine days in the aquarium at Nouméa, New Caledonia. The many small arms can be withdrawn into the shell's last chamber, and the entrance closed by the hood seen above the arms. (René Catala)

75. The **common cuttlefish** of Europe, *Sepia officinalis*, in a tank at the Den Helder Zoological Station in Holland. One of the two females is attaching black egg capsules, one by one, to the stick in the foreground. (Ralph Buchsbaum)

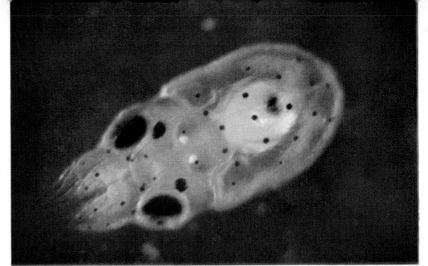

76. **A baby octopus** just hatched from the egg.
(Banyuls, France. Ralph Buchsbaum)

77. The **common octopus**, *Octopus vulgaris*, with a mass of egg clusters fastened to a rock in the aquarium at Marineland, Florida. Each egg is ⅛ inch long, and is attached to vertical strands supporting about 1000 eggs in each cluster. A female may lay 180,000 eggs in two weeks. (Marineland, Florida)

78–80. The **lesser octopus** of European waters, *Eledone cirrhosa*, shown crawling on the bottom of a tank, just taking off, and swimming. Like the common octopus, it feeds on fishes and even more on crabs. It ranges from the North Atlantic to the Mediterranean, rarely has a span of more than 3 feet, and has only one row of suckers on each arm. In contrast, the common octopus is mainly tropical and subtropical, extending north only to the English Channel. It has two rows of suckers on each arm, and in the Mediterranean may have a span of 10 feet. (Plymouth, England. D. P. Wilson)

82. A **serpulid tube worm**, *Serpula vermicularis*, fastened to a scallop shell. The red tentacles, or gills, are protruded from a pink or greenish hard calcareous tube 3 to 4 inches long. The worm lives below low-tide mark, and is widely distributed on Atlantic, Pacific, and other shores. (England. D. P. Wilson)

81. A **feather-duster worm**, *Eudistylia vancouveri*, a large sabellid annelid that lives in sand and mud flats on the American Pacific coast. The feathery tentacles, used in feeding and respiration, are protruded from a tough parchment-like tube, which extends deep into the substrate. (California. Woody Williams)

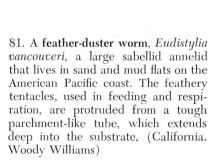

83. Several **sabellid fan worms**, *Spirographis*, shown here with the long tubes laid on sand in a tank of the Station Biologique, Roscoff, France. It lives upright, with the tube imbedded in sand and mud flats, from the English Channel to the Mediterranean. (Ralph Buchsbaum)

84. The largest **fan worm** in English waters, *Bispira volutacornis*, with an elegant double spiral of tentacles protruding from the tube. (England. D. P. Wilson)

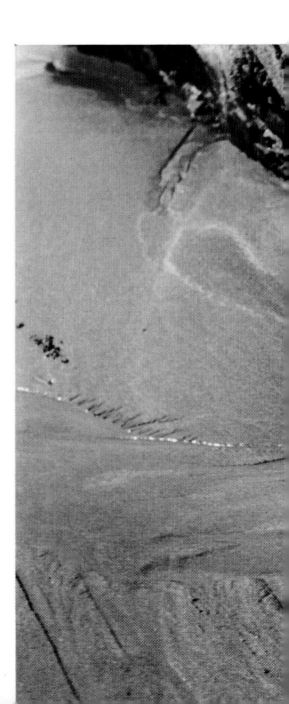

85. The **sea mouse**, *Aphrodite aculeata*, a scale worm, is here laid on its back to show the bristle-bearing, segmented appendages that line both sides of the body. It is 2 inches wide and up to 6 inches long, and the back is covered with matted bristles. Found on European and American shores, in sandy mud, with only the hind end protruding. (Plymouth, England. Ralph Buchsbaum)

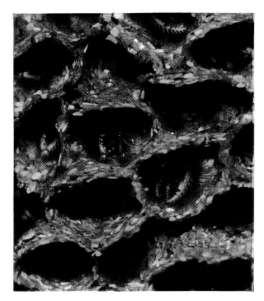

86 and 87. The **honeycomb worm**, *Sabellaria alveolata*, forms honeycombs of tubes (below) on wave-washed rocks near sandy bottoms that furnish the grains with which the tube is strengthened. At low tide the worms draw in their heads and stopper their tubes with two front feet (see enlarged portion of colony at right). (Widemouth Bay, England. D. P. Wilson)

88. A **peripatus**, *Macroperipatus geayi,* about 5 inches long, from the forest floor of Panama. Although of great interest as an animal transitional between annelids and arthropods, it is seldom seen. It lives mostly under leaf mold and logs in tropical forests and comes out at night to feed on small animals. (Ralph Buchsbaum)

89. A large **pill bug**, *Ligia pallasii,* which scurries about rocky cliffs, close to the water's edge, from Alaska to California. When the tide is out it ventures into the intertidal area to feed, but with the returning tide hurries back. (Oregon. Ralph Buchsbaum)

[continued from page 160]

from side to side as it shifts its weight from the one being moved.

The abundant little salt-marsh snails (*Melampus*), which breathe by means of a lung, hitch themselves along by clinging alternately with the forward half and then the hinder portion of the foot. As they do so they suggest a cautious child taking short, sliding steps on glare ice. By contrast, the curious little tube shell *Caecum* glides along on a ciliated foot, holding steady its blunt-ended limy cone with its many encircling rings.

Gastropods show tremendous variation in the degree of development of the shell. The horse conch *Pleuroploca gigantea* of Atlantic shores from North Carolina to Brazil, and an Australian marine snail *Megalotractus auruanus,* each with a 24-inch shell, share the distinction of being the world's largest univalves. On land the giant is *Achatina achatina* of African jungles, especially in Liberia, with a shell 8 inches long and 4 in diameter. All of these animals can pull well back into their shelters and remain hidden for days or even months if conditions are unfavorable.

In other gastropods, the shell offers so little space that it can serve only as a sort of badge, proving snailhood. Among sea butterflies (pteropods) it scarcely hinders progress as the animal swims freely near the ocean's surface far from land, waving a pair of winglike expansions from the sides of the foot. Or the shell may be lost altogether at a tender age, as in another sea butterfly (*Clione*), found in great schools, swimming in cold waters between the Arctic and New York, Scandinavia, the northern parts of the British Isles, northern California, and Japan. *Clione* serves as a major food source for several kinds of whalebone whales. The sea slugs (nudibranchs) and many land slugs also lose their embryonic shells and manage thereafter with almost none.

Some small snails lack a radula. Most of these are parasites on and in echinoderms, or they browse on the slime accumulating at the end of a clam's exposed siphon. Otherwise a radula seems important in rasping off minute particles of food, whether this is vegetable matter or flesh. Oyster drills and whelks use the radula to cut neat circular holes through the shells of clams and oysters, and then thrust the organ into the victim's shelter to remove the meat—killing the shellfish in the process. In tropical seas, many whelks and conchs with this habit are collected for human food and as bait.

Auger snails (*Terebra*) and cone snails (*Conus marmoreus;* Plate 59) have a barb at the end of the radula, connected by a duct to a poison gland near the gullet. These carnivorous snails use the radula as a weapon, "stinging" victims to subdue them. Some of the larger cone snails, whose shells are much prized by collectors, have been known to sting a hu-

man hand and inject a fatal dose of poison. For this reason they are quite honestly feared in the South Pacific.

Quite apart from any coiling of the body in relation to the shell, all gastropods go through a strange process found in no other group of mollusks. During their embryonic development, the body mass atop the head and foot undergoes a torsion through 180 degrees until the anus, mantle cavity, and any respiratory organs (ctenidia) come to lie at the back of the head instead of the rear of the body.

Among the majority of marine snails, from abalones and limpets to whelks, this arrangement persists. They are "prosobranchs," with the respiratory organs at the front. Other snails and all slugs undo the twist in one way or another, placing the respiratory organ at the rear again or replacing it with something else. These are the "opisthobranchs," such as sea hares (with a very reduced shell) and nudibranchs (with no shell at all), or the "pulmonates" in which the mantle cavity has become functional as a lung—these last animals usually are found in fresh

The sea butterfly *Clione* is a shell-less, swimming mollusk found in great schools in surface waters, particularly of the colder oceans, where it becomes an important food of whalebone whales. (Delaware Bay. William H. Amos)

When an abalone (*Haliotis*) is dislodged from its rocky support, it tends to curl the edges of its broad foot, here seen from below. (California. Ralph Buchsbaum)

Until the heavy growth of hydroids, moss animals, and seaweeds is cleaned from the red abalone (*Haliotis rufescens*), the attractive shell cannot be seen, although its breathing holes remain unobstructed. (California. J. A. Aplin)

water or on land. Curiously enough, the prosobranch snails are either male or female, whereas the opisthobranchs and pulmonates are hermaphroditic.

PROSOBRANCHS

Abalones (the word has four syllables, the final *e* being sounded) are also called ear shells or ormers. They are widespread vegetarians with definite preferences in location and habits. Man enjoys the big muscle attached to an abalone's shell so much that these animals are always in danger of extermination. Those used for food on the island of Guernsey in the English Channel (*Haliotis tuberculatus*) have virtually vanished. In California the large abalones of several kinds were in similar danger until minimum size limits were enforced on residents and shipment of both abalone meat and the handsome, iridescent shells from the state were forbidden.

Shells of the red abalone *Haliotis rufescens* are almost always encrusted heavily by hydroids, bryozoans, and plants. Water passing the abalone's gills emerges through three or four open holes in the shell as the animal browses on sea lettuce and kelps. The red abalone reaches breeding age at six years and a length of 4 inches. Minimum size for legal possession is now 7 inches, which may correspond to about twelve years of age since one thirteen-year-old specimen kept under observation was 8 inches long. Red abalones with 10-inch shells are now rare except in collections.

The green abalone *H. fulgens* has a flatter shell with six open holes and very little growth of other life on its shell. Yet it resembles *H. rufescens* in clinging to rock ledges where the water is fifty to seventy feet deep and consequently fairly free of wave action. The black abalone *H. cracherodii,* by contrast, is a surf-dweller, in the cracks of rocks through which waves plunge. Its shell is regularly clean and shining, with from five to eight perforations. Large numbers reach the legal minimum size for harvesting—5½ inches.

Apparently the black abalone feeds on microscopic plants, whereas the others take larger fare. The green abalone is particularly quick when a bit of seaweed strikes the long tentacles projecting under the mantle edge. It whirls and uses the anterior end of its foot to clamp the seaweed against the rock until the mouth can be brought to bear and the radula can rasp the plant into pieces small enough to swallow. This same whirling movement is a protection against starfish, one that is successful unless the abalone is too small or the sea star too large.

A limpet has the reputation of being able to cling to a rock more tightly than an abalone—more tightly, in fact, than any other animal. But an undisturbed limpet holds just tightly enough to keep waves from dislodging it. A sudden push from the side usually separates it from its rock surface. The merest touch, however, before the shove arrives is enough to induce a limpet to exert its full abilities as an animated suction cup. This suction has been measured as seventy pounds to the square inch of foot surface. That it is actually suction can be demonstrated by sliding a thin knife blade between the foot and the stone, letting air or water break the mucus seal; the animal will then be found to have lost all hold upon its support.

After growth is well under way, the shell of a limpet shows little of its spiral origin. The shell is tentlike as soon as a whorl or two have been produced, and thereafter additions are made evenly all the way around, keeping the shelter bilaterally symmetrical. A keyhole limpet (Plates 47, 48) has a hole at the peak like the crater of a volcano, and for this reason is sometimes called a volcano shell. The hole originates as a notch in the outer lip of the beginning shell. Later growth closes the notch, and the limpet goes on to make the shell symmetrical. But it continues to use the opening for discharge of wastes from the anus and for a current of water drawn under the shell at the anterior end by cilia covering the mantle surface.

The dunce-cap limpet *Acmaea mitra* of North Pacific coasts is the tallest of the true limpets. It reaches a shell length close to 2 inches and a height of 1 inch, and hence is probably the bulkiest of all limpets. Some other lower-spired species cover a greater area of rock. The largest of keyhole limpets is *Lucapina crenulata* of southern California and Mexico. It reaches a length of 7 inches and a width approaching 3. On the Atlantic coast of America, the eastern keyhole limpet *Fissurella alternata* ranges all the way from New Jersey into the West Indies and the Gulf of Mexico, but seldom attains a length of more than an inch.

One of the sea's strangest snails is the wearer of the "purple shell," *Janthina fragilis*. This eyeless, violet-colored animal drifts near the surface of all warm oceans, suspended from a raft of air cells in a mat of mucus. Often these creatures advance in large schools, yet the individual members appear able to find enough of their favorite jellyfishes to eat. Each *Janthina* is an expert at spearing small medusae on a long, prehensile proboscis.

Probably sea birds are *Janthina's* chief enemies. Against them it is camouflaged by its own color, and in addition it is armed with a glandular bag full of purple liquid. It expels this fluid into the surrounding water in a cloud, against which it shows no contrast. *Janthina* produces a floating egg raft too, and usually stays with it until the young snails hatch. Often both *Janthina* and its rafts are cast upon subtropical and tropical beaches as prizes for the curious.

Another oddity encountered by the beachcomber

Limpets that live high on the shore, like *Acmaea digitalis*, common along most of the American Pacific coast, must withstand extremes of temperature and drying. (Oregon. Ralph Buchsbaum)

is the sea collar, a capelike thin swirl of sand grains among which the eggs of the moon snail *Polinices* (Plate 55) appear as transparent dots when the collar is held up to bright sunlight. The moon snail itself has a tremendous foot, so large that the heavy, globular shell can scarcely accommodate it. The animal uses the foot as a bulldozer blade while plowing through the surface sediments of sandy beaches, feeling for clams it can hold while drilling through the shell to reach their flesh.

When *Polinices* is ready to lay eggs, she exudes a film of mucus from the foot and spreads this over the exposed part of her body, adding eggs at the same time as the mucus covering becomes impregnated with sand grains. When the mucus hardens to a leathery jelly, the parent snail slips out of a gap in the sea collar, leaving it on the sandy bottom. If the collar washes ashore, it may remain intact in very humid air. But if it dries out, the mucus becomes brittle and the collar extremely fragile. Sand collars are sometimes 8 inches across and 2½ to 3 inches high.

Polinices is so obviously too large for its shell that

The common European limpet, *Patella vulgata*, clamps down tightly when tide is out but moves about to browse on seaweed when water returns. (England. D. P. Wilson)

it seems incredible for any other mollusk to occupy space inside the doorway. Yet the boat shell *Crepidula* often takes up residence there. Actually the boat shell is not very selective about an attachment site, for it will even cling to others of its own kind until masses of as many as forty come to lie as a cluster on the bottom. *Crepidula* holds to its oval, boat-shaped shell by a horizontal shelf across the posterior end inside—and because of this shelf, the shell is often called the "quarter-deck shell" or "slipper shell."

Crepidula feeds on small plants and animals trapped in a mucus film spread over the gills on each side of its foot. About every four minutes, the mollusk twists its head to one side or the other and gathers the loaded mucus into its mouth. Small particles are swallowed immediately, but large ones may be stored in a pouch at the front of the mouth as emergency rations. These are used when *Crepidula* must clamp its shell down tight and hold on.

Freshly matured boat shells are males. Later they become bisexual, and still later completely female. At breeding season the mother snail produces about fifty or sixty membranous bags, each loaded with around 250 eggs, and guards these for the month until they hatch. The young swim freely for about two weeks, and then settle on some surface where they can become more or less permanently attached.

The edible periwinkle *Littorina littorea* is collected by the ton along European shores and sold roasted on the streets of London. About 1857 it was introduced into Nova Scotia and gradually spread southward, now well past Chesapeake Bay. The sexes are separate, the female being a little larger than the male, about ¾ of an inch in diameter and in height—a squat, thick cone, usually olive-colored but often banded with dark red or brown. Almost no one eats winkles in America. Other species of *Littorina* (Plate 56) are found on almost all of the world's coasts, rasping algae from the rocks or cleaning the film of vegetation from the surface of mud flats.

The old-maid's curl or worm shell *Vermicularia* starts out as a tightly coiled high spire, but the snail inside changes its construction habits after a few turns have been completed. It progresses with its building of new shell in a very straggling manner, producing a winding tube with lengthwise keel and grooves, often totaling 6 to 9 inches in length. In tropical waters these shells are found entwined among sponges and corals, where they suggest the products of tube-building worms. Occasionally they become grouped in tangled masses or attach themselves to oyster shells and other mollusks.

Conchs and whelks produce far more regular and massive shells. These are aggressive, carnivorous snails, whose large shells usually provide a "canal" for the siphon through which water is discharged after passing the gill, the excretory pore, and the anus. The queen conch *Cassis cameo* and the king conch *Strombus gigas* of warmer coasts in the Atlantic, Caribbean, and Gulf of Mexico produce shells 10 to 12 inches long, covering animals weighing up to five pounds. These shells are much sought for shipment to Europe (particularly Italy) as the material from which cameos are carved. The trumpet shell *Charonia tritonis* is similar but more slender; it reaches a length of 20 inches in the Gulf of Mexico and also in the Indian Ocean.

Cowries (*Cypraea* and other genera—Plate 58) produce massive shells too, with such strikingly handsome patterns that they are favorites with collectors. Yet the shell of a live cowry rarely shows unless the animal is disturbed, for the shell-secreting mantle covers its product almost completely. Many cowries have the habit of dissolving out the inner whorls of the shell, making more room for their bodies and salvaging the lime as material to be added in enlarging the outer whorl. In the South Pacific certain small cowries have served as money, and been carried like perforated coins strung on cords.

In former times even greater value was attached to the murex snail *Murex trunculus* of the Mediterranean, one of a large genus with perhaps a thousand species around the world. *M. trunculus* produces in its anal glands a brownish fluid which, upon exposure to air, oxidizes to a substance which man has used for thousands of years as a dye—Tyrian or royal purple. The ancient Tyrians did not know how to remove the glands. They obtained the secretion through the crude technique of crushing the whole body of the snail in bowl-shaped cavities along the rocky coast. They filtered the fluid and treated it in various secret ways to purify it, making the material a mysterious substance. It has proved to be one of the most beautiful, colorful, and permanent dyes for cloth. Yet the snail itself is almost equally striking, a predator that creeps rapidly and can swim too, in spite of a medium-weight shell with elongated siphon canal and a large number of ornamental ribs and spines.

A close relative of *Murex* is *Urosalpinx,* the oyster drill, which causes thousands of dollars' damage annually by cutting through the shells of oysters and clams and removing the commercially valuable meat, killing one victim after another.

Under surface of a limpet, *Acmaea,* at left shows the head and large muscular foot, mantle edge, and a feathery gill at left of head. Only sensory tentacles on the head protrude beyond the upper surface of the shell, at right. (Maine. Ralph Buchsbaum)

A top shell usually confined to a narrow tidal zone on European Atlantic shores is *Osilinus lineatus*. It lives on fairly bare rock covered by water about half the time. (England. Ralph Buchsbaum)

OPISTHOBRANCHS

Marine opisthobranch snails usually go through a shell-producing stage and then stop, or even obliterate the shell completely. Presumably these animals have an extremely disagreeable flavor, for almost nothing will eat them, with or without armor. Perhaps this is why the sea hare *Tethys californica*, which feeds on seaweeds, so often reaches a length of 15 inches and a weight of fifteen pounds. It has only a vestige of shell, completely hidden by large, fleshy folds of the mantle. The similarity to a rabbit is

suggested by a pair of upright ear-shaped organs (rhinophores) on the back of the head; they are believed to be organs of taste. If a sea hare is disturbed, it gives off a great flood of purple fluid, often concealing its own yellowish to greenish color (Plate 60).

Among the most bizarre of mollusks are the sea slugs or nudibranchs, which lack a shell altogether (Plates 61–69). They are fancifully colored and wear a highly decorative tuft of plumes (ceratia) upon the back as elaborations of the mantle. These have a respiratory role; gills are lacking. Nudibranchs creep over seaweeds and hydroids, browsing upon coelenterates and bryozoans. Aeolids (*Aeolis* and related genera) even digest away all of a coelenterate except its stinging cells, and transfer these weapons intact and undischarged into the surface tissues of the plume filaments and sensory projections. In this way the aeolid uses the hydroid's weapons long after the coelenterate itself has been absorbed as food.

In warmer seas far from land, the deep violet-blue nudibranch *Glaucus eucharis* creeps along on the underside of the surface film, scavenging for minute plants and animals. Branched extensions of its body make a strikingly symmetrical pattern as seen from air, but its color provides *Glaucus* with excellent camouflage over deep water.

Pond snails often travel in the same way along the water film, and waves of movement in the exposed foot can be watched as crosswise bands shifting from front to back. At intervals a pond snail presses its mantle against the surface film and opens a dark pore through which it can exhale and inhale a lungful of air. Land snails and slugs breathe with a similar lung cavity in the mantle. While active they display the pore every few minutes, closing it between one breath and the next.

The common snails include larger *Lymnaea* with right-handed shells (coiling clockwise as viewed from the open end), smaller *Physa* with a left-handed shell, and the wheel snails (*Planorbis*) with a flat spiral. Many of these creatures are a mixed blessing. They serve as important food for fish in which man is interested, but also as the intermediate hosts for dangerous parasites among the flatworms and flukes. Some fresh-water snails live as much as 120 feet below the surface of lakes, where the oxygen supply is very limited. Others thrive in marshes around Lake Titicaca in the mountains of southern Peru, 12,550 feet above sea level.

Terrestrial snails and slugs are mostly scavengers, feeding on decaying vegetation. A few are strictly carnivorous, some burrowing in pursuit of earthworms, others hunting for insects, other snails and slugs, and carrion. Slugs have been known to enter beehives, apparently raiding for honey.

Black turban snails, *Tegula funebralis*, form great clusters in crevices and on rocky surfaces from Alaska to Lower California. Their shells are afterward appropriated by small hermit crabs. (Oregon. Ralph Buchsbaum)

Scavenging slugs, such as *Limax maximus* (Plate 70) may reach a length of 8 inches. They can protect themselves by spurting out jets of milky mucus quite unlike the colorless, transparent film they secrete over the body surface and beneath the foot while traveling along. Until the mucus trail becomes covered with dust, the path of a snail or slug on land can usually be followed as a glistening ribbon. In places it may remain as a vertical rope, showing where the animal crept to the end of a leaf or twig, then let itself down in slow motion on a strand of its own secretion—like the Indian rope trick in reverse.

Land snails and slugs have a pair of eyes, each at the tip of an upper, retractile tentacle. If touched, the tentacle is inverted like a glove finger, pulling the eye down into the safety of the head. Yet if some animal nips off an eye-bearing tentacle, the mollusk can regenerate a new one.

Pond snails, by contrast, wear their eyes at the base of the single pair of tentacles on the sides of the head. These tentacles cannot be withdrawn, although they appear in position to correspond to the lower, retractile pair on land snails and slugs.

The custom of eating land snails in Italy antedates the Christian era. Snails became a delicacy in France in the latter part of the eighteenth century. Now Paris is the center for them, with more than two hundred million snails consumed annually during the season from September to April. Most of these are *Helix pomatia,* raised on vegetables and bran mash in snail gardens or snaileries fenced with wire netting—about ten thousand snails to each pen twenty-five or thirty feet square. No market of comparable size has been found for them in any other part of the world.

Shell collectors everywhere are attracted to a tree snail of Cuba and isolated bits of higher land in swampy parts of Florida and the Florida keys. These are the homes of *Liguus,* a tan-bodied animal with a 1½-inch banded shell the shape of a tear drop. Every isolated colony seems to have its own color pattern, although the diet in each is essentially the same: fungi and lichens growing on the bark of subtropical and tropical trees. During winter or extended dry weather, *Liguus* cements the rim of its shell to the bark and waits for a good rain that will allow growth of its food plants.

Among the largest of land snails (Plate 49), the most famous today is *Achatina fulica,* a native of Mauritius and perhaps also eastern Africa from Natal to Somaliland. These large snails weigh up to a pound, part of this a sturdy brown shell marked with streaks of purple, green, pink, or snow white. Both very young and old *Achatina* snails feed on decaying vegetation. But at intermediate ages they are active at night, attacking living plants and scav-

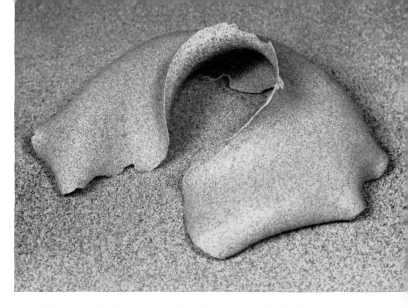

The eggs of the moon snail *Polinices* are embedded in a mixture of mucus and sand, forming the "sea collar" which is flexible enough while wet that waves can cast it unharmed upon the beach. When the collar becomes dry in the curio cabinet of a beachcomber, it is extremely fragile. Its form matches the upper surface of the foot of *Polinices* [see color plate 55]. (Massachusetts. Lorus and Margery Milne)

enging only for dietary supplements. Within six weeks each individual matures as a male, then changes to a female and begins laying batches of as many as three hundred pea-sized eggs month after month. A conservative estimate of over a billion offspring from each gravid female in five years could be translated, at a pound apiece, into more than half a million tons of mollusks, representing a frightful toll of vegetation.

In its African homelands, quite a number of different animals prey on *Achatina fulica.* Native people prize the snails as food and their shells as utensils and the raw material from which to carve spoons.

Common periwinkles, *Littorina littorea,* are gathered in great numbers for use as food. The largest of European periwinkles, they live on the lower half of the tidal shore. (North Wales. D. P. Wilson)

The handsome shell of the tiger cowrie, *Cypraea tigris*, is concealed by the enveloping mantle as the animal creeps along (left), but its spots show distinctly when the snail pulls back into its shelter (right). (Berlin Aquarium. Otto Croy)

Among the most wide-ranging land snails is the tiny (shell ¼ inch long) *Lamellaxis* (*Opeas*) *gracilis*, carried by commerce over the whole tropical world from a probable origin in America. In the United States it is found from South Carolina to Louisiana and in greenhouses. (Japan. Y. Fukuhara)

Together, these enemies of *Achatina* keep it in check.

In 1847 a shell collector who visited Mauritius took a few live specimens of *A. fulica* to Calcutta and released them in the Chouringhie Gardens just outside the city. There the snails had no obvious enemies, and the people—although often starving—refused to touch them as food. The snails multiplied and spread. By 1900 *A. fulica* had reached Ceylon and had become a serious agricultural pest. By 1911 it was common around Singapore and, with further human help, it island-hopped to Borneo. There, two decades later, a bounty was offered for the bodies and eggs of the snails, with no effect on their numbers. By 1933 *Achatina* was attacking rubber trees on Sumatra and Java. In that year too it reached Formosa, and was welcomed by the Japanese people on the island as an interesting food and potent medicine, although on no scientific basis. Living specimens were shipped promptly to Japan, and by 1936 some had been carried by Japanese people to Hawaii, where *Achatina* was soon out of control.

The Japanese took *A. fulica* to most of the islands of the South Pacific, either just before or during World War II. There the snails are providing more lasting devastation than all the bombs and artillery shells. They are still threatening to establish a beachhead on the North American continent, and they remain a potential pest perhaps as menacing as most of the fungus diseases or insect immigrants to reach the western hemisphere.

The Clams   (Class Pelecypoda)

One has only to mention clams, mussels, oysters, and scallops to realize how many bivalves man enjoys as food. If pearls are thrown in for good measure, the economic importance of the class Pelecypoda soars still higher. All of these creatures have a way of life geared to the ultimate in retirement—existence between two half shells in the seas or fresh waters, depending upon food particles that can be drawn in between the valves.

The fact that clams and their kin cannot be active on land and cannot fly is no reason to assume that their habits are completely monotonous. Various members of the class can leap or swim, tether themselves like captive balloons and then take off again, cement one shell to the bottom and lie indolently ever after, burrow many feet below the surface of the ocean floor, cut cavities in rock and timber, plow a furrow without getting stuck in the mud, creep up a plant stem, or lie back in the tropical sun and raise plants as food. Clams and their kin live in the greatest depths of the ocean, and also in the shallow waters at the source of every great river in the

In sheltered places, such as under fallen logs, slugs (*Limax*) deposit their glistening eggs. (Massachusetts. Lynwood M. Chace)

world. Some of these ways of life date back at least six hundred million years.

The class Pelecypoda is named for those members that can leap or tether themselves or burrow or plow or creep, for these are the ones in which the ventral portion of the body is extensible as a bladelike foot (*pelekys,* a hatchet, *pes, podos,* a foot). No pelecypod has a head—not even a radula to represent this region of the digestive tract. Essentially everything has been sacrificed to the various ways in which the clams and their kin draw food particles from the water into the mantle cavity, between the two great fleshy mantle lobes that secrete the two-part hinged shell.

The hinge of the shell introduces a special problem in growth, since nothing must interfere with the ability of the two valves to gape or to close while the animal is exposed to enemies. Consequently the hinge lags behind the growth of the shell, and enlargements are added eccentrically.

As in all mollusks, the outer surface of the mantle (particularly its edge) secretes the materials and lays down the molecules in precise orientation. This masterful accomplishment produces an outer horny layer (periostracum) protecting the limy shell from external erosion. Under this, calcium carbonate crystals lie in tightly packed prisms, forming most of the thickness of the shell. The innermost layer, to which

The large slug *Ariolimax columbianus* reaches a length of 8 inches in the humid coastal regions around Puget Sound, Washington. (Ralph Buchsbaum)

Mating slugs (*Limax*) have lowered themselves from a tree trunk by means of a mucus cord. While thus suspended their bodies entwine. (Massachusetts. Lynwood M. Chace)

additions are made discontinuously throughout the life of the animal, is of "mother-of-pearl," in which extremely thin layers of limy material alternate with equally thin films of horny material. These provide the diffraction of light that produces the iridescence for which these creatures are famous.

If a grain of sand or a small animal gets between the mantle and the mother-of-pearl layer of the shell, the soft tissues may become irritated enough to wall off the foreign object and then continue to deposit mother-of-pearl over its surface. This creates a pearl. It may be sperical, but more frequently it is irregular. "Cultured pearls" are the products of pearl oysters between whose shells a foreign object has been placed deliberately.

From season to season the abundance of food particles in the water varies markedly. When food is easily available, pelecypods usually grow rapidly; whereas during adverse times the mantle adds little to the rim and inner surface of the shell valves. Often these changes in the rate of shell production show as ridges on the outside of the shell. If growth is slow at only one period in each year, the ridges may indicate how many years the clam has been enlarging its shell. Great care must be used in making these estimates, however, for a storm can stir up the bottom sediments and induce pelecypods to cease feeding, simulating the malnutrition of a winter season and adding "growth rings" several times a year.

SWIMMING CLAMS

Over much of the world, the word "Shell" has come to be a familiar trademark, an emblem taken for a big corporation from the valve of the scallop *Pecten*. Scallops are swimming clams (Plates 41–43) whose shells bear "ears" at each end of the hinge. They are handsomely fluted in a radiating pattern as well as regularly wavy ("scalloped") along the outer edge.

Scallops swim by a gobbling movement of the shell valves, taking water in around the scalloped margin and expelling it in little jets through the "ears" at the hinge line. The edges of the mantle serve as valves in controlling this flow of water. They also bear many bright little eyes with which a scallop can keep informed of moving objects nearby.

When scallops complete a bout of swimming and settle to the bottom, they come to rest on the right valve. If they fall on the left valve, they immediately turn themselves over. Only a single large muscle controls these shell movements. It is the short, cylindrical morsel that is so delectable when fried in deep fat or served in cream sauce.

The flavor of an approaching sea star in the water or of an octopus is enough to start scallops into a different type of swimming—a flight reaction at much higher speed, with the hinge in advance. In this emergency reversal of the normal direction of swimming, a scallop's behavior suggests that of the octopus itself or of lobsters and crayfish.

These same reactions and ability to swim are found in the file shells (*Lima*—Plates 44–46), whose obliquely oval valves commonly bear close-set and overlapping edges across the ridges that radiate from the narrow hinge. In some species these edges suggest the teeth of a file. The two valves are of equal size and are mirror images in shape, whereas a scallop's upper (left) valve bulges more than the lower (right) valve. From *Lima* shells, a double fringe of long, slender, pale tentacles extend, often hiding the minute eyes between them at the mantle edge.

Lima has a diminutive foot from which the animal can extrude fine threads of a plastic material, the byssus. With these threads a file shell builds a crude tubular nest somewhat resembling those created by some of the wolf spiders. Usually the nest of *Lima* is under the sheltering bulge of a rock, and is open at both ends. This permits the 1-inch clam to create a feeding current through the nest, entering at one doorway and leaving at the other.

Scallops too, when quite young, can secrete byssus threads. Most of them give up the habit. *Pecten latiauritus* of America's Pacific coast is an exception, a small scallop that ties itself to kelp and other seaweeds by a single byssus strand. Sometimes it uses the byssus gland at the tip of its mobile tongue-shaped foot to hold temporarily to hard surfaces. By this means it can hitch its shell along, even up the vertical side of a glass aquarium.

TETHERED MUSSELS

Marine mussels (*Mytilus*—Plate 40—and *Modiolus*) are more expert at using byssus threads. They not only creep along by secreting one short thread after another from the extended foot, but can also hold fast to several dozen strands fanning out like guy ropes at a point of more permanent attachment.

Mussels the world over anchor themselves in this way to rocks and to each other, sometimes producing a "scalp" several inches thick over a sand bar and retarding erosion by waves. In France and other parts of Europe where *Mytilus edulis* is appreciated as food, the deep blue iridescent shellfish are cultivated in shallow coastal waters by providing them with tree branches driven into the bottom, or with other surfaces upon which they can attach themselves and feed. Cultivated mussels usually grow larger than their unaided brethren, and shells over 2 inches long are regarded as salable. The horse mussel *Modiolus* is a larger animal, often living partly buried in mud flats; its flavor is less attractive.

Byssus threads anchor far larger and more fragile shells in moderately deep and warm water. Pen shells (*Pinna*) are triangular or wedge-shaped, as

Garden snails, such as the *Helix aspersa* introduced into North America from Europe, glide out of damp corners at night and browse on a wide variety of plants, leaving glistening trails of mucus wherever they go. (California. H. S. Barsam)

much as a foot in length. In some species the byssus is coarse and black, but in *Pinna nobilis* of the Mediterranean it is silky, fine, and of a bright golden color. From this material in ancient times artisans wove "cloth of gold" (tarentine fabric), particularly in the Greek city of Tarentum (now called Tarento) under the heel of the Italian boot. Museums now display gold-cloth gloves made of this "marine silk," and point out how permanently flexible the material remains. So fine is the texture of this cloth that a pair of lady's gloves made from it can be crushed without harm into the space of a walnut shell. *Pinna* shells are a source also of black pearls.

OYSTERS AND OTHER FIXED CLAMS

One of the scallops, *Hinnites giganteus,* from the Pacific coast of America, shows how easy is the step from a free-swimming life to a permanently attached one. As a youngster it swims about, flapping its equal shells as though it were a *Lima* with a smoother shell and shorter tentacles. Then it slips into a crevice between rocks on the bottom and settles down. To the

The tree snail *Liguus fasciatus roseatus* is but one of many with strikingly colored shells in southernmost Florida. During the rainy season it feeds on fungi, but in dry seasons withdraws into the shell and attaches itself firmly to a tree. (Ralph Buchsbaum)

rock it cements its left valve, and begins to thicken both halves of the shell until they become quite irregular. There it reaches a diameter of more than 4 inches, still ready to snap its right valve closed and to squirt water at any animal that disturbs it.

Oysters (*Ostraea*) settle after an even briefer swimming experience. At an age of about two weeks the ciliated larva sinks to the bottom, forms a minute shell, and attaches itself to some solid object. This stage is known as a "spat." Unless it finds a suitable support it dies. But once "set," it proceeds to develop into a reasonable facsimile of its parent.

European and Pacific oysters begin their development while the fertilized eggs are retained in the gills of the female, whereas the Atlantic oysters of America shed both eggs and sperm, letting fertilization occur in the sea. Since a Maryland oyster may release sixteen million eggs at a time, and repeat the performance several times a year, oysters seem unlikely to die out unless the spats fail to find suitable supports upon which to set.

Oyster culture is largely a matter of providing an attractive bottom and preventing overcrowding so that each oyster will grow well formed and to a marketable size. Oystermen also try to reduce the number of sea stars preying upon growing oysters, and to find ways to discourage *Urosalpinx* and other carnivorous snails that thrive in oyster beds at the expense of the industry. Pearl oysters (*Meleagrina*) of warm seas and Japanese waters are cultured too because they appear to produce better pearls; the quality of their meat is low.

Pelecypods include quite a number of other fixed clams. Of these the hoof shells (*Chama*) of tropical waters and the eastern Pacific take the other alternative, affixing themselves by their right valves. Jingle shells (*Anomia*) hold the left valve down but in a very strange way. The valve next to the rock has a hole in it, and the closing muscle of the mollusk goes through the hole to an attachment area on the support. Both valves of a jingle shell are extremely thin, and they may be ridged or smooth and highly polished. If several left valves of *Anomia* are strung on a cord and shaken gently, they give the jingling sound for which the shells are named.

BURROWING CLAMS

Other pelecypods burrow into sandy and muddy bottoms, remaining out of sight for most or all of their lives. Among the most active of them are the bean shells or coquinas (*Donax*), which live in the surface sands between tide marks and just below low-tide level along many of the world's coasts.

A bird or a beachcomber can watch these ½- to 1-inch shellfish simply by standing quietly as waves expend their energy on a gradually sloping beach. As the water hurries in, it carries sand with it and apparently buries the *Donax* clams more deeply than they tolerate. By dozens or hundreds or thousands, they shove themselves up into the water just about the time the wave reaches its highest point. For a moment they may lie on their sides on the sand in the clearing, momentarily motionless water, feeding in the liquid that covers them to a depth of a few inches. Then the water rushes out again, rolling over and over those little clams that have not dug themselves down again. With the next wave the process is repeated.

In Florida, people collect *Donax* by the thousand, separating them from the sand with coarse sieves, as the distinctive ingredient for coquina soup. Others pick through the beach drift for empty shells of this kind and mount them on place cards as "butterfly shells." They are marked with suffused colors or with radiating bands in purple, pale blue, green, yellow, tan, and various shades of pink, but hardly any two of them are identical. In some places the accumulation of dead coquinas becomes consolidated into a soft limy rock that hardens upon exposure to air.

The Pacific Ocean, despite its name, tends to be violent on the coast of America. There the surf-dwelling clam *Tivela stultorum* is known as the Pismo clam. It is a far larger animal with a somewhat triangular shell. These clams maintain their position in the sand, always with the hinge toward the open ocean. They appear to use a jet of water from the mantle cavity beside the foot to aid themselves in pulling the shell into the sand.

In spite of the difficulty of collecting Pismo clams in the heavy surf, and the fact that man is their chief enemy, the annual census of this shellfish in California shows that its numbers are shrinking. Even a limit of fifteen 5-inch clams per person per day, plus a ban on all shipments and complete protection in some areas, has not halted the decline.

On sandy coasts throughout the world, razor clams live just below the surface, sometimes with the posterior end of the shell projecting slightly above the flooded beach. *Siliqua* has a rather short oval shell with a very sharp edge, *Ensis* an elongate and almost rectangular shell, slightly curved and suggesting the blade of a straight razor. The foot in each kind is at one end and is extremely agile. With it the clam is expert at digging in quickly if waves wash the sand away.

At slightly greater depths in beaches where the

Queen scallops, *Chlamys opercularis*, swimming about as they escape from a starfish. (England. D. P. Wilson)

The common edible mussel, *Mytilus*, attached to rock by fine but strong secreted threads. (England. Ralph Buchsbaum)

sand is mixed with mud and provides a firmer covering, burrowing clams of many other kinds live in constant readiness to jerk back into the buried shell. Only when undisturbed do they extend above the mud the siphon or "neck," which is actually part of the posterior end of the mantle, a part through which water and food enter and then water and wastes are discharged.

This is the way of life of the economically important soft-shell clam *Mya arenaria,* whose brittle, thin, oval shell averages less than 5 inches in length and bears a large spoon-shaped projection on the left valve at the hinge. The soft-shell is common on both coasts of America, having been introduced accidentally on Pacific shores along with Atlantic oysters. *Mya* is a favorite for New England chowders and clambakes. In the Arctic it is the principal diet of the walrus, which uses its tusks as a clam rake to dig the shellfish from the bottom.

An extremely popular clam with the same burrow-ing habits is the quahog *Venus mercenaria,* known also as the hard-shell clam, the little-neck clam, and the round clam. Immature ones, less than 3 inches in length, are called cherrystone clams. This is the shell from which New England Indians cut and pierced small beads as shell money (wampum) that could be carried as a necklace string.

West Coast Indians showed a preference for the bent-nosed clam *Macoma nasuta,* which lies upon its left side several inches below the beach surface and extends to the water above a long, slender, incurrent siphon. The excurrent siphon is a separate tube, equally slender but somewhat shorter, discharging into the sand near the clam. The asymmetrical bend in the incurrent siphon matches the upward bend of the bent-nosed clam's shell. Usually the incurrent siphon extends as much as three-quarters of an inch above the mud. It waves back and forth, turned downward and sucking in food particles from the surface sediments. At intervals of two to three minutes the clam retracts its siphon slightly and flushes out any inedible or coarse materials. At longer intervals it pulls the siphon well down into the mud and then extends it to the surface a few inches away, to sample a new feeding area.

The largest burrowing clam in the world is the edible geoduck [pronounced goo'ee-duck] of Puget Sound and adjacent coasts of British Columbia, Washington, Oregon, and northern California. *Panope generosa* may weigh as much as twelve pounds, but the 8-inch shell accounts for only a minor part of this. The shell is relatively thin and in a mature geoduck fails to cover the body. The siphons are almost as large as the body proper and stretch far enough to allow the clam to live three or four feet below the surface of the muddy bottom.

Geoducks constitute a sports fishery in Washington, with a bag limit of three per day enforced by wardens. Almost as strict protection comes from the animals' position in the beach. They are exposed only by tides lower than mean low (minus tides), and consequently are within reach of a man with a shovel for only a few hours a month.

Apparently it is only a small step from maintaining a vertical burrow in firm mud to boring into soft rock. The arctic rock-borer *Saxicava,* with a 1- to 1½-inch shell, holds tight with its foot while using the anterior end of the shell as a scraping tool with which to cut cylindrical cavities as much as six inches deep into rock and concrete. A later inhabitant of the same burrow in a breakwater or seawall may not be satisfied with the cavity, and may enlarge it or introduce a side branch. After a while the whole man-made structure is weakened and may crumble. The larger piddocks (*Zirfaea* and *Martesia*) show similar habits, using their 4-inch shells to bore into wharf pilings with disastrous results.

190]

One of the marine mussels (*Lithophaga*) is a tropical animal with a very different means for boring into rock. It secretes an acid that attacks limy materials, and uses this chemical means to excavate a place for itself. *Lithophaga* (the "rock-eater") protects its own shell by a thick brown horny material whose color, along with the shape of the shell, gives the animal the common name "date mussel."

At Pozzuoli, near Naples, Italy, visitors are shown the work of date mussels as conspicuous pits in the upright limestone pillars of the temple of Serapis. This edifice was built on dry land, and it now stands on dry land, some little distance above the waters of the Mediterranean. Yet in historic times, between the days of Roman civilization when the temple was constructed and the recent past, the land supporting the building must have subsided enough to let the sea cover the pillars, permitting *Lithophaga* to pit the surface. More recently the land has risen again, putting an end to the erosive action of the mollusks.

The burrowing habits of pelecypods reach an extreme in the wormlike borers that cause so much destruction to wharf timbers and hulls of wooden ships. The shipworm *Teredo navalis* may be as much as 24 inches long when fully grown, yet its shell consists only of two little ½-inch plates used as boring tools.

The minute swimming larva of the shipworm settles on a submerged timber and there transforms into the shell-bearing clam. It bores into the wood and continues to do so for the rest of its life. It becomes, in fact, a captive in its own burrow, for as the animal grows it scarcely enlarges the original opening. Instead, the shipworm excavates a bigger and bigger tube for itself deeper and deeper into the timber, and maintains connection to the sea only by way of two thread-sized siphon tubes. One of these brings in food particles and oxygen. The other discharges wastes (including powdered wood) and reproductive products. *Teredo* usually follows the grain of the wood, turning aside only to avoid a neighboring shipworm or a knot. Eventually the timber breaks apart, letting a dock collapse or a ship founder.

THE AGILE-FOOTED CLAMS

It would be difficult to find a greater contrast based upon a single body plan than between a shipworm grinding away, self-imprisoned in a timber from which it gets no nourishment, and a scallop or a cockleshell skipping through the water. The cockle (*Cardium*) is famous for the brittleness of its shell, which is obliquely spherical with rounded ribs. With its long and agile foot the cockle kicks itself along the bottom. Often it draws attention to itself, and a fish swallows it whole or a beachcomber picks it up. *Cardium magnum* of the Atlantic coast of America reaches 5 inches in diameter on shores from Virginia to Brazil. *C. corbis* of Pacific coasts is only

slightly smaller. In both, the extended foot is about as long as the greatest length of the shell.

A very different means of progression is found in the little fingernail clams of fresh water. The stouter ones (*Sphaerium*) and thinner kinds (*Musculium*) both live in pools of small streams and produce lightweight shells seldom more than ½ inch across. The foot is very slender and adhesive. With it the animal can glide up or down a plant stem as smoothly as though it were a snail or a flatworm.

The larger clams of fresh water plow a furrow in the bottom, leaving much of the shell exposed. The bladelike foot is extended well ahead of the body, diagonally downward into the mud. Into the tip of the foot the clam pumps blood, producing a knoblike swelling as an anchor. Then it shortens the foot by muscular contraction. If the anchor holds, the clam draws itself forward and downward a little. As the foot is made slender again and extended for another move, the clam's shell may be raised slightly. In consequence, the furrow of the fresh-water denizen usually has an almost regular pattern of greater

Coquina shells are also called wedge shells or butterfly shells. This species of clam, *Donax variabilis*, is only 1 inch or so long, occurs abundantly on sandy beaches from North Carolina to Florida, and is used to make soup. (North Carolina. Ralph Buchsbaum)

The commercially valuable razor clam of the American Pacific coast, *Siliqua patula*, lives on sandy beaches and can completely bury itself within about seven seconds. The one in the foreground has just done so, leaving only the siphons protruding. (Oregon. Ralph Buchsbaum)

and lesser width—greater where the foot pulled the shell deeper into the bottom.

The two size ranges of fresh-water clams represent two unlike families. The small ones (family Sphaeridae) lack a mother-of-pearl lining to the shell and are dull white inside. These clams retain the fertilized eggs in a brood pouch formed of the inner gill on each side of the foot, and release shelled clamlets. A viviparous parent may produce from two to twenty young at a time, but they breed repeatedly throughout the year.

The larger fresh-water clams (family Unionidae) are often called mussels. Their shells have been much sought in tributaries of the Mississippi River as material from which pearl buttons can be cut, for the inner surface of the shell is coated with mother-of-pearl. From fifteen to twenty buttons of different sizes can be made from one 5-inch valve. In *Anodonta* the shell lacks hinge teeth and the two valves are held in alignment only by the hinge ligament. In *Unio* and related genera, hinge teeth inside the shell give extra support.

Unionid clams have become strangely adapted to life in flowing fresh water. Instead of retaining the eggs in a viviparous habit, they discharge the young as larvae, called glochidia. Each glochidium has a pair of small, widely-spread valves, each terminating in a tonglike hook. It uses these to pinch into the skin of a passing fish or to hold to its gills if taken into the mouth. The glochidium thereupon becomes a temporary parasite, absorbing nourishment from the fish's blood stream. After a few weeks the larval stage ends with the glochidium freeing itself, dropping to the bottom wherever the fish happens to be, and changing to the adult form of clam. In this way

the unionids make use of fish to distribute their offspring, and depend upon the ability of the fish in resisting the current—staying in fresh water and not being carried to the sea.

A still stranger way in which a pelecypod depends for success upon the activities of another type of life was revealed recently in the giant bear's-paw clam *Tridacna* of the South Pacific. These mollusks lie hinge downward in coral reefs, usually in quite shallow water, and display a thick purple mantle over the coarsely fluted, exposed edge of the heavy shell. If a

A European razor shell, *Ensis siliqua*, with the foot extended. It is common on many sandy beaches, but can be found only by digging for it at low tide. (England. D. P. Wilson)

person examines the mantle surface closely, he sees little bright spots suggesting eyes. These are actually "skylights" admitting energy from the sun into "greenhouses" within the mantle. In these spaces, microscopic green algae grow and carry on photosynthesis. *Tridacna* uses its white blood cells to harvest the algae and, as an adult animal, seems not to use its digestive tract. It depends instead upon the plant food raised in the exposed parts of its body.

The bear's-paw clam has become world famous as a trap for unwary persons walking on a coral reef, for the shell valves will surely close tightly on a leg or arm accidentally thrust past the soft mantle folds into the interior cavity. Native people actually fear these clams very little, and often use a hammer to break a portion of the shell edge so that a hand wielding a knife can be slid into the interior to cut free as food the big muscle that clamps the shells together. *Tridacna* shells of small size are often used elsewhere in the world as bird baths and baptismal fonts. Large ones, weighing half a ton or more, are usually left in the reef, where the live animal continues to demonstrate how the giant of the clam world succeeds in getting enough to eat.

The Elephant-Tusk Shells   (*Class Scaphopoda*)

When white men first reached the west coast of America, they found Indians there wearing necklaces of almost cylindrical shells, each slightly curved and open at both ends. The Indians esteemed the shells according to their length, and used them for barter. A 1-inch shell had only slight value, but a 2-inch shell was equivalent in purchasing power to a shilling (then twenty-five cents)—equal to a dollar at present-day prices. Rare 3-inch shells were owned only by the wealthy chiefs.

An elephant-tusk shell or tooth shell seems made to order as a piece for a necklace, since it is open at both the larger end and the smaller. While occupied by the mollusk that secretes it, the large end is usually below the surface of the sandy sea bottom and the shell slants upward, exposing the smaller end. This latter is the place where water enters and leaves the shell, attending to the respiratory needs of the scaphopod merely through the walls of the mantle cavity, for no gills of any kind are present.

From the larger end of the shell, the elongated and bilaterally symmetrical animal extends a foot resembling a horse's hoof, using this as a digging organ. Behind the foot, at the edge of the almost cylindrical mantle, a cluster of ciliated tentacles arises around the mouth. They bring food particles to the mouth,

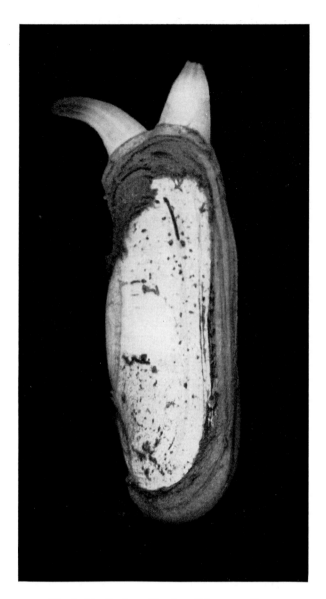

The jackknife clam, *Tagelus gibbus*, sometimes erroneously called a razor clam, occurs from New England to north Patagonia, and is often eaten where no better clam is available. (North Carolina. Ralph Buchsbaum)

the small ones to be swallowed whole, the larger ones to be rasped into fragments by use of the radula. The digestive tract bends in a U and opens at an anus, exposed from the larger end of the shell when the scaphopod is fully extended.

The sexes of elephant-tusk shells are separate, and the eggs are laid singly, the sperm discharged as a cloud into the sand through the pair of excretory tubes opening beside the anus.

The most widespread genus of these exclusively marine animals is *Dentalium*. The common tooth shell *D. entale* reaches a length of 2 inches in quiet sandy bays on both sides of the North Atlantic. The

[193

precious tusk shell of the North Pacific is *D. pretiosum*. In New Guinea, heavy tusk shells as much as 5 inches long are used by native people as decorations thrust through holes in the septum of the nose, in the lower lip, or in the ear lobes.

The Octopus and Its Kin

(*Class Cephalopoda*)

For almost everyone, the octopus holds a fearful fascination. This had led man to call it the "devilfish." Actually, octopuses are extremely shy, retiring creatures, eager to slither out of man's way. The biggest of them has an arm spread of about 12 feet, but the average octopus can barely stretch across a circle 1 foot in diameter. All of these animals seem completely unwilling to bite, even if provoked.

The same denial cannot include the octopus' kin, for some squids bite viciously if handled. Yet no member of the class Cephalopoda has been reliably recorded to have attacked a person without provocation. Admittedly, all of them possess a pair of armored jaws suggesting those of a parrot, except that the lower half of the beak closes outside the upper half. These jaws supplement a typical molluscan radula and aid the animals in tearing apart the crabs and other foods in their strictly carnivorous diet.

The distinctive feature of the octopus and its kin is the eight or more arms that extend from the head and are used in capturing food. They make the animal "head-footed" and give class Cephalopoda its name. Most cephalopods have also a pair of large eyes resembling those of man and other vertebrate animals to a degree that is uncanny, for the organs arise entirely differently in the embryo.

Millions of years ago, all cephalopods supposedly used the mantle to secrete an external shell, and were able to take shelter inside the secretion. Today this habit is continued only by two different "living fossils," the several species of *Nautilus* in the southwest Pacific and the strange little *Spirula* at the upper edges of the abysses in the Atlantic and Indian Oceans.

The common cuttlefish *Sepia officinalis* of the Mediterranean and eastern Atlantic (Plate 75) produces an internal limy shell of degenerate form—the "cuttlebone" sold to hang in cages with canaries and other pet birds. Squids, such as *Loligo,* gain some support from a concealed relic of the shell, the chitinous "pen," which may be shaped somewhat like the feather of a quill pen, or narrow and slightly curved like a sword blade. The octopus lacks all traces of a hard shell. Yet all cephalopods retain the U-shaped digestive tract which is helpful to an animal whose body is covered by a conical external skeleton.

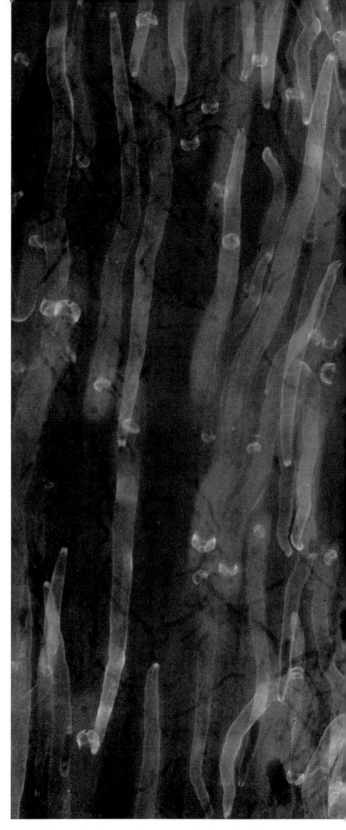

X-rays disclose a dense population of shipworms, both the larger *Teredo* and the smaller *Bankia,* as they sabotage a timber exposed to the sea. These degenerate mollusks use their small shell valves as boring tools in making chambers for their bodies. Apparently they use the wood only as a home, but the damage done is comparable to that of wood-eating termites on land. (Florida. Charles E. Lane)

Apparently the earliest cephalopods found difficulty in combining the activities demanded by predatory habits and a carnivorous diet with a slender body concealed in a heavy shell. As an adaptation helpful under these circumstances, they developed the unique ability of secreting gas into the spire of the pointed shell, giving it buoyancy and hence reducing the weight to be pulled around. The animal came to live in the enlarged open end of the limy cone, with the gas bubble above it. Addition of lime helped bring the shell into a horizontal position, but at the same time seemingly encouraged elongation of the animal in a direction truly dorsal in terms of its own anatomy. Few animals in the world are so high and so short and so narrow.

Shell-bearing cephalopods greatly improve their control over the gas bubble by dividing it with transverse shell partitions. The location of each of these is evident on the outside of a *Spirula* shell as a slight constriction, but the nautiluses show no external indications. The shell, in fact, is an object of outstanding beauty, one that appeals especially to mathematicians since its curvature (and the curvature of all internal partitions) follows the logarithmic spiral, with each turn of the shell about thrice as broad as the preceding turn.

Cephalopods are muscular animals, able to subdue struggling prey. They are alert, too, with a far larger and more complexly developed nervous system than is to be found in any other mollusk. Around the enlarged central ganglion above the mouth, they develop a good substitute for a skull, formed of cartilage tissue closely resembling that in vertebrate animals. At other points in the body also, cephalopods have cartilaginous rods and bars as stiffening supports. These give the whole animal a firmness that is unexpected from watching the fluid, graceful movements of a swimming, darting squid, or the lithe, sinuous flexibility of a live octopus.

The cynic who remarked that man is the only animal that blushes, or needs to, was not acquainted with cephalopods. Their blushes can put any other creature to shame, and may well be a means of communication. In the thin epidermis over all exposed parts of the body are small flexible bags of pigment—blue, green, yellow, brown, or red chromatophores—each surrounded by a set of radiating muscle fibers. When the fibers contract under the control of the nervous system, the little bag of pigment is suddenly stretched into the form of a flat disk parallel to the surface of the body. Its presence becomes noticeable as a spot perhaps $\frac{1}{16}$ of an inch in diameter, whereas when the fibers relax, the pigment sac rounds out and becomes invisibly small.

An excited cephalopod twinkles all over as the pigment sacs change dimensions. Waves of color may sweep along the body, like blushes in a variety of hues. At one moment the animal may be conspicuously banded and at the next a uniform wine red, and then may blanch uniformly to the ghastly bluish white so characteristic of dead octopus and squid offered for sale in fish markets.

The members of the genus *Nautilus* (Plate 74) are unique among living cephalopods not only in their handsome shells, often 10 inches across, but also in having about ninety tentacular arms, and twice as many gills (four), heart auricles, and kidneys as any other in the class. The arms, moreover, lack the firm-rimmed, muscular suction cups with which all other cephalopods cling to prey. And the eyes of nautiluses have no lens, making them operate as pinhole cameras—a type of visual organ unique in the animal kingdom.

All cephalopods except the nautiluses are armed with a gland secreting an intensely dark liquid, used by the animal as an emergency discharge beclouding the water and confusing the flavor trail by which an enemy might follow in pursuit. Long ago man began collecting the contents of this gland from cuttlefish in the Indian Ocean for use as a permanent ink—old-style India ink.

The males of eight-armed octopuses and ten-armed squids can be distinguished from the females by a strange feature of one arm—the lowest on the left side. It differs from the other arms in form and in the shape of the suction cups. The animal uses it to transfer into the mantle cavity of the female the transparent bags of sperm cells she needs to fertilize her eggs.

Fresh-water clams lie partly imbedded in sand or mud, with the shells slightly agape and the openings for water currents protruding. (Lynwood M. Chace: National Audubon)

The male octopus goes to an extreme in this final step of an elaborate courtship. He drops off the tip of the arm with its load of sperm bags deep in his mate's mantle cavity. Early observers found the still-living arm tips anchored securely there and concluded that they were parasitic worms entirely different from all others known because of the scores of sperm-filled cavities. To these "worms" the name *Hectocotylus* was given (*hecto,* a hundred, *kotyle,* a hollow vessel). When the true situation was discovered, the word came to be used as an adjective describing the peculiar arm as being the "hectocotylized" one.

The body of an octopus is rounded or saclike, usually with no fins (Plates 76–80). Ordinarily the animal crawls about on its flexible arms. But if frightened, it ejects water from the capacious mantle cavity through a narrow nozzle-like siphon. The water spurts forward, and the animal darts backward by jet propulsion.

The female octopus cements her eggs to a rock or other firm support. Some species attach them like punching bags, singly on short stalks. Others include a whole series of eggs in a slender string of jelly and affix the end of the string. For as much as three months, the mother octopus may stand lonely vigil over her developing offspring, not forsaking them even to find food. With her sucker-studded arms she polishes the outside surfaces of the egg coverings, keeping them free of dirt and fungus growths. Some kinds of octopus use their siphons as a sort of hose, sending jets of water among the egg strings and flushing out any minute particles that might contaminate them.

Squids, by contrast, lay many smaller eggs in cigar-shaped masses of jelly attached to the bottom and then go off, leaving the "dead man's fingers" to fate. Very few animals actually attack squid eggs, which suggests that they have an unpleasant flavor or toxic nature. When octopus eggs are left unattended through the death of the parent, fungi soon smother them.

Squids get far more effective use of jet propulsion, since their bodies are more cylindrical, tapering to a point and hence affording better streamlining (Plates 72 and 73). On each side the body bears a pair of horizontal muscular fins under exquisite control. With their help alone, a squid can hover, swim forward or back, or turn about sharply. Sometimes it uses the flexible siphon tip to direct a jet of water to rear or downward or to one side instead of forward, and gains an extra lift in this way.

Squids tend to hunt in packs, darting by jet propulsion through a school of fish and seizing victims by the head. Octopuses, on the other hand, are more solitary and bottom-dwelling. They may stalk a crab or wait for it to come within snatching distance. Al-

The sea butterfly (pteropod) *Creseis* is a delicate little free-swimming snail of the open ocean. It extends a pair of wing-like expansions of the foot from the larger end of the thin shell and flits through the water in company with many others of its kind. The specimens shown were dredged from Bikini lagoon in the South Pacific. (Fritz Goro: *Life* Magazine)

ways, however, they seize it from behind and thus avoid the crab's claws.

The extra two arms of squids, beyond the eight characteristic of octopuses, are considerably longer than the rest and are used in grasping prey. In the giant squid *Architeuthis princeps* of moderate depths in colder oceans, these prehensile arms may be 30 feet long on a 15- to 18-foot body as much as 5 feet in diameter.

Architeuthis is a real sea monster, the largest of all

Large clam, *Tridacna,* wedged among coral on Great Barrier Reef. The giant species of *Tridacna* may be 4 feet long and weigh up to five hundred pounds. (Fritz Goro: *Life* Magazine)

Four tooth shells (scaphopods), one with its three-lobed foot extended and two with the foot showing at the larger opening of the tapered shell. These are *Dentalium* from the beach at Roscoff, France. (Ralph Buchsbaum)

An X-ray photograph of a *Nautilus* showing the curved partitions separating the gas-filled chambers of the shell, and the living animal occupying the largest, outermost chamber of the spiral. See color plate 74 of this same *Nautilus*. (New Caledonia. René Catala)

known invertebrate animals. It must be a formidable adversary. Sperm whales, which feed almost exclusively on squids, often bear circular scars near the mouth, showing where the suction cups of a giant squid's arms grasped in the contest to avoid being eaten. Some of these scars are 5 inches across. The indigestible jaws of big squids found in the stomachs of these whales often exceed any from *Architeuthis* discovered dead, washed ashore. Consequently no one is sure how large the giant squid really grows.

No one knows either how many squids live in the sea. The number must be enormous, for seals dive to catch them and the toothed whales eat little else. Man's nets are too slow-moving and too obvious to fast-swimming squids for any reasonable sample to be caught from large boats on the ocean's surface. Consequently one is amazed, as were the adventurous scientists aboard the raft *Kon-Tiki,* when squids pursuing fish at night break through the surface water and tumble aboard a low craft. Or a person remains unconvinced that the echoes of depth-measuring equipment could be reflected back to the ship (indicating a phantom bottom about six hundred feet down at midday) largely because of squids congregated there—waiting at the edge of twilight in the water until the day above fades and lets them approach the surface to feed.

The slower squids in the deep sea (and perhaps also the sick and decrepit of faster-moving kinds) do get caught in the nets towed by oceanographic research ships. Many of them prove to have curiously gelatinous bodies and large numbers of light-producing organs along their sides and underneath. Very few of them are blind. Most have large eyes, even with the organs on swiveling turrets that can be aimed in many directions. Apparently they find food and mates by recognizing luminous patterns passing in the black water.

These depths are home to another "living fossil," one discovered toward the end of the nineteenth century and given the imaginative name *Vampyroteuthis infernalis,* the "vampire squid of the infernal regions." This improbable creature reaches a length of 8 inches and a diameter of 3 inches. Its blue-black body is literally pint-sized and wears at one end a group of eight tentacles linked together by a web. *Vampyroteuthis* is not an octopus, for it has two more arms, slender as feelers, kept curled up and tucked away in pockets outside the ring of webbed, sucker-studded arms. Yet the vampire squid is not a true squid either.

Deep-sea *Vampyroteuthis* may well have the largest eyes in proportion to body of any animal in the world. A 6-inch specimen wears a pair of globular visual organs each 1 inch across, more than a third of the body diameter, and as large as those of many full-grown dogs. Toward the other end of the body the vampire squid can extend from a slit on each side a blunt projection 1 inch long, ending in a brilliant reflector suggesting those set along highways to glow a warning as each car's headlights approach. How they are used in the intense blackness of the abysses may eventually be learned.

The vampire squid itself is bedecked with light-producing organs of many shapes and sizes. Only the mouth and surrounding surfaces of the arms and webs are devoid of luminous spots. *Vampyroteuthis* may stalk its prey behind a black cloak of webbing stretched by tentacles ready to seize and hold. Or it may vanish from view by turning off its lights and pulling the silvery reflectors into the pockets from which they were extruded.

This strange little octopus-squid, linking two types of cephalopods, has been caught in the depths of most oceans, seemingly so far from the surface and the bottom (as well as from shores of any kind) that it is a truly pelagic creature. In its wandering life it is merely a deeper counterpart of the paper nautilus, *Argonauta argo,* a drifting denizen of the Atlantic and Pacific. The paper nautilus takes its name from the parchment-thin shell the 8-inch female secretes from the expanded ends of her two upper arms.

For many years, people familiar with the sea believed that the argonaut sat in her shell and raised her expanded arms as a sail, drifting before the wind. Now her ways are better understood. The shell is only a floating, boat-shaped egg case with a single compartment. It is not a product of her mantle and hence is not comparable to the true shell of a chambered nautilus.

The argonaut's shell may be as much as 8 inches long, but it has no known role except as a place of security for the young. The parent is free to leave it or return to it, swimming smoothly along as a completely independent little octopus. Her mate is much smaller (about 1 inch in length) and lacks the expansions on the upper arms. But he does contribute his share to the family venture: the tip of his hectocotylized arm, holding a supply of sperms for his mate to use when her fragile bark is ready.

When swimming, the octopus (*Octopus*) holds its eight arms close together and drives itself along by jet propulsion. The suckers on its tentacles are attached directly to the arms, not borne on short stalks as in squids and cuttlefishes. (Fritz Goro: *Life* Magazine)

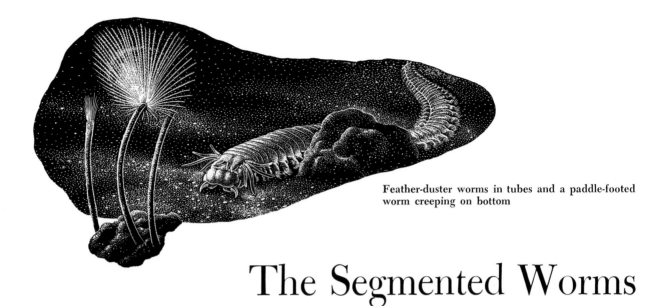

CHAPTER XVII

Feather-duster worms in tubes and a paddle-footed worm creeping on bottom

The Segmented Worms

(Phylum Annelida)

OF all the many kinds of worms, those with segmented bodies are surely known to more people than any others. Thus the inland angler seeks an earthworm as a lure, and the coastal fisherman realizes that in salt water a sea worm will remain attractive longer to fish, and therefore baits his hook with a ragworm.

Just about everyone sooner or later wades barefoot in a pond or stream where bloodsucking leeches live, and finds these parasites attracted to his own skin. In many parts of the world, pharmacies maintain a supply of live medicinal leeches, whether to take the color from a black eye or to extract "bad blood" from a patient.

The earthworm, the ragworm, and the leech are all segmented worms. The same phylum includes the far smaller *Enchytraeus* and *Tubifex,* worms sold in pet stores as food for aquarium denizens.

The rings that mark the body of an earthworm or ragworm are the features giving the phylum Annelida its name, from a French corruption of the Latin *anellis,* a ring. Each of the encircling grooves corresponds to the boundaries of an internal partition dividing the body into a series of almost identical segments. Many of these segments have not only a private portion of the worm's body cavity, but also a local exchange station (ganglion) of its nervous system, a pair of excretory tubules (nephridia), and access to the products of digestion both directly from the walls of the digestive tract and from blood vessels which extend through all segments from one end of the worm to the other.

The anterior segments of an annelid worm show specializations related to feeding. It is here that the worm has a particularly important part of its nervous system, even when no head is recognizable. Most annelids can survive loss of the hinder end of the body, and even regenerate new segments to take the place of those lost. But even when a worm's body is severed very near the anterior end, both pieces are likely to die.

Annelids are the most efficient animals of worm body plan. They live in the bottom muds of the sea's deepest abysses and in the almost oxygen-free sediments below deep fresh-water lakes. Others inhabit the open surfaces of glaciers high on mountain shoulders, and the foliage along jungle paths where passersby may furnish food. They perform midnight ballets at the dark of the moon in tropical waters, and till the soil in lands where winter's frost reaches far below the surface.

Annelids form an important part of the diet for many hydroids and anemones, corals and jellyfishes, flatworms and nemerteans, other annelid worms, crustaceans and insects, sea stars and serpent stars, fish, and a host of terrestrial vertebrates. Of the six thousand-odd kinds of living annelids, most swim or build shelters for themselves in the sea.

The Paddle-footed Annelids
(*Class Polychaeta*)

When a coastal fisherman picks up a clamworm to put it on his hook, he needs to look carefully and seize the animal close behind its apparent head. Otherwise he is almost certain to be bitten. The clamworm *Nereis* has a pair of horny jaws deep down in its body. To defend itself or to take prey, the worm everts its pharynx and exposes its two jaws, spreading them widely. It can give quite a painful nip as it presses the jaw teeth against a person's skin and then attempts to withdraw its pharynx.

A novice gives no thought to the fact that a more delicate victim would have been torn apart, a piece of it swallowed as the clamworm's dinner. He is too amazed as well as chagrined at having dropped his bait as though it were a snake.

Some kinds of *Nereis* are as big as small snakes. *Nereis virens,* found on both coasts of America in cooler water and in northern European mud flats as well, reaches a length of 18 inches in New England. Its body is a handsome reddish brown, showing an iridescent greenish sheen. From Long Island southward, shelly bottoms are home to *Nereis pelagica,* a more tapering animal rarely more than 8 inches in length. Sandy shores seem more suited to *Nereis succinea* (*limbata*).

On European coasts the sea worm used for bait is most frequently *Nereis cultrifera,* the chainworm or ragworm, whose "rags" are its paddles, which droop like wet cloth when it is removed from the sea.

In its native element, a sea worm's paddles are extremely important. Without them the muscles of the body wall could do little to promote locomotion while the worm was lying on the bottom or surrounded by water. But members of the class Polychaeta have the body wall extended into one pair of paddles (parapodia) on each of the many segments. Stiff bristles, for which the class was named, support the paddles and hold them almost at right angles to the body. The paddles may be slightly fleshy or mere thin vanes, yet they provide a hold on the water next to the worm and make efficient the locomotory movements of muscles in its body wall.

Among the largest of these paddle-footed swimmers is 3-foot *Nereis brandti* of America's Pacific coast. These worms, which are as broad-bodied as a garter snake, swim to the ocean's surface at night. Scientists sometimes wonder how a "sea serpent" of this kind would impress a slightly inebriated fisherman in a rowboat on a protected bay. He might need to do no more than shine a flashlamp over the side to see a few of the giants moving through the dark water, their paddles glistening in the light.

The Greek mythmakers peopled the Mediterranean with between fifty and a hundred nereids, and pictured them in human form, riding sea horses. Today's annelid worms in salt water can be almost as unbelievable when they ready themselves for reproduction. Even closely similar kinds show specific features in the methods used in starting a new generation on its way.

Nereis and its nearest relatives introduce alterations even in parts of the body not intimately connected with production of eggs or sperms. The eyes enlarge; the paddles change form; and for many years the sexual stages were believed to be members of a different genus (*Heteronereis*). They are still referred to as heteronereid individuals.

The male heteronereid is regularly much smaller than the female, and often almost white with sperm cells showing through the body wall. The female heteronereid is usually heavy with reddish eggs, and swims much more stiffly and sedately. The males spiral in dizzy paths.

On the Pacific coast of America, *Nereis vexillosa*

Clamworms such as *Nereis virens* are the fishworms of the sea. At night they swim or creep over the bottom, feeding on dead clams and other bits of food. By day they often reach food through the mud, burrowing up to it from underneath. (Long Island, New York. Ralph Buchsbaum)

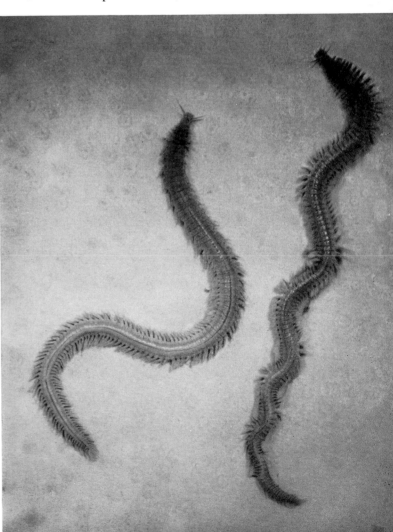

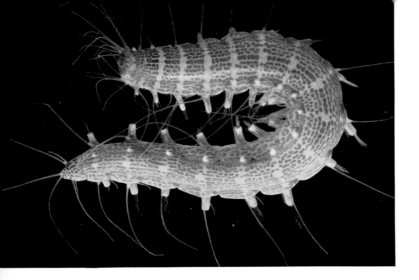

The paddles of *Hesione*, the bristle worm, are supported by stiff bristles and trail a long filament, giving a fringelike effect as the animal undulates from side to side. The head (top) bears eyes and several pairs of sensory tentacles. (Wimmer)

reaches sexual maturity during the spring and summer months when the extreme high tides at new moon come near midnight. One after the other the male heteronereids appear at the surface, each a mere ½-inch animal but swimming furiously. Females with red after-segments rise slantwise from the depths and join the crazed ballet. The males redouble their pace and commence shedding sperm cells as though they were stunt planes skywriting a message of welcome. This change in the water excites the female heteronereids, and they release their eggs through rents in the body walls of the loaded segments. By dawn, the survivors are spent.

On the New England coast, *Platynereis megalops* swarms for about two hours every night during the dark of the moon in summer months. In this species the male heteronereids appear to be in two parts: an anterior portion swimming violently with the maddest capers, and a posterior portion tagging along like a trailer, loaded with sperm cells. The females attack the males and bite off the segments containing the sperms. This mass the female heteronereid swallows in one long gulp. The sperms emerge into her pharynx, penetrate the segments where her eggs are waiting, and accomplish fertilization internally. Only after the event is complete will her body wall rupture and spill out the sexual products. Eggs of *P. megalops* cannot be fertilized artificially in sea water; some essential ingredient is missing.

Most famous of these nocturnal annelid ballets is the swarming of the palolo worm *Eunice viridis* in the South Pacific. There the big polychaetes live in holes among the coral reefs, hunting for food in the same general way as any *Nereis*. But at the third quarter of the moon in October and November come the "little rising" and the "great rising" for which the native peoples wait—ready to feast on the swarming worms.

At this season the palolo is mature, with eggs or sperm concentrated in a hinder part of the body. This posterior portion develops an eyespot and, at the appointed time, separates from the parent to swim to the surface and there mate like a heteronereid with other similarly dissociated individuals. This is actually mating by proxy, for the parent palolos remain in the rock crannies and develop new reproductive regions for the following year.

A very different polychaete worm swarms in the darkness near Bermuda. *Odontosyllis* partners find one another in the black water by bright luminescence. The little males flash like fireflies as they swirl near the surface. Each female glows steadily until a male reaches her and mating begins. Then her light goes out permanently, and so does his.

Nereids are inconspicuous as they prowl the bottom and tunnel through its surface sediments. Related worms, with added protection from enemies, can be more conspicuous in their foraging.

Among coral reefs of the Bahamas and West Indies, *Hermodice carunculata* moves about in apparent unconcern over the nearness of hungry fish. Its 8-inch body offers an attractive meal, yet few creatures molest *Hermodice* the fire worm. The soft-appearing white bristles on the rose-pink sides may suggest the texture of a Persian cat, but they are fine, stiff, brittle lengths of glasslike material that penetrate skin or the lining of mouth and stomach, producing agonizing pain. Brushing against *Hermodice* is like brushing against a hot poker. The burning sensation lasts for about an equal length of time, and is only aggravated by rubbing, since this drives the broken bristles even deeper.

Scale worms carry on their backs shields—overlapping plates in pairs—as armor. *Lepidonotus* has twelve such pairs, *Eunoa* fifteen, and *Halosydna* eighteen. These flattened worms, from 1 to 4 inches in length, are found on both sides of the North Atlantic where a beachcomber can discover them.

An even more astonishing polychaete of these same regions is the sea mouse *Aphrodite aculeata* (Plate 85), whose fifteen pairs of scales are completely hidden by a dense felt of long hairs, grayish down the middle of the rounded back, brilliant iridescent green and gold along the oval sides. Sea mice reach a length of 7 inches and a width of almost 3, far exceeding in size the mammals for which they were named.

The polychaetes that move about so freely are often grouped for convenience as "Errantia," the wanderers. Their counterparts are the more settled worms, the "Sedentaria." The latter build regular tubes and maintain a fixed address. Actually no sharp distinction can be drawn, for many of the wanderers are like *Nereis* in building mucus-lined tunnels in the bottom. *Cistenides,* among the supposedly sedentary types, fashions a beautiful slender tube of sand grains cemented together, and drags it over the sea floor like a trailer motorist in his mobile home.

One of the chronic burrowers, *Arenicola marina,* is known as the lugworm by fishermen on both sides of the North Atlantic. Other species of the same genus dig homes in the mud flats of the Pacific. These stout animals reach a length of more than 15 inches, with extra encircling wrinkles concealing the fact that the bristle-bearing trunk part of the body has only about twenty-one segments. Tufts of bright red gills mark the sides of each of these segments, but are lacking on the more slender, tail-like, posterior extension of the animal.

Arenicola lacks teeth in its eversible pharynx, but uses the organ as a burrowing tool in the sandy mud. While feeding, the worm engulfs the bottom material almost indiscriminately, swallowing a lump about every five seconds. It continues at this pace for from half a minute to a minute, then rests about twice to three times as long. From a quarter to a third of each day is spent in feeding, with occasional trips to the surface of the mud flat to expel a coil of sand from which the food materials have been digested.

The presence of *Arenicola* in a beach can often be suspected from the circular holes at the ends of the tunnels and the neat coils of castings which accumulate and erode into miniature volcanoes around some of the openings. In reproductive season, these worms enclose their fertilized eggs in great tongue-shaped masses of jelly as much as eight inches long, three inches wide and an inch thick, anchored at the small end in the sea bottom while the larger portion flops back and forth with each wave. After the enclosed eggs hatch, the developing worms use the jelly as food and continue to live in the enlarging cavity. Eventually they have more than a dozen segments and are beginning to resemble their parents; at this stage the small worms escape and the jelly disintegrates.

The parchment worm *Chaetopterus* builds a U-shaped tube lined with a tough secretion suggesting sheepskin. At the bend of the U the creature rests, waving its fan-shaped paddles (parapodia) to propel water past its body. The current brings both oxygen and particles of food; the latter are captured in a remarkable bag of mucus secreted by a pair of wing-like parapodia extending to the tube wall near the anterior end of the body. At intervals of about eighteen minutes, *Chaetopterus* stops pumping water, rolls its mucus net into a ball, and swallows it. Then it begins fanning again. Each ball of food contains virtually every microorganism in approximately a cupful of water pumped through the tube.

Although *Chaetopterus* rarely leaves the seclusion of its tube, it is a luminous animal. At night the pro-

The polychete worm *Eunice* is an active animal, hunting for bits of food among rock crannies and swimming or creeping by means of bristle-bearing paddles on each body segment. (Wimmer)

truding tips of its parchment tube may glow from the reflected light. No one is sure whether this attracts minute animals useful as food or has some other significance in the life of the worm.

On mud flats from New England to Georgia, the presence of another tube-builder, *Diopatra cuprea,* can be inferred from the conspicuous "chimneys" it constructs. These extensions of the vertical, three-foot tube project several inches above the bottom and are reinforced externally with bits of shell, plant debris, and seaweed fragments. The worm itself may be 1 foot in length, ½ of an inch in diameter. While covered by quiet water it extends from its tube a strikingly handsome pair of scarlet gill plumes, each treelike, with whorl after whorl of branches arising from a pulsating spiral central stem.

Tide pools and wharf pilings are home to some of the most spectacularly beautiful polychaetes, the feather-duster worms (Plate 81). Many of them are known more correctly as sabellids. They build tubes as much as eighteen inches long, and from the open end extend a pair of stubby, armlike organs (palps), each bearing a spray of gaily banded, feathery gill plumes which serve also in trapping food. In many cases the worm detects the merest shadow falling on the plumes, and snaps back out of sight into its tube.

[203

The parchment worm *Chaetopterus* lives in a U-shaped tube in muddy bottoms. Its bizarre paired paddles pump through the tube a current bringing oxygen and food, and help manipulate the mucus bag with which food particles are trapped. (Massachusetts. George G. Lower)

usually attaching their larger and irregularly coiled tubes to the shells of large mollusks.

A few exceptional polychaetes live in fresh water. Largest of these is *Nereis limnicola,* found in lakes and streams of California, close to the Pacific Ocean. Others inhabit remote Lake Baikal in Siberia. Even better known is the tiny, gill-bearing *Manayunkia* discovered in a Philadelphia suburb but now known also in the Great Lakes, where it builds tubes attached to stones. Its blood contains a green pigment (chlorocruorin) rather than the red hemoglobin found in most other annelid worms.

Some minute worms, all of them less than ⅕ of an inch in length, as adults resemble juvenile stages of polychaete worms. For years they were suspected of being "missing links" and received the name "archiannelids." Now it appears that they are merely degenerate types. Each of them has but five or six segments and develops neither parapodia nor bristles. On the dorsal surface, bands of cilia mark the boundaries of the segments; the ventral surface is rather uniformly ciliated. Some species are transparent, others bright orange or translucent white. *Polygordius* is almost as slender as a hair, and is a salmon-pink; it lives under stones on both sides of the North Atlantic and in the Mediterranean. *Dinophilus* is more oval in outline, and occupies similar sites around the world.

The Bristle-footed Annelids *(Class Oligochaeta)*

An earthworm maintains its grip upon the soil with the bristles that give the class Oligochaeta its name (from the Greek *oligos,* small, and *chaeta,* a bristle). Each segment of the animal has four pairs of glassy bristles which can be detected as roughnesses when a finger is rubbed along its sides or undersurface.

The worm has muscles with which to tilt the bristles forward or back, and it uses this simple control to determine whether the alternate contractions and extensions of its body will shift it ahead or toward the rear. If an earthworm tilts the bristles to slant backward and extends them to catch upon the soil, it is ready to move forward. The bristles then permit any portion of the worm to slide ahead, but prevent it from slipping backward. If the worm tightens its longitudinal muscles and shortens itself, the anterior end of the body holds to the creeping surface while the posterior end skids forward. When the worm contracts its encircling muscles and relaxes the longitudinal set, its body lengthens. The bristles in the posterior segments hold fast while those in the anterior region slip easily, and the worm moves ahead.

After a few minutes the whole headgear emerges slowly, mushrooming to a diameter of perhaps 3 inches like the cloud from an erupting volcano. Cilia covering the surfaces of the gill plumes then begin driving water against them. Any food particles are trapped in a mucus film carried down channels to the mouth.

Serpulids (Plate 82) are mostly smaller worms, with gill plumes seldom over ½ of an inch across. They have gone one step further than the feather-duster worms in that one part of the gill plumes has become a "stopper," pulled into place in the tube opening like a cork in a bottle as the worm jerks back into the security of its shelter.

Serpulids build limy tubes that coil or spiral. *Spiorbis* attaches to seaweeds a white, snail-like shell, often no more than ⅛ of an inch across. *Hydroides* and *Serpula* range widely, often to moderate depths,

→

Fan worms (sabellids) are annelids that extend from their parchment-like tubes a lovely crown of feathery tentacles with which suspended food particles are gathered and oxygen obtained. (Bimini. Fritz Goro: *Life* Magazine)

The large burrowing terebellid worm at left, *Amphitrite johnstoni,* shares its burrow, and probably a little of its food, with a smaller guest (commensal), the scaleworm *Gattyana cirrosa.* (England. D. P. Wilson)

To retreat, the worm simply tilts its bristles in the opposite direction and repeats the cycles of changes in body length, time after time.

This method of locomotion is adequate for oligochaetes wherever they live. A very few, such as the very slender, 2½-inch *Clitellio* worms found under stones in the intertidal zone, and the white, 1-inch *Enchytraeus* worms among living and dead plant debris in the same regions, can tolerate salt water. A few creep over glaciers, apparently feeding on microscopic plants in the film of water that melts when sun reaches the ice surface. These are "glacier worms." But most oligochaetes live in fresh water or in soil, on all continents and major islands with the exception of Antarctica and Madagascar.

Oligochaetes in fresh water inhabit their realm from top to bottom, and tend to be world-wide in distribution, perhaps carried from place to place in the

mud on the feet of migrant wading birds. Little *Dero,* scarcely ¼ of an inch in length, secretes a slender tube below a duckweed leaf, and slips in and out (or reverses itself) at astonishing speed. *Dero* captures small crustaceans (chiefly water fleas) that come to rest against the undersurface of the miniature floating plant.

Bright red or brownish members of the genus *Tubifex* thrive where the bottom mud is rich in organic matter, and can manage with almost no oxygen. Often they become conspicuous as an assemblage forming a carpet in polluted water. If undisturbed, each worm clings to the upper end of its individual slime tube, a tunnel extending downward into the bottom. Its inch-long slender body waves in the water, creating a feeding current. Yet the merest commotion is enough to send every *Tubifex* instantly into its refuge.

Many fresh-water oligochaetes reproduce asexually, simply by dividing the body transversely into two, each half regenerating the missing region. Often the regeneration is essentially complete before the individuals separate. Sometimes several offspring of this kind are being formed at the same time, one after the next in a chain.

Otherwise the bristle-footed worms mate in the manner that has become familiar from observations of earthworms. Each oligochaete is both male and female. At mating time a pair of equal size lie with anterior ends overlapping, facing in opposite directions. Sperm cells are passed from each worm to the other, and collected in special flask-shaped chambers opening to the outside by small openings. Then the worms separate, each to use the store of sperms in fertilizing a batch of eggs.

When the eggs are ready, the worm secretes a slime tube around its body, heaviest and charged with a special protein in the region of the clitellum (the saddle-shaped thickening so conspicuous a short distance back from the head end). Slowly the worm moves in reverse, sliding the slime tube like a girdle over the anterior end. As the thick part of the tube passes the sperm cavities, these discharge their load into the space between the worm and the slime tube. Opposite the ovaries, the eggs are extruded into the same space and fertilization occurs. Gradually the worm works out of the slime tube, and the latter purses up to form a lemon-shaped cocoon enclosing the developing young. By the time they escape from the cocoon, they are miniatures of the parent.

Quite recently, scientists have discovered that the common earthworms emerge from the cocoon with the full adult number of segments. In *Lumbricus terrestris,* the flat-tailed night crawler, this is about 150. In the barnyard earthworm *Eisenia foetida,* which Izaak Walton called the "brandling," the total is only about 95 segments.

The clitellum, too, has a definite position. That of

Lumbricus extends from the thirty-second to the thirty-seventh segment as counted from the anterior end. In *Eisenia* the glandular enlargement lies in segments twenty-five through thirty-two. The cocoons produced are similar, about the size of a grain of wheat in *Lumbricus,* slightly smaller in *Eisenia.* Those of the giant 11-foot earthworm *Megascolides australis* of Australia are almost three inches long and half an inch in diameter—about two-thirds as thick as the slender worm itself.

Some kinds of South Asian earthworms appear able to regenerate new individuals from both parts if they are cut in two. Earthworms in the northern parts of Europe and Asia, Australia, Africa, and the Western Hemisphere cannot do this. They will replace four or five segments at the anterior end, and this may be the most they will do even if the loss there is as great as ten segments. On the other hand, a cut between segments eleven and thirty-six is almost sure to kill the worm.

If its first thirty-five segments remain intact, a well-nourished worm may regenerate a new posterior end and add segments closely matching the number amputated. Somehow the worm is able to install replacements bringing the total almost exactly to the tally at hatching age.

In most soils, earthworms constitute about half of the entire weight of animal life. Half a ton of earthworms to the acre is an average figure. In rich soil it may reach twelve tons to the acre, which could be regarded as a fair indicator of fertility. Appreciation of the earthworm's role in the soil is far younger than a knowledge of its use in angling. Juliana Berners, a nun in an English Benedictine convent, gave clear instructions for finding and using worms as bait in the fifteenth century. Aristotle referred to earthworms inelegantly as "earth's guts," but he recorded no knowledge of where they came from or any value they might have.

Not until 1777 was the value of earthworms to plant economy guessed at by the English naturalist Gilbert White, who wrote:

> Earthworms, though in appearance a small and despicable link in the chain of nature, yet, if lost, would make a lamentable chasm. For to say nothing of half the birds, and some quadrupeds which are almost entirely supported by them, worms appear to be great promoters of vegetation . . . the earth without them would soon become cold, hard-bound, and void of fermentation, and consequently sterile.

Less than a century ago, Charles Darwin published a fuller account, *The Formation of Vegetable Mould through the Action of Worms,* a book drawing together extensive observations which showed how much of the humus matter in the soil came from leaves and other plant debris pulled by earthworms into their subterranean tunnels. The passageways also serve vegetation by admitting oxygen and rain. Darwin summarized his discoveries with the statement:

> The whole of the superficial mould [topsoil] over any such expanse has passed, and will again pass, every few years through the bodies of worms. The plough is one of the most ancient and most valuable of man's inventions; but long before it existed the land was in fact regularly ploughed and still continues to be thus ploughed by earthworms.

Darwin collected the castings over sample areas of ground, and dried and weighed the material collected. He estimated that between seven and one-half and eighteen tons of material were annually brought to the surface by worms in each acre of ground. Later scientists found that the amount of earth-moving actually ranges from two or three tons per acre per year in light soils to more than a hundred tons in some tropical parts of the world.

The conspicuous saddle-shaped clitellum of earthworms secretes the cylindrical sheath which becomes the "cocoon" for developing eggs. (Bavaria. Otto Croy)

Earthworms use their soft sucking mouths to seize plant debris on the surface of the ground while they are extended from burrow openings at night. Although these worms have no eyes, their skins are sensitive to light (except red light), and each individual will draw back into its tunnel if illuminated. Anglers often hunt them with a ruby lens on a flashlamp, taking advantage of the animal's blindness to this part of the spectrum useful to man.

All over the world, earthworms have many natural enemies. The national bird of Australia, the kookaburra or "laughing jackass," is actually a kingfisher whose remote ancestors gave up diving for fish and took to earthworms instead. Elsewhere moles tunnel after earthworms. Skunks dig them out or pounce on

The European medicinal leech *Hirudo medicinalis* has its larger sucker at the rear end (below). This leech is still being imported for sale in the United States, although it thrives in many ponds in America as an introduced animal. (P. S. Tice)

them at the surface. Owls eat amazing numbers and feed them to their young. Robins and other birds use earthworms as an important part of their diet.

Recent experience in Ann Arbor, Michigan, has emphasized the extent to which earthworms bury leaves and robins eat earthworms. In that city, prized elm trees were sprayed heavily with insecticide to check the spread of bark beetles carrying the Dutch elm disease. Poison-coated leaves fell to the ground in autumn, and were pulled by earthworms into their burrows for winter meals. The worms digested the plant matter without noticeable harm from the insecticide. But when the robins arrived the following spring, at the end of northward migration, the fliers encountered poison-charged earthworms. The robins ate so many worms that they succumbed to the insecticide. Soon Ann Arbor's formerly abundant robins were no more.

The Leeches   (*Class Hirudinea*)

Most leeches will take a blood meal from a vertebrate animal if they have an opportunity. Only a few, however, require this food, having become truly parasitic. The rest get along quite well on a mixed diet of snails, insect larvae, crustaceans, and small bristle-footed worms, swallowing these victims whole into the capacious crop portion of the digestive tract.

Leeches swim gracefully by undulating the body. Those that are flattened make especially rapid progress. At the end of the journey, however, all leeches settle down and hold to something solid by use of a muscular suction disk just ventral to the anus at the posterior end of the body. Most leeches have a second suction disk surrounding the mouth, and often stitch themselves along from place to place like an inch worm, holding to the bottom with one sucker and then the other alternately.

The saliva of blood-sucking leeches contains a powerful anticoagulant (hirudin), which prevents formation of a clot. It may also serve to preserve a blood meal, since, if permitted, a leech will usually swallow enough to last for several months. Almost as rapidly as the blood is taken in, the leech's excretory organs (nephridia) dispose of the water, concentrating the meal for maximum nourishment. A half-ounce leech has been known to gorge itself with two and one-half ounces of concentrated blood and then survive with no more to eat for fifteen months.

The leeches include a number of exceptional animals radically unlike other members of their class. One (*Acanthobdella*) has bristles and retains a true body cavity in adult life; otherwise leeches lack bristles, and the body cavity of the embryo is obliterated by a meshwork of connective tissue, muscles, and expanded portions of the blood system.

[continued on page 225]

90. The **barber-shop shrimp**, *Stenopus hispidus*, trails its tremendously long white antennae and large banded front pincers when it uses its tail fin as a water scoop and darts backward out of danger. It scavenges for food on coral reefs and wharf pilings throughout the West Indies. (Marineland, Florida)

91. The **Californian mantis shrimp**, *Pseudosquilla bigelowi*, burrows in ocean bottom mud, digging in at an angle of 45 degrees to a depth of as much as four feet. At the mouth of the burrow it waits for small fish to come within snatching distance. (Scripps Institution of Oceanography. D. P. Wilson)

92. The **prawn**, *Palaemonetes*, hides among eelgrass and floating seaweeds in northern, cooler waters of the North Atlantic. (Delaware. William Amos)

93. The **pond crayfish**, *Procambarus blandingii acutus*, often migrates in considerable numbers at night, traveling from one pond to another. (Illinois. John Gerard: National Audubon)

94. The **burrowing crayfish**, *Cambarus diogenes*, digs its home close to a stream, excavating a chamber three or four feet below the soil surface where water will seep into it. A mud chimney several inches high is built around the burrow opening. (Illinois. John Gerard: National Audubon)

95. The **common green crab**, *Carcinides maenas*, of America's North Atlantic coast, dines on a variety of young clams and marine worms, such as this beak-thrower (*Glycera*). (New Jersey. David C. Stager)

96. The most familiar **edible crab** in American Pacific coast markets is *Cancer magister*, often 7 inches across the body. It lives mostly on deeper sandy bottoms, feeding on fishes. In summer, breeding pairs come to the shore. These, and also young crabs, can be dug up at low tide from rockbound sandy pools. (Oregon. Ralph Buchsbaum)

97. A cornered **crab** will back, if possible, into a pile of seaweed and prepare to defend itself with pincers ready. (Maine. Eliot Porter)

98. The **land crab**, *Cardisoma carnifex*, with a body about 8 inches wide, is found around the shores of the Indian Ocean and on islands of the East Indies as far as Samoa and Tahiti. It eats fruit and dead animals, including fish, but seems to prefer fresh water for an occasional bath. (London Zoo. Ralph Buchsbaum)

99. The **ghost crab**, *Ocypoda arenaria*, haunts sandy beaches from Long Island to Rio de Janeiro, roaming freely at night but spending most of each day in a U-shaped or Y-shaped burrow in the sand. (Florida. William J. Jahoda: National Audubon)

100. From Boston southward on America's Atlantic coast, the **fiddler crab**, *Uca pugilator*, occurs in small armies that run as groups over the sandy shores. The male (left) has an enormous "fiddle" claw, used in courting the female (right) and in defense. (Florida west coast. Charles Lane)

101. The **land hermit crab**, *Coenobita rugosa*, of East African coasts, is known as a "soldier crab" because it hunts in large numbers, climbing trees and bushes, eating fruits, carrion, and animals slow enough for it to capture. This specimen in the London zoo carried a borrowed marine snail shell 3¾ inches in length. As the crabs grow they appropriate larger snail shells (Ralph Buchsbaum)

102. The **robber crab**, *Birgus latro*, of islands in the South Pacific is able to climb coconut trees and knock down the husk, which it then opens with its large pincers to get at the meat inside. (Bora Bora. Jerome and Dorothy Schweitzer)

103. The **sponge crab**, *Dromia vulgaris,* carries on its back, like a beret, a concealing piece of sponge, held securely by the highly modified last two pairs of legs. (France. Ralph Buchsbaum)

104. The large **hermit crab** of the American Atlantic coast is *Pagurus pollicaris,* common from Maine to Florida. This one has its soft abdomen securely protected by the heavy shell of a whelk, *Busycon,* a carnivorous marine snail. (Marineland, Florida)

→

107. Large **hairy-legged tarantulas** from Central and South America often reach countries far from the tropics in bunches of bananas where they have hidden during a nighttime hunt for insects, small lizards, and mice. (Roy Pinney)

105 and 106. (Above) The **giant whip scorpion** or **vinegarone,** *Mastigoproctus giganteus,* is a fearsome-looking but harmless denizen of the Sonoran desert in Arizona. (Eliot Porter) (Below) Only two of North America's scorpions have a deadly sting, and even they are reluctant to use the venom-bearing tail tip except in defense or to subdue a struggling insect seized in the pincer-tipped legs. (Roy Pinney)

108. On yellowing green foliage this **spider** is well camouflaged, but on the bark of a pine tree in a sandy woodland it is a good target for wasps and birds. (Berlin. Otto Croy)

109. The **wolf spider**, *Dolomedes*, runs lightly over the ground and also ventures out upon the surface of ponds and streams in search of insect prey. (New Mexico. Eliot Porter)

110. **Wolf spiders**, such as the members of genus *Lycosa*, drag with them wherever they go the silk-covered ball of eggs from which spiderlets will emerge. (Delaware. William H. Amos)

113. The female **black widow spider**, *Latrodectus mactans*, wears a bright red hourglass mark on the underside of her spherical black abdomen. She defends her nest with a bite that is dangerous to man. (Texas. Andreas Feininger)

111 and 112. Some **spiders** make a specialty of hunting for prey below the surface of ponds. *Dolomedes* carries a film of air caught in hairs over the body as it dives (above), but sheds the water quickly upon returning to air with a victim (below). (William H. Amos; and John Gerard: National Audubon)

114. The **banded garden spider**, *Metargiope trifasciata*, builds an orb web but spends many hours repairing holes made in it by heavy insects that break through and escape. (New Mexico. Eliot Porter)

115. Immature stages of the **velvet water mite**, *Limnochares*, have six legs and live as parasites on water insects. The adult (left) swims readily and clambers over the shore while scavenging for prey. (Delaware. William H. Amos)

[continued from page 208]

One leech in southern Chile (*Macrobdella valdiviana*) reaches a length of 30 inches as a burrower in soil, probably depending for food on earthworms and insects; otherwise the 12-inch horse leeches (*Haemopis*) acting as predators in ponds and lakes over much of the world hold the record for size.

One leech (*Haemodipsa*) in the moist jungles of southern Asia is terrestrial, and stays on foliage or tree trunks beside animal trails as much as 11,000 feet above sea level in the Himalayas. Holding firmly by its posterior sucker, it reaches out its slender 1-inch body, ready to catch a victim and be carried while collecting a blood meal. The bite is painless but is often followed by an ulcer due to infection of the wound. And a few dozen of these leeches can withdraw substantial amounts of blood, since each is unwilling to drop off before its dimensions resemble those of a small cigar. Other leeches live in ponds and streams, the sea, and wet soil.

Marine leeches are encountered on sharks and rays, although smaller kinds attack a variety of bony fishes. *Branchellion* is a very active leech which is as much as 9 inches long, highly distinctive because the sides of its dark-colored body bear lobed, fleshy, overlapping gills. *Pontobdella* has only little tubercles over the surface of its 3-inch cylindrical body. Both of these attack skates, but *Pontobdella* appears to favor sharks, especially the hammerhead shark. Smaller leeches, 1 inch or less in length, are sometimes found among the gills of bony fishes. Smooth-bodied *Piscicola* is commonest on flounders, attaching itself to the upper side. *Trachelobdella,* with conspicuous transverse wrinkles, seems less selective.

Even the method by which a leech's sperm cells reach the eggs seems bizarre. Each leech is a hermaphrodite, with both ovaries and testes. At mating season, one leech deposits on the back of another a small mass of mucus loaded with sperm cells. The mass remains cemented in place until the body wall becomes irritated and develops an open sore. Through this gap in the body defenses the sperms penetrate and work their way through the blood spaces to the ovaries, fertilizing the eggs there. Meanwhile the mucus mass drops off and the skin heals over.

In fresh waters the turtle leech *Placobdella* is often found clinging to the skin at the base of the hind legs of pond turtles, including snapping turtles. While unmolested, its body remains broad, flat, and handsomely patterned in yellow on a green background. But if disturbed, *Placobdella* drops off and curls into a ball that sinks quickly to the bottom.

Glossiphonia, the common flattened leech of running water, has a similar shape and color pattern. Both of these leeches are interesting because they lay their eggs in large gelatinous capsules, and each parent carries a capsule attached to the undersurface of the body until the young hatch out. Sometimes the young leeches cling for a week or more to the parent's back, and drop off one at a time. This may help get them distributed more widely as the parent swims about.

Other leeches ordinarily deposit their eggs in a flat cocoon, attaching this to a stone or other firm support in the water. In a few kinds the parent remains close to the eggs and protects them from disturbance for as much as three consecutive months.

The common bloodsucker *Macrobdella* is dark olive-green, with a thin body as much as 6 inches long and ½ of an inch in width. It frequents ditches and pond margins hunting for food of many kinds: frog's eggs, tadpoles, worms, and insect larvae. It is particularly sensitive to any vibrations in the water, however, and comes swimming to get a blood meal from fish, frog, turtle, cow, or man.

Picnickers should know that it is far easier to get an attached leech to drop off by sprinkling a little salt on its body than by pulling at the slippery, elastic animal itself. The same recipe is effective with the jet-black or chocolate-brown *Herpobdella,* which manages to get a blood meal occasionally despite the fact that its mouth has neither jaws (as have *Haemopis* and *Macrobdella*) or a stabbing muscular proboscis (as is found in *Placobdella* and *Glossiphonia*).

The medicinal leech *Hirudo medicinalis* has gone somewhat out of fashion, although it may still be purchased over the counter of pharmacies in big cities of America, and more readily on the European continent and throughout Asia. It is cultured deliberately in fish ponds, especially carp ponds, in Europe and the Orient, and has become a relatively docile animal. Medicinal leeches released in New World lakes and streams have often succeeded in colonizing American waters.

Hirudo medicinalis is so easy to handle that it will attach itself where guided. With its clot-liquefying enzyme hirudin it can remove the color-producing evidence of a bruise or a black eye. Or, in the hands of primitive medicine men, it will draw off load after load of "bad blood" in the practice of blood-letting. Application of a little salt to the engorged leech induces it to disgorge; the freshly washed leech is then ready for another meal.

So common was this use of leeches in the Middle Ages that physicians became known as "leeches." In 1846 the French physician Moquin-Tandon calculated that between twenty and thirty million leeches were used annually in his country. By 1863 the hospitals in Paris were requisitioning close to six million leeches a year, those in London another seven million. The requisitions usually specified full-grown 5- to 6-inch adult leeches because these have the largest capacity for blood.

CHAPTER XVIII

The Arthropods
(*Phylum Arthropoda*)

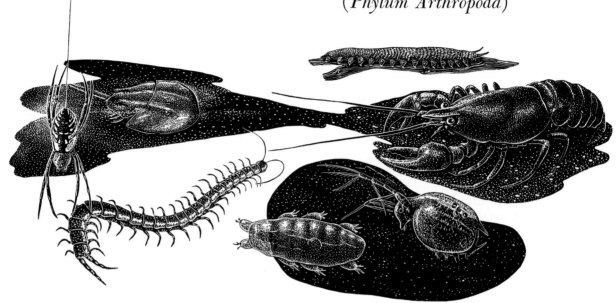

(Upper left) Orb-weaving spider and horseshoe crab; (upper right) velvet worm and lobster; (lower left) centipede; (lower right) bear animalcule and water flea

OF all the invertebrates, it is only members of the phylum Arthropoda that have mastered flight. Indeed, no other phylum of animals is so widely distributed, from pole to pole, from the greatest abysses to the highest peaks, from glacier to boiling spring, as well as from the driest desert and saturated salt lake to the felt of moss kept perpetually wet by the misty spray from a waterfall.

It is tempting to refer to the arthropods simply as "the insects and their kin," for the insects, which belong to this phylum, constitute three-quarters of the known kinds of animals. With other arthropods, insects share the possession of an external skeleton composed of hard cuticle, and jointed legs—the feature from which the entire phylum derives its name. Typically, the hard cuticle is molted at intervals, allowing the animal to grow by a succession of steps during the few hours while the body wall is flexible. Typically, too, each segment of the body bears a pair of jointed limbs. Commonly each leg ends in a pair of claws.

By interpreting these features liberally and watching for others that are found in arthropods about which no argument can be raised, it is possible to gather into this huge phylum two minor groups— the tardigrades and the onychophorans—which show affinities to other phyla as well. The remaining ar-

thropods can be subdivided easily into those with true jaws and those without.

The "mandibulate" arthropods have as appendages a pair of mandibles that do not end in claws. Instead, they work from side to side as chewing or crushing organs, or are modified in ways making them useful in piercing or sucking. The mandibulates also have antennae, either two pairs as in crustaceans or one pair as in centipedes, millipedes, and insects. Moreover, their body appendages tend at the base to show a forked character.

Arthropods without true jaws are spoken of as "chelicerate" because they all have associated with the mouth a pair of pincer-tipped appendages, the chelicerae. Chelicerate arthropods all lack antennae. Their body appendages are never forked at the base, and the first pair behind the chelicerae are usually modified into fingering organs, the pedipalps. Chelicerate arthropods include the marine horseshoe "crabs," the arachnids (the terrestrial spiders, scorpions, ticks, and mites), and the sea spiders.

The Bear Animalcules
(*Class Tardigrada*)

An almost infallible method for collecting live bear animalcules can be applied after a day or two of rainy warm weather. Put a fist-sized clump of damp moss into a pint bottle half full of water, shake vigorously for five minutes, remove the moss, strain the water through a pocket handkerchief, and examine the residue on the cloth with a strong lens or a low-power microscope. Nearly every clump of moss in the world is home to a few bear animalcules. But they are minute creatures—rarely more than $\frac{1}{25}$ of an inch in length.

The name "tardigrade" refers to the slow steps taken by the bear animalcule as it lifts its stout body along on four pairs of stubby legs. Three legs arise on each side, and a fourth is at the posterior end. All legs end in a little cluster of four or five claws or hooks that are movable and help the animal cling to a moss plant, a lichen, a bit of bark, or a shingle on the roof. A tiny eyespot adorns each side of the body just forward of and higher than the first pair of legs.

Bear animalcules are scavengers, feeding on both animal and plant matter sucked into the small mouth or cut free through use of a pair of sharp teeth. Each individual combines the organs of both sexes, but the feature most effective in insuring the continuation of bear animalcules in the world is their ability to lose a little water, become dormant, and be blown in the inactive state as dust particles. As a result, most tardigrades are cosmopolitan and can be collected as easily in the arctic as in the tropics, in Africa, America, Eurasia, or Australia.

Tardigrades can remain dormant for years, and then become active again in a few minutes when wet or exposed to very humid air. It is after rains that they climb about and can be shaken free from a support. Some bear animalcules inhabit ponds, particularly temporary pools. A few are marine, and creep in the capillary water film between sand grains on the beach, or cling to the surface of sea cucumbers, sea fans, and other slow-moving or attached animals.

Bear animalcules are so uncomplicated anatomically that biologists have often been uncertain of their proper place in the animal kingdom. Sometimes the tardigrades have been simply left in a little phylum of their own, sometimes grouped with nematode worms in the phylum Aschelminthes.

The Velvet Worms

(Class Onychophora)

Almost 150 years ago, the Reverend Landsdowne Guilding was poking about, searching for snail shells on the hilly slopes of the island of St. Vincent in the West Indies. Under a rotting log he found an inch-long brown animal. It moved slowly, and he mistook it for a slug. Since it did not have a shell he popped it into a vial of preservative solution, and did not examine it carefully until many months later. In 1825 he described the strange animal for science as a mol-

The head end of a peripatus, shown in color plate 88, here greatly enlarged. Thousands of minute papillae give the skin of a peripatus its unique velvety texture. (Panama. Ralph Buchsbaum)

lusk, *Limax juliformis,* curiously equipped with a series of lumps along each side of the almost cylindrical body as though it were a centipede. That the "lumps" were really legs never occurred to him.

Not until many years later did anyone examine a living velvet worm and realize how neatly it handles its more than two dozen pairs of stubby legs. Each leg ends in a flexible knob armed with a pair of claws. From these the name of the class Onychophora ("claw-bearing") is derived. On its unusual legs the creature (Plate 88) glides over the ground, latching each leg temporarily to some support by expert movement of the claw-bearing knob.

A pair of projections at the head end, which the Reverend Mr. Guilding mistook for the tentacles of a slug, are actually flexible antennae. They bear no eyes and curl out of harm's way, whereas the tentacles of a land snail or slug carry eyes and draw back inside the head like an inverted glove finger. Velvet worms do have a pair of simple eyes, one on each side of the head. But these organs are more like those of some polychaete worms than of any mollusk.

The West Indian velvet worm was eventually recognized as a creature that superficially resembled a caterpillar but was not an insect. It was neither a centipede nor a millipede. It had many features in common with annelid worms, yet was no annelid. It was a "walking worm," and so it received the generic name *Peripatus.*

[227

Other animals of the same general type have now been found living on every continent except Europe. Each one may be referred to as a peripatus (spelled without a capital), although the eighty-odd different kinds are now placed in a dozen genera and two different families.

Wet forests conceal these animals, from within a few feet of sea level to high in the Andes of South America. Various kinds of peripatuses are found as far north as Mexico and as far south as the Cape of Good Hope. One kind in Panama and adjacent countries reaches a length of 5 inches and the diameter of a lead pencil; it is *Macroperipatus geayi*. Best known of the velvet worms, however, are *Peripatopsis capensis* from South Africa and *Peripatoides novaezealandiae* from New Zealand.

Creatures of this body form have been walking the earth for at least five hundred million years. They may well have been among the earliest animals to creep out upon the land. Today's velvet worms are all terrestrial, extremely retiring in habit, and seldom seen except by naturalists who hunt them out. Perhaps this is because the peripatus avoids air containing less than 90 per cent of full saturation with water vapor. In so limiting themselves, the velvet worms parade in the open only at night or during rains, while the relative humidity is close to 100 per cent. By day they take shelter in the ground, or under stones and rotting logs, or between the leaf base of a palm tree and the trunk.

Every velvet worm has an amazing means of defense. On each side of the thick-lipped sucking mouth a small papilla marks the opening of a duct from large salivary glands. From these glands the animal can spit a blob of sticky secretion resembling clear rubber cement. Within seconds the liquid becomes opaque white and fairly firm. If a peripatus ejects its special slime at an annoying ant or other small attacker, the aim is usually excellent and the insect is effectively restrained.

Whether velvet worms use their salivary cement

Fairy shrimps (*Eubranchipus vernalis*) appear suddenly in meltwater ponds in springtime. They swim about catching microscopic green plants as food, and reproduce before migrant birds arrive or other potential enemies awake from hibernation. (Pennsylvania. Ralph Buchsbaum)

to subdue insects as prey is still questioned. Most peripatuses appear to eat dead insects and worms which they find as they explore among the leaf litter and bark crevices. But in the southern hemisphere some velvet worms live in termite nests, devouring dead termites. Whether they occasionally take a live termite has not been determined.

In captivity, some individual velvet worms will accept bits of liver. Some will seize live termites, other small insects, and woodlice. Most will feed readily upon freshly-killed flies and grasshoppers, cockroaches, and crickets. Others refuse food of all kinds, and within a few weeks die as a result of their hunger strike.

Occasionally a peripatus makes the mistake of spitting on its own back. The slime hardens, affixed firmly to the wrinkled, pebbled, water-repellent skin. In a few days, however, the velvet worm frees itself from the inflexible encumbrance by shedding the outer layer of the skin. This ability to molt is one of the ways in which a peripatus earns a place for itself among the arthropods. Another feature assumed to have similar meaning is the pair of bladelike jaws in the mouth. And a velvet worm breathes in a manner most like some of the centipedes, millipedes, and insects—using branched air tubes (tracheae) admitting air through openings on the surface of the body to inner organs.

Unlike that of typical arthropods, however, the skin of a velvet worm never develops a rigid cuticle. Molting tends to be by patches, rather than of a complete body covering at a time. In this respect a peripatus seems more akin to some of the annelid worms. Such resemblance extends to the excretory organs as well, for each leg base of a velvet worm carries the opening of a nephridium—the kind of organ serving annelid worms in much the same way that the kidney does a vertebrate animal. No other arthropod has nephridia.

Each peripatus is either a male or a female. Often the sexes can be distinguished in that the males have two or three fewer pairs of legs than the females. Male velvet worms sometimes seem unaware of sexual differences, for they may deposit a package of sperm cells upon the back of another male almost as readily as upon the body of a female. Only in the latter instance, however, does the skin develop an ulcer below the sperm packet and white cells from the blood open a passage through the skin. In this way the sperms are admitted into the body cavity, where they can migrate directly to the ovaries. For as much as a year, the arriving sperms may all be absorbed and used as nourishment for the developing eggs. Then, with the eggs finally ready for fertilization, another swarm of sperm cells can initiate the steps whereby a fertilized egg grows into an embryo and then a new individual.

One Australian kind (*Ooperipatus*) lays large yolk-filled eggs. Most other velvet worms retain the embryos inside the mother's body until the young are ready to be born as ½-inch facsimiles of the parents. Some South American peripatuses develop a connection between mother and unborn offspring that is analogous to the placenta of mammals. Across this bridge the parent furnishes her young with food and oxygen and attends to the disposal of wastes, including carbon dioxide.

Pregnancy in peripatuses may last for more than a year, and a female may even be carrying two different generations of young at a time. Often the mild excitement of being caught and placed in captivity is enough stimulus to cause a pregnant mother peripatus to expel her babies. For several weeks they may remain with her, and then wander off on their own—quite capable of feeding themselves.

The Crustaceans

(*Class Crustacea*)

People who enjoy seafood are likely to think of crustaceans as lobsters and crabs and shrimps. A whaler is prone to regard the class Crustacea as chiefly krill—the shrimplike denizens of the open oceans upon which whales feed so extensively. Inlanders may be more familiar with the crayfishes or crawfishes that resemble lobsters in body plan but thrive in fresh waters. The twenty-five thousand different members of class Crustacea include not only these animals—obviously "crusty" ones—but also an astonishing array of others, from water fleas to barnacles and fish parasites. Many are delicate microscopic creatures that drift in the waters of ocean and lake as plankton.

When the lobster and its many relatives are viewed as a group, the chief feature in common beyond their arthropod nature seems to be possession of two pairs of antennae. Other generalizations are subject to many exceptions. Most crustaceans are marine animals, but some live in rivers and lakes. A few inhabit the land, their gills modified in ways that require no wetting to be useful in respiration. The majority of crustaceans walk or creep or swim with their feet downward; a few regularly swim inverted. Most crustaceans live out their lives in waters illuminated by the sun. Yet others burrow in the bottom, and a surprising number inhabit the lightless abysses of the oceans.

PHYLLOPODS

Those crustaceans that regularly swim inverted are best known from the fairy shrimp *Eubranchipus* and the brine shrimp *Artemia*. Both are members of

Brine shrimps (*Artemia salina*) swim inverted in brine so concentrated that crystals form on their undersides. These phyllopods are found only in salty lakes, where they reach a length of a little under ½ inch. (Great Salt Lake. Fritz Goro: *Life* Magazine)

the order Phyllopoda. They drive themselves along in shallow water by successive waves of motion in the leaflike gill-feet, which are combined respiratory and swimming organs. They manipulate food with their leg bases, chewing it a little before swallowing it. Yet phyllopods have a clearly defined head with a pair of compound eyes, and a slender abdominal tail projecting behind the thorax with its paired gill-feet.

Fairy shrimps appear and disappear so suddenly that magic seems the only explanation. They occupy very temporary pools, such as meltwater from snow banks, and go through their growth stages so rapidly by feeding on microscopic algae that suddenly a clear new pond is occupied with inch-long swimming animals of iridescent colors—red, flesh-colored, greenish, bronze, or bluish.

Male phyllopods pursue the females, reaching for them with relatively huge claspers that extend from one pair of antennae. Mated pairs swim in tandem, the female often with dark spherical eggs filling a pair of large brood pouches at the base of her ab-

The water flea *Daphnia pulex*, less than ⅛ inch long, swims by jerking the large, branched antennae. (Japan. Y. Fukuhara)

dominal tail. The eggs drop out, sink to the bottom, and either develop promptly into a new generation of young or remain dormant until the pond dries up. Then the eggs can stay for years if necessary, until conditions are right again for hatching. They may blow as dust and fall into other temporary pools, starting other sudden swarms of fairy shrimps.

Brine shrimps ½ of an inch long are almost as unbelievable as they disport in salt-saturated bays of Great Salt Lake, Utah, and other bodies of concentrated sea water. Often they swarm in astonishing numbers in the artificial pans where man evaporates brine to get salt. In these places *Artemia* finds abundant microscopic plants of salt-tolerant types, and

few enemies, since most fish cannot endure the salt. Flamingoes may compete in filtering out the algae, and take small brine shrimp as well.

CLADOCERANS

Both salt water and fresh have their water fleas, members of order Cladocera. These creatures extend their antennae, legs, and abdominal tip through the gap in a bivalved carapace saddling them like the blanket on a pet dog. A water flea's second pair of antennae are remarkably long and bear a fringe of bristles or hairs that make the organs effective as swimming oars. A single compound eye occupies a central position in the head, but it can be shifted by muscles.

The most familiar of the water fleas in ponds and lakes is *Daphnia,* adults of which reach a total length just over ⅛ of an inch. In surface waters these pinkish or flesh-colored motes dance all day, while sweeping into their mouths microscopic algae.

Small fish eat enormous numbers of *Daphnia* and other cladocerans. Yet the rapid reproduction of these little crustaceans makes good all losses. For much of the year only female *Daphnia* can be found, and each releases another brood of fifty young ones every eleven or twelve days entirely by virgin birth (parthenogenesis). When living conditions deteriorate or autumn approaches, however, some of the young released mature as males and fertilize a final crop of eggs for the year. These "winter eggs" are resistant to freezing and to desiccation. The parent coats them in an extra shell (an ephippium) which may have air cells providing buoyancy. As the pond dries up, wading birds often become loaded with these armored eggs in the mud on their feet, and then wash off the living load in another pond where conditions are more suitable for water fleas.

Some of the larger cladocerans are carnivorous. *Leptodora* is an especially fierce one, sometimes reaching a length of ½ of an inch. It rows rapidly with winglike antennae in pursuit of smaller water fleas, insect young, and water mites. Like so many of its crustacean victims, *Leptodora* tends to swim at somewhat greater depths at midday, but comes to the surface in the late afternoon and feeds there until the sun brightens the sky in the morning.

COPEPODS

Members of another order of small crustaceans, the order Copepoda, swim by jerky, oarlike movements of the antennae. The name "copepod" comes, in fact, from the Greek *kope,* an oar. But the swimming antennae of a copepod are its second pair, not the first. And the body is usually a streamlined pear shape, with segmentation clearly visible through a microscope.

The largest of the free-swimming copepods is less

than ½ of an inch long. Those of average size are so small that they are easily overlooked, even when a cupful of pond water or sea water contains several hundreds of them.

The copepod encountered most frequently in fresh water is *Cyclops,* named for the one-eyed giant of Greek mythology. *Cyclops* seldom reaches a length of $\frac{1}{16}$ of an inch and appears to the unaided eye as a translucent milky white mote jerking along slowly through the water. It does have a single eye in the middle of the front of the head. If the individual is a female with eggs, her two egg masses may be almost as large as she is and suggest saddle bags. If a male is attending his mate, he holds to her with his second pair of antennae and they swim in tandem hour after hour while he transfers enough sperm cells to fertilize several batches of eggs.

Copepods in the drifting plankton near the surface, whether in fresh water or the ocean, tend to be highly transparent and colorless. Those associating with the bottom in shallow water may be pink or green or blue, whereas those in the black abysses of the ocean are more often black or blood red. All of them use fans of bristles on their feet to gather in microscopic plants or other nourishing particles as food. Often digestion is rapid enough that the digestive tract remains inconspicuous even when the body itself is glass-clear.

Most copepods hatch as six-legged, one-eyed creatures and undergo a number of molts before this "nauplius" stage is succeeded by the adult body form. An adult usually has many pairs of legs and no eyes, or one, or several. Yet the role of eyes is not easy to demonstrate, for even eyeless copepods tend to make long vertical migrations every day, swimming downward around daybreak and up again in late afternoon.

Some of these daily journeys are spectacular. The abundant marine copepod *Calanus finmarchicus,* about the size of a big grain of rice, travels from its daytime hideaway 1100 to 1500 feet below the surface to the topmost 150 feet of water at a speed of about 150 feet per hour. Before dawn it heads down again, diving about three times as fast.

These movements are not dependent upon light or the availability of food, for they are shown by captive animals in an endless ring-shaped tube at the same times of day in complete darkness. For a ½-inch crustacean to travel up a thousand feet and down again each day at half an inch each second is equivalent to a man's dog-trotting for the same length of time at four miles an hour—covering forty-six miles daily to reach a vegetable plate!

The number of animals performing these vertical migrations daily in the sea is unimaginable. With the copepods go slightly larger crustaceans and the small fish that prey upon them. With the small fish go larger

fish and squids in fantastic abundance. So dense is this migratory population during the day that the most modern sonar depth-measuring devices on shipboard sometimes cannot distinguish between the DSL (deep scattering layer) and the true bottom. The "phantom bottom" reflects the sound waves but offers no discernible resistance to the line and lead weight with which depth was formerly tested.

Directly or indirectly, the copepods provide a tremendously important link between the microscopic green algae that create foodstuffs in the sea with the energy of sunlight, and the multitude of larger animals that live far from shore. Vitamins elaborated by the algae and transferred into the copepods and then into the carnivorous crustaceans of the krill turn up in the oil of whale livers and then in the bottled concentrates for human dietary supplements. Proteins of plant cells, transformed into copepod proteins, are reorganized into the flesh of herring and salmon, cod and tuna.

Some copepods turn the tables on the fish, attacking these larger denizens of the ocean and sucking their blood or lymph as food. Many a marine fish,

The one-eyed *Cyclops* is a fresh-water copepod. This is a male, about $\frac{1}{10}$ inch long; the female usually carries a cluster of eggs attached to each side of her body. (P. S. Tice)

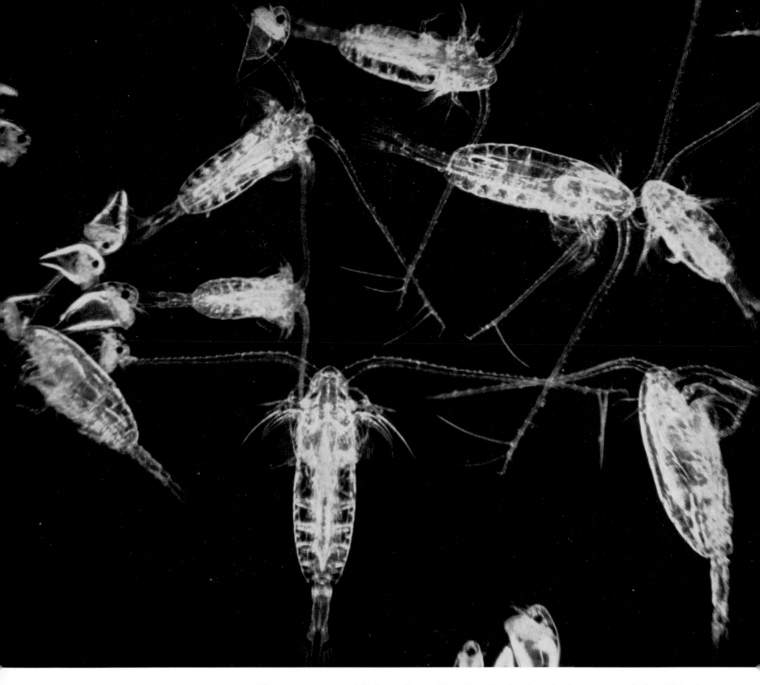

The marine copepod *Calanus finmarchicus* is only the size of a large grain of rice. This abundant crustacean makes amazing daily migrations between depths of 1500 feet and the topmost 150 feet of water. Also shown are a few, smaller cladoceran *Evadne*. (England. D. P. Wilson)

when freshly caught, is found to have small, flattened crustaceans scurrying over its surface. Others may be discovered clinging to the gills or the lining of the mouth, taking nourishment through the thinner, softer parts of the fish's skin. These are likely to be *Argulus,* the fish louse, a copepod with two prominent suckers on the under surface. Still other copepods go through an ordinary nauplius stage and then attack a fish, embedding themselves and growing larger as almost formless parasites. Yet when the female parasitic copepod produces eggs, she extrudes them in two egg pouches suggesting those of tiny, independent *Cyclops.*

OSTRACODS

The nauplius stage found in copepods appears to be an important first step in the life history of many crustaceans, both small and large. It is the first free-swimming stage for members of order Ostracoda, creatures a microscopist is likely to encounter while examining a bit of oozy mud from the bottom of a pond or a fragment of the floating algal mat at the surface. Ostracods have an almost egg-shaped, bivalved shell rarely more than $\frac{1}{16}$ of an inch in length, hinged at the back and capable of being closed entirely by contraction of a special muscle. These crustaceans are omnivorous scavengers which climb or cling on duckweed or other submerged vegetation by use of the same slender swimming legs that can be extended through the gap in the shell. *Cypris* is one of the common genera.

BARNACLES

Barnacles, which are crustaceans too (order Cirripedia) go through first a nauplius stage and then a bivalved form called a "cyprid" stage because of its resemblance to an ostracod. It is the cyprid stage that attaches itself to some solid object by means of the first pair of head appendages. Thereafter for a short time the young barnacle ceases to feed. It transforms itself into the degenerate adult form, secreting around its body a hard limy shell composed of several separate movable pieces. Inside this shell the barnacle is a prisoner, unable to move from place to place. It is attached to its covering by the region corresponding to the back of its neck, a fact that led an eminent biologist to describe a barnacle as an animal lying on its back, kicking food into its mouth with its feet. Much of what is known about barnacles comes from the monumental research work of Charles Darwin—work that established his reputation as a professional scientist fully a decade before the appearance of *The Origin of Species* in 1859.

Wharves and pilings, as well as ship bottoms and floating timbers, often bear a lively covering of gooseneck barnacles (*Lepas*), each holding to the support by means of a flexible leathery stalk that holds the shell-covered portion of the animal out into the surrounding water. Gooseneck barnacles usually have a shell composed of five limy plates, and present a somewhat flattened appearance suggesting a strange kind of clam attached by its siphon.

Barnacles attached to rocks are more often of the acorn type (*Balanus*), in which a conical ring of four closely fitted plates is closed at the top by two additional movable plates. When the latter are spread apart, the animal reaches out feather-like feet and combs the adjacent water for microscopic food particles. These are pulled into the cavity of the shell and there transferred to mouthparts that consolidate the catch and pass it to the mouth proper.

Both plankton organisms and the detritus from partial decomposition of living matter are acceptable food to barnacles. Upon a diet of this kind the acorn barnacle *Balanus nubilus* of Puget Sound on North America's west coast reaches a diameter of nearly a foot, and becomes an attractive item of food for human beings.

Man usually regards barnacles as "fouling" organisms that fasten themselves to ship bottoms and greatly increase the frictional drag of the hull upon the water. Barnacles also find a place on or in the skin of whales. *Coronula,* the commonest barnacle of

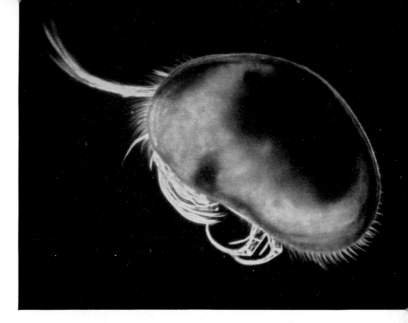

This fresh-water ostracod, whose head end is at the left, is less than 1/25 inch across its enclosing bivalved shell. Antennae and legs, which can be extended between the valves, beat and kick the animal along. (Illinois. P. S. Tice)

whale skin, may reach a diameter of 3 inches. Often this acorn barnacle, in turn, supports a few of the gooseneck barnacle *Conchoderma,* which is unusual in that it has only minimal shell covering and its feeding organs are enclosed in little hoods opening in the direction toward which the whale swims. From the appearance of its paired hoods, *Conchoderma* is called the rabbit-eared barnacle.

The step from being an embedded barnacle to one living a parasitic life may not be very big. It has been taken by a number of cirripedes, which thereby became "root-headed barnacles." The best known of them is *Sacculina,* since it attacks a variety of crabs, including the widespread green crab *Carcinides maenas* of the North Atlantic's shores and several different common kinds on the Pacific coast of America.

Sacculina reaches its victim while still in the free-swimming cyprid stage, but thereafter follows a truly amazing course. The *Sacculina* larva pierces a hollow bristle on the crab's body and through it frees into the crab's blood stream a few cells that float about inside the victim until they come to rest at the junction between the crab's stomach and intestine. There the cells attach themselves and grow on nourishment from the crab's blood while extending a mass of rootlike processes throughout the body of the host.

The growing *Sacculina* parasite invades and destroys the crab's reproductive organs. This not only terminates the host's ability to reproduce but alters its sex hormones until, at the next molt, it assumes female body form regardless of its inherited sex. Female body form includes an apron-shaped abdomen, which effectively protects *Sacculina* when the latter creates an opening in the crab's body wall on the under side at the base of the abdomen and extrudes a

Gooseneck barnacles, *Lepas anatifera,* on a floating bottle. (England. D. P. Wilson)

The rose-colored acorn barnacle *Balanus tintinnabulum* is one of the largest barnacles of the southern California coast. It reaches a width of 2¾ inches and is common on boat bottoms, wharf pilings, and rocks. (California. Woody Williams)

large shapeless mass. This bulbous extension becomes filled with eggs, which develop parthenogenetically to the nauplius stage and then escape to infect more crabs.

ISOPODS

A number of other crustaceans, ranging from ½-inch to larger sizes, become familiar to many people because they can be found alive or washed up on sea beaches. Still other crustaceans thrive in damp places on land far from any body of water. Under fallen logs, stones, and even human possessions in many a cellar, little oval flattened crustaceans known as sowbugs or slaters are often common. They are members of the order Isopoda, a name that indicates the various pairs of legs to be about equal in length.

Many isopods take advantage of their flexibility to curl up into a ball when disturbed. From this habit they have acquired the name "pill bugs," and been likened to miniature armadillos. Members of the common genus *Armadillidium* are particularly ready to exhibit this method of self-protection.

A pill bug of the seacoast is *Ligia* (Plate 89). Like the more inland members of *Oniscus* and *Porcellio,* it is more flattened and shows less tendency to curl up. Sowbugs are all scavengers, a few reaching ¾ of an inch in length. Their gills are greatly reduced but still serve in air for respiration. The females carry a batch of eggs with them in a brood sac formed by flat projections from the legs.

In fresh waters, whether stationary or slowly flowing, the isopods are represented by a 1-inch aquatic sowbug, *Asellus.* It tolerates stagnation better than many other creatures, and creeps over muddy bottoms eating refuse of all kinds. Females seem always to be carrying eggs or a brood of recently hatched young, with one generation succeeding another every five to eight weeks from very early spring throughout the summer.

Around wharves in salt water, the cosmopolitan wharf louse *Idotea baltica* is an isopod reaching a length of 1 inch or more. It shows surprising agility as well as awareness of its surroundings by expertly dodging the fingers of small boys who try to capture a specimen. It takes full advantage of its flattened body by scuttling into crevices.

The ⅛-inch gribble *Limnoria lignorum* goes even farther by burrowing into submerged timbers, often to a depth of half an inch or more, weakening docks and other wooden shore installations. Often pilings become eroded to an hourglass shape at low-tide mark primarily from the activities of this isopod.

AMPHIPODS

Whereas isopods tend to be flattened and broadly oval, members of the order Amphipoda are more usually compressed from side to side, and hence more flea-shaped or shrimplike. Fresh-water scuds with this form include the ½-inch *Gammarus* and *Hyalella,* both acrobats of no mean ability. Their repertoire includes swimming or climbing submerged vegetation by using the legs on the thorax, and leaps produced with the aid of longer appendages on the abdomen. Most of the world's seacoasts have species of *Gammarus,* which feed on both living and dead vegetation. All scuds provide fish with important food.

The conspicuous amphipods on sandy beaches are the ½-inch beach fleas, such as *Orchestia agilis* and *Talorchestia longicornis.* These creatures hide in vertical burrows in the wet sand or among piles of seaweed, where they can remain in humid surroundings or explore for food. If the seaweed is disturbed the beach fleas display the bouncing leaps for which they have been named.

The order Amphipoda includes some astonishing animals as well. One of them is *Caprella,* the ½-inch skeleton shrimp, whose body is a series of elongated cylindrical segments bearing two pairs of slender, hook-ended legs near the head and three more pairs at the rear. With these appendages the skeleton shrimp clings to seaweeds, hydroids, corals, and wharf pilings. It moves in slow motion with the gait of a measuring worm while stalking animals it can snatch with its anterior appendages. Some skeleton shrimps are grayish and translucent, others cream-colored or reddish.

Another strange amphipod is *Paracyamus,* the whale louse, which resembles the skeleton shrimp in size and body parts, but which is broader, more flattened, and constricted between segments. Its legs are more powerful grasping organs than those of *Caprella.* Whale lice creep in large numbers over the surface of huge whales, hooking their legs into the skin. They grasp a firm hold while gnawing out pits in which the body of the amphipod is protected from water rushing past the swimming whale. The entire nourishment of a whale louse is taken at the whale's expense.

Still another member of order Amphipoda is the glassily transparent *Phronima sedentaria,* whose head is so elongate as to suggest that of a horse. It is occupied almost entirely by the compound eyes. Inch-long *Phronima* captures one of the equally transparent colonies of the tunicate *Salpa* (p. 288) and takes up residence in the hollow, barrel-shaped tunic. It is carried along by the salp colony, and feeds on the larger animal particles entering the colony's central cavity. *Phronima* even uses this adopted home as a brood chamber for her own young.

Crustaceans more than an inch long tend to be more familiar to us, and to be valued either as human food or as nourishment important to large fish in

Rocks are often almost coated by the shells of acorn barnacles (*Balanus*). The two pieces of the shell that close the cavity can be drawn apart to let the barnacle use its feet to kick food into the mouth. (England. Ralph Buchsbaum)

which man is interested. A majority of these crustaceans have at least a superficial similarity to shrimps and lobsters. Their paired compound eyes are on movable stalks, and at least the first few segments of the leg-bearing thorax are fused together with the head to form a cephalothorax with shield-like top and sides (a carapace). This lends some rigidity to the fore part of the body, and often corresponds to use of the tail fin as a scoop in swimming backward, as is so characteristic of lobsters and crayfishes.

OPOSSUM SHRIMPS

Among members of the order Mysidacea the carapace does not extend far enough backward to cover all of the leg-bearing segments. Mysids are almost entirely pelagic, and their legs are all forked paddles suited for swimming but not for walking. These creatures are called "opossum shrimps" because the female carries her eggs beneath her thorax in a pouch formed of special plates. The young usually hatch in the nauplius stage and transform into the shrimplike adult form.

Mysis stenolepis is one of the most important mysids to man, for it is a major item of diet for such commercial fishes as shad and flounder. They find the mysid in abundance near shore, often among tangles of eelgrass. Sometimes a person can detect

The sowbug *Oniscus* is about ¾ inch long. Like other sowbugs it is a terrestrial isopod common under bark of fallen trees, or logs, or stones. (Hugh Spencer)

The pill bug *Armadillidium* is one of the terrestrial isopods that are ready at a moment's notice to roll up into a compact ball. (Switzerland. Otto Croy)

mysids there at night, seeing them from a skiff as little darting constellations of bright lights. Marine mysids carry their light-producing organs with them, but the few representatives of this order in the Caspian Sea and in large lakes of Europe and North America follow a different rule applying to all crustaceans in fresh water: they lack luminous organs.

EUPHAUSIDS

Krill, the principal food of whalebone whales, are pelagic crustaceans of the order Euphausiacea. Their appearance is even more shrimplike than that of mysids, for the euphausid carapace is fully developed, shielding the bases of all of the swimming legs. Euphausids carry their eggs below the slender abdomen. Most members of this order are a brilliant red, and when numerous they color the ocean's surface until whalers refer to it as "tomato soup." Wherever this color is widespread, whalebone whales can be expected.

At night euphausids may be equally noticeable because of their bright luminescence. When a ship disturbs them, they glow for minutes at a time, making the waves visible far astern. The underside of the first four abdominal segments bear light-producing organs. Usually another pair are located on the outer surface of the eyestalks, where they shine like electric torches into the water close to the mouth. The compound eyes have components facing in this direction too, and it seems likely that the animal actually jacklights its food (copepods) at night. In many euphausids the compound eyes are strongly bilobed, one portion seemingly directed upward and perhaps used to identify the abdominal lights of other krill. The other portion faces forward and downward, apparently for use in feeding.

LONG-TAILED DECAPODS

True shrimps, along with lobsters, crayfishes, and crabs, all belong to the order Decapoda. As the name suggests, all of them have ten thoracic legs. These include the large pincer-tipped appendages of North Atlantic lobsters as well as the smaller legs used in walking over the bottom. A number of pairs of appendages are associated with the mouth as food-handling organs, and still additional pairs below the abdomen serve in holding the eggs until they hatch.

Shrimps and prawns are free-swimming decapods, usually with a compressed body (Plates 90, 92). *Peneus setiferus* is the most important commercial shrimp of American Gulf Coast waters, with about 100,000 tons taken annually. In Europe its place is taken by *Crago septemspinosus* (also known as *Crangon vulgaris*), a denizen of sand flats and tide pools on both sides of the North Atlantic. On the American west coast the commercial shrimp is *Crago franciscorum*.

Commercial fishermen often refer to larger individuals as prawns and smaller ones as shrimps, but some of these men have learned to distinguish between the true prawn *Palaemonetes vulgaris* (Plate 92), in which the second pair of legs bear the largest pincers, and *Crago,* whose first pair of legs are the biggest and have a transversely closing finger, and *Peneus,* in which the third pair of legs bear the prominent grasping organs.

Tide pools and coral reefs are home to pistol shrimps, the "gunmen" of coastal waters. In these burrowing members of the genus *Crangon* (= *Alpheus*), the pincer on one of the front pair of legs is enormously enlarged, although borne on a slender limb. The movable claw near the end of the large handlike part is the hammer of the "pistol," cocked by the animal to jut out at an angle of about 90 degrees. The shrimp fires its pistol by snapping the hammer joint against the palm portion with amazing force, producing a sound audible all over a large room if one of these animals is in an aquarium.

The pistol shrimps use their weapons both to defend themselves and to obtain prey. The shock produced in the water is enough to stun a passing fish of usable size. In the South Pacific, returning fishermen are said to be able to learn the direction to the fringing reef around a coral island by hanging over the side of the boat and thrusting the head into the water. The crackling sound of pistol shrimps can then be heard all the way from the reef crevices.

The lobsters of North Atlantic coasts are members of *Homarus,* a genus whose name is derived from the old Scandinavian word for the animals. Epicures delight in the delicate flavor of the muscles in the large pincers and abdomen ("tail"). In consequence, more research work has been done on *Homarus* (and the similarly delectable oyster) than on any other invertebrate food harvested from the sea.

South of the Bay of Biscay in Europe, the lobster of Atlantic and Mediterranean waters is the spiny *Palinurus,* named for Aeneas' helmsman who fell asleep at the wheel and tumbled overboard. *Panuluris* is the spiny lobster of the Pacific and of Atlantic waters extending from North Carolina to Brazil. Spiny lobsters lack pincers altogether, and use their long and extremely strong antennae as whips to ward off enemies and to discourage competitors while feeding. As in *Homarus* and the various kinds of crayfishes, the tail meat of spiny lobsters is mostly muscles used to flex the abdomen, to drive the body backward through the water at each flick of the spread tail fan.

Throughout the spiny lobsters' range—as far south as the Cape of Good Hope—this tail meat is sought by native peoples and commercial fishermen alike. At the docks in Capetown, South Africa, the abdomens of millions of living spiny lobsters are ripped

From curled-under tail to the tip of antennae, the giant beachhopper *Orchestoidea californiana* may be 2½ inches long. It lives in a burrow beyond reach of the highest waves, and emerges at night to feed. (Oregon. Ralph Buchsbaum)

off annually by hand to be quick-frozen and shipped to markets in the United States. The still-struggling bodies are pushed into the sea as waste. Those who regard this practice as cruel have been met with a ruling by the local Society for the Prevention of Cruelty to Animals: by definition, only a vertebrate animal can feel pain.

All true lobsters, whether with pincers or spines, are scavengers. Yet they often engage in cannibalism. Apparently this is due to a chronic need for more lime than the environment provides, since the habit disappears when broken shells of mollusks or sand dollars are distributed on the bottom. Most of the weight of a lobster's exoskeleton is the lime that impregnates it and gives it rigidity. Yet at intervals each lobster sacrifices its hoard by molting the old covering, growing about 15 per cent in weight inside each new covering before it too must be shed. A thirty-four-pound, 23¾-inch *Homarus* is a record catch. *Palinurus* sometimes grows almost as large.

Crayfishes (Plates 93, 94) have much the same

The skeleton shrimp, *Caprella aequilibra,* is an elongated amphipod about 1 inch long. Caprellids crawl about on seaweed, as shown here, or on eelgrass or hydroids. (England. D. P. Wilson)

body plan as North Atlantic lobsters, but they live in fresh waters. Curiously enough, they are almost entirely absent from the tropics, which divide the astacids (such as *Astacus* and *Cambarus*) of Eurasia and North America from the parastacids of South America, New Zealand, Tasmania, Australia, New Guinea, and Madagascar. Africa itself has no crayfishes at all.

The largest crayfishes are the Tasmanian *Astacopsis franklinii* of surprisingly small streams. These creatures reach nine pounds in weight. American crayfishes are considerably smaller. Yet in the lower Mississippi Valley they are hunted at night for food, either for the tail meat itself or to give flavor and protein to the thick soup known as crawfish bisque. In the same regions, crayfishes often are a pest to rice farmers, for they graze at night on the rice and then retire to the concealment of shallowly subterranean burrows in which water stands for most of the year.

Lobsters, crayfishes, shrimps, and prawns are often grouped as the long-tailed decapods, the Macrura. With them should be included the hermit

crabs, which adopt empty snail shells as covering for their unarmored abdomens. Hermits (Plates 101, 104) are very common on every coast. They become familiar to beachcombers because they run about in daylight where the water is quite shallow, or come out on land in search of food.

The appendages which in a lobster form the sides of the water-scooping tail fan have become modified in hermit crabs and serve in holding to the inside of the snail shell. When disturbed a hermit draws back quickly into its shelter, often leaving only the tips of its two big pincer claws exposed, simulating protective doors. When left to their own devices, however, hermit crabs investigate every empty snail shell they encounter, often trying out an alternate for size. In this way they trade shells at frequent intervals and keep up with their own growth. To human collectors of shells, this habit can be most aggravating. A collector who leaves a fine specimen beside an ant nest for the ants to finish cleaning may find that a hermit crab has come along, carried off the collector's shell, and left an old, dirty, worn one of a common kind.

Largest of the hermit crabs is *Birgus latro,* the robber crab of South Pacific islands. After the customary juvenile period in the sea, the robber crab becomes progressively more terrestrial. Young ones may use a large snail shell or a small coconut as a cover for the abdomen. But gradually a robber crab's armor becomes heavier and the crab ceases to burden itself with shells. At the same time its abdomen twists toward a symmetrical position, although on its undersurface the crab has abdominal appendages developed on only the left side.

With its great pincers, the robber crab can open a variety of containers; it has earned its name by feeding from human utensils. It can also hammer and pick at a coconut husk until it reaches the contents of the seed within. If necessary, the crab climbs coconut trees and cuts the nuts from their attachments. Islanders who enjoy *Birgus* as food are said to take advantage of this habit by winding a thick layer of cloth around coconut palms well above the ground. The crabs will pass the cloth in climbing the palm, but on the downward return to the beach, they respond to the cloth as though it were the ground and let go of the trunk. *Birgus* is heavy enough that a fully-grown one, more than 1 foot in length, is likely to cripple itself by the fall and be unable to run away —letting the islanders capture it.

TRUE CRABS

True crabs are the short-tailed decapods, the Brachyura. Their bodies seem to be entirely cephalothorax because the abdomen is held curled underneath, usually fitting between the bases of the legs. In female crabs the abdomen forms a broad flat apron, whereas in males it is narrower and comparatively inconspicuous. When a female crab is carrying her eggs attached to abdominal appendages, she lowers the apron at intervals and uses it as a scoop to drive water among the developing young.

True crabs tend to run sidewise, "crab-wise," rather than forward or back, although they can progress fairly rapidly in any direction. Often the body is elongated transversely too. For crabs with this body form, the name *Cancer* has come down from ancient times. This is the type of crab for which the zodiacal constellation is named, and the sign astrologers apply to those born in the month following June 22, when the sun enters this portion of the sky.

Cancer crabs (Plate 96) are rock crabs, whose hindmost pair of legs is fitted for running. In this respect they differ markedly from the commercial blue crab of America, *Callinectes sapidus,* whose last pair of legs end in flat, oval paddles. *Callinectes* is easy to recognize because its body extends to each side into a long, sharp spine. It is sold as the "hard-shell crab" or held in a pen until it molts and is then put on the market promptly as the "soft-shell crab." Actually, any freshly molted arthropod has a soft shell.

The blue crab is an active swimmer. So is its near relative the green crab, *Carcinides maenas,* although *Carcinides'* hindmost legs are merely flattened into oars without losing their use in running (Plate 95). Green crabs cause serious losses to shellfishermen by eating young clams, oysters, and scallops.

Far stranger in appearance is the common spider crab *Libinia,* found on muddy bottoms along the Atlantic coast of America. The spiny sac-shaped body and long-segmented cylindrical legs suggest either a spider or, because of the pale ivory color, a creature composed of bare bones attached to a sort of skull. The giant of all crustaceans is a Japanese spider crab, *Macrocheira kaempferi,* found in deeper waters well offshore, where it achieves a reach of 11 feet from claw to claw.

On many beaches, particularly in the tropics, ghost crabs (*Ocypoda,* Plate 99) make their homes well away from the water. *Ocypoda,* the "sharp-footed one," has been described as the "rabbit of the crustaceans," for it races over the beach away from enemies. Its compact body may measure 2 inches across and 1½ from front to back, and the legs straddle as much as 8 inches.

When a ghost crab is ready to disappear down its U-shaped or Y-shaped burrow in the sand, it lowers its prominent eyestalks from their normal vertical position into protective grooves along the front edge of the carapace. In less temperate latitudes, toward the extremes of their range, ghosts even hibernate in the dunes back of the beach and show clearly how independent of water they have become as adults. Their gills, so necessary at younger stages, have practically disappeared, leaving empty chambers under

Cave crayfishes are usually white, blind, and dependent upon their especially long antennae. The body is small and unpigmented, and the pincers as well as the legs are unusually slender. (Missouri. Ralph Buchsbaum)

The spiny lobster *Palinurus,* lacking pincer-tipped legs, depends on the whip action of its heavy antennae for protection when it ventures from crevices among rocks. (France. Ralph Buchsbaum)

The mole crab *Emerita* (*Hippa*) *talpoida*, more than 1 inch long, burrows in sandy beaches and sand bottoms on both coasts of America. Its feathery antennae serve to strain food particles from the water. (Delaware Bay. William H. Amos)

the edges of the carapace where the body wall is thin and blood comes close enough to the surface to be aerated.

Beaches patrolled by ghost crabs at night are often the marshaling grounds by day of fiddler crabs (*Uca,* Plate 100). Most fiddlers are less than 1 inch from side to side and considerably shorter from front to rear. Yet each male carries an absurdly big claw (the "fiddle") on one side or the other. The "bow" is the corresponding pincer-tipped foot on the opposite side, used in feeding.

Female fiddlers have two "bows" and no "fiddle." They eat ambidextrously. Males use the oversize claw in courtship gestures and in defense. Often, when the big claw has been clamped firmly on an attacker, the crab sheds the whole arm and scampers off. At

The house centipede *Scutigera forceps* frequents damp places in houses, where it preys on undesirable household insects. It rarely bites and should be welcomed. (Vienna. Eric Sochurek)

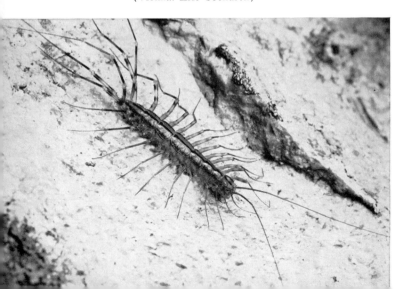

the next molt the loss is made good. On the damaged side a new claw of "bow" size appears; and where the crab had an undamaged "bow" it now has a new "fiddle." In this way the fiddler crab changes its handedness for feeding and courtship. And for this same reason almost exactly half of the males in any army of fiddlers is right-handed, the rest left-handed.

MANTIS SHRIMPS

Of all the crustaceans, the most intelligent may well be the mantis shrimps (order Stomatopoda, Plate 91). The bodies of these animals range from 2 inches long to somewhat more than 1 foot in the giant *Squilla mantis*. A few kinds are magnificently colored. All of them suggest a lobster that has lost its prominent antennae, its big claws, and the rear portion of the carapace. The tail fan is not quite so well developed. Yet when a mantis shrimp curls its powerful abdomen under, it darts backward just about as suddenly as any lobster or crayfish. In some places, stomatopod tails are sufficiently easy to take to be used as human food.

Mantis shrimps are predators that creep about or wait in a burrow mouth or an opening in a big sponge, watching for a fish to come within reach. Then the largest and most posterior of the mouthparts is suddenly opened like a jackknife, the blade being the outermost segment. It fits into a groove in the portion of the appendage against which it is folded.

In some mantis shrimps the blade is sharp and smooth. In others it bears strong sharp spines. But the snatching action with the blade is so fast as to put to shame the praying mantis, the insect for which these crustaceans were named. With its weapons a mantis shrimp can slash a small fish in two or, especially if the stomatopod is large, inflict a very severe wound.

The stalked eyes of a mantis shrimp are freely movable, not only in swinging motions that might compensate for change in position of a mate or some potential victim, but also through rotations. This allows the animal to use different parts of its compound eyes for examining objects nearby. To everything in its surroundings a stomatopod is alertly responsive. Quite quickly it accepts food and forms associations in an aquarium, achieving these conditioned reactions much more rapidly than the ghost crabs which seem so eminently trainable on land.

The Centipedes

(*Class Chilopoda*)

Every child learns to recognize a centipede as a "hundred-legged worm." But not many people take the time to count a centipede's legs. Most of the common ones have 15 pairs (Plate 117), and members of two different families hatch from the egg with even fewer, then gain another body segment and another pair of legs at each molt—just in front of the last segment. The extremely long and slender *Geophilus* found in rotting logs may possess 173 pairs of legs. It hatches with the full quota, as do other members of its family.

The fifteen hundred different kinds of centipedes are all carnivorous. The giant is *Scolopendra gigas,* of Boca Grande Island off the coast of Trinidad in the West Indies, which reaches a length of 12 inches and a width of 1 inch. It is fond of mice and occasionally catches a lizard, but feeds mostly on the larger tropical insects on rocky hillsides.

The smaller centipedes of temperate climates move quickly, their long antennae reaching out ahead in search of earthworms, insects, and other prey. The flattened body of the centipede and the fact that its legs are attached at the sides permit the animal to slip easily in and out of crevices while hunting. Victims are killed with venom from glands opening in the highly modified first pair of legs, which serve as jaws.

Despite the usual aversion shown by man to any animal that can defend itself with poison, large centipedes are esteemed as human food in some parts of Polynesia. The islanders hold the centipede by its two ends and roast it over a small fire, then chew the toasted middle portions as a delicacy.

A comparatively harmless member of many households throughout the world is the cosmopolitan house centipede *Scutigera forceps,* whose fifteen pairs of banded legs are so very long and slender that the creature holds them in a bent position, suggesting a multilegged spider. The body itself may be 2 inches long, light brown with three dark lengthwise stripes. Although *Scutigera* rarely bites a human being, it can do so if roughly handled. Its venom causes a reaction comparable to a wasp sting.

A few centipedes can be seen at night by their own light, but the significance of the light is still unknown. *Geophilus electricus,* one of this luminescent kind, with a very long, threadlike body, is found in many parts of Europe.

The Millipedes *(Class Diplopoda)*

The common name millipede ("thousand-legged") is a far less accurate description of these animals than is the class name, which indicates that each segment of the creature's body bears a double pair of legs (Plate 116). A millipede with fifty segments to the body, hence two hundred legs, is an

Many of the common cylindrical millipedes curl up like a watch spring if disturbed. The head is at the center of the spiral, and the animal lies on its side— a position in which the armored back protects the many legs. (Pennsylvania. Lorus and Margery Milne)

especially long one. Most possess between thirty and forty segments and bear the jointed legs along the underside of the cylindrical body. When disturbed, a millipede may curl up on its side like a watch spring, with the head at the center of the spiral and the legs protected by the armored body.

No one need fear to handle a millipede and to watch the waves of movement sweep along its legs. These animals are mostly harmless scavengers, eating decaying plant material. They have no venom, although some millipedes include hydrocyanic acid in their scent glands and might poison a mouse that ate too many of them. The scent glands appear to produce an odor unpleasant to some potential enemies.

In wet weather millipedes sometimes attack living vegetation and damage crops, particularly subterranean roots and tubers. *Julus terrestris,* a burrowing kind, is often called a "wireworm" and regarded as a mild pest. Occasionally it causes serious losses by eating the sprouts from seed grain as the crop emerges through the ground. This species shows some parental care for its eggs. The female constructs a dome-shaped nest from earth mixed with salivary secretion, and lays her eggs through the hole at the top of the dome. The nest is then sealed with another bit of the same cement-like material, and the parent goes off, perhaps to repeat the process elsewhere. The young hatch with only three pairs of legs, but at each molt they add new pairs on new segments, acquiring four more legs at each molt.

About 6500 different kinds of millipedes are known. In the tropics, some reach a length of 8 inches and include dead insects and other bits of animal matter in their diet. In California, the millipede *Luminodesmus sequoiae* is luminous; its eggs are not.

The Horseshoe "Crabs"

(Class Merostomata)

When Sir Walter Raleigh led his expedition to the New World in 1584–1585, he fully expected to encounter strange kinds of animal life. To help people in the Old World become informed about any unusual creatures, Sir Walter brought with him two naturalists: Thomas Hariot, who would write accurate accounts of whatever was encountered, and John White, who would prepare watercolor drawings. The reports of these men, published in England in 1588 and 1590, made known for the first time a very ancient type of life now familiar to many people as horseshoe "crabs."

Actually, the modern name is a corruption of a very good description given in 1870 under the name of the "horse-foot crab," for the main part of the animal's body does have the form of a horse's foot—not a horseshoe. Thomas Hariot used the Indian

The horseshoe "crab" *Limulus polyphemus*, a living fossil whose nearest kin today are scorpions and spiders, breeds each spring in shallow waters. Females deposit eggs in a beach near high-tide mark, and accompanying males deposit sperm on the eggs. (Florida. Allan Cruickshank: National Audubon)

name "seékanauk," and remarked that "it is about a foot wide, has a crusty tail, many legs, like a crab, and its eyes are set in its back. It can be found in salt water shallows or on the shore."

John White added, in the caption to his drawing showing these animals, that as the Indians "have neither steel nor iron, they fasten the sharp, hollow tail of a certain fish (something like a sea crab) to reeds or to the end of a long rod, and with this point they spear fish, both by day and by night."

Horseshoe crabs run along the bottom with a curious bobbing gait, or burrow shallowly in search of a variety of food: seaweeds, young clams, dead fish, marine worms. Or they swim inverted, sometimes to the surface of the sea. At the end of a swimming bout, they may sink to the bottom and alight upon their backs. The stiff, pointed tail is then used as a lever in righting themselves.

Seen from above, the horseshoe crab's body is clearly armored but divided at a transverse hinge into a larger forward part and a smaller hinder part. The first bears the two large compound eyes and a pair of smaller simple eyes, and the second ends in the highly movable tail. The front portion of the body is a shield covering the four pairs of walking legs and two additional pairs of appendages associated with the mouth. The mouth itself is an oval, lengthwise opening between the leg bases. It gives the class Merostomata its name from the fact that the mouth extends over several segmental regions of this portion of the body.

Most members of class Merostomata are known only from fossils. The class includes both the horseshoe crabs (order Xiphosura—"sword-tailed") and the extinct eurypterids (order Eurypterida) or sea scorpions. All of these animals seem strange in using the spiny bases of the walking legs for chewing the food, as though the animal's shoulders took the place of jaws.

Horseshoe crabs represent a style of life that has existed in similar situations essentially unchanged for at least 175 million years. All of the near relatives of these creatures have been extinct for even longer, for horseshoe crabs are not crabs at all. They are most similar to modern land scorpions and spiders, and quite unlike any of the crustaceans.

From below it is easy to distinguish the sexes among horseshoe crabs. In place of a pincer-tipped chelicerae on each side in front of the mouth (as in the female), the male has sturdy leglike appendages ending in grotesque hooks. With this armament he can cling to the rear of a female's shell for days or weeks at a time and be towed along by her until she is ready to deposit eggs. In both sexes the next pair of appendages are the pedipalps, used in feeding.

The hinder portion of the body has a triangular outline and bears below it a series of overlapping transverse plates attached at their forward edges. Each of these plates protects a pair of gill books, of which the individual "leaves" are the respiratory organs. When a horseshoe crab swims, it flaps the plates with the gills and jerks the legs in a rhythm that propels the body along like an animated wash basin.

In springtime the horseshoe crabs migrate to shallow water, and the males hunt out the larger females. Sometimes a "cow" crab is seen pulling a chain of four or five males, each clipped to the rear of the one ahead. When her eggs are ready, the cow crab drags her escort on shore at some sandy spot while the tide is at its peak, and there burrows into the beach to lay. Weeks later, and long after the parents have separated and returned to deeper water, the young crabs emerge from the sand. They have virtually no tail and bear a superficial resemblance to the extinct trilobites; so the larva has come to be known as the "trilobite stage" of development. Soon it transforms into a diminutive horseshoe crab.

At intervals each growing animal gets too cramped in its shell and sheds it, molting to a larger size. Unlike other arthropods, however, the line of weakness which breaks and liberates the horseshoe crab does not run down the midline of its back. Instead, a horseshoe crab splits along the forward rim of its carapace and creeps out, as though escaping from its own mouth. The cast shell is left seemingly intact, and waves often cast it ashore where a beachcomber can pick it up.

Young and comparatively soft-bodied horseshoe crabs fall prey to true crabs, fish, and many birds, including particularly gulls. Those that survive become comparatively immune to attack. Eels often follow horseshoe crabs into the breeding shallows and gulp in the eggs as fast as they are extruded. Coastal Indians used to eat horseshoe crabs, and according to Thomas Hariot they were "good food." In more recent times, coastal fishermen have built traps to capture horseshoe crabs for use either as cheap nourishment for pigs and chickens or to be dried and ground as fertilizer.

The horseshoe crab encountered by Sir Walter Raleigh's expedition was *Limulus polyphemus.* Today it is known from the Bay of Fundy all along the Atlantic coast to Key West, and at a scattering of places in the Gulf of Mexico as far as Yucatan. Formerly it may have been present in the West Indies, for old books on the natural history of Jamaica include illustrations of this animal.

Counterparts of *Limulus* occur in the Orient: *Carcinoscorpius* and *Tachypleus* along the coasts of China, Japan, the East Indies, and one species as far as India in one direction, the Philippines in the other. *Carcinoscorpius* readily invades brackish shallows, and has been found in the Hugli River at Calcutta,

ninety miles from the open sea, in water that is practically fresh.

The Spiders and Their Kin   *(Class Arachnida)*

In Greek mythology, Arachne was a Lydian girl who grew so proud of her ability as a weaver that she challenged the goddess Athena to a contest. For this impertinence Athena changed Arachne into a spider and condemned her to weave forever with silk from her own body.

Most members of the class Arachnida are indeed skilled weavers, and the silk they produce is one of the most marvelously versatile materials in all nature. But with some 29,000 different kinds of arachnids known, wide variation is to be expected. This is the second most varied class of animals, exceeded only by the insects.

SPIDERS

Spiders (order Araneae) are constricted conspicuously between a cephalothorax and an unsegmented abdomen. Their webs can be found almost anywhere on land. Charles Darwin reported them near the Equator in mid-Atlantic on the remote, isolated, guano-covered cluster of rocks known as St. Paul's Island—halfway between the bulge of Africa and the bulge of South America. The British expert on spiders, Dr. Thomas H. Savory, recorded jumping spiders trailing silken threads at 22,000 feet above sea level on Mount Everest, a good 4000 feet above the highest plant and with no other animal life for company. He concluded that cannibalism was their only way of existence, and in this they had to depend upon a continuous immigration of more spiderlets, riding the mountain winds on balloons and parachutes of self-made silk.

Wherever a spider travels, whether by running or leaping, it ordinarily spins out a fine strand of silk on which it can go back in an emergency. In addition, most spiders produce webs of some kind.

Early in the 1800's, the French entomologist P. A. Latreille classified the webs of spiders into four main groups: those of circular form suspended in a vertical plane, such as the familiar orb web of the garden spider; those with supporting strands in all directions, such as the house spider weaves in window corners, or with a horizontal sheet of web among bushes or on the ground, such as the work of the doily spiders; those of funnel shape, expanding from some crevice or natural hole in which the spider waits for prey to pass; and tubular webs spun in a hole dug by the

The giant orb-weaving spider *Nephila clavipes* stands guard over her eggs, which are fastened to a leaf. Until the spiderlets hatch, she lets her 8-foot web go untended. (Florida Everglades. Lorus and Margery Milne)

The orange-and-black garden spider *Argiope aurantia* weaves a platform with zigzag runways at the center of her spiral insect trap, and waits there until vibrations tell her that a victim has blundered into the tanglefoot. (Connecticut. Andreas Feininger)

spider, often closed by a fitted lid, such as the trap-door spiders produce.

In and near the tropics of both the Old World and the New, spiders of the genus *Nephila* weave orb webs between tall trees. Some of these webs are eight feet in diameter, and so sturdily constructed that they sometimes catch small birds and bats as well as quite large insects. When a victim blunders into the net, *Nephila* behaves in much the same way as the smaller but heavier garden spiders, such as *Argiope* (Plate 114). The orb-weaver runs to the side of the prey and expertly rotates the captive in the net while spraying over it multiple strands of silk that reduce struggling and prevent escape.

A spider has exquisite control over the spinnerets from which the silk emerges. Every spider has three or four different kinds available, each reaching the outside world through a different shape of tube. One product is the firm dry cord with which the orb-weaver constructs the radial strands of her web—lines that can be walked on without a foot adhering to the silk. Quite different is the sticky and elastic thread which is used for the spiral of the orb web—the tanglefoot to which victims will adhere. Far finer strands are those by which a spider lets itself down or which it pays out behind. These fibers are so uniform in diameter and so unaffected by changes in temperature and humidity that they have been in considerable demand as material for the cross hairs in telescopic sights. Still another kind of silk is the material in which the eggs are encased. Often it is a warm brown, or pink, or saffron yellow.

The common house spider, *Theridion,* hangs her silken spherical cases full of eggs in the irregular nest she constructs in some corner. She watches the egg cases, for if one of them falls, she hurries down and rescues it. Wolf spiders (Plates 109–112), such as the common small *Lycosa* of beach and woodland and the large *Dolomedes* of fresh-water margins, usually affix the ball full of eggs to the spinnerets and drag it after them wherever they go. Their eyes are useful in finding insect prey which can be run down or pounced upon, but a wolf spider seems to recognize her egg ball only by touch. If she becomes separated from it she pays no attention unless it chances to come into contact with her hindmost legs or abdominal tip. Only then will she fasten it in place and run off with it.

Dolomedes not only runs dry-shod over the surface of ponds after insects but occasionally creeps down a plant stem or wharf piling into the water and catches fish. During these underwater expeditions, the spider's hairy body seems silvered by an air film held among the bristles. The European water spider *Argyronecta* takes additional advantage of this load of air. The creature spins a dome-shaped nest in the water of a pond, anchoring the dome to bottom vegetation with strong lines. Then, on trip after trip to the

The mother wolf spider carries a silk-covered mass of eggs with her, held by her spinnerets, until the young emerge. (Florida. Andreas Feininger)

surface, the spider brings loads of air below the dome, combs them off as a series of bubbles, and goes above the water again for a fresh cargo of gas. The air released under the dome accumulates as one big bubble, and in this anchored diving bell the spider can live well below the surface of the pond, sallying forth at intervals to capture aquatic prey.

The largest spiders, such as the bird spider *Avicularia* of South America and the false tarantula *Eurypelma* of the southwestern United States and Central America, hunt chiefly at night by touch and perhaps by hearing. They overwhelm their prey by sheer strength, and often capture earthworms, mice, and small lizards. Occasionally these spiders are carried to big northern cities in bunches of bananas and create a panic among fruit-handlers, who fear them without real cause (Plate 107).

Poison from the cheliceral fangs is the chief weapon of smaller spiders. The venom is secreted by large glands opening at the tips of the chelicerae, making these appendages into efficient hypodermic needles. The spider seizes a captive in the fang portion of the chelicerae as though in a pair of ice tongs, and injects a small amount of poison from each side. The venom acts both as an anesthetic and as a digestive juice of high potency. In a short time it liquefies the body contents of an insect. Then the spider carefully inserts the fangs again and uses them as drinking straws through which to suck out the liquid.

These differences in habit related to size explain why large spiders, like large scorpions, make interesting pets and rarely use their venom. Their poison is actually less virulent and cannot hurt more than a bee sting. Smaller spiders and scorpions have a more potent poison, and a medium-sized individual may be really dangerous. Actually man needs to fear only a very few kinds.

A spider whose venom has been fatal to fully grown men on many occasions is the black widow, *Latrodectus mactans* (Plate 113), which occurs from Canada to Tierra del Fuego. Its abdomen is almost spherical, glossy black, and as much as ½ of an inch in diameter. Below the abdomen is a red spot that may be hourglass-shaped or rectangular. Probably most bites from the black widow are suffered by people who accidentally disturb a mother *Latrodectus* in a privy or cellar corner where she is defending her eggs in an irregular nest similar to that of the house spider. The male *Latrodectus* is much smaller than his mate, as is usual among spiders, with a body less than ¼ of an inch long. He is harmless to man.

The diminutive males of *Nephila* and other orb-weavers often make little webs of their own at the periphery of the big web of their mutual mate. At intervals they twitch the strands of the main web as a courtship gesture. If the relatively huge female is well fed, it is fairly safe for a male to approach her. Otherwise she is likely to seize him as though he were a fly, and digest the would-be suitor.

Most spiders have eight simple eyes like bright jewels around the forward portion of the cephalo-thorax—the leg-bearing subdivision of the body. The arrangement of the eyes and their relative size differ from one genus to another. Jumping spiders, such as the little pepper-and-salt-colored *Salticus*, have one pair of eyes enlarged enormously. With their help the spider can gauge distance and identify prey, abilities demonstrated by frequent leaps to a small branch as

Young wolf spiders often ride on their mother's back for several days after they emerge from the egg, and then venture off one by one. (Florida. Andreas Feininger)

much as fourteen inches away, or atop a fly that settles within a comparable distance. Jumping spiders use their eyes also in following a complicated code of semaphore-like signals through which the males seek to excite a female into permitting an approach.

Other arachnids probably depend far less upon vision, although elaborate claims have been made. For a while it was believed that the white crab spiders found on white daisies in midsummer would change color to a butter yellow within a few days if transferred to a yellow flower. But this camouflage seems fortuitous. Crab spiders are white in midsummer and yellow in autumn, whether on white flowers or on yellow ones. They change hue gradually, and happen to match a common sequence in flower colors. That they often match the flower upon which they crouch while waiting for an insect to visit and be caught may be helpful in concealing them from spider-eating birds. But insect victims are unlikely to detect the waiting spider in a flower so long as the spider remains motionless until its prey is within snatching distance.

SOLPUGIDS

A constriction between the cephalothorax and the abdomen is obvious also in the spider-like solpugids or "false spiders" (order Solpugida) of tropical and subtropical countries. The solpugid abdomen, however, is clearly segmented.

Solpugids are harmless, for they lack venom, depending upon crushing insect prey between the formidable-appearing fangless chelicerae. For the most part, solpugids are denizens of arid lands, venturing out at night. They range in size from barely more than ½ of an inch in length to nearly 3 inches. They run nimbly and will defend themselves if disturbed. At such times the solpugid is seen to be using three pairs of legs in locomotion and holding free of the ground the front pair, as well as the leglike but pincer-tipped pedipalps.

SCORPIONS

A true scorpion (order Scorpionida) is obviously segmented, the head bearing chelicerae suggesting lobster claws, the thorax of four segments each with a pair of walking legs on the undersurface, and the segmented abdomen broad in front but tapering to a more cylindrical portion that ends in a curved, poison-injecting sting. Scorpions are largely nocturnal, hiding under rubbish during the day or remaining in little holes dug with the pincer-tipped chelicerae.

In ancient times, a scorpion was feared almost as much as a lion. Both are among the animals represented in the zodiac—constellations of stars in the band of sky through which the sun, moon, and planets seem to move. *Scorpio,* one genus of scorpions, is thus the astrologic birth sign for people born in the

Some larger, thinner huntsman spiders are welcomed in tropical and subtropical homes as the answer to flies, roaches, and other household insects. This one, *Heteropoda venatoria,* on the wallpaper of a Florida home, has a 3-inch span. (Lorus and Margery Milne)

A wolf spider, its feet clothed in water-repellent hairs, can run dryshod over the surface of ponds and streams. (Herman Eisenbeiss)

A safety line is spun by the jumping spider *Phidippus audax* even during a leap to a finger tip. (Colorado. Walker Van Riper)

month following October 24, when the sun is between the earth and that constellation.

Scorpions feed principally upon insects and spiders, grasping them in the chelicerae and tearing them to pieces or crushing them for their juices. Only if a victim offers real resistance, or if the scorpion is threatened by some enemy, is the sting brought into use. Then the abdomen is arched forward over the body (Plate 106) and the poison-bearing tip thrust in vigorously.

Medium-sized scorpions, such as the 2- to 3-inch *Centruroides sculpturatus* and *C. gertschi* of the American Southwest, have enough poison to be dangerous, and it may be virulent enough to cause occa-

The male jumping spider (*Phidippus audax*) uses similar postures in courtship display and when threatening a rival. This one is stimulated by his own image in the mirror. (Colorado. Walker Van Riper)

sional human deaths. In Egypt and other tropical and subtropical countries, scorpion-stung people are frequent enough so that an antitoxin has become a medical necessity.

Truly large scorpions, such as the 10-inch kinds in equatorial Africa and tropical America, are comparatively inoffensive. Only toward other scorpions are they hostile, and this habit is so characteristic of scorpions of all kinds that they lead solitary lives. Even well-fed females usually resort to cannibalism, devouring the mate who has just fathered the next generation of young.

Scorpions bring forth their young as diminutive individuals, active and ready to fend for themselves. Yet the offspring often cling to the mother's back for many days after birth, riding with her wherever she goes. From careful inspection of a mother scorpion with her brood, it is easy to see that many sizes of young are present. Ordinarily they are born one or two at a time over a period of many weeks, rather than the whole litter within a day or so. In some scorpions, a placenta-like tissue is formed within the parent, permitting readier transfer of food and wastes between the mother and her unborn young.

WHIPSCORPIONS

Arachnids include a variety of creatures suggesting scorpions but entirely harmless to any animal larger than an insect. The tailed whipscorpion *Mastigoproctus* (Plate 105) is a formidable-appearing denizen of dark corners in tropical and subtropical lands. Its abdomen suggests the broader basal part of the corresponding region of a true scorpion, but ends in a long, flexible extension, the tail, with no venom.

Tailless whipscorpions are equally retiring members of the order Pedipalpi. In all whipscorpions the pedipalpi are powerful and are used in grasping and crushing spiders and insects as food. The first pair of legs usually suggest whips—long, slender appendages ending in a flexible lash, used in the dark as the animal feels its way about. In a large whipscorpion, these legs may stretch 6 inches from side to side.

PSEUDOSCORPIONS

Diminutive pseudoscorpions (order Pseudoscorpionida) are encountered prowling for still smaller insects among the stones along a sea beach. The largest of them reach a length of about ¼ of an inch, but most are less than half this size. One of them invades libraries, where it is known as the book scorpion, *Chelifer cancroides*. Its flattened body, somewhat suggesting that of a bedbug, is admirably fitted to gliding between the pages. The creature runs about on its four pairs of legs while holding up and forward a greatly enlarged pair of pedipalps ending in pincers. These are used in seizing tiny insects, such as the young of silverfish and book lice (psocids), found

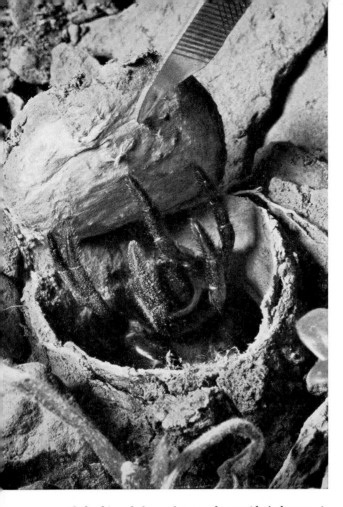

If the hinged door of a trapdoor spider's burrow is raised carefully, the spider may remain with her feet clinging to the silken covering of the door; otherwise she drops quickly down into her vertical burrow.

The trapdoor fits the doorway perfectly, but the spider usually builds its hideout where runoff rain water will not flood over the doorway and soften it. (Florida. Photographs by Andreas Feininger)

among old papers. The abdomen of a pseudoscorpion is broader than its cephalothorax, and it is clearly segmented.

Pseudoscorpions are amazingly systematic about building nests, using these as places in which to molt, hibernate, and raise young. The chelicerae secrete silk needed to cement together sand grains and bits of vegetable matter into stationary or movable pouches. A bag of this sort carried about affixed to the mother's body forms a brood pouch into which the eggs are laid. They hatch there and the young remain in the pouch, getting nourishment from glands upon the mother's body, exposed to them through the opening at the top of the pouch.

HARVESTMEN

An arachnid familiar to most people is the daddy longlegs (see illustration on page 252) or harvestman spider (order Phalangida). Its body is small and very compact, its bristle-slender legs tremendously long. No one need fear to handle a harvestman, but a naturalist should be very gentle to save the animal from losing a fragile leg or two. Only at the next molt can it make good such a loss.

If left to their own devices, harvestmen use the second and longest pair of legs to explore the surrounding territory before moving on. Apparently vision with the two eyes in a little tubercle on the back is inadequate, and touch takes its place. Often a harvestman can be found standing quietly, waving these sensitive legs in the air. Probably this habit has led to the old bit of folklore which claims that a dairy farmer can tell where to find his cows by watching the direction in which a harvestman points.

Phalangids have no venom and no silk glands. They depend for food on mites, small spiders, tiny insects, and other harvestmen. They deposit their eggs in crevices or under stones, and ordinarily remain solitary throughout the active months. During winter, however, harvestmen often congregate by the dozens or the hundreds. In the spring they can be found still standing with their slender legs interlaced, even swaying in unison as though dancing to music undiscerned by human ears.

TICKS AND MITES

In man's economy, few arachnids rank higher in importance than the mites and ticks. These members

[249

The crab spider *Misumena* spins a safety line as she lets herself down (left). At any time she can climb back up again (right). (Colorado. Walker Van Riper)

of the order Acarina have the whole body fused into a single piece, and are peculiar too in going through a very different, six-legged larval stage followed by transformation into the eight-legged adult.

Ticks are mostly larger than mites, and live as parasites on land-dwelling vertebrate animals. Mites include many that are helpful to man through their predatory habits, eating the eggs of plant lice (aphids), attacking insects and nematode worms in the soil, prowling over the surface of plants and of the ground, and hunting even in shallow ponds. Most mites are external parasites, particularly in larval stages. Water striders and damsel flies are often found carrying on their bodies little red lumps that are the blood-sucking immature individuals of the big predatory red mites found swimming in ponds or along the shore (Plate 115).

When a parasitic mite or tick feeds, it thrusts its whole head into the skin of the victim. There the parasite is held in place through use of a dartlike anchor located just below its mouth. In ticks the outer surface of the anchor bears recurved teeth, and these hold so firmly that a pull on the body of a tick is likely to break off its head in the wound rather than remove it. In mites the anchor is smooth on the outside, allowing the parasite to be brushed off quite easily.

The mite affecting most people directly is the chigger, usually a member of the genus *Trombicula*. In the Old World these unpleasant creatures are called harvest mites. They lie in wait upon vegetation until a vertebrate animal brushes against the plant. Then anywhere from one to a hundred may be "painted on," and promptly begin spreading over the skin. At a chosen site, each mite bites and discharges into the wound a drop of digestive agent which opens a tubular path far enough into the skin to enable nutritious lymph to well up and provide the mite with a meal. Soon the chigger drops off of its own accord, seldom remaining on the skin for more than from one to seven days. On the ground it completes its development and, if a female, eventually mates and lays a batch of eggs from which a new generation of young ascend a grass stalk and wait for a host to pass.

The action of a chigger is intensely irritating, leading the host (whether man or rat or quail or snake) to scratch vigorously, often breaking the skin and admitting serious infections. The extent of distraction from mite bites can be evaluated on domestic fowl in a hen house infested with the chicken mite *Dermanyssus gallinae*. The hens spend so much time scratching that they feed less frequently, become malnourished, and cease to lay reliably.

Mite pests seem to be found on every hand. The "seven-year-itch" is caused by the itch mite *Sarcoptes scabiei* of man and hogs. This creature burrows under the skin and reproduces there. Related mites,

A mother scorpion *Tityus serrulatus*, with newborn young clinging to her back, stands safely under the arch of her sting-tipped abdomen. (Switzerland. Othmar Danesch)

The whip scorpion *Stegophrynus* has a body about 1½ inches long. It is harmless to any creature too large to be crushed between the first pair of appendages. (Singapore. M. W. F. Tweedie)

living in the hair follicles, cause mange in many kinds of mammals.

Beekeepers are familiar with Isle of Wight disease, a fatal epidemic in hives of cultivated bees that become infected with a mite that invades their tracheae and suffocates the insects.

The pest known as "red spider" in gardens and orchards is actually a vegetarian mite. Severe infestations can be recognized from the loose webs covering leaves upon which the female mites have laid their eggs. Other mites attacking plants cause cancerlike growths of characteristic forms, each known as a plant gall.

Ticks have an equally bad reputation for transferring diseases from one animal to another. Texas cattle fever is an infection of the sporozoan (a protozoan) *Babesia bigemina,* transmitted by the tick *Margaropus annulatus.* The larvae, called "seed ticks," are about $\frac{1}{32}$ of an inch in length. After gorging themselves on blood, they drop off the steer and transform into slightly larger, eight-legged nymphs. Soon they again climb a grass blade and catch a passing animal. After gorging again, the nymphal tick drops off and matures to the adult, either a $\frac{1}{10}$-inch male with an oval brown body, or a $\frac{1}{2}$-inch female of rectangular outline, whose color may be yellowish to slate gray. These adults again seek a steer and mate upon its back after another blood meal. The female then drops off and layers her five thousand eggs on the ground, where they hatch, starting another generation of seed ticks on its way.

Rocky Mountain spotted fever is a rickettsia disease transmitted by the widespread tick *Dermacentor,* a parasite found commonly on dogs. It attacks coyotes and many other wild animals in the western United States. Some of these are reservoirs of infection for spotted fever. If an infected tick bites a human being, the person is almost certain to contract the disease. If proper medical care is not given, the outcome can be serious or even fatal.

The Sea Spiders

(Class Pycnogonida)

A skin diver who sits quietly watching a clump of kelp, a sea fan, or a coral head may well discover a spider-like creature moving with the utmost deliberation among these. Sea spiders mostly possess four pairs of very long legs, each pair arising from a sepa-

Harvestmen are seen most often at harvest time. Their widespread legs well earn them the name "daddy-long-legs." (Colorado. Walker Van Riper)

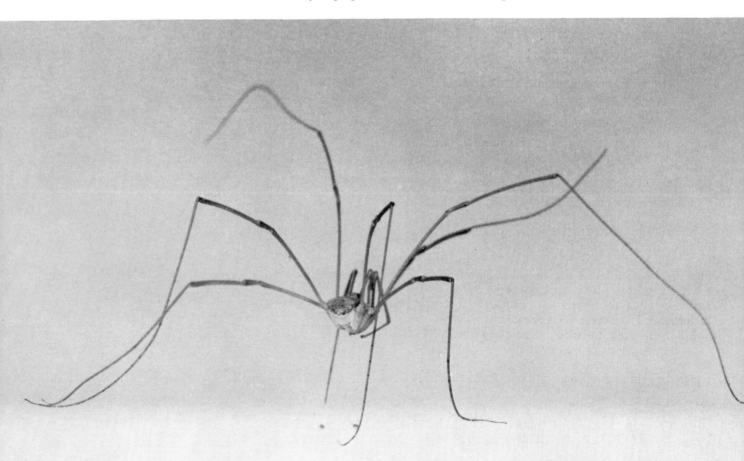

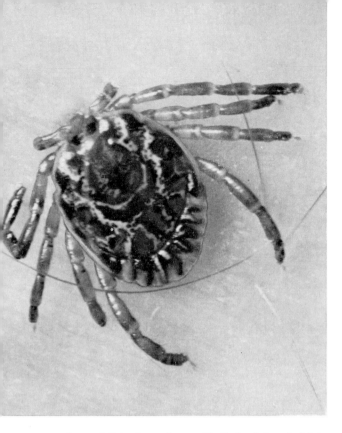

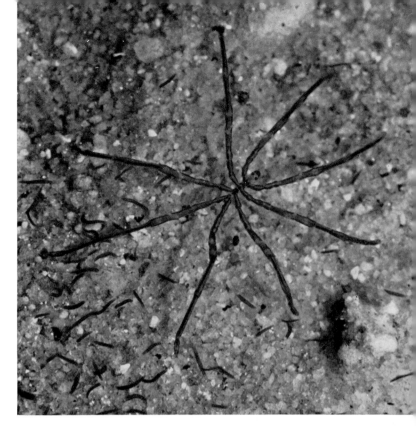

A wood tick, shown here with its beak inserted into human skin, can transmit serious diseases. This one became attached in a Panama rain forest. Related kinds are common in temperate woods. (Panama. Ralph Buchsbaum)

The eight legs of a sea spider (pycnogonid) seem joined to one another rather than to a body, for the latter is so very small. The legs accommodate lobes from the digestive tract, perhaps because there is no room for them in the body. (France. Ralph Buchsbaum)

rate segment of the body. But the skin diver will scarcely be able to detect the animal's unsegmented abdomen, and may wonder whether it has been lost. Actually it is extremely minute, so small that it can provide space for almost no part of the digestive tract. As though in compensation, the legs are somewhat broader toward the base and accommodate lobes of the alimentary canal.

If the sea spider is a female, she will have a slender head ending in a minute sucking mouth—almost a beak. If a male, he will possess additional appendages on the head, including a pair of small jointed legs held downward and backward. These little legs are the "ovigerous" pair, used by the male to carry ball-shaped masses of eggs laid by his mate.

At the junction of the head and the first segment of the body bearing walking legs, a sea spider has a small eminence with two to four simple eyes—a turret of visual organs that may keep the animal informed of movements of fish and seals in the surrounding water. To none of these does the pycnogonid react in an obvious way. It merely clings, swaying gently with water movements, or progresses at a sloth's pace from one point to another.

In coastal waters, sea spiders are mostly small, seldom spanning more than 1 inch in diameter. The abysses are home to far larger kinds, including the giant *Colossendeis,* whose legs span as much as 24 inches. Pycnogonids have been collected from as deep as twelve thousand feet below the surface, and the five hundred different kinds known include representatives from all of the world's oceans. They seem particularly common in the frigid waters of the Arctic and Antarctic.

Sea spiders seem to subsist as adults on microscopic algae, but a number of kinds go through juvenile stages parasitic upon or within coral animals, jellyfishes, nudibranch mollusks, clams, and sea cucumbers. The young hatch from the egg equipped with only three pairs of legs. Additional body segments and leg pairs are acquired at metamorphosis. Some pycnogonids do not stop when four pairs have been acquired but continue with the same body plan until they have five or even six pairs of legs.

[253

CHAPTER XIX

The Echinoderms

(Phylum Echinodermata)

(Left) sea star, serpent star and sea cucumber;
(right) sea lilies and (below) sea urchin

ONE of the delights in visiting the seashore is to find sea stars (starfishes) and sea urchins, brittle stars, and sand dollars. Or perhaps a sea cucumber. Their symmetries, their strange movements, are fascinatingly different from those of any creature found on land. Even after a naturalist has enjoyed years of acquaintance with echinoderms, they remain a great enigma. Almost none of their actions resembles the activities of other kinds of animals. Yet in their embryonic development and some features of the adult animal, they show remarkable similarities to chordates such as ourselves.

The name echinoderm comes from the Greek *echinos,* a hedgehog, and *derma,* the skin. The word is most suited to sea urchins, whose bodies are armed with movable spines.

A sea urchin or sand dollar differs from a sea star or brittle star in that its skeleton is composed of interlocking plates that cannot be moved. The stars, by contrast, can be real contortionists if given time to change position. When first picked up a star may seem stiff. But its skeleton, just inside the skin, consists of separate pieces, each hinged movably to neighboring ones. Muscles keep the star from feeling flexible in human hands. Sea cucumbers may have granules of lime embedded in the skin, but the body wall is comparatively soft.

A century and a half ago, the great French zoologist Baron Georges Cuvier grouped the echinoderms

with the jellyfishes as "radiate" animals. But when the development of echinoderm eggs is followed, each embryo is found to develop into a bilaterally symmetrical larva. Later it takes on a modified radial symmetry with five similar sectors. Since the animal develops no head end, it comes to show distinctly only an oral surface bearing the mouth and an aboral surface opposite this.

Sea cucumbers are unique among echinoderms in giving up the radial pattern after acquiring it. They lie over on one side, and thereby gain anew a distinction between right and left, between upper and lower surfaces.

Sea lilies are found almost exclusively at depths that neither a beachcomber nor a skin diver can explore. They live permanently attached by long, slender stalks to the bottom, and are so fragile that their remains are unrecognizable when washed ashore. Their more modern relatives, the feather stars, inhabit also waters nearer land. They begin a sedentary life, but become detached and can swim gently by convulsive flapping of the arms.

In all of these animals the body cavity is subdivided, one portion forming a water-vascular system peculiar to echinoderms. This system consists of a ring-shaped tube encircling the gullet, and five radial tubes ("canals") extending into the five sectors of the body. This hydraulic system receives its fluid either from the body cavity (in sea lilies, feather stars, and sea cucumbers) or the outside world of sea water. In the latter case it enters through a pore connected to the ring canal by a slender tube (the "stone canal") whose walls are stiffened by deposits of lime.

In sea cucumbers, sea urchins, and sea stars the water-vascular system serves in locomotion. Its radial canals communicate with an extensive series of short, paired tubes, each with a muscular bulb and an elongated, hollow tube-foot that projects from the body surface. A tube-foot combines muscular and hydraulic mechanisms. It is extended by contraction of the bulb, forcing liquid into the cavity of the tube-foot; muscles in the walls of the tube-foot control the direction of extension.

The tip of a tube-foot is a small, glandular suction disk by means of which the echinoderm can attach the sticky tube-foot to solid objects. Contraction of longitudinal muscles of the tube-foot shortens it and forces water back into the bulb, pulling the echinoderm along or shifting the movable object to which it holds. Teams of tube-feet also cooperate in carrying the body, in policing its surface, or in supporting bits of seaweed, rock, or coral as a shade against strong sun in shallow water.

Echinoderms maintain an important fluid in the body cavity, taking the place of blood. It is shifted from place to place by patches of cilia. In this fluid, ameba-like cells move around freely, serving much as white blood cells do in vertebrate animals. Some sea cucumbers have red blood cells too, but with a hemoglobin differing chemically from that of vertebrates.

In their response to the environment, echinoderms manage with a minimum of complexity in the nervous system. It consists primarily of a ring around the gullet, parallel to the ring canal of the water-vascular system. From the nerve ring extend radial nerves that branch profusely. In most echinoderms they end blindly, yet appear able not only to coordinate the movements of the animal but also to report on chemical substances in the surrounding sea, on conditions of light and shade, on vibrations of many kinds. Free nerve endings thus take the place of specialized sense organs.

Echinoderms generally are very casual about reproduction. In most instances, parents never meet. They merely cast their eggs and sperms into the sea, each to find the other by sorting themselves out in the surface water from among a thin soup of reproductive products of many species. Retention of the eggs and some degree of maternal care are found in each class, however; often they are correlated with life in polar waters.

Members of this phylum use many of the same basic body features found in the vertebrates, but emphasize each in a very different way. As in the chordates and no other phylum of animals, they de-velop an internal skeleton. But instead of coordinating that skeleton with muscles as a device important in locomotion, they hide inside it as a shelter. Radial symmetry seems to imply a readiness to withdraw, moving away from molestation in any direction. Yet with this different approach to life, often paralleling ways found among coelenterates, the echinoderms occupy every habitat available in the seas, from oozy muds at the greatest depths to the sandy beach and the most wave-pounded rocky coasts.

The Crinoids (*Class Crinoidea*)

These delicate and often colorful creatures are unique among echinoderms in that they live with the oral surface uppermost. For food they depend upon capturing small animals and plants drifting past them in the sea, reaching out for this nourishment with arms that may be more conspicuous than the body to which they are attached. Usually each arm is fringed along both sides with a row of short, tapering branches, and suggests the fronds of a fern or the petals of a lily.

Most crinoids have five arms, each forked near the base—producing ten flexible appendages. In many species the arms continue to branch and rebranch with increasing size of the animal. Sea lilies rarely have more than 40 arms; some possess only 5. Feather stars may produce up to 200 arms. Most of the many-armed forms are from tropical and subtropical seas. Cold-water or deep-sea forms usually bear 10 arms.

Modern crinoids gather food by means of a method believed to have been used by all primitive echinoderms. Along a ciliated groove in the upper, oral surface of each arm and its side branches, delicate finger-like tube-feet respond to the arrival of each food particle by bending quickly inward. This action throws the food into the mucus-filled groove, where it becomes entangled and is swept to the mouth.

Sea lilies remain for long periods, and possibly for life, anchored to the bottom, mostly in water from 600 to 15,000 feet deep. Feather stars seldom venture below 4500 feet. Sometimes they swim languidly to the surface, or can be found near shore in shallow water. Feather stars living where sunlight reaches them often have beautiful colors, perhaps exceeded by no other marine animals. Some are bright red, others purple, green, orange, golden, white, black, or even variegated.

All living crinoids belong to the same order. All go through a swimming embryonic stage that is slightly gourd-shaped, encircled by several rings of cilia, and bearing a little tuft of sensory hairs at one end. As skeletal plates begin to form, the embryo comes to rest on the bottom, becoming attached there.

SEA LILIES

Until 1873, sea lilies were believed to be extinct, represented only by fossils in ancient rocks. Then, at the dawn of oceanography, scientists aboard the famous British research ship H.M.S. *Challenger* began peering at animals from the sea bottom, brought to light in special sampling dredges. Among the collections, they found sea lilies still alive. About eighty species are now known to live in the oceans, each animal with an upright, flower-like body supported from the bottom mud by a slender stalk. For them the name of the class Crinoidea is particularly appropriate. It comes from the Greek *krinos*, a lily, and the ending *-oid*, similar to.

A dredge dragging along the sea bottom on the end of a mile of steel cable is not particularly gentle. It gathers indiscriminately, often breaking off forms of life attached in the ooze. In consequence, no one was certain for many years just how modern sea lilies were anchored. Then, as oceanic telephone cables were raised for repairs, a few stalked crinoids were found attached to them. In most cases they ended in a set of remarkably rootlike extensions, wrapped around the covering of the communication wires. Other sea lilies have a stalk tapering to a curled end, capable of wrapping around solid objects. Or they wear a set of grappling hooks, or a bulblike swelling, or a flat circular disk. All of these are able to resist most pulls that would tend to dislodge the animal from the bottom sediments.

The stalk itself is supported by a long series of skeletal pieces, giving it a jointed appearance. In living crinoids the stalk may be as much as 20 inches long. In members of one suborder it is ornamented at intervals by short tendril-like extensions (cirri). Apparently these sea lilies sometimes break away from the bottom and thereafter move from place to place, propelling themselves by awkward movements of the branching arms or holding temporarily to firm objects with the cirri. Members of another suborder have no cirri or only rudimentary ones, or cirri only at the attached end of the stem.

Often the skeletal pieces of the stalk have made highly resistant fossils. The flower-like crown, which is the main body of the animal, is less sturdy. Yet intact fossils have been found with stalks over 70 feet long and as many as 200 branches of the five arms. Altogether more than 5000 kinds of extinct sea lilies have been discovered, some of them dating back nearly 700 million years. Probably modern seas are less hospitable to sea lilies and they can be regarded as "living fossils," and perhaps as candidates for extinction.

Recent work by oceanographers in arctic waters has led to the discovery of a few kinds of stalked crinoids in large numbers at a depth of barely fifty feet. Apparently they take advantage there of the wealth of microscopic food that thrives, in turn, because upwelling currents bring dissolved nutriment from the bottom.

FEATHER STARS

Feather stars (Plate 135) are the best-known of crinoids, with about 550 different species. They begin life much as do the sea lilies. But after establishing themselves on the bottom with a slender stem, they break away from its upper end and thereafter lead a free existence. Around the area where the stem was attached, each feather star wears a cluster of cirri and uses these for holding to submerged objects. It then spreads its arms gracefully to the sides, usually curling their tips upward, and waits while small particles of food drift within range of its cilia-driven feeding currents.

Along the Atlantic coast from the Arctic to Long Island, New York, a grayish feather star with brown bands is found at depths from 90 to nearly 6000 feet. It is one of the many species of *Antedon* found on both sides of the Atlantic, and uses its ten long arms in the characteristic swimming movements. With mouth upward, the arms spread as much as 8 inches across. Five of them move down with delicate side branches (pinnules) spread while the alternating five arms rise with pinnules drawn together. If the animal becomes inverted by swimming into a current, it may settle to the bottom and there right itself. The arms on one side are used as levers to raise the body from the surface while the opposite arms reach around and catch hold.

On the eastern side of the Atlantic, another *Antedon* clings to seaweeds in comparatively shallow water, and British trappers of seafoods find it temporarily attaching itself to the wicker traps set for crabs and lobsters. In Jamaica and Barbados, British West Indies, a *Tropiometra* with brownish golden arms clips its cirri to coral rock in water as little as six feet below low tide. These tropical animals are more suitable for a skin diver to examine, for they do not break to pieces (as *Antedon* does) when touched. If freed from the bottom by chiseling loose the piece of coral, they will let go of their own accord and seize the diver's fingers tenaciously in their cirri as the next best support.

Feather stars are most abundant in the waters of the Sulu, Celebes, and Banda Seas, in a triangle pointed at New Guinea, Borneo, and the north island of the Philippines. They are fewest in the Atlantic and eastern Pacific, and clearly favor rocky bottoms or coral reefs in preference to sand or mud. The smallest adult feather stars, 1 inch across, live in the West Indies and in abysses of the Pacific Ocean. The largest is *Heliometra glacialis*, reaching 3 feet in diameter in ice-cold water at the west side of the Okhotsk Sea north of Japan.

[continued on page 273]

116. This **giant millipede** from Tanganyika, about 8 inches long, is still not fully grown. Such millipedes attain a length of 11 inches and are often seen parading after a rain in equatorial Africa. They are harmless scavengers, living on decaying vegetation. (London Zoo. Ralph Buchsbaum)

117. A large **centipede**, *Scolopendra heros*, usually 4 or more inches long. Found in Mexico and in the southern United States. (Arizona. Eliot Porter)

118–121. A **starfish**, *Pisaster ochraceous*, turned
on its back, rights itself by twisting its arms and
pulling with hundreds of vacuum-cupped feet.
This is the common starfish of surf-beaten rocks
on the American Pacific coast. Specimens range
from 6 to 14 inches across and occur in several
color phases. (Oregon. Ralph Buchsbaum)

122. Despite its name, *Pisaster giganteus capitatus* is usually smaller than its relative in Plates 118 to 121. This variety of a more delicate and more colorful species of *Pisaster*, with relatively few but large spines, is found from Southern to Lower California. (Cy La Tour)

123. The **long-armed starfish** of European waters, *Luidia ciliaris*, has close relatives on the American side of the Atlantic. Like most specimens from well-fished waters, it shows evidence of having regenerated parts of several arms, probably after mutilation by fishermen's trawls. It feeds on starfishes, sea urchins, and sea cucumbers. (Roscoff, France. Ralph Buchsbaum)

124. The **common European starfish**, *Asterias rubens*, feeds mainly on bivalves, and is abundant on beds of mussels. Two American relatives, the more northerly *Asterias vulgaris* and the more southerly *Asterias forbesi*, do great damage to east-coast oyster beds. Roscoff, France. Ralph Buchsbaum)

125. The **blood-red starfish**, *Henricia sanguinolenta*, is found near shore but ranges down to more than three thousand feet in the North Atlantic. A similar species lives on the American Pacific coast. (Roscoff, France. Ralph Buchsbaum)

126. The **sea bat**, *Patiria miniata*, about 5 inches across, and red, yellow, or purple in color, occurs on protected rocks and on sandy bottoms from Alaska to Lower California. The short spines are arranged in small concentric clusters. (S. H. Rosenthal, Jr.: Rapho Guillumette)

127. The many-rayed **sunflower star**, *Pycnopodia helianthoides*, with up to twenty-four arms, ranges from Alaska to southern California. Perhaps the largest of starfishes, it often measures 2 feet across. It becomes limp when exposed, and even if handled gingerly may shed an arm or two. (Washington. Ralph Buchsbaum)

128. The **spiny sun star,** *Crossaster papposus*, with up to fifteen arms, feeds on other starfishes. It is found around the world in northern waters and as far southward as the English Channel, New Jersey, and Vancouver. (Roscoff, France. Ralph Buchsbaum)

129. The **cobalt-blue starfish**, *Linckia,* up to 12 inches across, is the most common and conspicuous starfish on the Great Barrier Reef flats. Unlike other starfishes, *Linckia* lies exposed in bright daylight. Members of this genus are the only starfishes that can, and often do, regenerate a whole starfish from a piece of one arm. (Allen Keast)

130. A little **starfish**, *Ceramaster placenta,* brought up from a depth of 480 feet near the Bay of Biscay, and photographed in a tank at the Plymouth Aquarium, where it lived for at least a year. (D. P. Wilson)

131. The **common European brittle star**, *Ophiothrix fragilis,* shown at about the size of the largest specimens, are more often half this size. Especially fragile, when handled they may throw off all the arms in pieces. Underwater cameras reveal that in favorable spots the floor of the English Channel is carpeted with dense masses of this species. (D. P. Wilson)

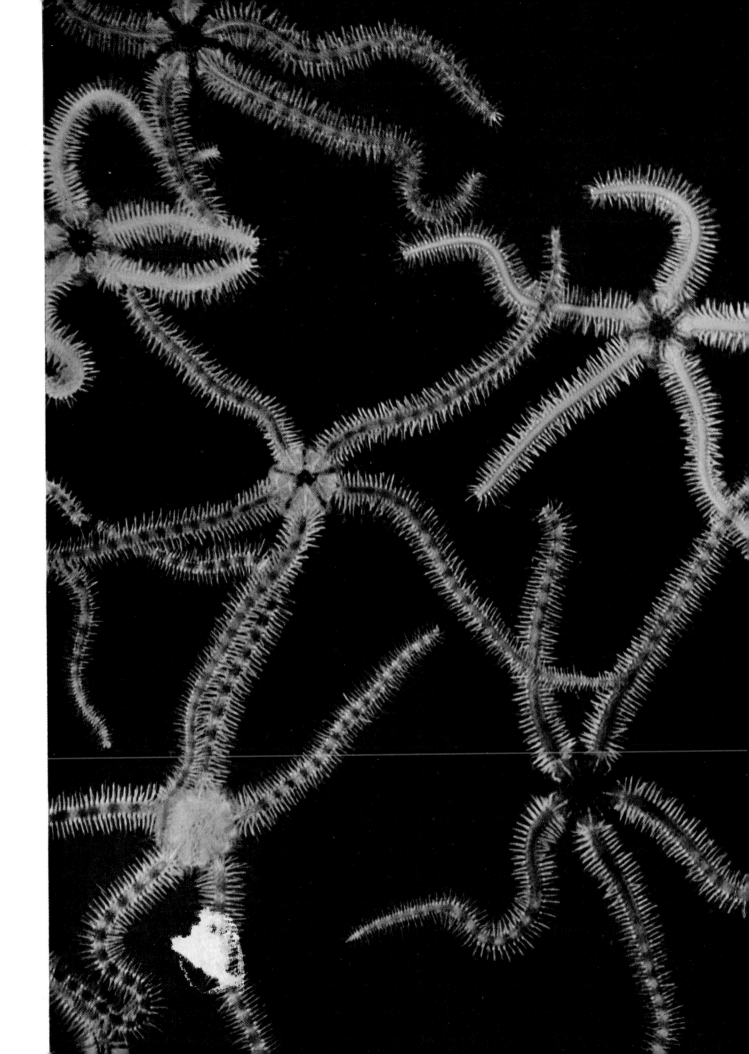

132. Underside of the central disk of *Ophiocoma*, revealing the star-shaped mouth of this beautifully patterned **brittle star** of the South Pacific. (Great Barrier Reef. Jerome and Dorothy Schweitzer)

133. **Brittle stars** near shores are usually insinuated under stones or in the holdfasts of seaweeds. These two (same species as in Plate 131) were clinging to a dead sea fan (Plate 12) in a tank at the Station Biologique, Roscoff, France. (Ralph Buchsbaum)

134. A **common basket star** of the American Pacific coast is shown here in a tank at the laboratory of the University of Oregon. Seen from the underside, the animal displays the star-shaped mouth and five arms. Each arm branches repeatedly, and the tiny end branches curl and uncurl ceaselessly. (Ralph Buchsbaum)

135. A **feather star**, or **stalkless crinoid**, has branched arms with short side branches that make the arms look feathery. The animal lies with mouth and arms turned upward. (New Caledonia. René Catala)

136. The **European edible sea urchin**, *Echinus esculentus*, up to 6 inches across, with a red shell and movable white spines, is found from Norway to Portugal, usually below low-tide mark. Only the ripe ovaries are eaten, either raw, like caviar, or cooked. (Plymouth, England. D. P. Wilson)

137. The **giant red urchin**, *Strongylocentrotus franciscanus*, which may also be purple, is more than 7 inches across. From Alaska to Mexico it frequents the deeper tide pools and rocky channels. (Ralph Buchsbaum)

138. The **purple sea urchin**, *Strongylocentrotus purpuratus*, has almost the same range as its larger relative in Plate 137, but is seldom more than 3 inches across and occurs in great beds, especially in surf-swept areas. In soft rock each urchin sits in its own pothole. (California. Woody Williams)

139. A close-up of the **mouth of a sea urchin** reveals the five white teeth that grind the seaweeds and animals on which it feeds. (West Indies. Fritz Goro: *Life* Magazine)

140. A **reddish sea cucumber**, *Cucumaria miniata*. It lives under rocks in temperate or cold waters around the world. In the quiet of an aquarium it spreads the branched tentacles that surround the mouth and shows three of the five rows of tube-feet by which it clings. Behind it is a **white sea cucumber**, *Eupentacta quinquesemita*, with two double rows of longer tube-feet. (University of Oregon Marine Laboratory. Ralph Buchsbaum)

→

142. Patches of the **colonial golden-stars sea squirt**, *Botryllus schlosseri*, encrust rocks, wharf pilings, boat bottoms, and seaweeds on protected Atlantic shores. The yellow-accented individuals have separate mouths but are arranged in starlike or oval clusters that share a vent. (Brittany, France. Ralph Buchsbaum)

141. A **sea cucumber** found around the world in tropical waters is *Holothuria impatiens*, here shown ejecting long, bluish white, opalescent, and very sticky threads. Shot out from the rear of the aroused animal, these threads can confuse or immobilize an enemy. (Great Barrier Reef. Allen Keast)

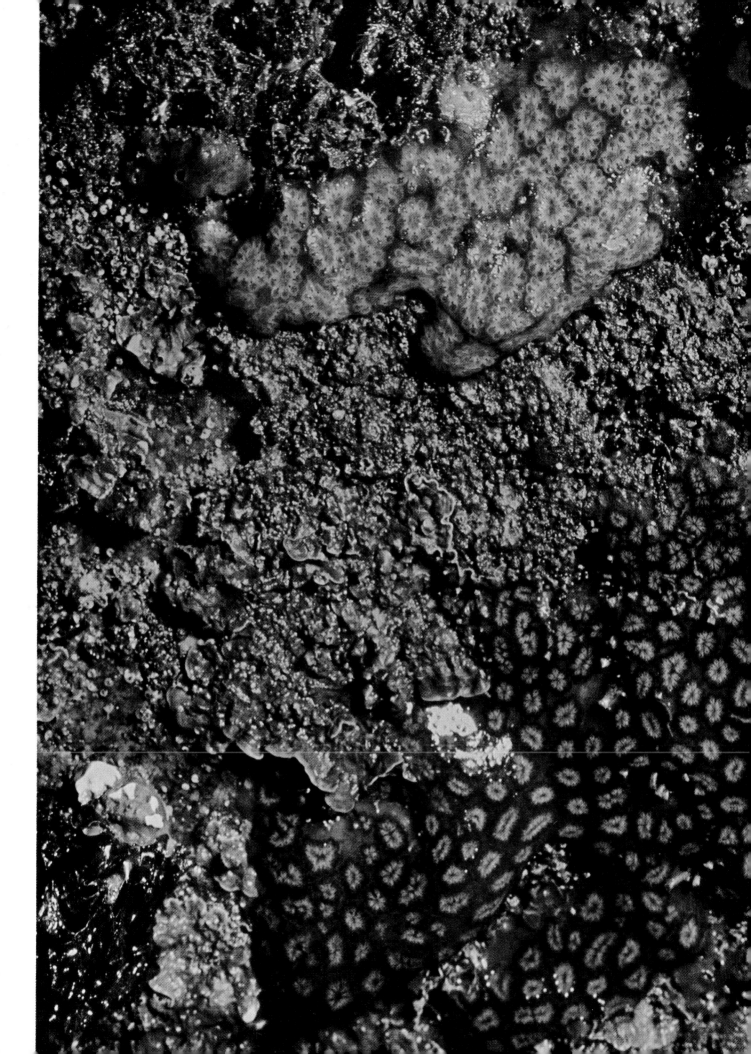

143. The **sea peach**, *Tethyum pyriforme*, is a sea squirt whose size, shape, and color suggest a peach. The feeding and respiratory current goes in one opening and out the other. (Passamaquoddy Bay, Canada. N. J. Berrill)

144. Clusters of **stalked tunicates** are common on stones and wharf pilings on many shores. In *Clavellina lepadiformis*, 1 to 2 inches high, the individuals are separate but rise from a common base. The two body openings are close together. (Plymouth, England. D. P. Wilson)

[continued from page 256]

Sea Cucumbers

(*Class Holothuroidea*)

A person need wade out only knee-deep around many of the Florida keys to encounter, lying conspicuously exposed on the muddy bottom, large sausage-shaped creatures 1 foot or more in length and better than 2 inches in diameter. Against the pale gray surface on which they lie, the contrast may be striking: dark brown with light spots, or brick red with raised lumps of black or dark brown. They are sea cucumbers (Plates 140, 141), with a name given them (*Cucumis marinus*) in the first century A.D. by Pliny, the Roman elder and encyclopedist.

Upon closer examination, none of the usual clues is evident to show which is the head end of the animal. As it lies there quietly, both ends of the cucumber appear to be doing something. At one end, an opening appears, sometimes as much as 1 inch in diameter. If the water is shallow, a current may be noted pouring out of the opening. Or the sea cucumber may be taking in water just as rapidly. The movements of the opening and the slow enlargements and contractions of the whole body suggest a sort of underwater whistling. Actually, they are breathing movements and, in this unusual animal, occur at its rear end.

As though further to astonish the beachcomber on tropical and subtropical shores, a sea cucumber may be found from which a fish's head projects. The fish is very much alive, and the cucumber's breathing movements simply take in water or expel it around the fish. If nudged, the fish may swim out, exposing a slender tapering body as much as six inches long.

Usually a minor drama follows at once. The blenny-like fish turns back immediately to the side of the sea cucumber and moves about along the surface, evidently searching for the respiratory opening again. Often the sea cucumber closes the aperture tightly, as though to keep the fish from returning to its refuge. But eventually the need for oxygen becomes too great. The cucumber opens again, the fish slips in either tail first or head first (and turns around immediately).

The cavity into which the fish goes is the cloaca of the sea cucumber, a chamber serving not only respiration but also as a common exit for wastes from the digestive tract and sex cells from the reproductive system. Sea cucumbers are unique in having a pair of generously branched "respiratory trees" extending blindly from the cloaca far forward in the body cavity. Through their walls oxygen and water pass, keeping the other internal organs aerated and maintaining the plumpness of the cucumber's body.

At the opposite end of the animal a set of tentacles moves slowly, obtaining food. In most sea cucum-

bers, including the large kinds found near shore in tropical and subtropical waters, these soft organs around the mouth shovel the surface mud into the digestive tract, letting the animal get the nourishment from a great assortment of microscopic life, especially diatoms. The gritty residue is expelled from the cloaca, and sometimes accumulates into conspicuous heaps. The late Professor W. J. Crozier estimated from measurements of the cones of debris that the sea cucumbers on each acre of bottom in one region off Bermuda would pass between 100 and 200 pounds of sand through their bodies annually.

Substantial amounts of the nourishment obtained by a sea cucumber are stored in its body wall. There the food reserve usually gains protection from a slimy, leathery skin in which are embedded little limy secretions of remarkable variety. Some are microscopic plates perforated by many holes. Others are knobby rods, or anchor-shaped, or resembling a concrete bird bath or a wheel with spokes but no rim. Each species has its own distinctive limy granules. Only a few kinds lack them altogether.

Many of the larger sea cucumbers that live close to shore supposedly discourage attack by fish and crabs through the presence of a poison (holothurin) in their skins. If extracts of it are injected into mice, they die quickly. The presence of certain sea cucumbers in an aquarium tank may be enough to poison any fish present. With some of the large subtropical and tropical cucumbers, the effect sometimes persists in a tank for weeks after the echinoderm has been removed and the water changed repeatedly.

Large cucumbers belonging to the genera *Holothuria* (Plate 141) and *Actinopyga* have ready a truly astonishing defense against animals that molest them. Associated with the region where their respiratory trees open into the cloaca they have short tubules of red, pink, or white color. If the echinoderm is disturbed seriously or repeatedly, it slowly turns its body until the cloacal opening faces the molester, then performs a general contraction and proceeds to send out the slender tubules in great numbers. The blind ends of the tubules may be enlarged; almost always they are very sticky. And as they emerge from the cloacal opening, they become darting, adhesive threads that, in a minute or less, can so enmesh a crab or lobster that it is immobilized. The cucumber frees itself from the tubules and moves slowly away as though nothing had happened.

With provocation these and many related sea cucumbers will perform a far more amazing trick. With a single powerful contraction they turn themselves partly inside out—throwing out the respiratory trees, the reproductive organs, and sometimes some of the intestine as well. All of these emerge suddenly through the cloacal opening as a tangled mass over and around a crab or fish. From these too the cucumber separates itself, as one of the most spectacular instances of self-mutilation and evisceration in the animal kingdom. Until new organs are regenerated, the sea cucumber continues its breathing movements, drawing sea water directly into its body cavity. In six weeks or so, the animal recovers completely and is ready to repeat the performance if irritated sufficiently.

In many parts of the South Pacific and along Oriental coasts, people deliberately annoy these large sea cucumbers and gather up the extruded organs (particularly the ovaries of a female) as meat for the soup pot or delicacies to be eaten raw. More widespread is the custom of preparing holothurians as "trepang" or "bêche-de-mer." Usually the animal is eviscerated, its body wall boiled, then dried or smoked. In the Indo-Pacific region the product is very popular as an ingredient for soups or as gelatinous tidbits. Great quantities of trepang are sold commercially to the Chinese.

Trepang from the Mediterranean is almost two-thirds protein, whereas that from the Indo-Pacific averages between one-third and one-half protein. Apparently the protein constituents are completely digestible, and the method of preparation removes all toxic materials.

Since the sea cucumbers in which the little pearl fish *Carapus* seems an unwelcome guest are exactly the ones producing fish poison and sticky threads and eviscerating themselves when irritated, a person can only marvel that the pearl fish is able to use the cucumber's cloaca as a refuge. Actually, *Carapus* gets enough space for its body by sliding its tapered tail well up into one of the cucumber's respiratory trees. Yet the fish seems never to trigger the common responses and is completely immune to the poison.

The potency of the poison to fish in general is well known among natives on many South Sea islands. On Guam, for example, people cut the common black sea cucumber in two and wring the contents of its body cavity into tidal pools to drive the fish to the

The feather star *Antedon bifida*, found on European Atlantic shores and in the Mediterranean, may be red, orange, yellow, or purple. It attaches itself temporarily to rocks by use of a circlet of appendages (cirri) on its back, and holds the mouth up to receive food collected by the feathery arms. (France. Ralph Buchsbaum)

surface. In the Marshall Islands, similar sea cucumbers are pounded and the mangled remains dropped into pools at low tide, stupefying the fish enough that they can be caught easily. Yet the poison is not feared by the natives. It is harmless to human skin, and fish caught through its use are often eaten raw with no ill effects.

About 500 different kinds of sea cucumbers have been found, living almost exclusively on or in the bottom sediments. Most of them are dull colored, and only a few have contrasting spots or stripes. Yet they pursue their lethargic way of life on minute food in so many different levels of the sea that a surprising variety of form and body build is represented.

Something in common can be seen between a child solemnly licking its fingers to clean them of jam, and a big sea cucumber in its normal method of feeding with ten or more profusely branched tentacles, each like a shrubby tree. The cucumber spreads its tentacles over the sea bottom and rubs them around, gathering food particles in the mucus coating. Then, one at a time, the animal thrusts a loaded tentacle into its mouth, closes fleshy lips around it, and pulls out the tentacle all clean and ready for reloading.

Sea cucumbers acting in this way can be found in cooler waters between low-tide mark and 1200 feet below the surface. *Cucumaria frondosa,* found in tide pools along rocky coasts on both sides of the North Atlantic, is one that presents a particularly magnificent set of bushy tentacles when fully expanded. Along the body of a *Cucumaria,* five lengthwise tracts of short tube-feet show the five-parted symmetry so obvious in most echinoderms.

In *Thyone,* the whole body is studded with tube-feet and curved into a broad U. Ordinarily these animals bury themselves in the bottom with only the cloacal opening and the bushy tentacles exposed. If a *Thyone* is dug out and then placed on the sea floor, it usually needs three to four hours to work itself into the hidden position again.

Some other sea cucumbers with bushy tentacles have a scale covering. Usually these animals rest on a solelike area of the lower surface, and give the general appearance of an armored slug with tentacles instead of gills. They creep from place to place, and can climb the vertical walls of a glass aquarium at fair speed. *Psolus* has tube-feet only around and under the creeping sole, whereas *Psolidium* extends degenerate tube-feet that lack sucker tips through holes in the body scales.

Psolus antarcticus carries as many as 22 young along with it, holding to smooth areas of the creeping sole. *Cucumaria parva* has been seen holding plant material against its body, helping keep young in place. Other species of these two genera have pockets in the body wall, usually around the anterior end, in which the eggs develop.

These large sea cucumbers in a coral reef of the South Pacific face the danger of being collected and prepared for human food as "bêche-de-mer" or "trepang." (Great Barrier Reef. Fritz Goro: *Life* Magazine)

Large tropical and subtropical sea cucumbers usually have twenty tentacles, but each of these feeding organs has an expanded tip and cannot be withdrawn into the body as is done by cucumbers with bushy tentacles. *Holothuria* is one genus of particularly inert and sausage-like sea cucumbers, with no obvious flattened surface to indicate a ventral side. *Actinopyga* has a creeping sole, as has *Stichopus.* Both of these live in exposed positions on mudflats, reaching record lengths of 40 inches and a diameter of 8 inches. *Actinopyga* differs from *Stichopus* in that the anus opens into the cloaca through an armament of five limy teeth. *Stichopus* lacks these teeth, but has the ability to raise its body in waves of movement, like a giant caterpillar walking, and shift the animal far more rapidly than use of its tube-feet would permit.

Close relatives of these cucumbers live in the great depths of the ocean. There *Bathyplotes* appears to drift well above the bottom for most of its life, supported by a float extending around the rim of its creeping sole. *Mesothuria intestinalis,* a grayish white animal often tinged with pink or violet, is sometimes found also near the surface. It covers its body with debris, as though to hide from enemies, and has been found to begin adult life as a male, later transforming into an egg-laying female.

Molpadonias are sea cucumbers with a conspicuous tail, often found buried in the bottom mud with only the tail tip and cloacal opening exposed. These animals lack tube-feet, or have them only around the anus, perhaps used there in keeping the cloaca free of sediments. The feeding tentacles are fleshy, sometimes with a few finger-like extensions at the ends.

According to Japanese scientists, molpadonias feed particularly rapidly. An individual may move from 125 to 150 pounds of bottom sediments through its 7-inch body annually in extracting nourishment. One of this type of cucumber is *Caudina arenata,* found from Rhode Island to the Gulf of St. Lawrence between 100 feet below the surface and low-tide mark. Its tail tip can be found exposed from the sandy mud, and used to capture the buried cylindrical animal. The body may be 1 inch in diameter and 7 in length, in hues ranging from deep purple to flesh-color.

Some sea cucumbers are wormlike, lacking tube-feet and respiratory trees. Usually the body wall is very thin, often translucent, and the animal itself is more active than most other holothurians. Several kinds with this shape of body burrow in the mud and can bury themselves in five to six minutes. Others, while only partly grown, swim to the surface at night by a curious twitching movement of the body, suggesting a scissors kick.

Synaptula is one of the commoner wormlike sea cucumbers. It can be found clambering among seaweeds and through coral reefs. When fully extended a *Synaptula* may reach a length of 3 feet, yet be no more than ½ of an inch in diameter. Some members of this genus have openings through the wall of the intestine in the female, through which sperms from sea water reach the eggs in the body cavity. Thus fertilization is internal, and the embryos develop for some time in the body cavity before being cast out into the sea. The young of *Chiridota rotifera,* a wormlike sea cucumber of shallow water in the West Indies, reach the same body form as the parent before they emerge, and this sea cucumber is truly viviparous.

Sea Stars *(Class Asteroidea)*

For many people, a starfish, better called a sea star, is a clear symbol of marine life (Plates 118–130). They are aware that animals of this type are never found in fresh water or on land. Sea stars are strictly bottom animals, chiefly of the margins of the sea. They range in size from less than ½ of an inch in diameter to more than 3 feet across, and in shape from regular stars with five or more arms to pentagonal and almost circular. Yellow, orange, pink, or red are the commonest colors, but gray, green, blue, and purple ones can be found.

Most sea stars take mollusks as their favorite food, but some eat sea urchins, sea cucumbers, and other sea stars. A few catch small fish and shrimps. Perhaps a majority will devour carrion on the bottom. Sea stars of certain kinds swallow soft mud and digest the organic matter, as do so many other echinoderms.

A sea star's arms are actually part of its body rather than appendages. If one of these animals is turned upside down to expose its mouth surface, each arm is seen to have a lengthwise groove filled with moving tube-feet. Within each arm the star has also one or two branches of its reproductive organs, and often extensions from the digestive tract as well.

If the inverted sea star is balanced for a few seconds on the back of a person's wrist, it may take hold firmly enough to hang from the human hairs after the wrist is turned over. Its grip is not strong enough to pull out the hairs, but once attached in this way, it seldom will let go.

This trick is not due to tube-feet, for stars have none of these organs on the aboral surface. Instead, it is a demonstration of strange little modified spines (pedicellariae) by means of which the animal ordinarily polices its body. Each pedicellaria commonly has the form of a pair of pincers, or of a little clam shell lying in a minute pocket of the surface. The parts open or close under muscular control. Sea urchins are the only other animals in the world with pedicellariae.

Between the pedicellariae over much of the star's aboral surface, small domes of soft skin show where the body cavity is separated from the sea by only a thin layer of tissue. Here the blood can exchange carbon dioxide for oxygen. Elsewhere the outer surface of the star, like the lining of its digestive tract and the corresponding parts of sea urchins, crinoids, and brittle stars, is covered by cells with cilia. These propel a thin film of mucus from glands and, on the outside of the body, efficiently keep it clean by sweeping away any debris that falls on it.

One or more madreporites, flat plates perforated by many holes, can be found on the aboral surface of a sea star. Through these the water-vascular system is connected to the ocean. Most sea stars have only one madreporite, and naturalists have often used this landmark as a guide in trying to learn whether a sea star is actually so versatile that it will travel with equal readiness in all directions, letting any arm lead the way. Some few kinds and occasional individuals seem to show a distinct preference. For the rest, the radial plan extends to habits, and all arms are equivalent.

When a star rights itself after falling on the bottom with mouth up, it shows little partiality for one way or another. Yet for a patient observer, the star's movements provide a wonderful demonstration of its remarkable flexibility and muscular control. The creature may take anywhere from two to ninety minutes to get back on its tube-feet.

Some stars turn over by use of the "tulip method." Slowly they bend all of their arms in the same direction, perhaps raising them around the mouth like the petals of a tulip. The disk of the body becomes rounded and the animal is no longer in balance. It topples to one side, and then proceeds to curl the under arms and take hold of the bottom with its tube-feet. Eventually it reaches the ordinary outspread position, mouth downward.

Other stars use the tulip method in reverse, bending the arms away from the mouth, rising up like an inverted flower until they topple or can grasp the bottom with extended tube-feet on some one or two arms.

A great many stars, when righting themselves, accomplish the same end with far less obvious movement. Just the tips of one or two arms (usually two) curl under, away from the mouth side of the animal. Their tube-feet gain a hold on the bottom and, with this beginning, the star proceeds to walk under itself, the region of bend shifting nearer and nearer the disk of the body. Finally the remaining arms may be raised free of the bottom, and the slow somersault is complete. Or the folding may continue all the way to the tips of the opposite arms, none of them ever being elevated into the water.

The tube-feet of sea stars are stout organs. Yet, unless the star is climbing a vertical surface, they appear to push rather than to pull. Muscles in their walls serve to aim the tube-foot as it is extended by hydraulic pressure from the water-vascular system. Contraction of longitudinal muscles shortens the tube-foot and expels the water.

It is on tube-feet slanting away from the animal in a backward direction that real force is applied. As these tube-feet are inflated with water, they push the body along very much as a man's feet push against the ground in walking. A sea star strides very slowly on a multitude of tube-feet all out of step with one another. But in this way it can walk on soft mud as well as on hard surfaces to which it clings.

At the end of each arm, a star has one or more tube-feet of a different sort. They lack suckers and appear to be feelers, especially sensitive to vibrations and chemical substances in the water. With them a sea star can be repelled by a salt crystal or attracted to a piece of clam.

In all but certain deep-sea starfishes, each arm has at its tip a small cushion-like area that bears a cluster of simple eyes. In most species this light-sensitive area appears as a red spot. Often a creeping star curls the tips of its arms upward, as though to peer vaguely in the direction of movement by aiming the eyespot at the surrounding bottom.

Nearly 2000 different species of sea stars have been discovered, the greatest number from northern parts of the North Pacific Ocean. Living sea stars all belong to three great orders, separated upon inconspicuous details of the pedicellariae and skeleton. Familiar and remarkable sea stars are included in each of the three.

THE EDGED SEA STARS

A majority of deep-sea stars belong to the order of "edged sea stars" (Phanerozonia), the record for depth being held by *Albatrossaster richardi,* dredged from 19,700 feet below the surface near the Cape Verde Islands. This order has many members too in waters a beachcomber or skin diver can reach.

Edged sea stars usually have a sharp boundary between the upper and lower surfaces. Along the margin of the often broadly joined disk and the arms, especially large skeletal plates commonly form two rows (*Ceramaster,* Plate 130). These marginal plates, together with the ones that cover the upper surface with a kind of mosaic pavement, give rigidity to the sea star.

Many edged sea stars have pointed tube-feet with no suction tip, and live normal lives with neither pedicellariae nor an anus. These are all features of the common, sluggish mud star *Ctenodiscus crispatus,* and of the various kinds of *Psilaster, Astropecten,* and *Leptychaster* encountered along muddy coasts of the northern hemisphere.

Ctenodiscus crispatus itself is a short-armed, blunt-tipped creature with a broad yellow disk. It sinks itself just below the surface of mud flats from shore to depths of at least 6000 feet along coasts of both the North Pacific and North Atlantic. Full size—3 to 4 inches across—is probably reached by the time it is three years old, showing that the mud star is really efficient at extracting food from the sediments carried to its mouth by a veil of mucus propelled by the ciliated cells of the skin.

The arms of *Psilaster, Astropecten,* and *Luidia* (Plate 123) are pointed and far longer than those of *Ctenodiscus. Psilaster andromeda* needs about four years to reach the full 4-inch spread of its slender arms, feeding on small urchins, little clams, mussels, and microscopic life in surface sediments. Recently-dead *Psilaster* are often washed ashore, for they live in waters as shallow as 60 feet and from there to more than 2500 feet below the surface on both sides of the North Atlantic—from Delaware Bay to Greenland and down the eastern shores to the Cape Verde Islands off the westward bulge of Africa. A gelatinous secretion on the aboral surface of this star makes it slimy to the touch.

The -*pecten* of *Astropecten* is the comblike fringe of spines attached to the marginal plates. Many of these stars are large ones. *A. articulatus* and *A. cingulatus* both reach 10 inches in span. The former lives in comparatively shallow water from New Jersey to the Gulf of Mexico, and can be bright orange or purple above and yellow below with orange-red marginal plates and purple spines. *A. cingulatus* inhabits deeper water and usually is colored more drably.

Still other species of *Astropecten* are the commonest shallow-water sea stars in the Mediterranean. They compensate for lack of suction cups on the tube-feet by having particularly large mouths, and engulf astonishing numbers of small animals. One individual of *A. auranciacus* from the Mediterranean was found to have swallowed ten scallops, six *Tellina* clams, five tusk shells (scaphopods), and several snails. Another species in the same region dines regularly on young sea stars, brittle stars, bivalves, snails, segmented worms, and assorted crustaceans. Snail shells regurgitated by *Astropecten* stars along the Pacific coast of America are so intact and empty that hermit crabs adopt them while house-hunting.

Leptychaster arcticus has a larger body disk than members of *Psilaster* or *Astropecten* and differs from them in lacking spines on the marginal plates. Fully grown individuals seldom exceed 1¼ inches in diameter, but they are well worth examining closely since this is a sea star that may brood its young. It is found in cooler coastal waters of both the North Atlantic and North Pacific.

Brooding in these stars seems related to low temperatures and, as among sea cucumbers, to echinoderms that produce larger eggs than is usual, hence with plenty of yolk as stored food. In *Leptychaster uber* of the northwest Pacific and *L. kerguelenensis* from close to Antarctica, up to thirty young are carried in depressions of the greatly stretched aboral surface of the parent.

Edged sea stars whose tube-feet have suction tips are better able to hold a shellfish while attacking it as food. The largest group with this characteristic (family Goniasteridae) includes perhaps the most brilliantly colored sea stars of Australian waters, and has representatives in many other parts of the world as well. Thick, massive plates border the broad-based arms, and the whole aboral surface is commonly roofed by a mosaic of skeletal pieces under a smooth or granular skin. *Mediaster aequalis* is studded above and below with compact little paxillae, giving the appearance of everlasting flowers in a honeycomb pattern. It is found in shore waters along the Pacific coast from Alaska to California.

The largest sea star of the Atlantic coast of America is *Oreaster reticulatus* of Florida, the Bahamas, and the West Indies. The name *reticulatus* refers to the network pattern evident on the upper surface, where the parchment-thin skin sags a little between the mesh of the bar-shaped skeletal plates. Like others of its family, it is a massive animal, quite thick in the middle. Specimens measuring 16 to 20 inches across are often displayed as trophies of the sea. They may be almost any color from deep purple through maroon, orange, green, or bluish, with bright yellow points where the skeletal plates join one another at prominent rounded spines. *O. nodosus,* brilliant in red and blue, is equally admired in the Indo-Pacific.

The marginal plates in *Linckia* (Plate 129) are much less evident on the more-or-less cylindrical arms. The whole body is clothed in rounded or squarish plates, often with a pebbled surface. *L. guildingi* inhabits tropical waters of all oceans. *L. colombiae,* which grows to as much as 4 inches across, can be found on rocky shores from Los Angeles, California, to the Galápagos Islands off Ecuador. All of these animals show spectacular powers of regeneration, for even a piece of an arm less than ½ of an inch long can reorganize itself into a whole new sea star. At least part of the body disk must accompany a whole arm for such a fragment of any other kind of sea star to regenerate the missing parts.

THE SPINY SEA STARS

A connoiseur of sea stars recognizes those with conspicuous spines over much of the upper and lower surfaces as being very different from any of the edged sea stars. These features are marks of a spiny sea star (order Spinulosa), the skeleton of which usually consists of a network of limy bars or of plates overlapping one another. The boundary between oral and aboral surface is rarely evident on the body or arms, and while the tube-feet always have suction tips, pedicellariae are rare.

One of the commonest spiny sea stars of western Europe and the Mediterranean is *Asterina gibbosa,* which is covered on both surfaces by tufts of small spines. It is found along the Atlantic coast of Africa as far as the Azores, and is known to vary its diet of mollusks with meals on sponges and sea squirts.

The red or orange sea bat, *Patiria miniata* (Plate 126), is almost equally familiar along the Pacific coast from Lower California to Alaska. Its oral surface is decorated with tufts of spines in the form of little fans fitted together, whereas the aboral surface is granular, with curved plates forming an attractive pattern. It seems to be particularly omnivorous, often eating seaweed, sponges, sea urchins, squid eggs, or spreading its thin surface against surfaces upon which diatoms are growing. It will digest them away from even the glass side of an aquarium.

Sometimes the appetite of a spiny sea star cannot be predicted from an examination of its body. The broadly pentagonal *Anseropoda placenta* of western Europe and the Mediterranean is a burrowing species of wafer thinness. Yet it engulfs other echinoderms, snails, little clams, and a great variety of small crustaceans—even hermit crabs. It seems impossible for any animal to eat so much and stay so thin.

The blood star, *Henricia sanguinolenta* (Plate 125), is seldom more than 3 inches across, but its rich red color and graceful pointed arms make it a favorite with beachcombers from Greenland to Cape Hatteras on the western side of the Atlantic, and to the Azores on the eastern side. Some individuals are rose-colored, others orange, or purple, or even mottled with creamy yellow. The arms are always smoothly curved from aboral to oral surface, and the groove containing the tube-feet is usually narrow.

Both *H. sanguinolenta* and *H. leviuscula* on the Pacific coast of America stay hidden in dark crevices during the winter months while they brood their relatively large eggs. *Henricia* larvae omit the usual free-swimming larval stage, and remain concealed among the parent's incurved arms until they have transformed into miniature stars, ready to glide on their own along the bottom.

The sun stars *Crossaster* and *Solaster* have a broad body disk and many arms. *Crossaster papposus* (Plate 127), found in the Pacific Ocean along coasts as far south as Vancouver Island and in the Atlantic to New Jersey on the west and the English Channel on the east, is easily the handsomest of them. It may have from eight to fifteen arms, each tufted conspicuously with spines. The whole aboral surface wears a sunburst of color perhaps more striking than on any other echinoderm.

Solaster endica, by contrast, has slender arms and no raised tufts of spines. It lives on both sides of the Atlantic in cool water, and is usually a bright purple. On Pacific coasts it is represented by *S. dawsoni.* Sun stars are voracious creatures, eating large numbers of smaller sea stars as well as sea anemones, bivalves, and snails. Like *Henricia,* they have no free-swimming stage, but develop directly. Older individuals have more arms than younger ones.

Pteraster miliaris is one of several cushion stars found in shore waters of Scandinavia, the British Isles, down the Atlantic coast of America to New Jersey, and along cooler shores of the Pacific. The pinkish red body is covered by a membranous skin draped from circlets of slender spines, as though it were a tent roof. The membrane extends as a web around the short, bluntly rounded arms, which may span 6 inches. The skin over the aboral surface actually conceals a cavity used as a brood pouch for the young and in respiration. Water enters it through pores below, and emerges through a large cloacal opening near the middle of the upper surface.

THE FORCEPS-CARRYING SEA STARS

The special enemies of shellfishermen are sea stars which, upon close inspection, prove to bear pedicellariae raised above the surface on short stalks able to turn in various directions. Most of these forceps-carriers (order Forcipulata) have long, rounded arms and a small body disk. They include many of the most persistent destroyers of clams, mussels, and oysters.

The forceps-carriers include the familiar stars of wharf pilings and tide pools all over the world. *Asterias amurensis* inhabits the Pacific coast from Alaska to Korea, *A. vulgaris* the Atlantic coast from Labrador to Long Island, *A. forbesi* from Maine to

Sun stars are denizens of shallow temperate seas. Their arms vary in number, usually from seven to thirteen, but may total as many as seventeen. The exposed surface often wears a sunburst of color. (Maine. Ralph Buchsbaum)

the Gulf of Mexico, and *A. rubens* (Plate 124) the northern shores of Europe. All of them have a rough body surface and four rows of tube-feet in the groove below each arm. They also have two types of pedicellariae: some with straight forceps, and others of a cross-bladed type. *A. vulgaris* in Maine sometimes reaches a span of 17 inches.

In opening a shellfish, these stars mount it with the mouth opening directed toward the place where the clam would gape if the mollusk did not clamp its valves together. Then, with almost every tube-foot affixed to one valve or the other, the sea star applies the force of its body muscles. A pull of 7 to 10 pounds has been measured, tending to open the shell.

Contrary to widespread belief, the sea star need not wait for its victim to tire. A force of this size is sufficient to bend the shell of clam or oyster, making it gape a fraction. Even a hundredth of an inch is enough for the sea star. Through the narrow slot it slips its even thinner, everted stomach and proceeds to digest the shellfish deep in the shell. For much of the time the sea star does not even bother to hold the valves apart. It lets them clamp on the extruded stomach except at such times as a stream of liquefied products of digestion are ready for transfer into the sea star's body.

Not all forceps-carriers have the same tastes. On the Pacific coast of America, *Astrometis sertulifera* is expert at feeding on the large chiton *Stenoplax* clinging to the rocks. *Pisaster brevispinus* on sandy bottoms hunts for sand dollars, and the flavor of an approaching star of this kind is distinctive enough to sand dollars that they will cease feeding and burrow

The starfish *Asterias forbesi* extrudes its stomach to envelop the small dead fish which will be its dinner. (Virginia. Robert Bailey)

out of sight when *Pisaster* comes within two feet of them; half an hour after this star has passed by, they come up again and resume feeding. They may have an opportunity to repeat this vanishing act many times, for *Pisaster* is believed to be one of the longest-lived of sea stars, reaching an age of twenty years.

In the Indo-Pacific, *Coscinasterias calamaria* is a spinier star with from seven to fifteen arms. It opens brachiopods as food, using the same method as *Asterias* employs on clams. The giant twenty-rayed *Pycnopodia helianthoides* of the Pacific coast from southern California to the Aleutians often eats whole sea urchins. In Puget Sound this sea star attains a diameter of 22 inches. Apparently its mouth and appetite are in proportion (Plate 128).

The Echinoids *(Class Echinoidea)*

Among the denizens of tide pools and seashores, the sea urchins and sand dollars are second only to sea stars as popular trophies. The smallest of them are sand dollars barely ½ of an inch in diameter when mature. The largest a skin diver can retrieve are black

sea urchins with a shell 6 inches across; long, slender spines usually add another 10 or 12 inches to the space needed to accommodate the prize without touching. In much deeper waters live urchins with leathery, flexible shells almost a foot across. The largest urchin known is a leathery specimen of *Sperostoma giganteum,* taken off Japan; it measured nearly 13 inches in diameter.

Echinoids come in many different shapes: sea urchins as regularly symmetrical as a doorknob; flattened sand dollars and sea pancakes; broadly pointed sea arrowheads; and heavy-bodied heart urchins. Even their empty shells are things of beauty, for without the skin covering them, they reveal a handsomely regular pattern of limy plates joined immovably. Knobs on certain plates are the balls of ball-and-socket joints for spines under individual muscular control—the armament from which echinoids get their name, suggesting *echinos,* the hedgehog.

As a sea urchin moves along a submerged rock or the bottom, its spines seem constantly to be readjusting themselves. Between them and often beyond them, slender tube-feet may extend as feelers ready to detect the approach of food or enemy. Other tube-feet bear the weight, except in a few kinds of urchins in tropical waters that progress on their spines or lurch forward by lifting themselves on their mouthparts. Their tube-feet arise in five radiating areas, regions evident in an empty, cleaned shell from the rows of circular holes through which the tube-feet extended in life.

Pedicellariae on long stalks also reach about, seizing on particles and transferring them as though hand to hand around the body to the mouth, or defending the urchin against attackers. The commonest type of pedicellaria among echinoids has three jaws coming together only at the tip. Special ones are glandular, with a poison sac in each jaw producing a toxic material. Each pedicellaria has its own nervous control and can act independently in policing the body surface.

Echinoids replace tube-feet, pedicellariae, and spines when these are damaged or lost. Cracks in the shell can be mended, but new plates are produced only during normal growth, keeping up with the enlargement of the enclosed parts of the body.

Probably sea urchins occasionally live to be older than eight years, but their growth is most rapid while young. The common green urchin *Strongylocentrotus* of the North Atlantic and North Pacific attains a body diameter of about ¼ of an inch by the end of its first year, ⅝ of an inch in the second year, 1 inch at three years, 1⅝ at four years, 2 inches at five years, 2⅜ at six years. Off the Norway coast this urchin reaches a top diameter of about 3 inches.

In sea urchins and sand dollars the mouth is equipped with an amazing dredgelike device with as many as forty separate pieces, serving to control five teeth that come together toward the outside and the center of the oral surface. Aristotle, who discovered this organ in the fourth century B.C., described it as resembling "a horn lantern with the panes of horn left out," and it has been called "Aristotle's lantern" ever since. With it a sea urchin can chew a wide variety of foods and possibly also excavate living spaces in rocky shores.

So great a range of different echinoids inhabits the coasts of the Indian Ocean and Malaya that those areas are regarded as the world center for shore-inhabiting kinds. In all directions from that center the number of unlike types of echinoids decreases. It shrinks too in progressively deeper water, and below fifteen thousand feet none is known. Temperate and polar seas have the largest number of individuals, whereas in the tropics, communities of urchins are less frequent although the number of different kinds is more impressive. In the Arctic, urchins often congregate in such abundance that it would be impossible for a skin diver to set down a foot between one urchin and the next.

About 750 species of living echinoids have been identified, most of them members of groups with representatives in shallow water. Some of these can be recognized at a glance.

SEA URCHINS

Hatpin urchins, the bane of waders and skin divers, are the most respected echinoderms in tropical and subtropical waters. They include also the largest of the regular echinoids to be found near shore. Much larger ones, which belong to family Echinothuridae, are found in very deep waters.

The spines of these urchins may be 1 foot long, shaped like needles, jet black, fragile, hollow and probably poison-filled. They penetrate human skin easily, break off, and cause intense stinging pain. Eventually the lime of the spine is absorbed. Whorls of minute teeth around each spine resist extraction, and the material of the spine itself tends to crumble in a pair of tweezers.

No one who has watched these big urchins on a reef or experimented with them in an aquarium tank has any doubts about the role of the long spines. The urchin keeps them in constant motion, and responds to any shadow by turning even more spines in that direction. With only a general sensitivity to light in the black skin covering the shell, the urchin seems very well aware of any change in its surroundings affecting the illumination falling upon it.

The hatpin urchin of the Mediterranean and tropical eastern Atlantic is *Centrostephanus longispinus,* a black-bodied animal with brightly colored spines kept constantly in motion, the tip of each spine tracing a small circle in the water. *Diadema setosum* of the East Indies and *D. antillarum* of the West Indies

and Florida keys present the same formidable appearance. Commonly they cluster in cavities of coral reefs, and all of the really large ones seem to have protection of this sort.

When stirred into movement a hatpin urchin can travel at from one to one and one-half inches per second, "walking" on the tips of shorter spines over the oral surface. This is about sixty times as fast as the maximum for the common sea urchins of New England coasts on their multiple tube-feet.

Cidarid urchins differ in that they bear two very different sizes and types of spines. The large ones may be as long as the diameter of the shell, and are widely spaced and covered by a wooly, hairlike material to which foreign particles often cling. Their small spines, by contrast, are as spotlessly clean as those of other sea urchins. Some of the small spines form a whorl around the base of each large spine.

Of cidarids, *Cidaris tribuloides* is familiar in tropical parts of the eastern Atlantic, and from North Carolina to Brazil, throughout the West Indies, and in Bermuda. It reaches a diameter of 2¼ inches and is mottled in various shades of brown. Often its large spines carry such a crust of moss animals (bryozoans) that the bands of purplish red and yellow are concealed.

In scientific circles the sea urchins that have become most distinguished are plain purplish brown, measuring between 1 and 2 inches in diameter, with the anus in the middle of the aboral surface clearly equipped with four or five large plates acting as valves. These urchins are poorly armed, usually lacking glandular pedicellariae and bearing only moderately slender spines about half as long as the width of the shell. Shorter spines around the mouth wear shiny caps.

These urchins of the genus *Arbacia* have provided experimental biology with study material to a degree paralleled only by the fruit fly in genetics, the white rat in nutrition, and the frog in investigations of muscle action. The most famous of them is *Arbacia punctulata,* found from Cape Cod to Florida and throughout the West Indies. *A. lixula* lives in the Mediterranean and along tropical coasts of the eastern Atlantic. *A. stellata* is a very similar urchin occurring from Mexico's Baja California to Peru along the eastern Pacific.

Most of the familiar sea urchins are not hatpin urchins or cidarids or distinguished members of the genus *Arbacia.* Instead, they are of types with solid spines and an abundance of all four types of pedicellariae.

On shores from the Carolinas through the West Indies, the good-sized, somewhat flattened urchin whose solid, white spines against a darker body give it a shaggy appearance, usually proves to be *Lytechinus variegatus.* Close to the limit of low tide,

The hollow spines of the hatpin urchin *Diadema setosum* are a menace to skin divers, for they readily penetrate the skin, break off, and cause bad wounds. This one rested in a coral pool at low tide on the Great Barrier Reef. (Fritz Goro: *Life* Magazine)

where waves break over it and the sun is particularly bright, *Lytechinus* often uses the tube-feet on its aboral surface to hold pieces of seaweed and bits of coral or stones as a shield and shade. In deeper water this habit is less frequent.

Echinus miliaris, found in British coastal waters, tends to conceal itself in the same way. Apparently it is a less active animal than its close relative, the edible urchin *E. esculentus* (Plate 136), for the latter remains clean as it forages about for a mixed diet of shellfish, tube-building worms, crustaceans, small echinoderms, and hydroids.

The "sea egg" of Barbados and other islands in the West Indies is *Tripneustes ventricosus,* a particularly common urchin sought for human food at seasons when the orange-colored ovaries are loaded with eggs. Native people collect large numbers of them, break them open, and either eat them raw or roast them on the half shell or fry the ovaries as though they were an omelet of hen's eggs. In Italy the egg masses of sea urchins are marketed in coastal towns as "frutta di mare." The favored Mediterranean species is *Paracentrotus lividus.*

Recent immigrants to New England sometimes seek out the largest specimens of a green sea urchin, *Strongylocentrotus droehbachiensis* (recipient of one of the longest scientific names on record). It takes the place of *Arbacia* north of Cape Cod. It is found also on northern European and Pacific coasts. This animal is like *Arbacia* in being mostly a vegetarian, feeding on seaweeds of definite kinds. Along the Canadian east coast, it has become addicted to a diet of cannery wastes. In the Baltic Sea, it often varies its diet with hydroids, tube-building worms, and other foods. The big purple or red *Strongylocentrotus franciscanus* (Plate 137) is sought by Italians in California for its tasty ovaries, which are eaten raw.

A fair number of different urchins bore into rock, seemingly by working on it with the hard teeth of the Aristotle's lantern or by abrading it with spines. Another possibility is that they keep the rock so free of plant particles that erosion is hastened. Any loose particles are probably removed by the tube-feet. In any case the process is slow.

The commonest boring urchin along rocky coasts from Norway and Iceland to the Cape Verde Islands is *Psammechinus miliaris.* In the Mediterranean and farther down the west coast of Africa, *Paracentrotus lividus* has the same habit, and can be found in honeycombed rock—a dark green animal with spines of bright green, violet, and brown. *Strongylocentrotus purpuratus,* a purple urchin along the Pacific side of North America, not only cuts cavities in hard rock but has done extensive damage to steel posts used as wharf pilings in California. Its food consists mostly of plant materials.

If one of these boring urchins is disturbed, it attempts to wedge itself at the bottom of its cavity. Possibly this is its protection against wave action too. Yet when the tide is in these animals apparently wander away from their holes, feed on algae or other material, and then return to the security of the home they have prepared. Sometimes an urchin becomes imprisoned in its cavity, having opened a big enough room but not enlarged the doorway through which it entered at a smaller size and younger age.

On rocks of various Pacific islands, *Colobocentrotus atratus* demonstrates a very different technique in resisting wave action. Its aboral spines are all short, flat, bladelike organs that shield the body from debris carried in the surf. Similar spines around the somewhat flattened body suggest the petals of a daisy. These too seem to aid the animal by using the force of a wave to hold the body against a rock.

Heterocentrotus mammillatus is the slate-pencil urchin of the Indo-Pacific and Hawaii. Its slightly flattened spines may be ½ of an inch in diameter and 5 inches long. The lime of which they are composed is hard and white; it can be used to make clear, erasible marks on old-fashioned writing slates.

THE CAKE URCHINS AND SAND DOLLARS

A bit of broken shell from a cake urchin or a sand dollar shows many differences from any fragment of a sea urchin's test. The limy plates are thicker and little vertical struts (such as no sea urchin possesses) extend as braces between the aboral and oral surfaces.

The intact shell of a cake urchin or a sand dollar shows, too, a bilateral symmetry through slight elongation and in the displacement of the anal opening toward the edge of the shell, on either the oral or the aboral surface. The aboral surface itself bears a striking pattern of five petal-shaped marks (petaloids) corresponding to the tracts of tube-foot holes in a sea urchin's shell.

Over much of the oral and aboral surfaces of both cake urchins and sand dollars, short tube-feet extend singly through a multitude of small openings. Along with inconspicuous pedicellariae they serve to keep the body clean and perhaps also in feeding. Those on the undersurface aid the spines in locomotion and in the digging movements by means of which these animals sink themselves in the surface sediments.

Cake urchins are oval creatures with no distinct edge to the shell. The common *Clypeaster* is covered by a dense, furlike coating of short dark-brown spines. *C. rosaceus* is known as a "sea biscuit" in the West Indies. *C. subdepressus* burrows shallowly in tidal areas from North Carolina to Brazil.

Sand dollars are very flat, the edge of the body thin and distinct. Most of those known live along sandy shores of America and Japan. *Echinarachnius*

The slate-pencil urchin *Heterocentrotus mammillatus*, with its great clublike spines, is more than two handsful in size. (Great Barrier Reef. Fritz Goro: *Life Magazine*)

parma reaches a diameter of approximately 3 inches along the Atlantic coast from New Jersey northward, as well as around the Pacific from Vancouver Island to Japan. Its petaloids end abruptly, as though incomplete.

From Nantucket to Brazil, the sand dollar *Mellita testudinata* has pointed petaloids and develops notches in the rim of the body. These become surrounded as slots when the sand dollar grows. In the Gulf of California, certain members of *Encope* acquire even more distinctive slots and holes, and are popular as "sea arrowheads." *Echinodiscus auritus,* the yellow or purple "sea pancake" of Africa's east coast, excels most other sand dollars in size and thinness of the body. The shells of many of these animals can be ground up in water to make an indelible ink.

HEART URCHINS

It is easy to tell a heart urchin from a sea biscuit, even though both have a bulky oval body and a heavy shell. The heart urchin has only four complete petaloids on its aboral surface, and the mouth is a transverse slot somewhat anterior of the middle on the lower surface. The anus is well posterior. Internally the shell is braced, but the animal has no Aristotle's lantern.

Heart urchins are burrowers, usually covered with fine short spines that slant backward as though combed. If large spines are present, they too are aimed in a way that offers little resistance as the animal works along through the muddy bottom.

Spatangus purpureus, a violet-colored animal, excavates chambers for itself in the mud along shores in western Europe, the Mediterranean and the west side of Africa. Its presence can be suspected from the small hole kept open between its chamber and the water above. Mucus secreted by the heart urchin keeps its cavity from shedding mineral particles while extremely long tube-feet are extended from the petaloid areas through the hole in the chamber's roof to scavenge for food over adjacent areas of bottom.

The Serpent Stars

(Class Ophiuroidea)

By far the most active of all echinoderms are the serpent stars. Yet because most of them are of small size and retiring habits, they are less familiar than sea stars and sea urchins. They are often called "brittle stars" because of their readiness to throw off parts of their arms when disturbed. Each arm may break into many pieces. A few kinds go so far as to discard the upper part of the body as well. Then the missing portions are regenerated.

The five arms of a serpent star (only a few have six or seven arms) are distinct from the disk-shaped or pentagonal body. On the oral surface they lack the grooves as well as the sucker-tipped tube-feet found in sea stars. Only a pair of minute soft swellings at each joint in the arms represent the tube-feet. Apparently they are primarily sensory.

Flexibility of the arms in most serpent stars is mostly in a horizontal direction. The animal curls them around irregularities of the bottom and lifts its body along, ordinarily holding it above the surface on which the arms rest. The arms commonly are five to six times as long as the diameter of the body, but in some serpent stars the proportion reaches as much as fifteen times.

The arms are so flexible that they suggest a serpent's tail, giving the common name to the animals and also the word for the class to which they belong (from *ophis,* a serpent, and *ura,* the tail).

Serpent stars frequently cluster together in astonishing aggregations. The tangle of arms becomes impressive enough to suggest that the group forms a more efficient trap for suspended food matter than is possible for a single individual.

The mouth at the center of the oral surface has five sharp teeth but no Aristotle's lantern. Close to the mouth is the opening through which the water-vascular system is filled.

Serpent stars feed on a wide variety of bottom material and take advantage of opportunites to include flesh in their diet. They scavenge from the tide line to at least twenty thousand feet below the surface, and are found on every type of bottom in all seas at all latitudes. A few burrow, but most creep over and cling to seaweeds, sponges, hydroids, corals, and other attached forms of life.

Most serpent stars are either male or female, and they free their reproductive products into the sea. Some do brood their eggs, providing this parental care until the young are miniatures of the parent. Some serpent stars are hermaphrodites, with both ovaries and testes. A number of six-armed species reproduce by transverse division of the body, followed by regeneration of the missing parts by each half.

Almost all of the sixteen hundred different species of serpent stars have unbranched arms. One order is exceptional: the basket stars (Plate 134). These creatures live in deeper water, and somehow control a profusion of arm branches, walking about on the branch tips or coiling them about submarine growths. *Gorgonocephalus,* the gorgon's head basket star, is a big one, with a body as much as 4 inches across and arms repeatedly branching to a total length of 1 foot or more. If a living specimen is placed in fresh water, it will die in an expanded position, completely relaxed. Then it can be preserved to show the great maze of slender branchlets. Otherwise it curls up in a confused mass.

Serpent stars with unbranched arms seldom have a body disk more than 1 inch in diameter (Plates 131–133). A good many of them have remarkably extensive geographic range, some being truly cosmopolitan in coastal waters. The long-armed serpent star *Amphipholis squamata* is one of the most widespread from the subarctic to the subantarctic. It is particularly abundant around the British Isles as a grayish white or faintly bluish denizen of tide pools. It is hermaphroditic and broods its young internally, hence is viviparous.

Ophiactis savignyi is circumtropical, and is distinctive in having square teeth. Small, young individuals with six arms can often be found in the cavities of sponges; there they reproduce by transverse division of the body. Eventually, however, they reach a larger size and become solitary. Then, after a final fission, each half grows only two new teeth and two new arms, becoming a five-armed serpent star. Thereafter it is an adult, reproducing only by sexual means.

Some serpent stars are quite colorful and show a range of coloration from one individual to another. This is particularly obvious in the common daisy brittle star *Ophiopholis aculeata* found from Long Island Sound to the Arctic, and in the spiny serpent star *Ophiothrix angulata* of shallow waters from Chesapeake Bay to the West Indies and Rio de Janeiro. The first-named actually spreads downward to a

The five-holed sand dollar *Mellita testudinata* has five rays and a covering of movable spines that identify it as a flattened relative of sea urchins. It digs into sandy bottoms along the Atlantic coast of America and in the West Indies. (Delaware Bay. William H. Amos)

depth of over six thousand feet—ten times as deep as *O. angulata* is found.

O. aculeata has a body just under 1 inch across and arms to 3½ inches long, and may be red or blue on the body, deeper red or green or brown banded with white on the arms. *O. angulata* seems always to show a color difference between the banded arms and the body: the latter may be red, pink, yellow, brown, green, blue, or purple—almost the full spectrum among the individuals in a single tide pool.

At night a number of different serpent stars can be found along the shore because the arms luminesce. *Ophiacantha bidentata,* whose arms often appear to be knotted, is dark brown by day but bluish gray in the dark; it inhabits the Atlantic and Pacific, as far south as Portugal and South Carolina, California and Korea; it is commonest between thirty and fifteen thousand feet below the surface. *Ophioscolex glacialis,* whose 5-inch arms and 1-inch body are covered with a thick skin, varies from purple to yellow in daylight; at night its body is invisible but the arms are a bright violet, contrasting with muddy bottoms from Virginia to Greenland.

CHAPTER XX

(Top to bottom) salp, lancelet and sea squirt

The Invertebrate Chordates

(*Phylum Chordata*)

IF it were not for the existence of sea squirts, salps, and lancelets, the phylum Chordata would consist only of vertebrate animals—those with a vertebral skeleton or backbone. But sea squirts, salps, and lancelets do exist. This fact necessitates a broader view of the qualifications for membership in the phylum Chordata.

This subdivision of the animal kingdom takes its name from the notochord, a stiffening rod of characteristic construction serving as the first, inner, skeletal support of the body. A notochord consists of a fibrous sheath around a multitude of translucent cells whose turgid condition provides firmness with flexibility.

Possession of a notochord prevents a chordate's body from telescoping as an earthworm does when its longitudinal muscles contract. Instead, a notochord-bearing creature bends from side to side, undulating as a fish does. Lancelets retain the notochord throughout life, whereas sea squirts, salps, and vertebrates possess one only during larval or embryonic stages of development. No member of any other phylum has a notochord.

Above its notochord, a chordate has a tubular dorsal nerve cord, which may be enlarged at the anterior end into a true brain. This part of the animal arises in a uniform manner in all chordates from sea squirt to man, a procedure quite unlike any of the ways in which a nervous system develops in members of any other phylum.

Chordates also show a third feature, found elsewhere only among acorn worms (hemichordates): a series of openings between the pharynx region of the digestive tract and the outside of the animal. Gill slits of this kind are used throughout life by acorn worms, sea squirts and salps, lancelets, and such vertebrates as lampreys and fish. The tadpole stages of amphibians use gill slits. Reptiles and warm-blooded vertebrates possess pharyngeal clefts only during embryonic development.

The invertebrate chordates include a few hundred members of the subphylum Urochordata (sea squirts, pyrosomes, and salps) and about thirty different kinds of lancelets in subphylum Cephalochordata. These names refer to the fact that in urochordates the notochord is restricted to the tail region, whereas in cephalochordates it extends to the anterior end of the body.

Invertebrate chordates resemble one another in being exclusively marine and in possession of a peculiar pocket, the atrium. Water from the pharynx passes through the pharyngeal slits into the atrium, and then to the outside world through a permanent opening, the atrial pore. This current of water is maintained by cilia on most inner surfaces of the pharynx. It brings particles of food which become entrapped in a film of mucus secreted over the same pharyngeal surfaces. Cilia also move the loaded mucus into a groove along the length of the pharynx and within this narrow passageway as a food-charged rope into the gullet and stomach. Thus the invertebrate chordates are filter feeders, depending upon plankton and detritus particles for nourishment.

The Sea Squirts and Their Kin (*Subphylum Urochordata*)

Most sea squirts consist simply of a saclike body permanently attached to some solid object or buried shallowly in the ocean bottom. One body opening admits a current of water. The other serves for the escape of the same current as well as of wastes and reproductive products.

The tadpole stage of most sea squirts could swim through a buttonhole quite easily. Even in a shallow dish with a black bottom, their tadpole-shaped bodies are so transparent that it is easy to overlook them. Yet the tail contains the complete notochord and the slender nerve cord extending from a slightly enlarged hollow brain in the dorsal portion of the body. A light-sensitive simple eye and a minute organ of balance are embedded in the walls of the brain.

The anterior end of the larval sea squirt is occupied by the adhesive organs with which the creature will attach itself at the time of transformation into adult form. Already, however, it shows a small mouth (incurrent opening) well forward on the dorsal surface, leading into a capacious pharynx. Gill slits through the pharyngeal walls communicate with the atrium, which opens dorsally farther back on the body. The small stomach is connected by a short intestine ending in the atrium, nearer the excurrent opening from which water is discharged.

When a sea squirt larva attaches itself and transforms, it literally stands on its face while absorbing and obliterating its tail, notochord, sense organs, and so much of the nervous system that only a solid ganglion remains, with nerves extending to the few internal organs. At the same time the dorsal surface becomes distorted through great enlargement of the pharynx, until the incurrent and excurrent openings are raised like two spouts on the squat body. Externally the body surface secretes a covering of cellulose as the tunic from which the attached animal gains another common name, "tunicate" (Plate 144).

When a beachcomber disturbs a sea squirt, the creature usually contracts. On a rock between tide marks this event is made obvious by two little jets of water, one from the incurrent opening (mouth) and the other from the excurrent (atrium). If a person wearing slacks inadvertently steps beside a large sea squirt on the beach, one or both jets may easily go up inside the trouser leg and reach the knee, to the walker's sudden dismay.

Along the Atlantic shores and also in California, a common sea squirt with incurrent and excurrent openings close together is *Ciona intestinalis*. Its pale golden-yellow tunic and body wall are so transparent that the inner organs can be seen through them. The height of the slender body ranges from about 1½ to 2½ inches. Its favorite sites for attachment seem to be rocks, floats, and submerged timbers.

Tethyum pyriforme, the sea peach (Plate 143), is of the right size and shape to earn its name, and varies in color from orange to yellow, suffused with pink or red. It is a strikingly handsome member of the coastal population from Maine northward in cold, shallow water.

Sea grapes are clusters of *Molgula manhattensis*, the commonest sea squirt along North America's Atlantic coasts from Massachusetts southward. Each "grape" is almost spherical, about 1 inch in diameter, and greenish yellow in color. The surface appears soft and spongy, and often serves as a site for the attachment of other kinds of animals.

Many sea squirts reproduce by budding as well as by sexual means. They often build large, complex colonies coating the surface of stones, sea walls, and pilings (Plate 142). The various colonial species of the genus *Amaroucium* are popularly called "sea pork" from the translucent gray, tough tunic linking one individual to the next.

In addition to the attached sea squirts (class Ascidiacea), the urochords include several types of free-swimming pelagic animals. Appendicularians (class Larvaceae) never metamorphose from the swimming, tadpole-like larval stage. Instead, they develop reproductive organs and reproduce their kind without ever "growing up." Their whole lives are spent as minute creatures swimming in upper levels of the sea, where they secrete complicated food traps of mucus in the form of a lemon-shaped house. Every few hours the trap is discarded because it becomes clogged with particles unsuitable as food, and the appendicularian spends about thirty minutes creating a new one into which it can move.

Members of class Thaliacea are transparent animals that reach far larger size or group themselves together into colonies big enough to handle easily. Among the most spectacular of them are the pyrosomes (*Pyrosoma*), found swimming gently in the sea, either near its surface or far down in the depths. *Pyrosoma* means "fire body," and refers to the fact that in the dark these colonies can be detected as luminous cylinders moving slowly through the water.

Each translucent cylinder consists of hundreds or thousands of ⅛-inch sea squirts arranged radially around a lengthwise central cavity, like the separate parts of a pineapple around the hole where the core

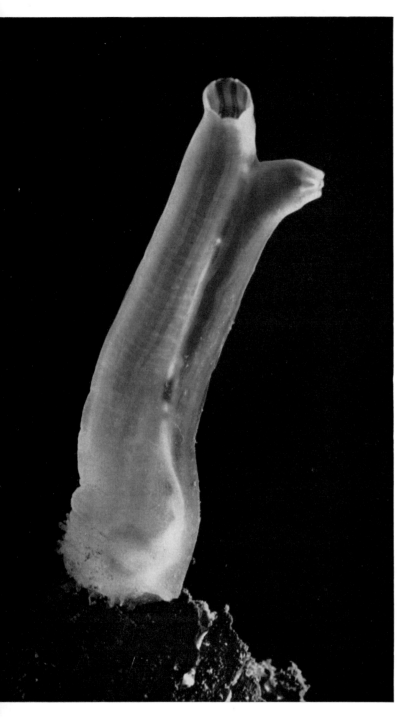

Tube sea squirt, *Ciona intestinalis*, 5 inches high, filters food out of the water that is drawn into the opening on the left and discharged through the temporarily closed one on the right. (England. D. P. Wilson)

cavity. The combined flow is enough to propel the colony endwise—jet propulsion of the mildest kind.

Pyrosomes found near the surf or netted from the sea usually fall in the size range from 1 to 5 inches long and from ⅜ to ⅞ of an inch in diameter. Occasionally a really large one is collected at night, when the display of its luminescence is so vivid. One pyrosome colony 4 feet long and 8 inches in diameter was brought up and handled by scientists and crew aboard an oceanographic research vessel. Before preserving their trophy, the men amused themselves for half an hour by writing their names in light on its surface—merely by tracing a finger tip gently over the outer ends of the small animals that composed it.

None of the other thaliaceans is colonial. They are known as salps, and they combine a barrel-shaped body with extreme transparency. Many of them are evident in the water only as a regular series of hooplike muscle bands, seemingly with no connection. Slow pulsations of these muscles drive water in through the mouth opening at one end, through the huge pharyngeal sieve, and out of the atrial opening at the other end.

One crustacean of almost equal transparency (*Phronima*) is sometimes found riding along in this transparent-walled cavity. Nearly always it turns out to be a female feeding on larger food particles swept in by the salp, and using the pharyngeal basket as a convenient place in which to raise her young.

Salps reproduce both sexually and by budding. Often the buds develop into fully grown individuals while still attached to the parent. In this way, long, delicate trains of salps arise. In *Doliolum* the budded individuals migrate over the surface of the parent and attach themselves temporarily to a dorsal projection, taking places in three rows of remarkable regularity.

The Lancelets

(*Subphylum Cephalochordata*)

Along sandy coasts of most oceans where the water is as warm as in North Carolina, southern England, the Mediterranean, or Japan, if a shovel is thrust suddenly into the wet beach at the low-tide line and the handle pulled back sharply, little translucent flesh-colored animals may jump out and bury themselves rapidly close by. If a person is quick, a few can be captured. Each turns out to have a flattened slender body pointed at both ends, but no paired appendages or very obvious fins. It is a lancelet, a link between the vertebrates and the more widely known kinds of invertebrates.

Through sand that is very wet or under water, lancelets can swim almost as easily as a minnow in

has been removed. Each individual of the colony takes water and food particles through incurrent openings on the outside of the colony, and discharges the water again from atrial openings into the central water itself. They emerge, wriggle a few inches, and dive in again so quickly that one naturalist realized he could not tell whether they swam mouth forward or tail first. To learn the answer, he caught some lancelets and carefully dipped the tail of each into a harmless dye. Then he released them in an aquarium with a sandy bottom. Some dove into the sand mouth first. Others went tail first. But when they swam around of their own volition, the mouth was always in advance.

Undisturbed lancelets rest in the sand with just the mouth exposed. Water drawn into the pharynx passes through oblique S-shaped slits into the atrium and emerges into the sand about two-thirds of the way along the ventral surface. The anus opens farther back, at the base of the narrowly fin-bordered tail.

The reproductive organs, either testes or ovaries, form a series of block-shaped bags that bulge into the atrium and release their products into the water being discharged through the atrial opening. Fertilization occurs outside the body, and the development of the embryo follows a pattern closely comparable to that in many vertebrates. The early stages, however, suggest the steps in growth of an echinoderm embryo. For this reason, lancelets have been of special interest to scientists, and are still known by an outmoded generic name as "amphioxi." "Amphioxus" merely indicates "pointed at both ends."

Bibliography

BERRILL, N. J. (1951). *The living tide.* New York: Dodd, Mead.

BORRADAILE, L. A. and POTTS, F. A. (1958). *Invertebrata: a manual for the use of students;* with chapters by L. E. S. Eastham and J. T. Saunders. 3rd ed. rev. by G. A. Kerkut. Cambridge: Cambridge University Press.

BRANDT, K. and APSTEIN, C. (1901–1941). *Nordisches Plankton. Zoologischer Teil.* Kiel: Lipsius & Tischer.

BRONN, H. G. (1859–1948). *Klassen und Ordnungen des Thier-Reichs.* Leipzig: Winter'sche Verlagshandlung.

BUCHSBAUM, RALPH (1948). *Animals without backbones.* Chicago: University of Chicago Press.

BURTON, MAURICE (1954). *Margins of the sea.* New York: Harper.

CAMERON, T. W. M. (1951). *The parasites of domestic animals.* Philadelphia: Lippincott.

CARTHY, J. D. (1958). *An introduction to the behavior of invertebrates.* London: Allen & Unwin.

CHANDLER, A. (1955). *Introduction to parasitology.* New York: John Wiley.

CLOUDSLEY–THOMPSON, J. L. (1958). *Spiders, scorpions, centipedes and mites.* New York: Pergamon.

COKER, R. E. (1947). *This great and wide sea.* Chapel Hill: University of North Carolina Press.

COMSTOCK, J. H. (1948). *The spider book.* Ithaca, N.Y.: Comstock.

COUSTEAU, J. Y. and DUMAS, F. (1953). *The silent world.* New York: Harper.

DAKIN, W. J. (1950). *Great Barrier Reef.* Melbourne: Australian National Publicity Association.

—— (1953). *Australian seashores.* London: Angus & Robertson.

DELAGE, Y. and HÉROUARD, E. (1896–1903). *Traité de zoologie concrète.* Paris: Schleicher.

DOBELL, CLIFFORD (1958). *Antony von Leeuwenhoek and his 'little animals.'* New York: Russell & Russell.

EALES, N. B. (1939). *The littoral fauna of Great Britain.* Cambridge: Cambridge University Press.

GALTSOFF, P., et al. (1937). *Culture methods for invertebrate animals.* Ithaca, N.Y.: Comstock.

GERTSCH, W. J. (1949). *American spiders.* Princeton, N.J.: Van Nostrand.

GRASSÉ, P. (1948–1949). *Traité de zoologie, anatomie, systématique, biologie.* Paris: Masson.

GRIMPE, G. & WAGLER, E. (1925–1944). *Die Tierwelt der Nord- und Ostsee.* Leipzig: Akademischer Verlag.

HALSTEAD, B. W. (1959). *Dangerous marine animals.* Cambridge, Md.: Cornell Maritime Press.

HARDY, ALISTER (1956). *The open sea: The world of plankton.* London: Collins.

—— (1959). *The open sea, II: Fish and fisheries.* London: Collins.

HARMER, S. F. and SHIPLEY, A. E. (1895–1909). *Cambridge natural history.* London: Macmillan.

HEDGPETH, JOEL, ed. (1957). *Treatise on marine ecology and paleoecology:* Vol. I, *Ecology.* New York: Geological Society of America.

HESSE, RICHARD, ALLEE, W. C., and SCHMIDT, K. P. (1951). *Ecological animal geography.* New York: Wiley.

HYMAN, LIBBIE (1940–1959). *The invertebrates,* Vols. I–V. New York: McGraw-Hill.

JOHNSON, M. E. and SNOOK, H. J. (1927). *Seashore animals of the Pacific coast.* New York: Macmillan.

KUKENTHAL, W. and KRUMBACH, T. (1923–1938). *Handbuch der Zoologie. Eine Naturgeschichte der Staemme des Tierreiches.* Berlin: Der Gruyter.

LANE, F. W. (1957). *Kingdom of the octopus.* London: Jarrolds.

LANKESTER, R. (1900–1909). *Treatise on zoology.* London: Black.

LE DANOIS, EDOUARD (1957). *Marine life of coastal waters.* London: Harrap.

LIGHT, S. F. (1954). *Intertidal invertebrates of the central California coast,* rev. Ralph Smith *et al.* Berkeley: University of California Press.

MACGINITIE, G. E. and MACGINITIE, NETTIE (1949). *Natural history of marine animals.* New York: McGraw-Hill.

MARSHALL, N. B. (1954). *Aspects of deep sea biology.* London: Hutchinson.

MINER, R. W. (1950). *Field book of seashore life.* New York: Putnam's.

PARKER, T. J. and HASWELL, W. A. (1940). *A text-book of zoology.* London: Macmillan.

PENNAK, R. W. (1953). *Fresh-water invertebrates of the United States.* New York: Ronald.

PRATT, H. S. (1951). *A manual of the common invertebrate animals.* Philadelphia: Blakiston.

RICKETTS, E. F. and CALVIN, JACK (1952). *Between Pacific tides.* 3rd edn. rev. Joel Hedgpeth. Stanford, Cal.: Stanford University Press.

ROUGHLEY, T. C. (1947). *Wonders of the Great Barrier Reef.* New York: Scribner's.

RUSSELL, F. S. and YONGE, C. M. (1936). *The seas.* London: Warne.

SCHULZE, P. (1922–1940). *Biologie der Tiere Deutschlands.* Berlin: Borntraeger.

SMITH, F. G. W. (1948). *Atlantic reef corals*. Coral Gables, Fla.: University of Miami Press.

SVERDRUP, H. U., JOHNSON, M. W., and FLEMING, R. H. (1942). *The oceans*. Englewood Cliffs, N. J.: Prentice-Hall.

TREMBLEY, A. (1744). *Mémoires pour servir a l'histoire d'un genre de polypes d'eau douce*. Leiden.

WALFORD, L. A. (1958). *Living resources of the sea*. New York: Ronald.

WARD, H. B. and WHIPPLE, G. C. (1959). *Fresh-water biology*. 2nd ed. rev. W. T. Edmondson. New York: Wiley.

WARDLE, R. A. and McLEOD, J. A. (1952). *The zoology of tapeworms*. Minneapolis: University of Minnesota Press.

WILSON, D. P. (1951). *Life of the shore and shallow sea*. London: Nicholson & Watson.

YONGE, C. M. (1949). *The sea shore*. London: Collins.

INDEX

NOTE : A numeral in parentheses refers to a color plate; a page number followed by an asterisk indicates a black-and-white illustration.

A

B

C

Cheilostomata, 153
Chelicerae, 226
"Chelicerate," 226
Chelifer, 248
Chigger, 251
Chilomonas, 23
Chilopoda, 240
Chink shells, 160
Chiridota, 276
Chiropsalmus, 76, 80
Chiton, 158*, 159 (38)
Chlamydomonas, 25
Chlamys, 189*
Chlorophyll, 21
Choanoflagellates, 26
Chordata, 14, 15
Chromatophores, 21
Chromulina, 22
Chrysaora, 80
Chrysomonads, 22
Cidarids, 281
Cidaris, 281
Cilia, 51
Ciliata, 51
Ciona, 287, 288*
Cirripedia, 233
Cistenides, 202
Cladocera, 230, 232*
Clams, 158*, 184
Clamworm, 201*
Clathrulina, 31
Clava, 72 (4)
Clavellina (144)
Cliona, 63
Clione, 177*
Clionidae, 64

Clitellio, 206
Clitellum, 206
Clonorchis, 125*
"Cloth of gold," 187
Clypeaster, 283
Cnidaria, 67, 68
Coccidians, 49
Coccidiosis, 49
Coccoliths, 23, 30
Cockle, 191
Cocoon, 206
Codosiga, 26
Coelenterata, 15, 67
Coenobita (101)
Coleps, 52
"Collar cells," 57
Colobocentrotus, 283
Colossendeis, 253
Colpoda, 52
Comb jellies, 115, 117*
"Compensation cavity," 151
Conchoderma, 233
Conchs, 177, 180 (51)
Cone snails, 177
Conjugants, 51
Contractile vacuole, 21
Conus, 177 (59)
Convoluta, 121 (36)
Copepoda, 230, 231*, 232*
Coquinas, 188, 191*
Coral reefs, 111
Corals, 97 (23–29), (31)
Corallium, 102
Cordylophora, 72
Coronate jellyfishes, 80
Coronula, 233

Corymorpha, 72
Coscinasterias, 280
Cowries, 181, 184* (58)
Crabs, 239 (95–104)
Crangon, 236, 237
Crania, 154
Craspedacusta, 74
Craterolophus, 77*
Crayfishes, 237, 239* (93), (94)
Crepidula, 180
Creseis, 197*
Crinoidea, 255
Cristatella, 152
Crossaster, 279 (127)
Crustacea, 229
Cryptochiton, 160
Cryptomonads, 23
Ctenidia, 177
Ctenodiscus, 277
Ctenophora, 15, 115
Ctenoplana, 118
Ctenostomata, 153
Cuboidal jellyfishes, 80
Cucumaria, 275 (140)
"Cultured pearls," 186
Cuttlefish, 194 (75)
Cyanea, 76, 78*, 80, 97
Cyclops, 231*
Cydippids, 116
Cypraea, 184* (58)
"Cyprid" stage, 233
Cypris, 233
Cysts, 19

D

Dactylometra, 76, 79*, 97 (7)
Daddy longlegs, 249, 252*
Daphnia, 230*
"Date mussel," 191
"Dead men's fingers," 99*
Decapoda, 236
Deep scattering layer, 231

Dendronotus (63)
Dendrophyllia, 110
Dendrosoma, 55
Dentalium, 193, 198*
Dermacentor, 252
Dermanyssus, 251
Dero, 306

Diadema, 281, 282*
Diadumene, 108
Dibothriocephalus, 127
Didinium, 51, 52
Difflugia, 29
Digenetic flukes, 125
Dinobryon, 22

Dinoflagellates, 23*, 24*
Dinophilus, 204
Diodora (47)
Diopatra, 203
Diphyllobothrium, 127
Diplomonads, 28

Diplopoda, 241
Doliolum, 288
Dolomedes, 244 (109), (111)
Donax, 188, 191*
Dourine disease, 27
Dracunculis, 137

Drilophaga, 139
Dromia (103)
DSL, 231
Dugesia, 122*
Dysentery, 29

E

Ear shells, 178
Earthworm, 204, 207*
Echinarachnius, 283
Echinococcus, 128
Echinodera, 140
"Echinodere," 140
Echinodermata, 15, 254
Echinodiscus, 284
Echinoidea, 280
Echinus, 283 (136)
Echiuroidea, 15, 157*
Echiurus, 157
Ectoprocta, 150
Ectyodoryx, 63
Edged sea stars, 277
Edwardsia, 105
Edwardsiella, 105
"Eelworms," 133
Eimeria, 49

Eisenia, 206
Eledone (78–80)
Elephantiasis, 138
Elephant's-ear sponge, 64*
Elephant-tusk shell, 193
Elkhorn coral, 112*
Elphidium, 31
Emplectonema, 132
Enchytraeus, 200, 206
Encope, 284
Encystment, 19
Ensis, 189, 192*
Entamoeba, 29
Enterobius, 138
Entoprocta, 15, 143*
Epiactis, 108 (16)
Epidinium, 21, 53
Ephippium, 230
Epistylis, 54

Epizoanthus, 113 (30)
"Errantia," 202
Eubranchipus, 228*, 229
Eucestoda, 127
Eudistylia (81)
Euglena, 24, 25*
Euglenoids, 25
Eugorgia, 101
Eukrohnia, 145
Eunice, 202, 203*
Eunicella, 102 (11)
Eunoa, 202
Eupentacta (140)
Euphausiacea, 236
Euplanaria, 122
Euplectella, 61*
Euplotes, 54
Eurypterida, 242

F

Fairy shrimp, 228*, 229
"False spiders," 247
Fan worms, 205* (83), (84)
Fasciola, 126
Feather-duster worms, 200*,
  203 (81)
Feather stars, 255, 256, 274*
  (135)
Filarial worms, 138
File shells, 187 (44–46)
Finger sponge, 63*

Fire worm, 202
Fish louse, 232
Fissurella, 179
Flabellum, 110
Flagellata, 16, 21
Flagellum, 21
Flatworms, 119, 123*, 124*
  (35), (36)
Flukes, 119*, 124
Flustra, 153
Food vacuole, 51

Foraminiferans, 29, 30*, 31*
"Forams," 29
Forceps-carrying sea stars, 279
Forcipulata, 279
Forskalia, 76
Fredericella, 152
Fresh-water clams, 192, 195*
Fresh-water mussels, 192
Fresh-water sponge, 62*
"Frutta di mare," 283
Fungia, 109

G

Galathealinum, 148
Galatheanthemum, 104
Gammarus, 235
Garden snails, 187* (50)
Gastropoda, 160
Gastrotricha, 15, 139*, 140
Gattyana, 206*
Gemmules, 59, 64
Geoduck, 190
Geonemertes, 131
Geophilus, 241
Gersemia, 101
"Glacier worms," 206

Glaucoma, 20
Glaucus, 182
Globigerina, 30
"Globigerina ooze," 30
Glochidium, 192
Glossiphonia, 225
Glottidia, 155
Golfingia, 156*
Gonactinia, 104, 106, 108
Gonionemus, 69*, 74*
Gonium, 25
Gonyaulax, 23
Gordian worms, 141

Gorgonia, 102
Gorgonians, 101, 102*
Gorgonocephalus, 285
Grantia, 60
Gregarina, 49*
Gregarines, 33, 49*
Gribble, 234
Guinea worms, 133, 137
Gymnodinium, 23
Gymnolaemata, 153
Gyrodactylus, 124

H

Haematococcus, 25
Haemodipsa, 225
Haemopis, 225
Haemoproteus, 50*
Hairy stinger, 97
Halichondria, 62 (1)
Haliclona, 62
Haliclystus, 77*, 80
Haliotis, 178*
Halosydna, 202
Halteria, 53
Harenactis, 105, 108
Harvestmen, 249, 252*
Heart urchin, 284
Hectocotylized arm, 197
Heliometra, 256
Heliopora, 101
Heliozoans, 31
Helix, 183, 187*
Hemichordata, 15, 146
Hemosporidians, 49
Henricia, 278 (125)
Hermissenda (62), (64), (69)
Hermit crabs, 238 (101), (104)

Hermodice, 202
Herpetomonas, 27
Herpobdella, 225
Hesione, 202*
Heterocentrotus, 283, 284*
Heterodera, 136
Heteronemerteans, 132
Heteronereis, 201
Heteropsammia, 109
Hexacorallians, 98
Hexactinellida, 60
Hinge, 185
Hinnites, 187
Hippa, 240*
Hippopodius, 75, 76
Hippospongia, 57*
Hirudin, 208
Hirudinea, 208
Hirudo, 225
Holothuria, 273, 275 (141)
Holothuroidea, 273
Holotrichs, 52
Homarus, 237
Honeycomb worm (86) (87)

Hoof shells, 188
Hookworms, 137
Hoplonemerteans, 132
Hoploplana, 124
Hormiphora, 117
Horny corals, 101
Horse conch, 177
Horsehair worms, 141*
Horseshoe "crabs," 225*, 242*
Hyalella, 235
Hyalonema, 61
Hydatid cyst, 128
Hydatina (57)
Hydractinia, 72
Hydra, 73
Hydras, 72*, 73*
Hydrocorals, 74
Hydroides, 204
Hydroids, 67*, 70*, 71* (4) (5)
Hydrozoa, 70
Hymeniacidon, 62
Hymenolepis, 128
Hypermastiginads, 28

I   J   K

L

M

P   Q

R

S

T

Thalassicola, 31
Thaliacea, 287
Theridion, 244
Thorny corals, 113
Threadworm, 138
Thyone, 275
Ticks, 249, 253*
Tiger cowrie, 184* (58)
Tivela, 189
Tjalfiella, 118
Tokophrya, 54
Tooth shell, 158*, 193
Tracheae, 228
Trachelobdella, 225
Trachyline medusas, 74
Tree snail, 183, 188*
Trematoda, 124

"Trepang," 274, 275*
Trichina worm, 136
Trichinella, 136, 137*
Trichodina, 54
Trichomonads, 27
Trichomonas, 28
Trichonympha, 28
Triclads, 121
Tridacna, 192, 196*
Triopha (67)
Tripneustes, 283
"Tripoli stone," 32
Trochophore, 156
Trombicula, 251
Tropiometra, 256
Trypanosoma, 27*
Trypanosomes, 26, 27*

Trumpet shell, 181
Tsetse fly, 27
Tubastrea, 111
Tube anemones, 104, 114 (32)
Tube-foot, 255
Tube shell, 177
Tube worm, (82)
Tubifex, 200, 206
Tubipora, 101
Tubulanus, 132* (37)
Tubularia, 72 (5)
Tubulipora, 153
Tunicates (144)
Turbatrix, 135
Turbellaria, 120
Turbellarians, 119*, 120
Tyrian purple, 181

U   V

Uca, 240 (100)
Umbellula, 103
Unio, 192
Urechis, 157
Urnatella, 143
Urochordata, 286
Urosalpinx, 181

Vacuole, 51
Vampire squid, 199
Vampyroteuthis, 198
Velamen, 118
Velella, 75
Velum, 70
Velvet worms, 226*, 227
Venom, 245
Venus, 190
Venus' flower basket, 61*

"Venus' girdle," 115*, 118
Veretillum, 103 (10)
Vermicularia, 180
Victorella, 153
Vinegarone (105) (106)
Virgularia, 103
Vitamins, 231
Volvox, 25, 26*
Vorticella, 54, 55*

W   X   Z

Wampum, 190
Water fleas, 226*, 230*
Water spider, 244
Water-vascular system, 254
Webs, 243
Wedge shells, 191*
Whale louse, 235
Wharf louse, 234
"Wheel animalcules," 138
Wheel snails, 182

Whelks, 177, 180 (104)
Whipscorpion, 248, 251* (105), (106)
Whipworm, 138
"Whiteweed," 69, 71
"Wireworm," 241
Worm shell, 180
Wrinkled purples (54)

Xiphosura, 242

Zirfaea, 190
Zoantharia, 104
Zoantharians, 98
Zoanthids, 104, 113 (30)
Zoochorellae, 22
Zoomastigina, 26
Zoothamnium, 54
Zooxanthellae, 22, 111

THIS BOOK has been printed and bound by Kingsport Press, Inc. Color engravings by Chanticleer Company. Design and typography by James Hendrickson. Color layout by Nancy H. Dale.